I0797883

ALSO BY ROBERT M. DOWLING

*Eugene O'Neill: A Life in Four Acts*

*Slumming in New York: From the Waterfront to Mythic Harlem*

# COYOTE

## THE DRAMATIC LIVES OF SAM SHEPARD

ROBERT M. DOWLING

SCRIBNER

NEW YORK AMSTERDAM/ANTWERP LONDON

TORONTO SYDNEY/MELBOURNE NEW DELHI

Scribner
An Imprint of Simon & Schuster, LLC
1230 Avenue of the Americas
New York, NY 10020



First Scribner hardcover edition November 2025



Interior design by Kyle Kabel

Manufactured in the United States of America

1 3 5 7 9 10 8 6 4 2

Library of Congress Control Number: 2025937484

ISBN 978-1-5011-9573-0
ISBN 978-1-5011-9575-4 (ebook)

*To*

*my mother,*

*Janet B. Kellock (1931–2020),*

*and*

*my mentor,*

*Jackson R. Bryer*

There are certain times and certain places in which tragedy can be written. Times of great and apparently sudden change. Times when the ground is shifting so fast that there is not one world but two, a past that is melting into the future, leaving a present in which cause and effect break down, in which there is no consonance between intentions and consequences. Places in which this change is still so visible in its entirety that it can be dramatized. And there are writers—very rare ones—who have both the instinctive understanding of the change that is happening and the sense of form with which to embody it, allowing them both to plumb the depths of that tragedy and to transcend it. When these three things—time, place and writer—come together, something extraordinary can happen in the theatre.

—Fintan O'Toole

# CONTENTS

# COYOTE

## PROLOGUE

# EXILE

"Exile must be a terrible thing," said Norton sympathetically.

"Actually," said Amalfitano, "now I see it as a natural movement, something that, in its way, helps to abolish fate, or what is generally thought of as fate."

—Roberto Bolaño, *2666*

"Duarte," Sam Shepard scoffed to a reporter. "The Orange orchards. Have you ever been there? It's where I grew up on an avocado ranch. Tractors. Horseshit. Beep-beep."[1]

Samuel Shepard Rogers, in fact, spent his teenage years in Bradbury, California, an extension of the larger San Gabriel Valley town of Duarte, then known for rock quarries, cement plants, and a cancer center. Its homes were swept by hot desert winds and adorned with timeworn trailers, aluminum awnings, and Astroturf. Those in the surrounding area called Duarte "Rock Town," but Bradbury was a haven above that valley of ashes. Twenty miles northeast of Los Angeles, the township is nestled at the foot of the San Gabriel Mountains, a forlorn cascade of brown swellings and ridges that signal to eastward itinerants they have arrived in the Mojave Desert, the driest zone in North America and home to Death Valley, the hottest place on Earth.

Duarte and its clutch of nearby townships—Monrovia, Arcadia, and Pasadena to the west, and Azusa, Glendora, and Claremont to the east—form an apron along the San Gabriel foothills. For Shepard, this region "stuck with me not so much as a fond memory but as a jumping off place. They hold a kind of junk magic." Azusa's slogan is "Everything from A to Z in the USA." "And it's just like that," Shepard said. "A collection of junk."[2]

Formerly a vast expanse of avocado orchards, citrus groves, and vineyards, the exurban valley in which Shepard was raised had been settled by "people who couldn't make it in the big city," he wrote. "They got so far and just quit the road. Maybe some just ran out of gas. . . . It was a temporary society that became permanent. . . . It was a car culture for the young. For the old it was just a dead end." Characters in Shepard's plays arrive onstage the way the valley's inhabitants arrived there—fearful and unsure of themselves, their ambitions thwarted by an unseen hand:

> They crash around in this space for a while making a certain kind of rough music and then disappear again. Nothing's figured out or decided for sure. Nothing's final. . . . Everybody's caught up in a fractured world that they can't even see. What's happening to them is unfathomable but they have a suspicion. Something unseen is working on them. Using them. They have no power and all the time they believe they're controlling the situation.[3]

Shepard spent his weekends as a teenager cruising around the valley in his metallic blue '32 Ford Deuce Coupe with black Naugahyde upholstery and a bucket rumble seat.[4] To pay it off, he worked two summers at Cowley's Horse Ranch in Chino for "a buck and a quarter an hour, all day long."[5] He'd often sit in his Deuce Coupe at A&W Root Beer stands, in the high school parking lot, at Bob's Big Boy, or "racing some chump in a Hudson Hornet on a Friday night."[6]

Shepard hung model airplanes from his bedroom ceiling as a boy, but those dangling toys, designed to ignite a child's sense of adventure, seemed only to add to the feelings of claustrophobia and dread that enveloped his home.[7] Far from objects of wonder and escape, the model planes appeared as spies planted by his dad, a former Army Air Force bomber, and thus reminders of his entrapment in what Shepard later claimed was a violent home life. He used to lie in bed obsessing over his terrors with his sisters asleep in their bunk bed in the next room. "Those nites locked up inside my blood, bones rigid, body of stone. Staring at the ceiling. Starving for a voice."[8]

Shepard and his father churned with seething resentments throughout his adolescence; and once "Steve," a byname to avoid confusion with his father, Sam Rogers Sr., shot up in height, they circled each other like a pair of six-foot-tall silverback gorillas. Shepard's mother, Jane Rogers, recorded in her diary, "Sam called Steve his nemesis."[9] Jane spoiled her son, but also adored her husband and couldn't bear the idea of separation. Yet her husband would disappear for days-long drinking binges, and Jane would find a load of laundry dumped in the kitchen from him, with a sharp reminder not to starch or bleach his shirts.[10]

Sam Sr. was convinced that his son, two daughters, and his wife were all conspiring against him: "It's like living in a den of vipers!" says Weston Tate, Shepard's portrait of his alcoholic father in the play *Curse of the Starving Class*. "Spies! Conspiracies behind my back! I'M BEING TAKEN FOR A RIDE BY EVERY ONE OF YOU!" Sam Sr. came to regard his only son as female. "Not exactly a woman but of the female persuasion," Shepard confided to a friend. "Not fruity exactly but suspicious."[11] As Shepard grew into manhood, he cloaked himself in a mantle of machismo so impregnable, he made certain that no unlucky soul would make that mistake again.

Shepard routinely suggested that his father beat him; but in his plays and interviews, this violence appears less than certain. A private notebook of his from 1974 offers a clearer picture. In an entry titled "Snake Eyes," Shepard contends that he'd surmounted his fear of his father the same way he overcame his fear of American violence, as he likened his father's deficiencies to the sins of the nation: "It's like when you finally see yer old man beating you up after years of beating you up & you see he's just crazy & weak & drunk & he hates himself more than he hates you & when he's beatin' the shit outa' you he's doin' it to himself. He's goin' backwards with poison & it's just sad 'cause he ain't got a chance. He'll go down like a bug in a drain. America's just like my

Dad." The Rogers clan "feels its catastrophe but can't pin it down, can't see it, can't do nothing about it," he wrote, as if his family existed, "just like America," with a murdered child buried in its backyard. "There's a secret in my family. In my family's blood."[12]

A school pal of Shepard's remembered a black eye before high school, after which Shepard became an athlete, and he could bat away drunken assaults. "His father beat him up a lot" before high school, the friend said, describing Sam Sr. as "a drunk and a failed jazz musician." "He was very strict, my father," Shepard acknowledged, "very aware of the need for discipline." But there was another side, one that Shepard's sister Sandy, whom his father indulged as lavishly as Jane did their son, was able to enjoy when her brother was gone. "There was no physicalness going on; it was all mental," Sandy said of her father and brother during his later school years. "My dad just wanted him to work. . . . On weekends, he would disappear, and my dad just wanted him to mow the fucking lawn. And he didn't want to do it. He was like that. . . . He didn't want to do this; he didn't want to do that. He just wanted to get out of there."[13]

"Like a lot of people who grow up in a little hick town, you just want out altogether," Shepard agreed. The drive-ins, drive-throughs, drag races, Ripple wine, and Benzedrine of his teen years did offer petty distractions, and Shepard had started experimenting with the high life by age twelve, after he'd stolen his first Chesterfield butt from his father's ashtray.[14] By sixteen, he was "totally addicted [to cigarettes] and indoctrinated into the strong belief that American manhood and smoking were synonymous." At that point, he drove down to Tijuana, Mexico, to smoke and drink and buy Benzedrine tablets and gawk at prostitutes and score a fake driver's license. "I felt I wanted to escape," he wrote in disgust at the memory, "but only into the mountains."[15]

Sandy Rogers attributed her father's relentless anger more to World War II than to his bloodline, as her brother did. Sam Sr. was, after all, a war hero, his Army Air Force uniform festooned with medals testifying to his valor across Europe, Africa, and the Middle East.[16] He'd flown forty-six combat missions as a B-24 bomber pilot during the war, and watched some close friends get shot down in their "flying fortresses." Once during the war while piloting a bombing mission, Sam Sr. watched the glass turret beneath the fuselage explode out from under him and take with it a close friend, his gunner, who fell to Earth with an unopened parachute. It was a story that haunted Shepard's childhood dreams and contributed to his fear of flying as an adult. Often when a plane flew overhead, Sam Sr. reflexively picked at a scar on the back of his neck that Shepard presumed was a result of war trauma.[17]

When Sandy was twelve, she borrowed his pocket knife and later slipped it back into his pants pocket while he was napping. "He jumped about four feet high and was scared to death. I know that was the war." On another occasion, a French teacher from the high school where Sam Sr. was teaching Spanish came over for dinner. The adults began talking about the Romanian village where the teacher, Frank Say, grew up, and "I remember my dad getting up and disappearing, and then finding out later that that was a village that they'd bombed, and he was shook."[18]

Shepard privately wrote about this period, "I lived on the edge of terror all the time." One fateful night when Shepard was eighteen, a demonic spirit, fueled by a drinking bender, took hold of Sam Sr. that his son later called his own personal "holocaust," "original banishment," or "Big Blow-Up."[19]

Shepard had been out with Stark, his prize-winning German shepherd. They were rambling by horses in neighboring fields, rows of alfalfa, avocado trees, and orange blossoms. Approaching the house, he observed his father drunk as usual, but his hands were drenched with blood. Jane had locked him out, at which point he had smashed one of the windows with a claw hammer and tore the front door off its hinges. Shepard stepped in to defend his shocked younger sisters in the hallway, and Jane was trapped screaming in the kitchen. The exploding windows sounded like twelve-gauge shotgun blasts.[20]

"You were there watching the whole time," Shepard later wrote in his father's voice. "I remember your beady eyes peering out at me from the hallway. You saw the whole thing."[21]

Being thrown out of his home would weigh heavily on Shepard, and the episode appeared in his writing well after his father's ignoble death. As he would later depict his exile in an autobiographical story, "The son then snuck out one of the broken windows, under cover of dawn, with a few books in a paper sack.... Stepping over the unconscious, bleeding form of his father he then jumped into [his car] and never stopped driving for the rest of his life."[22]

Shepard rented a second-floor room at the Motel 6 in nearby Arcadia with views across Huntington Drive of that shrine to old-time horse racing on the outskirts of Pasadena, the Santa Anita racetrack.[23] To pay for the room, along with betting on ponies at the track, he used money he'd saved working for a veterinarian, and he shagged balls at the golf course down the street.[24] "My greatest ambition," he recalled, "was to be a veterinarian at the Santa Anita racetrack."[25] Santa Anita was a magical place for Shepard, and he used to lie in bed dreaming of its mystery and grandeur. "It's the only place I ever longed to be a part of," he later wrote.[26]

Shepard owned a car, so he was able to land a part-time job as a newspaper delivery driver. Each morning he scanned the papers, but one day he paused on an advertisement for the Bishop's Company, a traveling theater troupe named in honor of the Methodist Bishop Gerald H. Kennedy that was scouting for actors. The audition terrified him, but the Bishop's casting directors appraised his boyish good looks and rakish blue eyes and hired him on the spot. In mid-June 1963, Jane and his little sister Roxanne drove him to the "Silver Eagle" Continental Trailways bus that would take him to Philadelphia.[27]

Shepard toured with the Bishop's as an actor and stagehand on the Northeast church circuit for over four months; but after a few performances in New York City, the company parked for a while at Times Square and he and a couple of others abandoned the company to try their luck on the Great White Way. After watching the tail of the red Ford bus rumble away down Broadway, trailing exhaust, Shepard scanned the shows advertised in bright colorful lights on the theater marquees. "Now I'm really in for it," he thought, and he was.[28]

INTRODUCTION

# THE SIDEWINDER'S HEAD

Samuel Shepard Rogers, after over a half century of hard work and equally hard living, passed away at seventy-three years old on July 27, 2017. Over the course of his improbable career, Sam Shepard, as he renamed himself at age twenty, received a Pulitzer Prize in 1979, and a record ten Obie Awards, the most prestigious prize for Off- and Off-Off-Broadway theater. His screenplay for Wim Wenders's Western cult classic *Paris, Texas* (1984) won the Palme d'Or at the Cannes Film Festival, and he won or was nominated for countless other honors. Shepard was also an actor onstage and on-screen, a screenwriter, a director, a musician, and a skilled equestrian and horse breeder. But it's his role as the "poet laureate of America's emotional badlands," the most daring theatrical innovator of his generation, that will endure.[1]

The *New York Times* greeted Shepard in the 1960s as an "acknowledged 'genius,'" though only one of his plays, *Operation Sidewinder*, premiered in a Broadway theater.[2] He adored the women in his life but was a compulsive philanderer; he was a movie and TV star but was dismissive of acting and loathed Hollywood; he walked and talked with a cowboy's swagger but was hounded by neurotic fears, of threats both real and perceived. (Ironically, in *The Right Stuff*, when he played the world's greatest pilot, Chuck Yeager, he was paralyzed by a fear of flying, or "falling" as he put it.)[3] He shied away from questions about his personal life, but writing, he acknowledged, was therapy for him:

"Writing is a way of bringing things back together a bit," he told *Rolling Stone*. "If I can at least write something, I start to feel that I'm gathering out of that lostness something that has some kind of structure and form, and something that, one hopes, can be translated to others."[4]

Shepard's tragic death by progressive muscular atrophy (PMA, an ALS-adjacent neurodegenerative disease) brought down the curtain on an electrifying career. His work chronicled the historical upheavals of American life in all of its outer splendor and inner chaos—from the 1960s countercultural revolution to 9/11 and the resistible rise of Donald Trump.

But contrary to the well-worn legend of an all-American hick from the sticks who unwittingly happened upon his accomplishments, the scores of interviews I conducted with friends, colleagues, and members of his family reveal a man fiercely driven to success, even in film acting, a vocation he publicly decried. ("It's like having a little oil well back there in the backyard," he joked about being a movie star. "You go and dip into it.")[5] Shepard composed over sixty plays, more than twenty of which would be produced in New York by the time he was twenty-eight. By his death in 2017, he saw fifty-six of his plays staged professionally and directed ten of them; wrote six screenplays for produced films, two of which he directed; helped doctor dozens of other screenplays; published ten books of fiction, narrative nonfiction, memoir, and poetry; and acted in over sixty television and film roles. Looking backward from 2014, Shepard quipped, "Oddly, I wasn't even fucking trying."[6]

In fact, Shepard could be nothing short of ruthless in his quest for notoriety. After he left California for New York, his friend Charles Mingus III implored me to understand over the course of numerous interviews, Shepard "strategically plotted out a career by being everything—all things to all people."[7]

Shepard was fascinated by Native American cultures, and he respectfully tapped their mythologies to inform his writing—the Chindi spirit of the Navajo; the sidewinder rattlesnake and Blue Star Kachina of the Hopi; and the broadly invoked coyote, hawk, crow, and horse. The mythical Coyote of folklore is usually a male half-human trickster and has multiple interpretations across tribal cultures, if primarily in the Great Plains and the Southwest. Depending on the tale, he might be loving or lecherous, tender or cruel, hilarious or cutting, a staunch individualist or a communal hero. Coyote is, like the subject of this book, "all things to all people."

In the fall of 1975, Shepard enjoyed a torrid affair with the iconic folk singer Joni Mitchell while touring on Bob Dylan's Rolling Thunder Revue. At the time, Mitchell gave him a pet name with her song about the dalliance, "Coyote," which became an instant folk classic. Before that, Patti Smith, another musical legend who'd fallen under Shepard's spell, listed "coyote" in her journal as one of her lover's favorite words, along with "Topeka, red dog, pistol, appaloosa, [and] outlaw." She loved his "coyote laugh," and his autobiographical character in their cowritten play, *Cowboy Mouth*, is described in the script as "a cat who looks like a coyote."[8] In Shepard's play *Back Bog Beast Bait*, a one-act written around the same time as *Cowboy Mouth*, his alter ego, Slim, actually transforms into a coyote. "Coyote" never stuck as a nickname, but as Mitchell and Smith intuited, the totem, notably in Native American cultures, bore the strongest likeness to the man. Much like Shepard, real coyotes can survive and even flourish in urban areas, however reluctantly, and in so doing, also like the playwright, their presence serves as a welcome reminder of the resilience of the wild. Coyotes expanded their range across North America, as Shepard did, but are associated, as he is, with the American West as much as Monument Valley, the saguaro cactus, or the Colt .45.

To the outside world, Shepard presented himself as a solitary artist in a perpetual state of exile. To those who knew him, one moment he could be gentle, funny, soft-spoken; the next, he could turn ornery and brutish, an "instant animal" as he put it.[9] The effort of managing this duality is a steady refrain in Shepard's work, as he drifted off into self-exile from friends and family. "Exile" is the word he settled on to prepare for one of his movie roles: "'Exile.' I knew it. There was no need for preparation. My whole life was a preamble. . . . I've exiled myself without wanting to."[10]

* * *

Shepard conjured a steady stream of plays he regarded as "a series of impulsive chronicles representing a chaotic, subjective world," and with them, he proved what an ambitious young American playwright might achieve without a Broadway imprimatur.[11] John Lion, founder of the Magic Theatre in San Francisco, where Shepard's stature as a leading playwright was fully realized, submitted that his impact on American culture was akin to the rock-and-roll idol Elvis Presley's. "Elvis Presley and Sam Shepard signify a change in the structure of American society that cuts much deeper than critical catch phrases like 'the birth of rock and roll' or the 'death of the American west,'" Lion observed. "They both apparently came from nowhere, reached the top of their profession with no formal training, rapidly became the stuff of popular myth. But beneath each persona lies an objective, calculating artist who has basically altered the way we look at things."[12]

Indeed, if Eugene O'Neill was the novelist of American drama and Tennessee Williams its poet, Sam Shepard was surely its musician. "Everything converges in music," insisted Shepard, himself a percussionist. "All of it: theater, directing, acting, and writing. All of the laws of music, you know, rhythm, dynamics, harmonies, discord, everything." "I like to look at the language and the inner rhythms of the play," he said of his 1980 tour de force *True West*, his personal favorite and most often revived play. "It's very related to music, the whole rhythmic structure of it. Rhythm is the delineation of time in space, but it only makes sense with silences on either side of it. You can't have a rhythm that doesn't have silence in it."[13]

Early in his career, Shepard was known for musically infusing his dramas with stream of consciousness monologues, or "arias," as they became popularly known. But rather than modernist stream of consciousness writing, Shepard said, "they were chants; they were incantations; they were spells. . . . They were a pulse." The *New York Times* drama critic Clive Barnes aptly dubbed these arias as "hand grenades thrown at an uneasy consciousness." The actor Joyce Aaron, Shepard's girlfriend in the mid-1960s, wrote an essay titled "Clues in Memory," which was meant to serve as a brief insider's guide for actors in Shepard's plays. In it, Aaron wrote of these arias, "You could compare it to jamming, or improvising on a single note."[14]

The impact of these arias on American theater history is incalculable. Eugene O'Neill, America's first serious dramatist, voiced a central problem of modern playwrights: How can a writer replicate the soliloquy of Shakespeare and melodrama once realism and naturalism had emerged with the plays of Henrik Ibsen, Anton Chekhov, and August Strindberg? How was it possible, he asked himself, to make apparent his characters' innermost feelings with realistic dialogue? Shepard's evolution away from O'Neill was to think of the "problem" of replacing the soliloquy as no problem at all: "In the conventional play," Shepard said, "the soliloquies always seemed to have this responsibility to realism or naturalism. But why? Why couldn't a character carry on an external monologue that was in fact an internal monologue just coming out? And why couldn't it be off the wall or exploratory, the way the inner monologue really is?"[15]

The musical attributes of Shepard's plays also allowed for comedy and tragedy in equal parts. "Sam hears his plays musically," the Irish actor Stephen Rea explained after Shepard added a laugh line during a rehearsal, "and the laughter is part of the music."[16] His writing was a psychological coping mechanism, and, on top of his musical ability, he had a wonderful gift for the most agreeable way to cope: a sense of humor. By all accounts, Shepard's wit was irrepressible. "One of the wonderful things about Sam is that he's funny," wrote his mentor, the avant-garde actor-director Joseph Chaikin. "There has to be a certain proportion of humor in everything he does. It's as clear as that there would have to be pepper on somebody's food or vegetables as part of a casserole."[17] When Chaikin was trying to recall a title of one of Shepard's plays, he asked the playwright for help. "A comedy?" Chaikin offered. "They're *all* comedies," Shepard said with a laugh.[18]

His offbeat sense of humor was a mixture of slapstick and existential dread that one critic described as "a funny thing happened to me on the way to Armageddon."[19] With humor, what pained Shepard most transferred into something outside of him, reified and distanced; then, through the writing process, the pain would drift away, however fleetingly. "I don't think you can do anything if you're right slap in the middle of it," he said of his use of what the postmodernists, with whom he was roughly affiliated, called "ironic distance" in autofiction.

> The only way I can do it is to step a little bit away, and the characters somehow become human. If you have enough distance that it becomes funny, if you can illuminate the humor, even though what they're going through is very raw, then it's possible. . . . If the humor drops away then it just becomes deadly—so deadly and remorseful that it's hard to enjoy. What humor brings to it is the "humaneness" of it.[20]

Shepard was one of those writers whose work is so distinctive that their name can be employed as an adjective. This started when he was only twenty-six, after *Newsweek*'s drama critic Jack Kroll applied the term "Shepardian" in a 1970 review of his play *Operation Sidewinder*, which merged the Hopi Indian religion with the 1960s call for Black revolution and white countercultural rebellion: "Shepard is one of those writers so resonant with the times that life seems to imitate them—the Indians at Alcatraz are a very Shepardian phenomenon."[21]

In 1979, the critic Jacques le Sourd incisively defined "Shepardesque" in a review of Shepard's jazz play *Suicide in B♭*: "The play is, well, Shepardesque—obscure, beguiling, with the fascinating Shepard mix of mythic vision and funny stage business, opacity and crystal clarity."[22] In 1996, the *New York Times* drama critic Ben Brantley defined "Shepardesque" as conveying "the falseness of memory, the gulf between men and women and, above all, the uncertainty of identity."[23] The Shepard chronicler David J. DeRose applied the term to dramas that "both thematically and theatrically [present] the world and the self as unfixed."[24]

One way to integrate these definitions is to say that a true Shepardian play is shot through with an overwhelming sense of fear. As Stephen Rea, who both acted in and directed Shepard's plays, observed, "The people are all dislocated and strange and unconnected in Sam's plays. It's all about this kind of terror—you know: the *horror*. The horror that's outside, that undefined outside world. Unseen, unknown terror suddenly striking. If you don't understand that about Sam's plays then you can't do them."[25] Fear is the guiding principle of Shepard's work—fear of authority, fear of flying, fear of war, fear of climate change, fear of failure, fear of abandonment, fear of loneliness, fear of heredity, fear of exposure, fear of death, and fear of our escalating estrangement from reality. "My terrors now have more to do with being alienated from life rather than dying or death," he said in 1988, less than a decade before the internet was to consume the world's populace, "but what's most frightening to me now, not only personally, but in everything you see around me, is this estrangement from life, people, things, everything, becomes more and more removed from the *actual*, removed from the *Earth*, to the point where people just don't know each other or themselves."[26]

Shepard's life, by his own numerous accountings, had been shrouded in an interminable fog of anxiety since his childhood in Southern California. "I was raised on a steady diet of fear & guilt," he observed. "In some ways I think it was probably this very state of anxiety & fear that brought me initially to . . . my interest in writing & art. So it's a double-edged sword maybe."[27] When I asked Joyce Aaron about the notion of fear as a controlling dynamic in his plays, she replied, "Terror's underneath all of them."[28] Similarly, Nancy Meckler, Shepard's longtime director, told me, "The way I rehearse Sam's plays is by helping the actors work from a state of fear. So we would improvise, they would do improvisations, from that state of fear. . . . When people are in a state of extreme terror, they can do or say anything to get through it. And that's the only reason they're saying it. They're just trying to get through it."[29]

When Shepard found himself in a panicked state, his road to recovery, as he put it, was "through getting totally identified with some function or set 'interest' like cattle or horses or writing & slowly the anxiety fades into the background."[30] Writing centered him, and without it, he said, he was lost. "Not having a play to write," one frustrated diary note reads, "is like being without a friend, homeless, in a state of wandering."[31]

This dysphoric self-portrait flies in the face of Shepard's self-invented image as a hard-as-nails cowboy. Again, to reconcile the contradiction in the man, we must go to the man himself: "There's nothing wrong with real *machismo*," he argued. "It's just that nobody knows what it means anymore. The original idea must have had its roots in what at one time was a sense of real courage in the face of danger; but it's been so distorted that it's now mostly externalized behavior that actually has to do with *pretending*, with *covering up*, with *fear*. So the more *macho* a guy appears, the more scared to death he usually is—you can bet your boots on that!"[32]

Once the lights go down in a Shepard play, it's understood that the auditorium will no longer be a safe space. His titles generally tip you off with words such as "unseen," "ghostly," "savage," "crime," "killer," "dread," and so on. (If they're upbeat titles like *Fool for Love* or *Simpatico*, he's messing with your mind.) After the curtain goes up, what follows aims straight for the amygdala. If this target is missed, it is not Shepardian. When the target is hit, Shepard's paranoia drifts away to release a sensation of clarity and awe. This is the reasoning the playwright Jack Gelber, a pioneer in American avant-garde theater, had in mind in his 1976 styling of Shepard as a New World shaman:

> Anthropologists define the shaman as an expert in a primitive society who, in a trance state induced by drugs or music or other techniques, directly confronts the supernatural for the purposes of cures, clairvoyance, the finding of lost objects, and the foretelling of the future. Sam Shepard . . . is a shaman—a New World shaman. There are no witches on broomsticks within [his plays]. That's the Old World. Sam is as American as peyote, magic mushrooms, Rock and Roll, and medicine bundles. . . . The emphasis is on the trip, the personal visions, the shamanistic goals fulfilled along the way—in short, the metaphysical. . . . Shepard's design is to promote a theatrical condition between the audience and actor similar to an ecstatic state which will allow him to fulfill his shaman's role within the play and between audience and actor.[33]

Shepard's motives for writing were rarely shamanistic, however. According to his sister Roxanne Rogers, "He doesn't write for anybody; he writes for himself."[34] Writing was a proactive form of psychic healing for Shepard, and if his audiences felt healed along the way too, it was a happy byproduct of his dramas, not the end goal. But his plays struck a psychic chord among his contemporary audiences and fellow artists, as they do now in our current Age of Insecurity.

Shepard's kinship with the horse becomes more understandable the further we recognize his dysphoric mind: horses were kindred spirits. Susanna Massie Thomas of the Secretariat Center in Kentucky describes the horse as always on alert—eyes wide apart, ears up, running in protective herds. "To the horse, a human, as with all predators, is initially terrifying," Thomas informed me. "Humans smell like meat eaters, their eyes are close together (forward in scope), their ears barely visible. We have to work very hard to convince the horse that we are their friends and not their foes."[35] As a teenager, Shepard felt like his father's prey, and later in life, the Oscar-winning actor Jessica Lange, his longtime romantic partner, and other friends used to tease him for his revealing "horse eyes," or a frantic look of desperation to bolt his surroundings.[36]

The terrifying physical and emotional violence that convulses Shepard's writing is in part what makes him so unambiguously American. "There's no way to escape the fact that we've grown up in a violent culture, we just can't get away from it, it's part of our heritage," he said. "I think part of it is that we've always felt somewhat helpless in the face of this vast continent. Helplessness is answered in many ways, but one of them is violence."[37] Shepard even believed that American-style violence was "touching" in a way because it was motivated by "humiliation": "This sense of failure runs very deep—maybe it has to do with the frontier being systematically taken away, with the guilt of having gotten this country by wiping out a native race of people, with the whole Protestant work ethic."[38]

* * *

Shepard's psychic journey was like a funhouse hall of mirrors, each mirror displaying a more contorted self than the last. It is the same for those of us who, following his erratic and tumultuous artistic career for decades, hunt for that place in time that might offer a conclusive portrait of the artist and man. As one progresses, the mirrors' warped forms consolidate and clarify, but by the end, we never arrive at a single definitive image. "When you talk about Sam," his closest friend Johnny Dark said, "are you talking about the 23-year-old or the 30-year-old or the 60-year-old? The theater Sam or the movie Sam? The guy at home or the guy at the bar? The funny, generous Sam? Sometimes they were different people."[39] No one knew this better than Shepard, and he hated it about himself.

Shepard had an emotional rough patch while in London in his late twenties, and he returned stateside a card-carrying member of a group dedicated to healing self-doubt. They followed what's called the "Fourth Way" (the other "ways" of holiness being embodied by Muslim fakirs, Christian monks, and Hindu yogis) but is better known by its followers as the "Work." The Greco-Armenian mystic George Ivanovich Gurdjieff taught that people sleepwalk through their lives. Gurdjieff invited his followers to wake up to their authentic selves and, as Johnny Dark, who introduced Shepard to Gurdjieff's Work, said, "destroy all false representations."[40]

Shepard made a Work-related declaration to another friend, the independent filmmaker Michael Almereyda, while shooting pool in South Dakota. Almereyda was watching Shepard play with a stunt double when the playwright announced, seemingly out of nowhere, "Personality is not the man. Personality is the *opposite* of the man."[41] Almereyda, interviewing him later at the Sundance Film Festival, urged him to expand upon his idea of personality. "Don't you have the feeling," Shepard responded, "that we all develop masks, layers of masks, and these masks make up a personality, a persona, and if you stripped these away what you come down to would be something completely different? An essence. Something more pure—or nothing at all."[42]

"'Who am I?'" Shepard asked in his midfifties. "As hackneyed and simplistic as this question might sound to us, it is one of the most important ones we can ask."[43] Once Shepard reached his late sixties, however, he rejected the basic premise of existential questioning. "We all walk around with this notion of 'I.' And it's not true: We're not this one entity. We're different aspects, different voices."[44]

One of Shepard's fragmentary identities was a man of unslakable appetites, mainly for alcohol and women. He'd struggled with alcohol for ages, he admitted in 2010 after getting a DUI in Illinois the previous year. "You sometimes use the excuse, 'I'm a writer, dammit, I can do anything I want,' but that doesn't work. In my later plays, especially, alcohol is there—not as a moral issue, but as a disaster. And in my case, it's a real disaster."[45] Sex for Shepard was a mysterious, thrill-seeking adventure, which at the same time fulfilled his need for connection (and literary inspiration). His womanizing was a great source of aggravation for the women in his life, whether they were his lovers or collaborators or some mix of both. "I felt totally at home on the road with Sam in the Southwest," the director Treva Wurmfeld said of filming her 2012 documentary *Shepard & Dark*. "That part was easy. . . . It's really the drinking and womanizing that makes him difficult. That part is pretty awful, but the rest of him is great."[46]

When I asked Shepard's friend and colleague Ethan Hawke what he thought about Shepard's inveterate drinking and notorious promiscuity, he considered the question psychologically:

> There's a reason why people are alcoholics or addicts or sex addicts—it makes you feel good, and if you're in pain, you want to feel good. And I always sensed from him that some part of him was in pain, and I think he was using alcohol and sex and different things to feel like he was alive, and to feel good and to feel better. It's always a temporary fix, but it always works. (What's the song, "Tonight the Bottle Never Let Me Down"?) . . . I can just picture him rolling his eyes at everybody trying to psychoanalyze him, because he was allergic to that line of thinking. In effect, what we all admire about him is he was willing to let the inner animal live—the id part of us. You never fucking knew what you were going to get with him, I swear.[47]

Shepard's love life plays a central role in the dramatic tension of many of his plays as well, making sex an "imaginative quest," in the novelist John Updike's meaning.[48] Jessica Lange, who was Shepard's partner for almost thirty years, the mother of two of his children, and a regular character in his plays, poetry, and prose after 1981, the year she met him, called Shepard "a great man, a natural man, which is rare." "I've been with a lot of men, and I've known a lot of men," she said after their first decade together. "And you know I've had romances with what you'd call famous men, and none compare to Sam in terms of maleness."[49] (She later disavowed this, saying, "I hate talking superlatives. There's obviously something. I've been with the man for 24 years. And I'm still crazy about him.")[50] On top of Shepard's inarguable sex appeal, he was also a Hollywood star, and his successful acting career paralleled his successes with women, who provided him with an overabundance of literary material along with the ephemeral pleasure that came along with his romantic relationships. "If I wasn't so fucked up," he concluded to Johnny Dark about his lifelong struggles with alcohol and sex, "I probably couldn't have written all those great plays."[51]

Perhaps it's no wonder, then, that Shepard was cryptic about his personal life, a guarded man who considered his privacy inviolable. "Somebody said a writer is someone who hides his secrets in print," Michael Almereyda recalled. "And that's true of Sam."[52] To Shepard, whose writing is infused with such deep personal stakes, the idea of a biography about him was a nightmare, even while he recognized its inevitability. "This is for you 'archivists' who snoop into other people's lives," he wrote in an archived journal, "hoping to solve some mystery or other about yourselves through others: YOU'LL NEVER FIND IT HERE!!"[53]

Still, Shepard hoarded material for future chroniclers. He judiciously saved his personal notebooks, letters, poetry, autobiographical sketches, travelogues, lists, timelines, reviews of his work, publicity notices, and media interviews. And Shepard's body of writing itself cries out for a biographical approach. This might sound odd about a man notorious for self-mythologizing, but listen to his own words: "I consider theatre and writing to be a home where I bring the adventures of my life and sort them out, making sense or nonsense out of mysterious impressions."[54]

Shepard was promoting his collection of stories *Cruising Paradise* when a journalist asked him point-blank, "To what extent are the stories fiction, and how much of them are real?" "It's all fiction," he replied uneasily. "I mean it's based on real stuff, but I've got to call it fiction."[55] Autobiographical material was vital because of the "stakes" involved, he said. "It's not just a good idea for a story. It's a life-and-death situation—and that [rare] kind of material is very exciting."[56] Ben Brantley described Shepard's gutbucket confessionals this way:

> For anyone at all familiar with Mr. Shepard's biography, it is clear that his most intimate experiences and feelings gleam piercingly throughout his work. In fact, his work may be the most intensely personal of that of any living playwright of his stature, which may account for the fact that his style (unlike, say, David Mamet's) has never been successfully imitated.[57]

Brantley's observation leads to a crucial point about autofiction: that a piece of writing is based on the writer's own life has never deflated its value or disqualified anything from being a work of fine art. Rather, it's the act of highly imaginative people processing their lives through writing without the burden of strict factual accuracy. This is often achieved, as with Shepard, by intensifying their singularity through surreal or abstract imagery, exaggerated characters, and verbal distinctiveness.

Shepard was endowed with an uncanny ability to conjure the fraught states of his particularly American psychosis out of otherwise ordinary conversations. A rumor had been floating around for decades, for instance, that Shepard's ex-wife, O-Lan Jones (née Johnson), herself an actor and playwright, was the actual author of his only play with an all-female cast, *Little Ocean* (1974).[58] When I asked her whether this was true, she responded unequivocally, "No, Sam wrote that." When pressed that the dialogue sounded more like her voice than his, she responded with a smile: "Well, I *said* most of it."[59] Certainly it's true that his writing is not inevitably factual. For that matter, anything that sounds suspect probably is. "He doesn't tell the truth," his sister Sandy slyly told me, then corrected herself by quoting O-Lan: "The facts aren't the facts, but what he says is the truth."[60]

O-Lan's stepfather, Johnny Dark, an unsung writer and photographer whom Shepard considered "an underground genius," was his best friend for fifty years. Dark told me about Shepard's troubled mind, and the ways that he hid it in plain sight. His writing in general, Shepard told him, was about "personal problems." Dark's tales of their fraternal adventures demonstrate how volubly Shepard revealed his private life in his work, and Dark told me how astonished he was that there were never any real-world consequences because the works exposed his actual behavior under the auspices of fiction. Shepard once told Dark about an intimate moment he enjoyed with Jessica Lange in a Los Angeles motel, for instance. "And then what happened?" Dark needled him. "Or will we read about it in your next play?"[61]

Nearing the end of his life, when a reporter asked Shepard why he didn't write a memoir, he responded, "If anybody wants to understand who I am, they just read my plays, or go see my plays, or read my books. I don't have to go beyond that."[62] That's fair, and has the advantage of being true, but it's the biographer's job to create the context around those works that give a reader a fuller understanding of where those ideas originated and how they correspond to his actual life. It's also a matter of giving shape and form to an otherwise serpentine career path.

As such, another Shepardian totem, like the coyote and the horse, is the venomous sidewinder rattlesnake, also native to the playwright's arid Southwest American territory. The trajectory of Shepard's career curiously resembles the trick-of-the-eye quality of the sidewinder: as you watch the reptile ascend the dunes, it appears to be wriggling backward. "What [Shepard] does from play to play is lunge forward," wrote the critic Richard Gilman, "move sideways, double back, circle around, throw in this or that, adopt a voice then drop it, pick it up again."[63]

No other reptile depends as much as the Mojave sidewinder on its family to survive. In their first few days, newly hatched sidewinders coil up together at the opening of a burrow to keep their bodies at a survivable temperature, much as Shepard used to feel the warmth and comfort of his two sisters at the Rogers homestead in Bradbury. Sidewinders without the support of their kin would not survive; but once they depart the burrow, they do so for good. Shepard did too, but came around to the life-giving yet equally venomous subject of dysfunctional family life. "Father, mother, brothers, sisters—you can't really cut yourself off from that. Why would you want to? Because family is the real heart and soul of what you're about as a writer. What it becomes, how it unravels, is part of your craftsmanship, but if you cut yourself off from it, all that's dead."[64]

There's an old gold prospector in one of Shepard's plays who speaks of the Hopi belief that a sidewinder's head, like this playwright's own astonishing mind, "has a door and if you keep that door open all kind a' wonders come to ya'."[65]

# PART I

# 1943–1971

We have all these galaxies inside of us. Huge, unknown territories. And if we don't enter those in art of one kind or another, whether it's playwriting, or painting, or music, or whatever, then I don't understand the point in doing anything. If you don't enter into these areas that are deeply mysterious and dangerous, then you're not doing anything as far as I can tell. . . . It's the reason I write. I try to go into parts of myself that are unknown.

—Sam Shepard

In the beginning was the Groove.

—Suzan-Lori Parks

CHAPTER 1

# SON OF SAM

Sam Shepard conjured a birth story of himself bursting forth from his mother's womb with a fully formed consciousness. "I plunged into the world head first," he wrote, "and, although covered with blood, my attitude was very friendly. I was not a mean person then." Outside his mother's hospital window, he saw "mammoth green icebergs" forming on Lake Michigan, and the nursing staff watched him climb out of his mother's belly and slide down to the cold, white-tiled floor. Upon reaching the windowpanes, he got his "first taste of what it's like to suffer."[1]

Jane Rogers's recollection of her only son's birth was more faithful to reality, if still through a starry-eyed lens. Samuel Shepard Rogers was born on November 5, 1943, in the hospital of an army basic training camp in the Fort Sheridan neighborhood of Highland Park, Illinois. Jane remembered the exact time, 3:20 p.m., because the army brats had just been let out of school, and she'd heard them below her window screaming and laughing and frolicking in the autumn leaves. She rejoiced in how "wonderful it was to have you laying close to me all pink and perfect." Shepard remembered her saying that he "never even cried when he came out.... He just slid into the world as quiet as a ghost."[2]

The Rogers family called him "Steve," or "Stevie," to avoid confusion with his father's name, and it stuck long past childhood; he's even listed more formally as "Steven Rogers" in his high school yearbook.[3] His father, Samuel "Sam" Shepard Rogers, was born in Crystal Lake, Illinois, on February 20, 1917. Jane was born the same year a few months later on July 16. Sam Sr. and Jane had known each other since second grade, when he first walked her to school in their hometown of Lombard, Illinois, and they began dating at fifteen.[4]

In 1939, Sam Rogers dropped out of Ripon College in Wisconsin after his freshman year to sign up for the military. He first served as a private in the Thirteenth School Squadron, then enlisted in the army on August 30, 1943, and trained as a pilot in the US Army Air Corps. He and Jane were married at Holy Trinity Church in West Palm Beach, Florida, on April 3, 1942, while he was stationed at Morrison Army Airfield. Shepard was conceived during Sam's flight training in Douglas, Georgia, where he'd arranged for Jane to hide in a field on base for several nights. As Shepard later described it, after learning "to fly B-24s and B-17s and drop bombs and what all," his father went off to "Italy, Holland, Germany, England, the whole shebang."[5]

On the day his son was born, Sam Sr. was stationed in California at Muroc Air Force Base, later Edwards Air Force Base, in the Mojave Desert.[6] Eventually it would be the home of the most elite test pilots in the world, a center of innovation for the aerospace industry, and host to the sound-barrier-breaking test pilot and war hero Chuck Yeager, "the fastest man in the world."

The Rogers family's roots in the United States ran very deep. Sam Sr.'s side descended from the *Mayflower* passenger Susanna White, one of four women who survived to attend the first Thanksgiving in Plymouth.[7] "It was anything *but* the ridiculous myth of Thanksgiving we've been handed down," Shepard wrote of his ancestor's experience, "where the Indians & Pilgrims all sat happily down at a long plank table eating turkey & sharing brightly colored corn. A terrible war broke out that almost devastated the entire population of native people—setting the stage for everything to come 200 years later with the greedy sweep Westward."[8] Susanna gave birth to Peregrin (pilgrim), or Peregrine, in 1620, making him the first English newborn to arrive in the Massachusetts Bay Colony.[9] Shepard routinely claimed that he was the seventh in a line of

Episcopalian, hard-and-fast alcoholics named Samuel Shepard Rogers. He was, though nominal discrepancies meant that technically—and for Shepard it mattered a great deal—he was Samuel Shepard Rogers IV. Nevertheless, as a young man of twenty, he would infuriate his father by rechristening himself "Sam Shepard."[10]

A self-described "spawn of the air force," Shepard described his upbringing this way: "Semi-rural. Crazy, insane family." And he received the fearsome notion about seven generations of troubled men from his father, Sam Sr.[11] On the Fourth of July 1977, Shepard completed a draft of a screenplay about his senior year in high school titled "The Seventh Son." The film was never produced, yet much of the plot, themes, dialogue, and character names were drawn from his 1976 tour de force *Curse of the Starving Class*, his first full-length autobiographical family drama. In "The Seventh Son," a heated discussion between the son and his father, whose eyes are "bloodshot and full of the despair of a resigned alcoholic," directly confronts Shepard's ill-fated bloodline:

> **Father:** Me? (he laughs) You scared of me? You shoulda' seen my old man. He was somethin' to be scared of. You shouda' seen his old man before him. All the way back down the line. Seven generations. What'd you think, you'd be able to escape somehow?
>
> **Wes:** Escape what?
>
> **Father:** The blood. Escape the blood.[12]

This stranglehold of heredity would become a refrain in Shepard's relationships and writing. A later avatar of Sam Sr., the drunkard father Weston Tate in *Curse of the Starving Class*, also believes he's been "infected" by his family's bloodline: "From being born, to growing up, to droppin' bombs, to having kids, to hittin' bars. . . . It all turned on me somehow. It all turned around on me."[13]

A year later, Shepard made it clear that his mother's heredity was his only hope. In a brief sketch titled "I Wonder What I'm Doing Here," he lists a "Statement of Character" that includes, among other personal traits, his age (33), vocation (writer), race (white), height (6' 1½"), weight

(160), eyes (blue), and ambition (Salvation). At the end, he scrawls, "FACE: Gaunt. Right eye more open than left. More susceptible to the world. Right eye is my mother's. Left eye is my father's. Right eye represents female principle. Left eye is male. Right eye represents good. Left bad. La Sinistra!" He wrote in hindsight that he'd desperately tried to resist the urge to adopt his father's despotic identity:

> I thought I had done my level best, everything I possibly could, *not* to become my father. Gone out of my way in every department: changed my name, first and last, falsified my birth certificate, deliberately walked and swung my arms in exact counterpoint to the way he had; picked out clothing the opposite of what he would have worn, right down to the underwear; spoke without any trace of a Midwestern twang, never kicked a dog in the ribs, never lost my temper over inanimate objects, never again listened to Bing Crosby after Christmas of 1959, and never ever hit a woman in the face. I thought I had come a long way in reshaping my total persona. I had absolutely no idea who I was but I knew for sure I wasn't him.[14]

From January to August 1944, his father flew B-24 Liberator bombers in forty-six combat missions across the European Theater in the Fifteenth Air Force out of Foggia, Italy. Their main objective was to bomb the oil and petroleum fields in Romania, the Nazis' primary fuel source. Sam Sr. came back from the war "greatly disturbed," according to his son. After returning stateside, he was transferred to army bases in Florida, Illinois, Idaho, Washington, Nebraska, Hawaii, and finally Guam.[15]

In Guam, where the Rogers family lived for twenty months, Japanese diehards hid out in the jungle and made desperate raids on the American military installations. His mother carried a holstered sidearm at all times, a loaded .45 automatic Colt with another clip in her handbag. "Me on one hip," Shepard remembered, "the pistol on the other." "All the women were issued with army Lugers," he said, and he remembered her taking aim and firing at furtive Japanese soldiers hidden among the mangroves.[16]

A photograph taken of Jane in Guam by Sam Sr. shows her in a beat-up Army jeep and pregnant with their first daughter, Sandra "Sandy" Amy Rogers, who was born there on September 9, 1947. A holstered pistol lies on her lap, while a beagle stands alert at her feet. "Stevie," a grinning, happy, towheaded toddler, is leaning over his mother's right shoulder from the back seat, clutching his knee as he grins and hams it up for the camera.

Sam retired as a first lieutenant of the Army Air Corps, what became known after World War II as the United States Air Force, and served as a captain in the Officers' Reserve Corps until 1955, his sleeves and lapels resplendent with campaign medals, service stars, and marksmanship badges. Next to him, Jane Rogers was an unimposing figure at about five feet three inches tall, but she had radiant, "glowing blue eyes," said a friend of Roxanne's. "They were intense. You looked at them and said, 'Oh, I'm not going to bullshit this person.'"[17]

After his retirement in 1949, the Rogers family lived for seven years at the home of Jane's maternal aunt, Grace Upton. Auntie Grace, as the family called her, lived in an adobe house in the affluent suburb of South Pasadena. While there, Sam Rogers studied Spanish at Occidental College on the GI Bill, and in 1952, he landed a position as a Spanish and Latin teacher at San Marino High School. The local paper reported that he was "older than most beginning teachers [because he is a veteran, but] demonstrates determination and enthusiasm which radiates to those with whom he associates." After eight years, Sam Sr. would become head of the foreign language department, along with supervising the foreign language and camera clubs.[18]

Jane Rogers had attended Pasadena City College before Sam Sr. went to war, then transferred to Occidental College as an English major. She was hired in 1958 to teach second grade in Pasadena at Polytechnic School, an elite feeder school for the nearby California Institute of Technology, and she would hold the post there until her retirement in 1985. Jane was a beloved teacher for students such as the future television writer and actor Mike White (*Freaks and Geeks*, *The White Lotus*). "Get rid of this," she'd scold him while miming an *X* across a page,

Jane encouraged White to write an adaptation of "The Emperor's New Clothes" in his second year. "She was my first development executive," he joked to the *Washington Post*.[19]

* * *

"Once he learned to run," Jane Rogers said of her son, "he never walked again." The first time Shepard ran away from home was at the age of six. He and two older boys, juvenile hall alumni according to Shepard, stole three bikes in South Pasadena and made their way down the cavernous, concrete strip of the Arroyo Seco (Dry Brook) to the Los Angeles River with the intention of riding to the city, which he'd only visited once or twice with Auntie Grace. "Los Angeles at that time in the fifties was a very exotic, distant place," Shepard wrote of this bike ride. "We rode past red shotgun shells faded by the sun, dead opossums, beer cans, Walnut shells, Carob pods, a Raccoon with two babies, pages of porno magazines, hunks of rope."[20]

After peddling through a pitch-black tunnel for what felt like hours, the boys were famished. They'd arrived at the city limits of Sierra Madre, which located them ten miles in the wrong direction. One of the boys had an uncle, though, who lived there and had a television. This was the first time Shepard ever watched TV, according to him, because his parents considered it bubble gum for the mind. Once the family did get a television set, Sandy Rogers recalled, "we only watched Dodger [baseball] games on TV. We couldn't watch anything else, only the games. Mom and Dad both thought TV was evil, that it was really bad for your brain."[21] "The thing is, Mom didn't like comedy," Roxanne specified on the subject of Jane Rogers and TV restrictions.

> It was fun that my mom was allergic to. We weren't allowed to go to movies. . . . My dad was very musical, but we didn't sing and stuff. I think if my mom had been a little bit more open, we would have had more music in the house. We had a lot of music with my dad, but my mom didn't like fun. It was this weird, Victorian, strange thing. She

was funny. My dad was funny. All of us were funny, but we couldn't have fun.[22]

*The Lone Ranger* was on at the uncle's house in Sierra Madre, auspiciously enough. It was the popular cowboy show's first season, 1949, and Shepard, revived after a spaghetti dinner served up by his partner in crime's aunt, was rapt. By the time the boys returned to South Pasadena, it was late enough for the local police to question them and radio for their parents. Shepard's mother picked him up, telling him his father said he might kill him if he returned. On the ride back to Auntie Grace's, Jane repeated over and over, "Now you've got a Police Record. You'll have that for the rest of your life." Once home, his enraged father whipped him three times with "the buckle-end of [his] belt," then stormed out without uttering a word.[23]

But seeing *The Lone Ranger* was worth every swat. Like so many Southern Californian kids, he wrote, "I wanted to be 'famous' for something. I wanted everything turned around where I was the one revered and instilling a sense of awe in other people, where other people wanted to know me and I held a certain sway over them, a certain power, a deep mystery."[24]

At seven, he drove with his father to stake out an investment property Sam Sr. bought in the Mojave in the resort town of Desert Hot Springs. Gene Autry, Al Capone, Frank Sinatra, and Cary Grant had all traveled there to enjoy the mineral baths and evade the paparazzi in a desert oasis, though Sam Sr.'s land was, Roxanne said, "literally a patch of dirt with a gas pipe shunted into it."[25] Shepard was seated next to his father at a local mahogany bar when they spied the character actor Gabby Hayes. The Hollywood celebrity was sporting a tuxedo and cavorting with two young women, "decked out in slinky cocktail outfits, dripping with jewelry and sex." This was the first time he'd seen a recognizable actor just living the dream, and he wanted what Gabby Hayes had. His mother was allergic to fun, and his father was scornful of it: "That's what fame and fortune'll get you," he'd sneered when they saw Hayes. "Couple a blond chippies and a shrimp cocktail."[26] What better way, then, for Shepard to rebel in his youth than to dream of becoming an entertainer himself?

* * *

One of the high points of Shepard's childhood was visiting his grandparents Helen and "Grandpa Sam" Rogers, who lived in a two-story home in Lombard, Illinois, just east of Chicago. The house abutted a large cornfield, which gave credence to Grandpa Sam's signing the occasional letter to the local paper "Plain Dirt Farmer," and it would become the setting of Shepard's masterwork *Buried Child*. "Grandma Helen" Dodge Rogers was a strict disciplinarian when it came to raising her children and grandchildren. "She was really tall and really scary," Sandy said. "Six kids and five of them were boys, and she ran that house."[27]

Jane's father, Fred "Pop" De Forrest Schook, who died in 1942, lived near the Rogerses in Chicago. Schook was a leading impressionist who studied under H. O. Tanner in Paris and taught at the Art Institute of Chicago for more than twenty-five years. Her mother, Amy Louisa (Bynon) Schook, Grace's sister, was his model before they married. As a result of Pop's profession, Shepard's home was always chockablock with his impressionistic paintings and Asian art designs that inspired his work. Despite Pop's dying before Shepard's birth, "he was an influence on Sam . . . in the genes," according to his sister Sandy. "Of course, my mother was very artistic. She didn't paint or draw anything but . . . she had an artist's eye."[28]

Shepard's maternal side, in short, endowed him with an appreciation for art and culture, while the paternal side provided him with the raw material—war trauma, alcoholism, the curse of heredity—to dramatize.

Roxanne De Forrest Rogers, the youngest of the three Rogers siblings, was born at Grace Upton's house on July 12, 1955. The following summer, the family settled at 1459 East Lemon Avenue in nearby Bradbury. (Grace Upton passed away a few months after their move, on November 13, 1956.) Shepard attended Lincoln Elementary School and South Pasadena Middle School, then matriculated into the class of '61 at the newly established Duarte High School in the fall of 1957.[29]

The Rogers' property was situated at the foot of the San Gabriels, with a three-acre, sixty-five-tree avocado farm and a converted greenhouse overlooking the San Gabriel Valley. "My parents set it up so it would be their little dream house," Roxanne said, "and their little dream family."[30] They owned horses, chickens, and sheep, enough livestock to qualify as a ranch. The land was so open, the Rogers kids could ride a horse to the store for candy, then ride on for hours.[31] "We were living in this very upper-middle-class neighborhood," Roxanne said, "but we weren't really upper middle class. We didn't roll that way." Still, having the master impressionist Fred De Forrest Schook as a father, Jane was reared among a rarefied cultural elite. As a result, she looked down her nose at the San Gabriel Valley from her lofty perch in Bradbury.[32]

Once an idyllic expanse of farmland, by the 1950s, the San Gabriel Valley was littered with gravel pits, tract housing, dive bars, and drive-in movie theaters. Looking back on this period, Shepard told a friend, the actor Clark Middleton, that the truest depiction of the valley was the LA-based crime writer James Ellroy's *My Dark Places* (1996), a memoir about Ellroy's mother's unsolved murder there:

> The San Gabriel Valley was the rat's ass of Los Angeles County—a 30-mile stretch of contiguous hick towns due east of L.A. proper. . . . Valley land was cheap. The flat topography was ideal for grid housing and potential freeway construction. The more remote the area, the more land your money got you. You could hunt coons a few blocks off the local main drag and nobody would give you any grief. You could fence in your yard and raise chickens and goats for slaughter. You could let your toddlers run down the block in their shit-stained diapers. . . . The San Gabriel Valley was White Trash Heaven.

"Fucked up" veterans seeking sanctuary arrived in the valley en masse, and the population exploded. With the people came smog and housing developments and an economic boom that changed the area's look, Ellroy wrote, "but did not in any way alter its Wild West character."[33]

* * *

Shepard's parents were minimally paid schoolteachers, and it showed. When they first moved to Bradbury, for instance, Sam Sr. became a DIY fanatic. "If my dad could make it, he'd make it," Roxanne recalled. "He didn't buy anything. He wanted to do it all himself, and he never got it done."[34] And he bellowed at Shepard that he'd help him come hell or high water.[35] "For eighteen years I was your slave," the response came later from his beleaguered son. "I worked for you hand and foot. Shearing the sheep, irrigating the trees, listening to your bullshit about 'improve your mind, you'll never get ahead, learn how to lose, hard work and guts and never say die.'"[36]

During brushfire season, Shepard would clamber up on the roof and help his father spray down the shingles to prevent their house from burning down. Sam Sr. refused to pay for proper irrigation for the avocado trees, so he'd make the children help him hand-water them with hoses. As Shepard grew older, he was tasked with plowing the avocado orchard, while using a bandanna to keep the dust from his throat.

Each boyhood memory forms a singular sense of an isolated and unseen self. Like all teenagers, he felt misunderstood and underappreciated, but what singled him out over the years was his astonishing recall of details and emotions that most think of hazily, if at all, once they've reached adulthood. It was an early education for a writer who wished to accurately express what it feels like to be in a state, as he always described it, of eternal anxiety and exile.[37]

* * *

Sam Sr. taught his son to play drums on a Ludwig kit they bought at a pawnshop, and Shepard set down his father's drill-sergeant style of instruction in his play *The Holy Ghostly*:

> It takes more than gulldanged imagination to be a great drummer. It takes guts. . . . You gotta' build up yer strength. You gotta' work on that left hand so hard you can do a triple paradiddle with yer right hand tied behind yer back. Ya' gotta' get yer right foot so strong it's

> like steel. Work with that ankle so hard that it feels like it's gonna' break off. Then when ya' reach that point where ya' can hardly stand the pain of it—that's when you start yer real practicin'. That's when yer work begins.[38]

Over time, Shepard started to pick up rhythms everywhere around him: "Oilcan rhythms, ratchet wrench rhythms. Playing cards in bicycle spokes. A string of rapid-fire, firecracker rhythms." Once he'd learned the basics, he dolled himself up in a pink checkered shirt with rolled-up sleeves, black pegged pants, a pink suede belt, and white buck shoes and joined a doo-wop band called Nat's Cats (named for their front man and clarinet player, Nat Henkins). They played school assemblies and penny-hops and in time added rock and roll to their repertoire, including covers of Jerry Lee Lewis, Chuck Berry, and the Coasters.[39] The local paper billed the band as "straight dance music, with variations, even including some rock and roll."[40]

In the fall of 1960, Shepard shared another mutual passion with his father over a full-bred German shepherd puppy. The dog was registered with the American Kennel Club as Amazon's Ark, but the family called him "Stark," or "Starkie" for short. That dog was what Roxanne called "the first revelation of Sam's eye for breeding."[41] Shepard carefully researched, at fourteen, Stark's family history before they bought him and concluded that the dog was an exquisite specimen from an impeccable bloodline. Shepard was an altar boy at the St. James Church, and a member of its choir, and although he later renounced religion, he prayed to God until his hands turned white before every dog show with Stark. If he won, he'd perform the same prayer in the exact same way for the next dog show. ("I was very superstitious about God," he joked.)[42]

Stark was awarded first place in several dog shows, and as a result, Shepard won real admiration from his father at last. In fact, Sam Sr. took on the burden of showing the dog after Shepard had long left the family. Before Stark, Shepard and his father had mutually branded each other as "losers," Roxanne said, until they got the dog. "My brother had set up this situation where they could be winners together."[43]

This kind of tender experience is conspicuously scarce in Shepard's writing about his father. "I kept remembering small occasions when we seemed to have something in common," he wrote to Sam Sr. when he was twenty-one. "Then somehow through some kind of subtle psychological reasons that common ground disappeared and we found ourselves competing for one reason or the other."[44]

Instead of reconciliation, Shepard carried around with him ghastly boyhood memories of his father's abuse to the end of his life. "My father had a real short fuse," Sandy admitted. "He had a really rough life; he had to support his mother and brothers at a very young age when his dad's farm collapsed. You could see his terrible suffering, living a life that was disappointing and looking for another. My father was full of terrifying anger."[45]

In July and August 1961, Sam Rogers participated in a six-week student Fulbright program called the Summer Seminar for Teachers of Spanish.[46] The Fulbright grant was for studying Spanish language and literature at the University of Bogotá in Colombia, where he traveled alone. While there, he cultivated an abiding love for the poets Pablo Neruda, César Vallejo, and Federico García Lorca. "One thing that I'll always be eternally grateful to him for," Shepard said, "is he introduced me to García Lorca when I was a kid, which is kind of unusual, *in Spanish* no less. . . . And that got me fascinated about poetry at an early age."[47] Sam Sr. also loved New Orleans jazz, and he passed his zeal for music on to his son as well. "I remember watching my Dad while he listened to his music," Shepard recalled. "I remember it was the only times I ever saw him happy. All the rest of the time he seemed angry or in a faraway dream about something like war."[48]

And to top it off, he was "gorgeous," Roxanne said. "He was like Chuck Yeager. He had that romantic image, like a big gorgeous Bobby Duvall."[49] Yet despite playing drums for a local Dixieland band and being a passionate and amiable teacher, at home Sam Sr. was poles apart from the charming war hero his students would have known. "My dad was frustrated with life because he had done everything right," Sandy explained:

> He came back from that war. . . . We had everything, we had a nice house, I had a little horse, we had good cars, a camping trailer. We had everything, and yet life was fucked. My dad was not happy with life. I don't know what he would have wanted to be or to do, but he was frustrated, and I think a lot of those guys were after the war. The American Dream was not good enough, even though you got it. Once you get it, then what?[50]

"The alcohol," Shepard said, "just completely deranged him."[51] The process was initially slow, and he hid his dependence for a few years, but his drinking worsened badly after Colombia. Then he started skipping classes, crashed his car multiple times, and became a tyrant to his son. After seventeen years at San Marino High School, he was fired without pension for drinking on the job.[52] By the time Jane divorced him in January 1968, Sam Sr. had already been living elsewhere for five years. His unquenchable thirst ultimately overwhelmed anything else meaningful in his life, especially his relationship with his son.

Sam Sr.'s anger was passed down to all of the Rogers children, but was especially acute with Shepard. "He worked very hard with his temper," Roxanne said of her brother. "It took a lot to set him off, but when he went off, he was lethal. But he wasn't a bully like my dad. He really tried to be conscious of his temper. Sammie knew it was our Achilles' heel. We all have it. It's a constant challenge. . . . I've never seen that rage in his acting. But it's there on the page, isn't it."[53]

Soon enough, Shepard inherited his father's lust for alcohol too, and after vomiting the first time he got drunk with Nat's Cats at fifteen, he drank steadily through his school years and beyond. Both men belonged to a long line of churlish drinkers, "liquid nitrogen in the bloodstream," Shepard called it. "He was a nasty drunk," Roxanne said of her father. "Wicked nasty. And of course Sammie also got worse when he got older." Later, when asked whether his father was violent with him, Shepard said, "Mostly when he was drunk. Yeah." Did Jane know? "Yeah." "Was she violent with you?" "No," he said, then changed the subject.[54]

In contrast to his father, Shepard adored his mother, whom he described as a "strong, solid woman, like a rock." When asked how she handled his father's outbursts, he called her "a very brave soul." Jane, unlike her husband, appears only sporadically in Shepard's work, at least in recognizable form. "She [had] a little bun. Very straight, but bright," a close friend described her. "She was tightly wound," the friend said. "She looked like a teacher, you'd know that just by looking at her, she was a schoolmarm." She was also a diligent parent. In his story "Majesty (Highway 101 South)," Shepard recounts a period when he briefly lost the ability to correctly identify object's names (e.g., he'd say "margarine" for "majesty"). "I remember the panic on her face," he wrote, "as though she suddenly thought she had a cabbage-head for a son on top of everything else she was worried about like the old man and taxes and the price of milk."[55] His father, he said, "went further and further off in the direction of being an outsider, mainly, in simple terms, of alcoholism. My mother was the opposite. Very together, figuring out how to get along."[56]

Although many of Shepard's father characters are true to the actual Sam Rogers, the mothers in his plays represent an incongruous assortment. The actual Jane was written out of Shepard's dramas almost as aggressively as the actual Sam was written into them. Still, he said later, "I couldn't have survived without her protecting me and reassuring me."[57] Roxanne had a theory about the comparatively absent mother in her brother's plays: "Sam was very, very close to my mom. They were psychically connected. I think because he knew of this connection with my mom, and she protected him so much, and had formed him so much, he didn't want to be thought of as so attached. Also, he wanted to protect my mom from the cloying eye of the public."[58]

* * *

Duarte High School's mascot was the falcon, and its student-run yearbook, *Halconado*, shows that Shepard lettered in basketball and track and was a cheerleader. On the track team, he excelled at the 880-meter relay and high-jump events, and he claimed to have broken the league record in the 220, albeit cranked up on Benzedrine. In November 1958, at age fifteen, he joined the 4-H club as a "Future Farmer of America" and entered sheep as a junior exhibitor in the Great Western Livestock Show in Los Angeles, the largest of its kind on the Pacific Coast. "I slept with my sheep," Shepard wrote. "I lambed them, sheared them, docked their tails, clipped their hooves, castrated ram lambs, fed them, wormed them, showed them & sold them." He was a natural farmer, to his father's amazement, and continued to win championships at nearby fairs and festivals. He also engaged in county fair pig scrambles, in which a pig is greased, a starting gun is fired, and the children race around to catch the terrified animal, "with the parents cheering & boozing & kids knocking themselves out on the field."[59]

Shepard had a snaggletoothed grin and tried to copy Burt Lancaster's toothy performance in 1954's *Vera Cruz* at school, though "one of the front ones was dead and brown and overlapped the broken one right next to it."[60] Other boys would gawk at his teeth, but the girls of the San Gabriel Valley didn't seem to mind, and late into adulthood his crooked teeth only enhanced his rugged mystique. "He's always been an attractive kind of guy," Sandy said. "I had friends who had things for him when we were young. I'd bring them home from school, and he'd take them up to the treehouse."[61]

As an aspiring veterinarian with a strong dose of horse sense, Shepard was hired at an Arabian horse ranch, owned by the Conleys of Bradbury and located in nearby Chino; he also worked, or at least volunteered, at another Chino ranch run by the notorious racehorse owner Rex C. Ellsworth. Shepard was sixteen, and these were his first real jobs, secured through the 4-H Club. The ranch was vaunted as a breeding ground for winners and home to a herd of two thousand cattle and over three hundred broodmares, stallions, and racehorses. The *New York Times* dubbed Rex Ellsworth "the nation's leading owner and breeder of Thoroughbred horses."[62]

Ellsworth and his trainer, Mesh Tenney, were true-to-life horsemen. They won the Kentucky Derby in 1955 and the Preakness Stakes in 1963, along with eleven other major wins; but Tenney was "the boss," and for Shepard, the incarnation of Western cool. Shepard only made $1.25 a day for his work "cleaning horse piss," he griped, but left with an adoration of American horse culture that lasted a lifetime. In his darkly ironic short story "A Man's Man," the titular character isn't based on Tenney, but at least in part on Shepard's supervisor, called Duane in the story, whom he also considered "a man's man." The two of them raced against the Kentucky Derby winner Swaps in Duane's Chevy, and Swaps won handily, to their delight. "I never heard of a horse beating a Chevy before, have you?" shouts Duane. "That's gotta be a first!"[63]

Once home in Bradbury, according to the story, Shepard awoke in Duane's truck from a deep sleep after one of the most memorable days of his life, only to look down and find Duane's hand resting on his privates. The appendage, Shepard wrote, "was just laying there limp, like a piece of raw hamburger. 'You're home,' Duane said, and returned his hand to the steering wheel with a meek smile that made me suddenly sorry for him." Shepard later confirmed that this was based on events he had experienced more than once. As late as 2010, while he was being interviewed for a documentary about him, these carnal abuses were still very much on his mind. "All these guys," men he looked up to, blue-collar carpenters and painters and horsemen, would wind up with their hands on his crotch as a teenager. The way he saw it, they were treating him like his father had, "like a chick."[64]

Shepard's character in "A Man's Man" steps down from the truck and sneaks through the darkness to spy his father through the kitchen window pouring himself a drink. "I kept waiting for him to turn the light out and leave the kitchen, but he just kept standing there and staring. What was going through his head? Was he waiting for me? I felt this panic start to boom up through my chest and ears. This old familiar fear. What was it about certain men?"[65]

On the surface, the boy Steve Rogers enjoyed about as all-American a childhood as they come. But the playwright Sam Shepard found little in his archetypal 1950s upbringing to inspire him as an artist; growing up in the '50s, he later grumbled, "sucked dogs man."[66] It was the unspoken truths happening behind the dreamscape, the forces of land development and Hollywood greed, of alcoholism and sexual abuse, of family secrets and private despair, that drove him to lift the veil on paradise and write about this New West. And once he'd reached adulthood, he incorporated both sides of his parents in near equal parts, specifically his mother's cold civility and his father's hot misanthropy. Under their influence, Shepard came to embody the insider and the outsider in American life, a split that would haunt him and his plays to the end.

CHAPTER 2

# FISHING IN THE DARK

By Shepard's senior year, the arthouse cinema movement had spread from New York to the West Coast; and in 1961, his friend Ed Cartwright took him to see his first foreign film, Luchino Visconti's *Rocco and His Brothers*. The language, culture, and landscapes were utterly alien to Shepard, but in these European films, he said as an adult, "there was never any story. . . . They always gave me the impression that they were trying to 'mean' something."[1] They also saw the French New Wave masterpiece *The 400 Blows*, François Truffaut's tale of teenage rebellion, which made a profound impact on Shepard. *The 400 Blows* "really stunned me," he said. He felt a kinship between himself and its main character, a misunderstood boy alienated by his parents.[2]

He later named the five movies that "meant" something to him during his teenage years, in this order: Stanley Kubrick's *The Killing* (1956), John Sturges's *Bad Day at Black Rock* (1955), David Miller's *Lonely Are the Brave* (1962), François Truffaut's *The 400 Blows* (1959), and Alfred Hitchcock's *North by Northwest* (1959).[3] Together, these films nicely encapsulate Shepard's adult obsessions: horse racing (*The Killing*), American masculinity (*Bad Day at Black Rock*), the passing of the Old West (*Lonely Are the Brave*), his own upbringing and family (*The 400 Blows*), and the slippery nature of identity (*North by Northwest*). Shepard was also aware that he was watching acting at its emotional heights, with the stars Sterling Hayden, Spencer Tracy, Kirk Douglas, Jean-Pierre

Léaud, and Cary Grant, respectively. He'd wanted to be Gabby Hayes as a kid; now he wanted to be a full-fledged movie star.[4]

Hence, along with drumming at school dances for Nat's Cats, he joined legions of Southern California's aspiring young actors and performed in high school plays, including in the Irish-themed musical *Finian's Rainbow* in 1961.[5] Shepard played the leading role of Og, the leprechaun, and, notably, at seventeen years old received his very first taste of theatrical glory in the press. The article was accompanied by a photo of Shepard as Og with the other lead actors that was captioned, prophetically, "TO STARDOM AND FAME": "Steve Rogers captivated the audience with his Irish brogue."[6] (Also prophetically, Shepard would have sung the showstopper "When I Am Not Near the Girl I Love.")

After graduating from Duarte High in 1961, Shepard entered the agricultural sciences program at Mt. San Antonio College, or "Mt. SAC." His long-term plan was to transfer after two years to the University of California, Davis, to study veterinary medicine.[7] Despite it being his first semester, Shepard was accepted into a competitive literature class with a cohort of intellectual misfits whom Shepard described, using the lexicon of the day, as "Beatniks."[8]

The local Beats lived in a big house where they played jazz records, talked literature and art, and smoked weed. Importantly, they introduced Shepard to Jackson Pollock's action paintings and the Irish playwright Samuel Beckett.[9] "Beckett turned my head around about thinking about theater," he said many decades later. "It doesn't have to be realistic, it doesn't have to be buried in this cause and effect, it doesn't have to be . . . dull."[10] He devoured *Waiting for Godot*, then *Endgame*, then *Happy Days*.[11] He was "knocked out of the saddle" by Beckett's spare dialogue mixed with scenic incongruity and absurdist plotlines.[12] "I didn't know what it was," he said about *Waiting for Godot*. "I couldn't place it as a play, a poem, a novel, or anything else. . . . It just struck me suddenly that with words you could do *anything*."[13]

Beckett inspired Shepard to seek out similar contemporary American playwrights at local bookstores, but he found none. "I couldn't understand why," he recalled. "They have a section called Modern Drama, you'd find Chekhov, Ibsen, Tennessee Williams and Eugene O'Neill, but that was it. Okay—they're great, but there wasn't anything that seemed to relate to now. There's a huge hole there. I was interested in this hole. Why don't I write something in that hole?"[14]

Armed with Beckett's plays as his touchstones, he managed that fall semester, 1961, to compose his first known play, *The Mildew: A One-Act Comedy*, under the byline Steve Rogers, for the student-run campus literary journal, *MoSAiC*.[15] The main character, Percival "Percy" Chambers Jr., is a self-described "respectable citizen" with a wife. As the play begins, Percy is seen "dressed in suit and tie and appears quite proper," pacing and smoking a cigarette on a street corner steeped in "a thick wet fog," lending notes of O'Neill's *Long Day's Journey Into Night*. He then breaks the fourth wall and addresses the audience, as Tom Wingfield does in *The Glass Menagerie* and the Stage Manager in Thornton Wilder's *Our Town*. He's waiting for a group of well-to-do friends, but they don't appear until his exit, bringing to mind Beckett's *Waiting for Godot*. Yet despite what it borrows from these benchmark modern plays, *The Mildew* reads like a classic early Shepard one-act, with its central theme of American male vulnerability, its evocation of tragic purposelessness with a down-to-earth sense of humor, its disdain for bourgeois pretension, and its resistance to any clear-cut interpretation. But he denounced it immediately, joking to his sister Sandy, "I hope they don't dig up my first play!"[16]

Shepard, for the time being, thus abandoned playwriting for acting and joined the theater troupe the Mt. SAC Players. The group was directed by the theater arts instructor Beulah Yeager, who became a strong advocate for him. He played a secondary role in Maxwell Anderson's *High Tor*; was cast in the lead as the lovable dreamer Elwood P. Dowd in Mary Chase's *Harvey*; and in his third and final semester, he played a lawyer in Eudora Welty's courtroom comedy *The Ponder Heart*. The game was on.

* * *

On Christmas Day 1962, once Shepard had dropped out of Mt. SAC after three semesters, Jane and Sam Sr. gave their son a newly published biography, *O'Neill*, a voluminous account of the life by Arthur and Barbara Gelb. ("You never gave a shit about school but there was nothing dumb about you," Sam Sr. told him later.)[17] The portrait of the dramatist as a man and artist, especially how a man turns into an artist, riveted Shepard. His margin notes testify that he was already well-read, with an immense store of intellectual curiosity. The notes include a striking range of cultural knowledge for a nineteen-year-old: his adoration of the Beats; his familiarity with the "meaningless meaning" of existentialism; the "self-actualization" of the psychologist Abraham Maslow; "the self-made man" of F. Scott Fitzgerald; the theatrical influences of Konstantin Stanislavsky, the Actors Studio, and Lee Strasberg ("the Method Man"), and much more.

The great playwright's journey offered Shepard a kind of roadmap for his own path. At the end of the chapter where O'Neill is wandering the high seas as a merchant mariner and living hand-to-mouth on waterfronts around the globe, Shepard gushed, "Experience is the greatest teacher!" At the point when O'Neill decides once and for all to become a playwright and famously declares that he was determined to be "an artist or nothing," he scrawled, "*Olé!*"[18]

On January 28, 1963, Shepard next saw Sidney Lumet's film adaptation of O'Neill's *Long Day's Journey Into Night* and later called it "the greatest play ever written in America."[19] O'Neill's masterwork, which he'd notably read prior to reading his other great influence, Samuel Beckett, convinced him he might be able to write about the American family in the same tragic vein. He told a close friend years later, "There was something wrong with the family [in O'Neill's play]. There was a demonic thing going on that nobody could put their finger on, but everybody knew the ship was sinking. Everybody was going down, and nobody knew how or why, and they were all taking desperate measures to stay afloat. So I thought there was something about that that felt similar to my own background, and I felt I could maybe write some version of that."[20]

* * *

In the spring of 1963, after having moved into a Motel 6 in Arcadia to escape his father, Shepard had two choices: accept a position to oversee a herd of three hundred Southdown sheep at one of the ranches in Chino, then return to school and study to be a veterinarian; or, after his success with the Mt. SAC Players, try his luck at acting.[21] He chose the latter, and the San Gabriel Valley Civic Players offered him a small role in Thornton Wilder's *The Skin of Our Teeth* at the San Gabriel Mission Playhouse.[22]

But he barely made it through opening night after getting involved in the casting for another supporting part. The Civic Players wanted to find a Black actor for the opening to play Wilder's Chair Pusher in a region that continued to be steadfastly segregated, and, at the last minute, Shepard thought he could find a solution for the casting.

Rumbles between white and Black students plagued the San Gabriel Valley's schools every spring. After segregation ended there in 1947, racially organized gangs would clash after a year's worth of racial animus at school, all tacitly encouraged by many white parents and teachers.[23] According to Roxanne Rogers, her father didn't play along. While Sam Rogers saddled his family with a number of burdens, racism wasn't among them. Roxanne remembered a time when she had a crush on a Black classmate when she was a teen, and her father blessed the pairing. "You just love who you wanna love," he told her. He nearly injured her when as a little girl, she unknowingly used the N-word in a children's rhyming song. Sam Sr. snatched her by the arm, lifted her high in the air, legs kicking off the ground, and yelled, "Don't you ever say that word again, or I will *swat* you! *Ever!*" It was the only time she could recall him disciplining her.[24]

Shepard's search for the Civic Players led him to one of the only Black men he was acquainted with, a tenuous affiliation at best, his schoolmate Charles Mingus III. Mingus was the legendary jazz bassist's son and a year behind him at Duarte High. Shepard found Mingus at a truck stop diner on Route 66 where, Mingus said, "everyone was Black," and offered him a paying role in the Civic Players' *The Skin of Our Teeth*.[25]

Shepard watched Mingus enjoy an ersatz tomato soup (a packet of ketchup mixed in hot water) and swore to him that if he took the part, he'd be the next Steve McQueen. Mingus agreed to do it, but soon discovered that as the only Black actor in the production, he'd been cast as the Chair Pusher, who is not designated as Black. So, on opening night, in the scene where the script (which Mingus hadn't had time to read) calls for his character to slide a wicker chair around the stage like a lowly servant, Mingus lost his cool. "No way, folks!" he shouted, hurling the prop into the audience. "Fuck you, Nazis! . . . If you want to see a chair pusher and get a coon show, come up here yourself." With that, the play stopped, and the other actors came after him. Mingus scrambled up a telephone pole to escape and looked down to see Shepard laughing his head off. "It's a good idea to be up there," he said. Mingus was relieved that Shepard didn't call him out, but was surprised at his attitude. "Well, I could have killed somebody," Mingus said. "Sam thought that was funny. That's what makes him scary. He thought it was hilarious." Shepard was nearly fired for suggesting Mingus for the part, but was allowed to remain for the three-evening run. The bigotry of the theater company had auspiciously brought Mingus and Shepard together, and their friendship over the following years powerfully helped to shape Shepard's artistic career.[26]

Soon after this debacle, Shepard was delivering newspapers for extra cash when he stumbled across a write-up about a traveling ensemble from nearby Burbank called the Bishop's Company. The Bishop's was "interracial and interfaith," and its members advertised the group as "America's first repertory company of professional stature to reunite the forces of religion and the theater."[27] ("The religious cover was a phony," Shepard scoffed. "We were really a bunch of frustrated actors who couldn't find a niche.")[28] Since their founding in 1953, the Bishop's mounted over five thousand performances across the country, and the pay was ten dollars per week, plus food, lodging, and transportation.[29]

Shepard auditioned for one of their traveling companies and was quickly accepted, though the casting call petrified him. By his account, he was so scared that he read the stage directions aloud and later suspected they hired everyone who auditioned.[30] In June, he boarded an eastbound Continental Trailways bus to Philadelphia and hit the boards on June 23 for their first performance, a production of Stephen Vincent Benét's *The Devil and Daniel Webster* at St. Peter's Church in Tunkhannock, Pennsylvania. Over the next four and a half months, Shepard toured around the Northeast in repertory as a cast and crew member for seven plays.[31]

The Bishop's Company tour gave him a taste of the itinerant life and deepened his rudimentary training in theater, greatly informing his vision as a developing playwright. The Bishop's theatrical dogma, one that was practical for a touring company but that Shepard would come to adopt as his own avant-garde staging technique before long, was to use no sets and minimal props. As the Bishop's folks told their young charges, "the setting is better found in the mind's eye."[32] He also appreciated their down-to-earth performance style: "I felt I had a handle on theatre in a non-scholastic, non-academic, non-literary way," Shepard remarked decades on. "I really understood what it was like to be an actor onstage facing an audience."[33]

* * *

On July 12, 1963, Shepard walked the streets of New York City for the first time. "What a fantastic place," he wrote with the breathlessness of a California teen. "I couldn't get over the millions of people just walking." It was then that he took in his first Broadway play, Edward Albee's *Who's Afraid of Virginia Woolf?*, then he saw the Paul Newman movie *Hud*, and Diana Sands (*A Raisin in the Sun*) in her avant-garde integrated revue *The Living Premise*. But it was his sojourn downtown that captured the romance of the city for him: "Greenwich Village was too much. There are book stores with everything under the sun—paintings, jazz—you name it!"[34]

The Bishop's toured through New England in August, and he found the "Yankee conservatives," as he called them, hopelessly parochial and racist. Larry Richardson, an actor in the troupe, was Black, and in a

Vermont town, "one of these idiots asked me . . . if Larry was an Indian. I guess he couldn't believe that his little cozy New England village could be shared with a Negro. Some of these people are so fanatical in their Yankee heritage that in some ways it's really worse than the South."[35]

That fall, they toured the mid-Atlantic states, and a rave review appeared in the local paper the *Daily Intelligencer* of Doylestown, Pennsylvania. It singled out Shepard, who played the Devil in *The Devil and Daniel Webster*, for delivering "the most subtle and suave performance of the evening." Shepard's Devil declares that he "stood on the first ship that carried the first slave from the Congo to America," and then foretells Daniel Webster's fate: "The future," he tells Webster, in an ironic line, given his own trajectory, "is not what you think. It is very dull."[36]

Shepard's taste of acclaim gave him the confidence to pursue a larger theatrical challenge. In October, he announced that rather than return home in December as planned, he'd stay behind in New York, where his final performance for the Bishop's was in the poet Marianne Moore's living room in Brooklyn.[37] "It's not quite as far-fetched as it sounds," he wrote to Jane. He reassured her that he'd found a place to stay "with two former Bishop's Company actors and one playwrite [*sic*]." He had saved eighty dollars and bought winter clothing at church rummage sales. He continued the letter, "I simply think I should take a chance here rather than go back to what I was doing, which was precisely nothing." Shepard had been offered a place with the Peterborough Players in New Hampshire the following summer, 1964, so he expected to get an Equity card. But if not, he heard there was plenty of acting work in downtown theaters located in a nebulous, quasiprofessional land called "Off-Broadway."[38]

* * *

Shortly after Shepard's twentieth birthday, he waved the Bishop's goodbye at Times Square. He was pining for a White Castle cheeseburger but wanted to save, so when he saw a blood bank with a sign in the window offering five dollars for a pint of blood, he went in. He and his Bishop's friends then found an apartment on West Forty-Fourth Street in Hell's Kitchen. "It's not a palace by any stretch of the imagination," Shepard said at the time, "but it's more than adequate."[39]

New York was both terrifying and exhilarating to Shepard. His new neighborhood, Hell's Kitchen, was riddled with ramshackle tenements, smoke-filled Irish pubs, tumbledown warehouses, sailors trawling for hookups along the docks, junkies pleading with dealers, and streetwalkers consulting their pimps. (Martin Scorsese would capture this mise-en-scène a decade later in his film *Taxi Driver*.) His first job was working as a security guard for the Burns Detective Agency, for whom he was stationed at the towering Con Edison plant on the East River. The pay was meager but it was enough to pay for his rent and cigarette habit. The job also freed up his daytime hours for auditions, but the competition was formidable: "It seems that everybody has decided that New York is the place to make it or something."[40]

Shepard's first potential break was an unnamed show in a theater, "really what one might call off-off-Broadway (Greenwich Village)," which opened on January 2, 1964, but led no further.[41] (The term "Off-Off-Broadway," or OOB, indicating the cramped spaces and artistic freedom of downtown theater venues in Greenwich Village, had just been coined a few years earlier by the *Village Voice*'s then drama critic Jerry Tallmer.) Shepard's dream to perform enough paid gigs to get his Equity card, which would guarantee a paycheck, health insurance, casting opportunities, worker's compensation, and a pension, didn't materialize. The once novel process of selling himself with headshots, the anxiety-producing auditions, the low pay, and the frantic scramble for his Equity card was all wearing thin. He was on the cusp of giving up when an alternative path in the entertainment industry presented itself through an old friend.

* * *

On January 27, 1964, Shepard read a gossip column in the *Daily News* about Charles Mingus III that pinpointed his old schoolmate's workplace: "Charles Mingus 3rd, son of the jazzman currently at the Five Spot, is himself a budding musician, but he earns his bread as a busboy at the Village Gate."[42] Right after reading the *Daily News* column, Shepard tracked him down at the Greenwich Village jazz club.[43]

Mingus also worked at a metal shop before heading off to bodyguard for his illustrious father, who was then receiving threats from the Italian mafioso Joseph "Crazy Joe" Gallo.[44] Mingus invited Shepard to share his cold-water walkup on Avenue C, with a sign on the door that read THIS DOOR'S A BAND-AID, where he gratefully moved into the railroad apartment's front room and kitchen, where the gas stove was located (Shepard was always cold). He arrived carting a new mattress and an old Chevy bumper for a footboard.[45] Along with a place to live, Mingus also arranged for him to work two nights at twenty-five dollars a week as a busboy at the Village Gate, a storied jazz and comedy club. About a fifteen-minute walk from their apartment, the Village Gate was the pulsing soul of Greenwich Village nightlife.[46]

Shepard quickly adopted the *nostalgie de la boue* of Greenwich Village, and to its east, the East Village (as it would soon be called) and, farther east, Alphabet City, where numbered avenues give way to lettered ones. In Tompkins Square Park, a dividing line between the two neighborhoods, Shepard observed junkie musicians busking for coins alongside elderly Polish couples feeding pigeons or reading a foreign newspaper. He was especially enthralled by the powerful influence of the Poles and Ukrainians around the neighborhood. Signs in foreign lettering, sausages and sauerkraut and blinis, giant mugs of beer being served by babushkas speaking indistinctly to one another in a foreign tongue. He felt as if he'd been transported to East Berlin.[47]

That was the fun part. But these poverty-stricken neighborhoods were in serious physical and moral disrepair. Landlords rebelled against zoning laws by burning their buildings to the ground for insurance money, so intermittent empty lots revealing only sky and rubble interrupted dilapidated rows of tenements. Their fellow Village Gate employees told stories of walking home late at night after work and being shot at, stabbed, mugged, and accosted, some more than once—especially in Alphabet City, where it wasn't uncommon before sunrise to have a bullet zing by your nose while you were walking home drunk or stoned from the club.[48]

One night after Shepard moved to Avenue C, he was startled awake by the sound of a woman shrieking on the street below. His mind raced as he stared into the blue flame of the stove and marshaled what courage he had. Shepard, now half-naked out on the street, saw a man pummeling the screaming woman. The storybook version ensured him that he would liberate a grateful damsel, trounce a villainous brute, and only then call for the police to clean up the mess. This wasn't happening in a storybook. When he approached, the couple turned, fell silent, and glared at him. "Fuck off!" the woman roared. Shepard spun around and hightailed it upstairs, while the couple carried on below. The incident taught him an important lesson about urban living: "I knew now to watch myself."[49]

Mingus had another roommate, his father's drummer, Dannie Richmond, who was much older than he or Shepard and lived in the back room of the railroad flat while recovering from a heroin addiction.[50] (Richmond later played for Joe Cocker and Elton John, and Shepard called him "the greatest drummer on two feet.")[51] Though there was little privacy, Mingus had French doors separating his art studio from the rest of the apartment, on which he'd mounted a montage of strip photographs of himself, taken at Woolworth's photo booths in California, zonked on Seconal (reds) in 1959 and tripping on LSD in 1961. Their nihilistic attitude toward convention was on full display, and a friend of Shepard's described the Avenue C apartment as "one of the worst you've ever seen.... If these guys ever heard of a laundry or ever heard of washing dishes it was not apparent any time I was there.... Everything was a mess. Dirty clothes and dirty dishes and dirty sink and dirty ... If they had a toilet I can't even remember." They even had a boa constrictor for a time. When it died, they left it on the floor to rot.[52]

Mingus was a visual artist, and that summer he was constructing an elaborate assembly of ten boxes with light, sound, visual sensors, and mechanized movement that would tempt people to observe objects they otherwise ignore. The idea, according to Shepard, was that "you don't have to go into an art gallery in order to see art because the real things are right on the street."[53] Shepard was awestruck by what emerged from Mingus's paintbrush too: "Charles is probably (without trying to be overdramatic) the only real artist I've ever known. That is to say he paints what he thinks and what he feels without worrying about whether it sells or not."[54] Though they were broke, Mingus received multiple offers for his artwork and rejected them all. His father even negotiated an art show alongside the work of the jazz maestro Duke Ellington, but he turned it down because, he believed, gallery goers were more interested in painter's names than in their art.[55]

That March, Shepard adopted a stage name, which debuted in print on March 12, 1964, in a small-town newspaper, the *Madison Eagle* of Madison, New Jersey. The *Eagle* announced "Sam Shepard" would appear in town with the seasoned actors Peter De Maio and Bill Martin in a revival of Christopher Fry's *A Sleep of Prisoners*.[56] Shepard altered his name, he said, because it was too corny after the "King of the Cowboys" Roy Rogers and his trusty steed Trigger, and he was relieved when he found out later that Steve Rogers was also the alter ego of Captain America.[57]

But Americans who followed the news through the 1950s and '60s equated "Sam Shepard" with only one thing: murder. Dr. Sam Sheppard was a neurosurgeon from Cleveland, Ohio, who, in 1954, was charged with bludgeoning his pregnant wife to death. The story made national headlines, and the US Supreme Court concluded in an appeal that the "carnival atmosphere" surrounding the trial had denied Sheppard due process. He was first sentenced to life but was released after serving ten years. An actor and coworker of Shepard's named Lee Kissman felt there was "a seditious allusion to the Ohio doctor Sam Sheppard" in Shepard's choice of stage names, since "outlaws hold an engaging spot in the American psyche, and it seems likely that Sam was not unaware this might turn a few heads."[58] Mingus also saw it as a marketing ploy. "The guy I knew would exploit that." People would buy tickets thinking, "I wonder what this guy who killed his wife and got away with it wrote?"[59]

"I almost forgot," Shepard wrote to his mother, "I've written three one act plays in my spare time and I'm going to see if I can find someone who's interested as soon as I get the courage."[60]

* * *

Shepard swore off stage acting by the spring of 1964, after he'd performed a coffeehouse show, a production with other former members of the Bishop's, and a rehearsal with the Harlem Writers Guild in a play produced by Juanita Poitier (wife of Sidney Poitier).[61] This all took passion, discipline, and hustle—the very traits his father had railed against him for lacking. Nevertheless, Shepard said after months of tryouts in New York, "the audition process was horrible. I didn't want to act anymore. I didn't want to be part of that machine, showing my picture and resume."[62] He wrote to his mother right before going onstage for another thankless show, "I was ready to go back to California and start school again and maybe teach or something."[63]

Any plans for Shepard to return were now cast off, however. He told Jane he planned to stay "because I've seen some other things that tell me life isn't as simple as that. I just couldn't get up every morning and do the same thing over and over no matter how much money I got or how good a 'position' it was. I also realize now that acting isn't everything either." Shepard ended by telling her about his newfound love of writing: "It seems to give me as much satisfaction if not more. I seem to be able to be more honest with my writing mainly because I do it when I'm alone. When you're in front of a lot of people there's always an awareness of them looking at you. Nobody looks at you when you write so there's no need to please anyone but yourself."[64]

In the meantime, Dannie Richmond regularly let Shepard into the back door of the Five Spot, where he could take in the world's greatest jazz musicians for free. "In the mid-'60s there were musicians who carried a certain kind of wisdom and power with them—like a shaman," Shepard said looking back on the experience.[65] One memorable night, he saw Sonny Rollins, Eric Dolphy, and Charles Mingus Sr. play at the Five Spot, where Rollins, sporting his Mohawk and shades, "blew the walls off the place."[66] But it was Mingus's stand-up bass performance that particularly ignited his imagination. "He was one of the first real artists I ever saw. When you saw him you knew you were in the company of something from another world."[67]

This wasn't Shepard's first foray into modern jazz, as he'd seen Miles Davis perform in Los Angeles when he was seventeen, but it was a revelation.[68] "That music calls you toward a certain approach," Shepard said, linking modern jazz with theater. "You don't feel obliged any longer to uphold the standards of Eugene O'Neill and Tennessee Williams."[69]

The emotional bond between jazz musicians and their audiences was a defining influence for Shepard's vision of how theater might work, but most important, it taught him how he might go about writing dialogue freed from realistic constraints, much like the Beats had been doing with jazz in their poetry and prose. Shepard played the drums, so he recognized the language of rhythm in Charles Mingus's artistry on the stand-up bass. What he heard was a "collage of rhythms and sounds," a polyrhythm, "rhythm on top of rhythm on top of rhythm," that could be just as powerfully applied to the theater.[70] "I was fascinated by the idea of merging that with writing, seeing if there was a way of evoking the same kind of collage in the writing of plays."[71]

That year, 1964, Shepard took in the live jazz shows of Ella Fitzgerald, Dizzy Gillespie, Nina Simone, Thelonious Monk, and of course Charles Mingus while bussing tables at the Village Gate, some of which opened with comedy routines by Woody Allen and Flip Wilson. The Gate's musical performers provided Shepard with a rich supply of rhythms to incorporate into his plays, and each song they performed was unique. Self-expression, not the unholy constraints of sheet music, mattered most to the jazz musician, and the same point could be made for Shepard's dramas: the audience's needs at any given moment change the nature of each singular performance. "Once the play opens it's both a death and a birth," Shepard said. "It's both things. It's no longer in a room with just 'us' . . . now suddenly it's being witnessed by all these strangers and it kills something right off. It also makes something else happen."[72]

Shepard returned home to listen to Charles Mingus's son, who spoke like his father played. Shepard's speech was slow and hesitant, but Mingus was a gifted monologist. His mind was a whirl of wild imagery, historical facts, cosmic truths, and mesmerizing anecdotes and aphorisms that spewed out in a hundred different directions. ("I have a superior education," Mingus boasted, "that does me no good because nobody else around me knows what the fuck I'm talking about.")[73] Mingus lived and worked, Shepard said, only with materials that evolved from his own "sphere of reference," a fancy way of saying that Mingus was no sellout.[74]

Shepard's reunion with Mingus, in sum, was fundamental to his metamorphosis from a California drifter looking for decent-paying theater work into an avant-garde artist of real stature. "There's a kind of otherness to the characters," Mingus said of his and his father's impact on Shepard's work. "He took our dialogue and turned them into plays." When asked for an origin theory of Shepard's apocalyptic monologues, or "arias," Mingus didn't hesitate: "He listened to me."[75]

One night at work, Shepard was stoned and plummeted into a trance as Nina Simone warbled Cole Porter's "You'd Be So Nice to Come Home To," during which he swooned and spilled candlewax onto a customer's crotch. "It looked like he'd come all over himself," he quipped. Mingus recalled the incident less amusingly: Shepard dumped a tray of plates and glasses on the man's lap; Mingus apologized, Shepard wouldn't. Either way, the maître d' hauled him into the kitchen and fired him on the spot. Outside on Bleecker, Shepard wistfully remembered, "I could still hear her voice coming right through the concrete walls: 'You'd be Paradise to come home to.'"[76]

Dosing his mind with psychedelics, amphetamines, and other drugs in Greenwich Village played a significant role in Shepard's artistic evolution as well. "I began experiments with various plants and growths," he wrote, resulting in "rhythm discoveries in space and time through packing up words and stretching them out along with their size and shape and sound. Once this got started lo and behold there came phantoms and ghosts speaking these words. At this point my acting stopped. . . . And things began to crackle." Subsisting mainly on a diet of "crystal Methedrine, crème soda, and liverwurst sandwiches," he wrote his second fully realized play, *The Rock Garden*, which he showed to another Village Gate waiter, Ralph Homer Cook.[77]

At thirty-six, Ralph Cook was much older than Shepard and the other waiters. An imposing man with bushy black hair, a black goatee, and penetratingly dark eyes, Cook had studied theater in San Francisco and was just then starting a ragtag theater company called Theater Genesis, named such, Cook decreed, because "here, now, in lower Manhattan the phenomenon is taking place: the beginning, the Genesis, of a cultural revolution." Plays produced under the helm of such directors cavalierly dispensed with traditional boundaries of dramatic form, and their stable of playwrights were encouraged to submit works with radical subjects that rebelled against the stranglehold of postwar conformity—all of which led to a revolution in American theater. Theater Genesis was designed, Cook wrote, "to serve the playwright at that point in his career when he needs to be produced with maximum freedom and with continuity." The foremost piece of advice Cook gave to each of his playwrights was the simple yet impactful maxim "Write what you know."[78]

Cook asked Shepard for another script to fill the evening, so he wrote his third known play, *Cowboys*, in two days, at which point, Shepard said, "things kind of took off from there."[79]

Theater Genesis was using St. Mark's Church in-the-Bowery, an Episcopal church at the epicenter of the East Village, Tenth Street and Second Avenue, as its main performance space. St. Mark's would, only a couple of years after Shepard's arrival, gain notoriety for hosting the storied Poetry Project, which showcased the work of the Beats and other off-center poets such as Anne Waldman, Joel Oppenheimer, Gerard Malanga, Jim Carroll, and Patti Smith. A reformed atheist now appointed "lay minister of the arts" at St. Mark's, Cook had independently put on Hemingway's one-act play *Today Is Friday* and a staged adaptation of Dostoyevsky's *The Grand Inquisitor* in lieu of Sunday sermons.[80] Theater Genesis, whose first and only production so far was the Reverend Malcolm Boyd's race trilogy *Study in Color*, used a crude stage in a second-floor storage room behind the choir loft as a seventy-seat black box theater. It was a humble beginning indeed for what would soon become one of New York's most influential downtown theaters, in large part thanks to Shepard. "He was in this vortex, and he had all the right stuff," Sandy Rogers reflected on her brother's good fortune in finding Ralph Cook and Theater Genesis. "He was there at the right time, with the goods, and he had something new."[81]

"I was breaking the ice with myself," Shepard remarked of these early days of emergence as an underground playwright in the East Village. "I can remember being dazed with writing, with the discovery of finding I actually had these worlds inside of me, these voices, shapes, currents of language, light—all the mysterious elements that cause anyone to make a journey."[82]

CHAPTER 3

# "JUNK MAGIC" AT THEATER GENESIS

Charles Mingus marveled at his roommate's self-assurance as a writer. "He could walk into a room with a typewriter and not leave until he finished a play," he said. "No revisions, just typing."[1]

Shepard would complete fifteen plays in just five years on this typewriter, and he maintained his devotion to the dependable tool, which he likened to an old Chevy, until the end of his life. "You're seeing a phenomenon," he said later of watching the hammers thwack ink onto the page. "You're seeing this apparition taking place. I don't mean to sound hocus pocus about it, but there's something taking place, and you're true to that."[2]

That summer, 1964, Shepard was writing quickly and hustling on the Off-Broadway theater circuit. Somehow he acquired Edward Albee's phone number, mustered his courage, and dialed. Albee was thirty-six but already a kingmaker of the theater scene after the successes of *The Zoo Story* and *Who's Afraid of Virginia Woolf?*. In Albee's sonorous patrician accent ("Awl-bee," he would correct people), the dramatist invited Shepard over to discuss a new script at his duplex in the West Village. Mingus agreed to join him for moral support, but when Albee, whether through nonchalance or lechery, answered the door wearing nothing but a beltless bathrobe, Mingus balked and hightailed it out of there.

Shepard went inside, handed Albee his latest play, a one-act about the Vietnam draft titled *Up to Thursday*, then raced off after Mingus.[3]

Shepard would astonishingly make his mark as an avant-garde playwright on the downtown scene with only a few months of networking and no production to his name. Other hopeful young playwrights such as Lanford Wilson, LeRoi Jones, Megan Terry, John Guare, María Irene Fornés, and Terrence McNally were also cutting their teeth at the makeshift drama venues in the churches, restaurants, and cafés that populated Greenwich Village and the Lower East Side, all of which were within easy walking distance of Shepard's Avenue C apartment. At this time, total production cost at any of these "theaters" was usually less than forty dollars. Most of the productions were free and open to the public, though hats were often passed around and coffee was sold.[4]

The four most notable Off-Off-Broadway houses were Theater Genesis, La MaMa Experimental Theatre Club, Judson Poets' Theatre, and Caffe Cino, and Shepard would stage his freeform one-act plays in every one of them. "New York was like that in the Sixties," he said later. "You could write a one-act play and start doing it the next day. . . . Nothing like that exists now."[5]

Edward Albee, along with the producers of *Who's Afraid of Virginia Woolf?*, Richard Barr and Clinton Wilder, had started a theater workshop for experimental new playwrights called the Playwrights Unit, which would finance an annual series called Theatre 1964. (This changed year to year; Shepard would appear in Theatre 1965.) In early August, before rehearsals at Theater Genesis for Shepard's world premiere as a playwright, Albee agreed to produce Shepard's work.[6] "I'll be able to write anything I want to," Shepard crowed to his mother, "no restrictions on content or form."[7] La MaMa ETC would soon join the Playwrights Unit and put on one or two more after Theater Genesis's double bill, which was scheduled for October. Despite the warm welcome by other Off-Off-Broadway theaters, Shepard recalled, in the downtown theater scene, "Theater Genesis became my home."[8]

The second play that Cook had asked Shepard to add to the evening, *Cowboys*, "was about me and Charlie [Mingus] on the streets of New

York," Shepard told a reporter, "because that's what we used to do in Duarte, play cowboys in the street, and when we got to New York we just kept doing it." "It seemed bizarre to me," he elaborated on his play's theme of dislocation, "this sense of being from a desert region, then suddenly being surrounded by immigrants, pigeons, and jazz musicians."[9] And so he wrote the twenty-one-page script consisting of two friends, Stu (Shepard) and Chet (Mingus), who are frightened of the city and find themselves on the street playing Cowboys and Indians.[10]

A fellow Village Gate waiter and Theater Genesis actor named Kevin O'Connor glanced over *Cowboys* and *The Rock Garden*, and at first blush thought they were "garbage." Later, he realized that "you can't tell with Sam's plays when you read them. You only know when you experience them. And when I did that, I realized that we were into gold."[11]

The cast started rehearsals within a week of Shepard's submission of *Cowboys*, and there was no budget. "I can remember getting props off the street," Shepard recalled. "We'd take Yuban coffee cans, punch a hole in them, and use them for lights. We did it all from scratch."[12] "But it was *exciting*," the Genesis member Georgia Hadler reminisced. They didn't care about not having money for a bigger stage or props or much else. They didn't care about Broadway, and they didn't care that Broadway didn't care about them.[13] They especially didn't care, Hadler emphasized, what outsiders thought when they came to see a show: "You could take acid and sit in the audience, and nobody's gonna be mad at you," she said. "Or you could shoot up [heroin] in the kitchen if you had to, and some people did. Not everyone was brilliant, but we felt brilliant."[14]

* * *

That summer, Shepard was seated on the stoop of a notorious drug dealer's apartment building at Tenth Street and Avenue C when a man climbing the steps noticed him scribbling in a notebook. This was Peter Orlovsky, a Beat poet and romantic partner of Allen Ginsberg. When Shepard told him he was writing a play, Orlovsky helpfully responded,

"You know, there's a woman around the corner on Second Avenue.... Why don't you take it over there and see if she'd want to do it?" So Shepard hopped off the stoop and over to Second Avenue and Ellen "Mama" Stewart's La MaMa Experimental Theatre Club. "And, there," he said, "was Ellen in all her glory. She usually wore really tight pants and kind of ballerina slippers and a glittery green thing. She was very sexy, you know." Shepard asked her straight up, "Would you be interested in this play?" With barely a glance at the script (either *Dog* or *The Rocking Chair*), Stewart gustily replied, "We're gonna do it baby!"[15]

Stewart also hired Shepard as a part-time waiter at La MaMa ETC. Located in a loft above a florist at 82 Second Avenue, at Fifth Street, the performance space was a short walk from where *Cowboys* was soon to be performed. Stewart, La MaMa's founder and namesake, was a transplant from New Orleans who supported her theater designing bathing suits.[16] La MaMa wouldn't make its name as a nerve center of avant-garde ingenuity until a few years later, when *Hair: The American Tribal Love-Rock Musical* staged its world premiere there in 1967, and by association La MaMa became a countercultural phenomenon.

Tom O'Horgan, who would direct *Hair*, had his directorial debut at La MaMa with a production of Jean Genet's *The Maids* during the same month Shepard enjoyed his world premiere as a playwright.[17] Shepard was serving hot chocolate during one of these showings of *The Maids* when police and firemen came into the café in hopes of finding some excuse to shut Stewart's shows down for obscenity. Genet's play was acted by three men in drag playing women's roles, a weird spectacle for the authorities who arrived midshow. "It was really a scene," Shepard said, "and the firemen shut it all down, and then [Stewart] would start it up again."[18] The theater venue was permanently shuttered that month, but Stewart just found a bigger space nearby.[19]

* * *

*Cowboys* and *The Rock Garden* opened at St. Mark's on October 10, 1964, for a three-weekend run.[20] For *Cowboys*, the stage was strewn with sand and gravel; two sawhorses were set up with blinking lights; and a recording made by Shepard and Mingus while driving around New Jersey with a tape recorder provided ambient street sounds for the show.[21] For Shepard, when the actors began to read his lines, the effect was transcendent: "It was quite amazing to me to recognize that putting on a play was an entirely different process from writing one," Shepard mused. "It was quite a shock to see actors take hold of what I'd written, and I suddenly realized what theater was all about . . . that it was this live thing that took place between the actors and the audience."[22]

The *New York World-Telegram* and *The Sun* printed an ominous word of caution to fainthearted theatergoers in their "Religious News": "Rough language will be ringing through the historic air of Manhattan's second oldest church building." But the article featured a conciliatory comment by the minister of St. Mark's, the Reverend Michael Allen, a tireless activist and advocate for the arts. "I'm not sure I approve of everything that will be said here," Allen told the reporter, but "how can a church minister to people unless it's willing to listen to them? . . . Our job is to help everyone in the parish. If there is a minority group, our job is to help its members be dignified, equal, respected citizens. If there are playwrights, it is to help them be playwrights." "What about the gospel?" the reporter asked. "I think," Allen replied, "that is the gospel." (Shepard and Mingus, as if to accentuate his point, painted FUCK GOD in large black letters on a wall inside the church.)[23]

Shepard had written to Jane Rogers in early August that *The Rock Garden* "really cancels out everything that I've written so far. I wrote it in four days and it was like piling everything into one suitcase." In fact, it was special to him well after he'd made it big. *The Rock Garden*, he said in 1991, "was sort of the beginning of something that reverberated from there, which I didn't realize at the time."[24]

*The Rock Garden* is an absurdist reflection on the ennui of growing up in a middle-class California home. Based on Shepard's relationship with his parents, *The Rock Garden* is a slapstick play that's performed deadpan. In the first scene, Shepard's character, Boy, is seated in a rocking chair wearing only his underwear, while his mother, Woman, is lying on a bed swaddled in blankets. The two perform a vaudevillian costume routine wherein Woman says that Boy's legs resemble her father's, and the teen, privately disgusted by his genetic heritage, exits and returns in pants; then it's his feet with shoes, then his torso with a shirt. In the second scene, father and son are discovered seated naked aside from their underpants. The father, Man, prattles on about mowing the lawn, painting the fence, and managing their orchard's irrigation, while the son periodically falls off his chair from boredom. When it's the teen's turn to reveal his own inner thoughts, he does so with an aria about sex: "When I come it's like a river. It's all over the bed and the sheets and everything. You know?" Boy delights over how to give a woman an orgasm and ends the play with the lines "I really like to come almost out and then go all the way into the womb. You know, very slowly. Just come down to the end and all the way back in and hold it. You know what I mean?" The father, in a state of shock, tumbles to the floor.[25]

Shepard's graphic sex talk showcased the group's "conspicuous heterosexuality," as Ralph Cook phrased it, which distinguished them from the more gender-bending fare less abashed theatergoers might find at La MaMa or Caffe Cino.[26] A friend of the stage manager's said Theater Genesis "did have a bit of a Boys' Club."[27] "They didn't hate women, but they didn't appreciate women," agreed one of the group's female volunteers. "They all held women at a distance."[28] And, of course, Cook's regular playwrights around this time—Shepard, Murray Mednick, Tony Barsha, Walter Hadler, Leonard Melfi, and Tom Sankey—were all men. Barsha referred to their communal "Macho Americano" attitude as the "Hells Angels of the Off-Off-Broadway scene. . . . A lot of pot, and a lot of women, and a lot of messing around in that area, so Genesis definitely had that reputation, and rightly so."[29]

But the collective sensibility of Theater Genesis, male or female, was that of all people involved in theater during the downtown underground scene: in equal measure tough, funny, cynical, talented, disgruntled, and steeped in the adventure of a lifetime. "Theater Genesis is a mix of counterculture ingredients," *Newsweek*'s drama critic Jack Kroll summed up their overall reputation Off-Off-Broadway, "a coolness that can explode like liquid oxygen, a dropout hipsterism, a polymorphous perversity of language and feeling, a Zap Comix mocking of straight heads."[30]

The final monologue in *The Rock Garden* was more pornographic than even some avant-garde audiences could endure. And yet one night, Lee Kissman (who played Boy) recalled, laughing at the memory, "I looked up from my perch out toward the audience and three nuns were sitting in the first row immediately in front of me. They seemed to be enjoying themselves; they didn't flinch." Still, Shepard's steamy theatrics and graphic dialogue did little to excite the critics. "All these guys said it was a bunch of shit," Shepard said, that he had "imitated Beckett or something like that." The most rancorous pan came from Jerry Tallmer's review in the *New York Post*, which reviewed only *Cowboys*, not *The Rock Garden*, and condemned Shepard as the latest proselyte of what he called Edward Albee's emergent "Theater of Assault." "In the Theater of Assault," Tallmer wrote, "the object is not so much to shock or awaken an audience as to attack it, directly, personally, unilaterally." Shepard's "psychic spleen" was in the tradition of Albee's *The Zoo Story* and Beckett's *Waiting for Godot*, and not in a complimentary way. "Mr. Shepard is angry at (a) everybody who must watch his play, (b) everybody in crowded, ugly New York City, and (c) everybody."[31]

Ralph Cook was apoplectic over the review. Tallmer had seen the second performance, before the production had settled into its own. And for two long weeks, Tallmer's was the dominant review. But later in the run another notice appeared, one that would single-handedly launch Shepard's career, written by Michael Smith, a playwright himself, who thought Tallmer was a "second-string critic."[32] While seated on a bench in Washington Square Park, Shepard read and reread the rave *Village Voice* review in stunned silence. In it, Smith argued that Shepard's plays defied categorization, and he warned other drama critics not to bother trying. "Shepard is feeling his way," he said, "working with an intuitive approach to language and dramatic structure and moving into an area . . . where character transcends psychology, fantasy breaks down literalism, and the patterns of ordinariness have their own lives."[33] And Smith was certain that these two short plays portended a great future for the twenty-year-old in the dramatic arts. "One comes away feeling that the playwright has kept some of his secrets, perhaps kept them from himself," Smith wrote, "but at least he has secrets to keep." Only a couple of years later, when Shepard was the poster child for the new underground theater, Michael Smith said that "I felt forever after as though I'd 'discovered' Sam Shepard."[34] And by critical standards, he had.

More accolades poured in. The future director and dramaturg Bill Hart, who would later room with Shepard, direct several of his plays, and serve as best man at his wedding, exited the church euphoric: "He had literally altered my consciousness." Lee Kissman drank often with Hart, and after the performance, they walked with Smith back to his apartment in the West Village, where, Kissman remembered, "they both were blown away. . . . Neither of them could stop talking."[35]

Another promising young playwright named Murray Mednick was also in the audience. Shepard had already seen a play of Mednick's and knew he had to meet him. Mednick and Shepard started playing pool regularly at the Blue & Gold Tavern, a popular East Village dive a couple of blocks from St. Mark's. Shepard was captivated by Mednick's "tough guy" walk and streetwise Brooklyn speech and mannerisms. "He never knew anybody like me," Mednick said, "a real Jewish intellectual. A real New Yorker." Mednick was equally captivated by Shepard's blend of homegrown Americana and bookishness. "Sam . . . read a lot. And that's what our friendship was mostly about—stuff that we read." But being friends with Shepard "wasn't so easy," he said.

> He beat you at everything—pool, he could ride horses. He was a good athlete. And he was good-looking. So if you go into a room, all the women were looking at him. Talented and intelligent, he had it all going. . . . It was just amazing that he had all these good things, and then, all of a sudden, he got famous.

This last came as a shock. "We were all just kids really," Mednick said.[36]

If not for Smith's bellwether notice in the *Village Voice*, and that paper's hungry downtown audience, Shepard might well have initiated his fallback plan to return to college and live a quiet life as a veterinarian in the San Gabriel Valley. Instead, only a year later, the maverick from California would be heralded by the country's most esteemed news source, the *New York Times*, as downtown's "generally acknowledged 'genius.'"[37]

"From the earliest day," Bill Hart agreed, "everybody thought of Shepard as the best—right away."[38]

* * *

Only a few days after closing night of his premiere bill, Shepard recruited a group of Theater Genesis players to act in his drama *Up to Thursday: A Short Play in Two Scenes*.[39] The troupe had ten days to rehearse at St. Mark's, after which they'd perform in workshop before a nonpaying audience at the Playwrights Unit's workshop space, "the Vandam," or Village South Theatre (now the SoHo Playhouse), just south of the West Village in Hudson Square. *Up to Thursday*, Shepard's first commercial production, had been chosen by Edward Albee's Theatre 1965 to be a part of its "Ten New Playwrights Series." The title *Up to Thursday* has no apparent bearing on the script, and Lee Kissman, who again played the starring role, admitted he wouldn't have known what it meant if Shepard hadn't told him. It referred to the script's unstated fact that the protagonist, Young Man, had "up to Thursday" before he was informed whether or not he'd be drafted.[40]

Theatre 1965 staged a free public performance of *Up to Thursday* on November 23, 1964, along with two other short plays at the Village South, then the workshop was revived for the first program of Theatre 1965's "Ten New Playwrights Series" at the Off-Broadway Cherry Lane Theatre on February 10, 1965. Shepard confirmed that his subject was the Vietnam draft in his first interview to appear in print. "On that certain specific Thursday I was supposed to go into the Army," he told the *Newsday* drama critic Allan Wallach for a feature on Albee's Playwrights Unit. "So this series of reactions leading up to that (event) amount to the play." (According to a girlfriend, he wasn't actually cleared from service until after writing the play.) Wallach reported that Shepard "has an apparent indifference to making money, formal writing courses, formulations about writing, and interviews."[41] The budding dramatist did, however, elucidate his desired effect on audiences: "I like to see someone stagger out of the theater, you know. I like to see some kind of chemical stuff going on between the person sitting in the seat and the things happening on stage."[42]

When *Up to Thursday* moved from the Vandam to the Cherry Lane Theatre, Shepard stepped into the Off-Broadway space for the first time, set his eyes on the proscenium, and gawked: "It looks like a big hole in the wall." The full cast from the original workshop remained except Mimi Levine, who had taken off to London with Elia Kazan, the master director of film and stage, to attend Winston Churchill's funeral. Joyce Aaron, an enchanting actress with a cascade of red hair, came in for an audition. Eight years Shepard's senior, Aaron was already a well-known presence on downtown stages. During her audition, she was asked to laugh, and her laughter was so infectious, Shepard started laughing too. He asked her out to dinner. "And then," Aaron said, "he never left."[43]

This was Shepard's first true romance.

At twenty-eight, Joyce Aaron had already been married and divorced twice before meeting Shepard. She was the adopted daughter of a middle-class family who had grown up modeling and performing in school plays. After college, she moved to New York to study acting with Sanford Meisner at the Neighborhood Playhouse. Meisner's approach to acting in the early 1960s, one that Aaron would apply to her relationship with Shepard, was to focus on the other actors more than yourself. Aaron's initiation to the Off-Broadway theater world came through a series of happy accidents: She was babysitting for the drama critic Richard Gilman, who attended one of her early shows and was so impressed with her acting, he introduced her to Joseph "Joe" Chaikin, founder of the Open Theater, whom she then introduced to Shepard.[44]

Joe Chaikin and Sam Shepard first met at a dinner party on the Upper West Side. The two quickly formed a bond and, after dinner, walked and talked for eighty blocks, all the way back down to Greenwich Village. Their conversation mainly revolved around LSD, but before parting ways, Chaikin invited him to a workshop at the Open Theater in their loft space in SoHo at 147 Spring Street, after which Shepard became tangentially involved with the group.[45]

Chaikin's ensemble company included the director Jacques Levy, who would soon take Shepard under his wing, and the young playwrights María Irene Fornés, Megan Terry, and Jean-Claude van Itallie, with whom he would more often collaborate outside the Open Theater. He attended workshops, and every now and then, Chaikin would ask him to write something for them, which he'd do. "I was always like in and out," he said, "contributing to the work just in little particles, in little pieces. . . . But I didn't know how to function there as a writer at all."[46] Chaikin was devoted to helping actors discover inner worlds while always keeping the spectators in mind. "What if Queen Elizabeth is in the audience?" he asked during an exercise. "Gandhi?" The mission of Chaikin's theater was "to bring about a kind of theatre immediacy—a presence, being present, in the theatre. To explore those powers which the live theatre possesses. What is it that's amazing about the theatre? It's the here and now, the existential encounter."[47]

In this way, Chaikin taught Shepard to be an adaptable artist for his moment. "He included it all," Shepard remembered. "Let's include the circus; let's include Japanese theater; let's include Strasberg; let's include Artaud, and find all the possibilities."[48] Chaikin also taught him that good theater forced audiences to reflect upon their mortality; if audiences were merely out for an evening of pleasurable entertainment, Chaikin would say, then they should "go to a football game."[49] Though Shepard made only fleeting contributions to the Open Theater, his relationship with Chaikin, whom he considered "the consummate theatre artist," would last for almost forty years.[50]

Joyce Aaron thus had critical connections that boosted Shepard's career the way Richard Gilman had helped hers. "I was a real mentor," Aaron said nearly six decades after facilitating her boyfriend's upward journey into the larger New York theater scene. "I recognized him. I really found him in a way." Aaron also introduced him to an agent, Toby Cole, who would serve as Shepard's literary champion and undaunted guardian for over a decade.[51]

Shepard moved in with Aaron at her apartment next door to La MaMa on Second Avenue. She began reading drafts of his plays out loud to him and soon enough realized that, as so many of his lovers, friends, and relatives would in the years to come, nothing they did together was private. "I never knew where our life—where *my* life—was going to turn up on the page, or later on some stage, but inevitably there was always some aspect of our experience together that I would recognize." But like his sister Sandy Rogers, Aaron never resented him or quarreled about his co-opting their personal life. "I never felt exposed by Sam," she said. "He transformed whatever he drew on."[52]

* * *

While the production of *Up to Thursday* led to a vital artistic and romantic connection, the critical responses were mixed. "They are apparently searching for another Albee but they didn't find one," the Associated Press quipped about *Up to Thursday*.[53] The *New York Times*, however, hailed Shepard's innovative use of everyday language in an otherwise abstract play and categorized his style as "theater of the absurd à la Abbott and Costello, but he cuts deeper."[54] Albee himself, though acknowledging Shepard's gifts as a burgeoning playwright, remarked that the scripts he yielded often "give the impression of being a mess."[55]

Shepard was likely never called on any Thursday by the draft board before he'd written his play, but he was feverishly determined to avoid fighting in Vietnam. To soothe his jangled nerves, Aaron helped him prepare for his actual draft board interview by encouraging him to process the ordeal as a performance: "We rehearsed what he was going to say and how he was going to act. The whole thing. I just made up the answers to their questions, and how to behave, and he was addicted, and he wouldn't be able to kill anyone." If the board asked him whether he believed he was fit to serve in the military, she said, "I told him say no, absolutely not."[56]

In the late spring or summer of 1965, he received what was called a "nut note," a letter from a certified psychiatrist informing the military he was mentally unfit for service. The fee for this was about five hundred dollars.[57] Prior to the impending escalation in Vietnam, draft boards were fairly slack in their decision-making, and nut notes were easily obtained. But soon after 1964's Tonkin Gulf Resolution, the nut note became an anachronism, as compliant psychiatrists were scarce once the government cracked down. Shepard also wrote home for an X-ray to prove he'd slipped a disc while working at Conley's horse ranch in high school, and he filled out the requisite form, checking yes to everything: "Do you wet the bed?" "YES." Do you take heroin?" "YES." The recruitment officer at Whitehall Street, where the line was predominantly made up of men in drag and druggies nodding off, said they could recommend a treatment program if he had a drug problem. Finally, the officer just said, "Get out of here," and presto, Shepard was 4-F.[58]

Draft fears abated, Shepard could focus on his third bill. La MaMa next staged Shepard's one-acts *Dog* and *The Rocking Chair*, which opened on February 10, 1965. *The Rocking Chair* is about a listless young man visiting a young woman in Boston. Still unpublished, the play is the earliest example of Shepard's attempts to exorcise his painful past with his father by projecting it onto the stage. *Dog*, also unpublished, reimagines Edward Albee's 1958 breakout *The Zoo Story*. A drunk, mutilated Black man convinces a wealthy white man that he is a dog, stuck in a prison of bourgeois security, and in doing so, renders him motionless.

* * *

Charles Mingus's father was close friends with New York's abstract expressionist painters, and one night, Mingus the younger brought Shepard to a party at the West Side apartment of Elaine de Kooning's lover, a friend but "a social climber, Gatsby-type guy." They got there, and the place was empty. In the refrigerator they found hypodermic needles on a steel tray for B-12 shots and a pint of orange and vanilla swirl sherbet laced with thousands of dollars' worth of LSD. Shepard ate a teaspoonful but didn't like the taste, so Mingus downed the rest. Mingus's acquaintance had been swept up by the Merry Pranksters, a hodgepodge band of touring LSD promoters led by the writer Ken Kesey, and they had "dosed him with massive amounts of drugs," Mingus said. "But nothing could be conceived of on the level I took it."[59]

Mingus felt all right after the trip subsided, still himself if perhaps more so, he said, whereas "Sam had a teaspoon, and he's been crazy ever since." Mingus had taken peyote, psilocybin, and mescaline, among a host of other psychedelic drugs back in Duarte, whereas Shepard had no prior experience with psychedelic trips, let alone maximum-grade Merry Prankster LSD.[60]

That night, Shepard arrived at Aaron's apartment seeking safe harbor to ride out this powerful dose of acid. While he was bouncing up and down on her bed and writing all over her walls, Aaron suspected that their mutual friend Charles Mingus was responsible. "She came up to me afterward," Mingus said, "and threatened to have me killed if I ever had anything to do with Sam again." To add to all of this, in mid-March 1965, Aaron left for Chicago for several months for an acting gig. Her departure panicked Shepard, as, in her view, "he was very dependent on me to make things go right and protect him. I was very protective of him, so he was losing that cover. . . . I kept the newspapers away. I kept people away. . . . He certainly didn't take care of those things himself. He was just writing. That's it. Writing was it."[61]

Alone in their Second Avenue apartment and overwhelmed with feelings of abandonment, Shepard banged out his legendary one-act *Chicago* in a single day. "The stuff would just come out," he shrugged, "and I wasn't really trying to shape it or make it into any big thing."[62] *Chicago* would become his most acclaimed and performed play of the 1960s.

*Chicago* presents another version of Shepard, again named Stu, in a bathtub having an apocalyptic vision that starts with fishermen and sea nymphs in a massive, sand-soaked orgy on a beach that lasts for years. They eventually build a house in which they weave many rugs and become smothered in the house filled with rugs. All the while, Joy, a character based on Aaron, calmly prepares for her journey and pays no attention to Stu's frantic outpourings, which she appears to take as false bravado. In the final scene, Stu breaks the fourth wall and directs the other cast members and the audience to therapeutically breathe in and out to stanch the panic he'd built up during the aria, then "there are three loud knocks from the back of the house," and curtain.[63]

The play's "movement," wrote Ralph Cook, who labeled such Theater Genesis plays "subjective realism," "is from Stu's minute particular subjective problem ... to the universal problem of Man's being civilized to the suffocating point of losing his balls."[64] They were losing their balls, Shepard added, "because they've been broken and crushed under some kind of gigantic weight called society, called culture, called politics, called labor, called poverty, called a thousand different names."[65] *Chicago* serves as a prequel to his one-acts *Red Cross* and *Fourteen Hundred Thousand* and the full-lengths *La Turista* and his unpublished and unproduced horror play about their first New Year's Eve together, "Replacement for Eight," which together form a cycle that revolves around Shepard's singular romantic and artistic partnership: a Joyce Aaron Cycle.

Theater Genesis staged *Chicago* on April 16 as part of a double bill with *The Customs Collector in Baggy Pants* by the Beat poet Lawrence Ferlinghetti. It was Shepard's bona fide breakout work, with high-profile revivals over the following year.[66] "What gives the play its delights," Stanley Kauffmann crowed in the *New York Times*, "is Mr. Shepard's ability to follow fast after the ephemeral half-thought that is usually unspoken." Other critics squabbled about its quality, but *Chicago* helped Shepard win his first of ten Obie Awards, downtown theater's answer to Broadway's Tony Awards. Also, in large part on the strength of that play, Michael Allen was able to draw real money for Theater Genesis.

The New School for Social Research, for one, gave the St. Mark's arts budget a lump sum of two hundred thousand dollars a year for two years (1966–68) in a sociological experiment to ascertain the extent to which street youths might find salvation in the arts. (Theater Genesis also received other substantial grants.) The money, according to Lee Kissman, was to fund Theater Genesis, St. Mark's newly conceived Poetry Project, and a short-lived underground film series. After only a year or so of work, playwrights and directors were getting paid about a thousand dollars per production. Actors and crew were also paid, though not enough to live without day jobs. Still, they got around thirty dollars for rehearsals and a hundred and thirty for performances. Most of them only paid forty or fifty dollars a month in rent.[67]

* * *

By early May, Shepard was fed up with being isolated in their apartment—Joyce Aaron wasn't supposed to return until July 8—so he hopped a train to Chicago, where she was staying at the Blackwood Hotel.[68] While in Chicago, he visited the Rogers family in Lombard, and his grandmother, Helen Rogers, immediately reported back to Jane and gave Aaron a hearty seal of approval: "She is good for [him] . . . intelligent, well-educated . . . friendly, warmhearted." Shepard, she wrote, "is not interested in being talented and hates the word success, only interested in getting his ideas over to people. He wants Utopia which looks almost impossible now & he is completely honest & he wants to do for others & hates all the cruelty & injustice that he sees in New York."[69]

Shepard's visit with the Rogerses of Lombard inspired him to write a somber, impassioned letter addressed to his father that expands upon what Helen Rogers only lightly observed. The letter is an eight-page-long paragraph written in the style of his consciousness-exploding monologues. Rather than lambasting his father for wrongdoings, he talks about visiting Sam Sr.'s parents and brother, and how their physical resemblance brought him to mind. He then confronts his father sideways, widening his parameters to encompass all of humankind and his place within it.[70]

"I've discovered the world," Shepard wrote. "Really. I feel like Christopher Columbus except without the patriotism." He'd arrived at an "awareness that the whole shmear goes on regardless of how many men get Ph.Ds or how many bombs this country continues to drop on Viet Nam in the name of peace and brotherhood.... There are people all over suffering from diseases that no one even knows the name for because they're diseases of the soul, of the spirit." And those responsible, the so-called leaders, were the architects of a mass advertisement for American life in the name of a cruel gaslighting operation called "freedom."[71] In the letter, Shepard outlines his ideal worldview, as opposed to that of the self-conscious masses of American strivers: "The self-conscious person goes nowhere," he wrote. "He's trapped forever in a cage of his own making.... He dies very slowly. If he could strip himself of everything, all his games, all his roles and stand there like a naked person he could start to become alive. He could see a fantastic infinity in front of him and all around him where living is everything."[72]

Shepard and Aaron celebrated the Fourth of July with friends on the shores of Lake Michigan in Milwaukee, Wisconsin. "One of the weird things about being in America now," he said, "is that you don't have any connection with the past, with what history means: so you can be there celebrating the Fourth of July, but all you know is that things are exploding in the sky."[73] This ambivalence toward the holiday inspired him to write his next one-act play, *Icarus's Mother*.

Shepard and Aaron tripped on acid with their friends, and Aaron remembered of the experience, "I became in that state like a baby, like an infant... and the only thing that got me out of it [was] Sam came over to me as I was this baby and brought a bottle of milk." According to Shepard, she was attempting to say the word "duck," then "moaned in a voice I'd only heard in animals giving birth.... It kept rolling out of her as her body unleashed itself. At the peak I thought for sure she was dying." And then, he observed, "she was instantly transformed. She started using words as though she's never known the lack of them."[74]

Aaron's production, the British playwright Ann Jellicoe's improvisational sex comedy *The Knack*, closed early, so they left Chicago for summer stock at the Playhouse in the Park in Philadelphia, the country's first "theater in the round."[75] They boarded at a campground, where Aaron would leave Shepard holed up in their cabin worrying over a bad case of crabs. ("He had crabs," Aaron confirmed.) One day, a maid entered to fix their room, and Shepard spun their interaction into another tragicomic one-act, *Red Cross*.[76] Everything was fair game to him.

That same summer, 1965, Shepard accepted his first screenwriting job for the film *Me and My Brother*, about the Beat poet Peter Orlovsky and his brother, Julius, who was a catatonic schizophrenic. The film was cowritten and directed by the photographer Robert Frank (*Pull My Daisy*, *Cocksucker Blues*), who'd enlisted Shepard, and starred the Orlovsky brothers and Allen Ginsberg as themselves. Julius disappeared during filming, and once he reemerged, he sank into a comatose state. It was obvious he required a replacement, and Joe Chaikin gamely accepted the role. (Christopher Walken, the up-and-coming acting star, played Robert Frank.) *Me and My Brother* was written over the next couple of years, but it wouldn't be completed until the winter of 1967.[77] The film remains an astonishing work of cinema verité, revealing the personal lives of the Beats and their fascination with madness.

Then, after traveling to a frustrating inaugural festival for Off-Off-Broadway playwrights at the Eugene O'Neill Theater Center in Waterford, Connecticut, Shepard resolved to get out of New York for a healthier stretch of time. "It was incredible luck to be around when something like off-off-Broadway was getting off the ground," Shepard recalled of this period, "but the 1960s were kinda awful. I don't even want to think about it." Asked why Shepard felt so negatively about New York in the sixties, Murray Mednick gravely responded,

> It was the war. It was the off-off Broadway movement, which was very competitive. It was the drug revolution. People were using, and it was a sexual revolution and people were fucking everybody. A lot of bad things were happening. It was very tense. There was a lot of betrayal.... It was a lot of revolutions on at the same time, and besides that there was street shit, street hassles. We were on the street a lot. It was dangerous.... And we did things that would be with us 'til we die.[78]

CHAPTER 4

# LOS TURISTAS

At twenty-two, Shepard wasn't much interested in foreign travel, but Joyce Aaron, a Latin American culture enthusiast who frequently visited Mexico, convinced him it was time. First, they flew to Los Angeles, then caught a connecting flight down to Mexico City, and on to Mérida on the Yucatán peninsula in August 1965. On the flight down from California, their airplane was assailed by gale-force winds from a hurricane, causing turbulence that was so extreme, Shepard swore he'd never fly again. But once they were settled in, the two found themselves so happy and at ease that the trip turned into a months-long excursion.[1]

"Mexico is what America should have been," Shepard said.

> Mexico still has heart, it still has extraordinary passion, it still has a sense of family and culture, of deep, deep roots. Some of it is awful—the poverty level, the oppression's awful, and stuff like that—but there are places you go in Mexico that just make you feel like a human being. The Indian culture is what I think does it for me. . . . It really is paradise.[2]

From the Yucatán, the couple traveled farther south to San Cristóbal de las Casas in the southern state of Chiapas; and from there, they left their luggage behind at a bed-and-breakfast to tour Chiapas and the rainforests of Guatemala.[3] After that, Shepard's "paradise" turned hellish. Upon returning to San Cristóbal, they decided to head back to Mexico

City, but in Oaxaca, they spent several days confined to their room at the Hotel Nacional in a "semidelirious state of severe dysentery."[4] They had no toilet, so they shared the sink. Sometimes they threw up together, first laughing at their predicament, then resigned to it. "I remember lying on a bare mattress," Shepard wrote, "staring up at a slow black ceiling fan and wishing I were dead. It was the only time I've ever actually wished I were dead, and I wished it with all my heart."[5]

Shepard, while ailing, somehow managed to write a three-act play that he called *La Turista*, the name that Mexicans sometimes use for the stomach virus that strikes visitors.[6] "In that state," he said, "any writing I could manage seemed valid, no matter how incoherent it might seem to an outside eye."[7] When it was time to return, Aaron discovered to her dismay that he was serious about never flying again. With sixty-five dollars left, they spent several days on a bus back to New York.[8]

* * *

Their excursion south of the border prevented Aaron from joining the cast for Shepard's next play, *Icarus's Mother*, about their Fourth of July acid trip.[9] In it, a group of five young picnickers are awaiting a fireworks display. They're assailing one another with sarcasm, pranks, and mental gamesmanship when a skywriting airplane flies overhead, intensifying and making visible a subliminal terror that lurks within them. Shepard said of the banter in *Icarus's Mother* that they're broadcasting outlandish emotions churning inside their heads, and the only reason we're even hearing it is that a play needs dialogue. "Like you can be washing the dishes and [have] an apocalyptic nightmare going on inside of you," Shepard said. "People at a picnic, yet inside they're in turmoil."[10]

In this way, Shepard served as a critical new voice in American theater: he was moving away from the "problem" of realistic dialogue and its limitations that Eugene O'Neill confronted. *Icarus's Mother*, at bottom, is a soliloquy that requires teamwork.

*Icarus's Mother* was produced in Greenwich Village's storied Caffe Cino, known as the birthplace of Off-Off-Broadway, where the motto was, "If no one's there, we'll do it for the walls." It was tight if more than fifty people showed up, and the stage was a small raised platform of about six by nine feet.[11] Joe Cino, the café's gregarious proprietor, came up with the idea to have Shepard's champion from the *Village Voice*, Michael Smith, direct the production. Smith would get to know Shepard in the process, and he also introduced Shepard to Caffe Cino's predominantly gay clientele. (Most of the gay and bisexual men in the downtown theater scene were unashamed about their sexuality, yet private about whom they loved.)[12]

One of the characters who made Joe Cino's café a popular attraction was its lighting impresario, and Smith's lover, John Patrick Kennedy Dodd. Johnny Dodd, as he was known, had already performed in two Andy Warhol movies by the time Shepard met him, and he later became a backstage legend, lighting punk rock acts and shows on Broadway. "He didn't know the conventional way of doing things," Smith said. "Warm and cool, etc. He just made it up."[13]

Shepard was dumbstruck when he first watched Johnny Dodd in action. He was following an actor with handheld lights and appeared very stoned, but Shepard considered him as integral to the performances as the actor. Dodd's lighting technique was simple: never stop moving. On those cramped stages, Dodd projected a kaleidoscopic effect for the benefit of the audience and the actors, Smith said, "colors changing, brightness changing, space is changing with the flow of the performance." *Icarus's Mother*, which opened on November 16, 1965, would be Johnny Dodd's first of many Shepard productions.

"I still think it's the best of Sam's plays to date," Smith wrote, "the fullest, densest, most disturbing and provocative. But it is terribly difficult to produce." He saw his attempt to stage it as a failure. To begin with, the five characters appear interchangeable aside from their sex (two women and three men). But when Smith asked the young playwright about this before rehearsals were to begin with a group of Open Theater actors, Shepard replied that he didn't care about character. For him, actors were strictly vehicles for delivering his language and imagery.[14]

"Shepard's focus is on creating a theatrical event," Smith wrote in a mea culpa in the *Village Voice*, "and any logical or psychological approach makes many of his choices appear arbitrary." His characters, he went on, contrasting Shepard with the playwrights Tennessee Williams and William Inge, "are not 'motivated' in a conventional way, not driven by the mechanistic psychology that lurks inside so many modern plays." Smith noted that the "so-called paranoia of the nuclear present" was the play's governing principle, but the day before opening night, Smith realized he should stop dealing with nonrepresentational *meaning* and focus on the damned picnic.[15]

This helped, but not enough. "I have no way of telling you what 'Icarus's Mother' is about," wrote Edward Albee. "But, then again, up until now, at any rate, what Shepard's plays are about is a great deal less interesting than how they are about it." Shepard didn't rewrite his early plays much at all, he admitted years later. "It was like 'Take it or leave it—if you don't like this shit, tough luck,' and go on to the next one," he said of his attitude composing the early plays. "They were explosions that were coming out of some kind of inner turmoil in me that I didn't understand at all.... They were just survival techniques, a means of putting something outside rather than having it all inside."[16]

Whatever his motives, Shepard's plays had become greatly admired in the avant-garde theater scene for their formlessness and raw originality, though some of his peers resented his swift ascendance. But La MaMa's Ellen Stewart herself said, "That's the boy, that's the boy to watch." Stewart nurtured Shepard's talent and even gave him a basement room to store his drum kit, where he would thrash away until inspired to write.[17]

* * *

In March 1966, Shepard and Aaron headed westward with another avant-garde playwright, Jean-Claude van Itallie of the Open Theater, to Minneapolis, Minnesota, with funding from a Rockefeller Foundation grant. On March 11, Shepard's *Fourteen Hundred Thousand*, along with van Itallie's *Where Is de Queen?*, premiered at the city's Firehouse Theater, a playhouse that had close artistic ties to La MaMa and the Open Theater.[18]

Minneapolis was frigid as usual that March. A photograph accompanying a local feature story about the avant-garde New York playwrights shows a twenty-nine-year-old van Itallie and twenty-two-year-old Shepard on the Firehouse Theater stage, open- mouthed and amusing themselves. Shepard appears especially relaxed, seated on a stool with his legs up to his chest, and—rebelling not just against the press's expectations but against the city's frosty weather—wearing a slim pair of dungarees, no socks, a leather jacket, and a fur fez.[19]

On a lark, Shepard declared that he was married to Aaron, and in the script, their fictional counterparts are also married; later, and in a letter to the *Village Voice*'s Obie committee, she's listed as "Mrs. Sam Shepard." "I felt like her husband," he wrote years later, "but for her it could never be real unless we were married."[20]

On March 4, Shepard and van Itallie took part in a discussion with a local audience at Minneapolis's contemporary art museum, the Walker Art Center. There to prepare Minnesotans for what they were about to witness, they brought balloons to liven up their act. As the locals began asking questions, the duo would each blow one up and grotesquely let the air out or pop them with a pin. "Why are you so hostile?" an audience member demanded. "This isn't art. We want meat! We want substance! Give us meat!" The next morning, they'd scheduled a radio interview but were in no mood to cooperate. Rewinding her tape for a third time, the interviewer turned away from the recorder and screamed, "You can't do this to me!" and showed them the door.[21]

On March 9, they joined a small group of students for coffee at the University of Minnesota's Union Gallery. The event was billed as a discussion of avant-garde theater as a "social weapon." The playwrights didn't look like stereotypical "theater people," a student noted. No long hair. No goatees. Instead, they were "casually dressed and plain-spoken." In fact, the student newspaper quoted Shepard as questioning the very term "avant-garde theater":

> Avant-garde is like a word invented by an advertiser who tries to define what's undefinable and prepare people for the theater.... People think that a play not understood by them somehow has some kind of secret that has to be knifed out of the playwright, so that it can be exposed and understood.... Art should be experienced, like an orange. What do you do with an orange? You experience it. You eat it, taste it, feel the juice on your fingers.... Analyzing has become a disease. Today we analyze, categorize—it's become a substitute for being.[22]

That said, the title of Shepard's play *Fourteen Hundred Thousand* refers to the number of books owned by a couple, Tom and Donna (Shepard and Aaron), and the action revolves around their construction of a massive bookcase in their Manhattan apartment. Donna's parents haul armloads of books up eight flights of stairs as the couple bicker viciously and slap paint on each other, while their friend, Ed (likely based on Bill Hart), helps with the move but guiltily admits that he needs to depart for his hideaway cabin in the woods. The play is an indictment of congested urban living and ends with the parents reading out loud from a book on the relative merits of "radial" versus "linear" urban planning (a monologue for which Shepard had to consult an architect). *Fourteen Hundred Thousand*, the third play in the Joyce Aaron Cycle, is notable for being an overtly environmentalist play, a point Shepard drove home in his program note by quoting the ancient Roman philosopher Seneca: "And the whole firmament shall fall on the divine earth and on the sea; and then shall flow a ceaseless cataract of raging fire, and shall burn land and sea, and the firmament of heaven and the stars and creation itself it shall cast into one molten mass and clean dissolve."[23]

"Fourteen Hundred Thousand Times, No," read the archly titled *Minneapolis Star* review. In it, the drama critic Lew Reeve mercilessly disparaged the double bill:

> If this is supposed to be satire, or commentary on the contemporary scene, it missed by a country mile. One qualification for success in

> such dramatic efforts is that the target must be identifiable. Firing a muzzle loader merely to carve a hole in the air is not productive of lasting results no matter how many buckets full of verbal stove bolts and harness buckles are spewed out.[24]

The Upper Midwest may not have had the stomach for avant-garde theater as yet, but that same month, back in New York, Shepard and van Itallie, with other tyro playwrights, were featured in a *Mademoiselle* magazine story on Off-Off-Broadway announcing the emergence of "the third stream" of theater in New York: "Much talk these days about that chronic invalid, the theatre, dying—at last. And it does look as though first-stream theatre (on and Off-Broadway) is in a bad way. But second stream theatre (campus, community, and festival) is booming, while third stream, OOB (meaning Off-Off-Broadway), is at its zoomiest."[25] Off-Off-Broadway stages were challenging traditional boundaries of dramatic form and rebelling against the stranglehold of postwar conformity—all of which led to a cultural and social revolution on the New York stage, one that would ignite young imaginations across the nation and abroad. Sam Shepard, it was clear, was now at the head of this pack.

*Mademoiselle*'s writer called Shepard "possibly the most original of the hundreds of playwrights being produced OOB." When asked why he wrote plays for such small theaters, Shepard replied, "It's an environmental choice—I have to work OOB. The plays can't be done anywhere else—economically or any other kind of way. Anywhere else the value systems are completely different—no experimentation.... You have to conform in a certain way."[26]

Shepard's earliest plays lacked structure, characterization, romance, and other familiar theatrical elements in favor of extreme, liberating, even irrational insights. Additionally, Off-Off-Broadway as it existed then was rooted squarely in the history of the moment, as Shepard swiftly came to understand. "How do you relate O'Neill to the psychological atmosphere around Vietnam?" he asked in hindsight. "It was very palpable, the psychological fire going on. Panic, terror, paranoia, all that shit that was happening—and there wasn't anything that responded to that climate."[27] For this reason, Shepard believed that the evolution of a "new underground theatre," as the critic Robert J. Schroeder termed it, was less a revolt against the commercial theater of Broadway and more a youthful reaction to historical forces at play—Vietnam, civil rights, free love—while satisfying the outsized personalities involved. "It was a phenomenon unto itself," Shepard wrote. "There was very little talk of the 'bad guys' uptown because the commercial theatre was felt as a totally alien world."[28]

* * *

Together with offering Off-Off-Broadway theaters a seemingly inexhaustible supply of one-act plays, Shepard also began playing live music in folk rock bands. "After a while I started reacting against that, this whole jazz influence," he said, and he started calling jazz "beatnik horseshit . . . sitting around and snapping your fingers." Rock and roll, however, represented "another kind of back-to-the-raw-gut kind of American shitkicker thing."[29]

Shepard's first band in New York was called the Heavy Metal Kid, whose lineup included Eddie Hicks, a steadfast anarchist from West Virginia, on guitar and harmonica; Shepard on Indian tablas; and Murray Mednick on the chanter, recorder, and tambourine. The band was named after a character in a William S. Burroughs's Nova trilogy, and Mednick described their sound as "acid rock." Then, in the fall of 1966, Shepard met an outlaw fiddle player in his late twenties named Peter Stampfel. Stampfel, along with the guitarist Steve Weber, was a member of the Holy Modal Rounders, an Appalachian-style country rock band credited with first applying the term "psychedelic" to rock music. The Rounders lived by the creed "If it doesn't make you feel horny it's not art." Weber, Shepard wrote, was "the first guy to ever walk barefoot on the Lower East Side . . . the first one to wear granny glasses with actual lenses . . . the first one to wear black vests without a shirt . . . the first one to use speed to come down from smack [*sic*]."[30]

The Rounders were recently offered a lot of money for a reunion show, so Stampfel returned to a Lower East Side pawnshop to redeem his fiddle, a "lacquered candy-apple green" instrument with "a pin-striped spider web painted on the back in black," which he'd hocked for amphetamines. Shepard approached him in the shop, and not long after, he left the Heavy Metal Kid and started playing for the Holy Modal Rounders and Stampfel's other band, the Swamp Willies, later called the Moray Eels ("More A" meaning "more amphetamines").[31] The Rounders soon landed a recording deal with ESP-Disk' records to record *Indian War Whoop* (1967), with the core band made up of Shepard, Stampfel, and Weber.

This was Shepard's induction into rock and roll history, and with it, the agony and ecstasy of crystal methedrine. It was a drug habit he had, on and off, for about five years. His personal record for days without sleep, he claimed, was five. (Stampfel's was two weeks.) The Rounders were a wild band, often, as with Shepard's plays, at their audiences' expense, but Shepard listed them alongside his other favorites of the era, which included the Beatles, the Rolling Stones, Credence Clearwater Revival, the Velvet Underground, and Dr. John the Night Tripper. He also recognized that unlike theater, popular music "is what's really good."[32] By tapping into contemporary music for his plays, Shepard realized, he could promote the explosive impact of rock and roll acts while also offering emergent playwrights a pathway into the hearts of younger audiences.

One day in July 1967, Stampfel stepped into their practice space on East Fourth Street and observed "this nearly bald scary-looking guy" battering away on Shepard's drums. "I thought some local hood had stormed in, and was Sam gonna be mad." The scary-looking guy turned around, and there was Shepard. He was fed up with the "Summer of Love" and the long-haired, rich-kid hippies encroaching on the Village, so he'd shaved off his rangy mane at a barber college on Fourteenth Street. But by doing so, he'd also derailed the possibility, from the ESP-Disk' marketing department's perspective, of appearing on their album cover of *Indian War Whoop*. Shepard grew it back long and straight, as before, but over time, he'd settle on presenting haircutters with the iconic street scene of James Dean huddling up on Broadway for them to use as a template for his own cut.[33]

* * *

While Shepard was rocking out with the Rounders, Joyce Aaron was angling to improve his visibility on the New York stage. Aaron was studying acting under Wynn Handman, the revered acting teacher who launched the careers of an astonishing cohort of superlative performers, including Richard Gere, Alec Baldwin, Mia Farrow, Christopher Walken, Michael Douglas, Frank Langella, Burt Reynolds, Raul Julia, John Leguizamo, and Denzel Washington, to name a few.

Aaron had invited Handman to see her perform in *Red Cross* at Judson Poets' Theatre, and the Off-Broadway impresario was enthralled. Handman was then staking his career on fledgling American playwrights and asked whether he could see more of Shepard's work, so Aaron sent him his first full-length play, *La Turista: A Play in Three Acts*. Handman saw Shepard as American theater's evolutionary step after Edward Albee's individualist-minded Theatre of the Absurd. "*The Zoo Story* was a milestone because it dealt with alienation—of the individual," Handman said. "By the late Sixties, it was about alienation of society. That's what Sam Shepard was about."[34]

An "unflappable Off-Broadway champion," as the theater critic Jeremy Gerard once labeled him, Handman had just founded the now historic American Place Theatre, a boutique playhouse in Hell's Kitchen forty-two feet below street level at St. Clement's Church. Its mission was to produce the debuts of American playwrights, and Handman's early roster boasted a number of heavy hitters, mostly famous novelists or poets trying their hands at drama for the first time. Robert Lowell, Joyce Carol Oates, Robert Penn Warren, Anne Sexton, and Philip Roth put on plays there, along with the radical Black playwrights LeRoi Jones and Ed Bullins. To be affiliated with Jones (soon known as Amiri Baraka) was a great honor for Shepard. Jones was an advocate of the Black Arts

Movement—plays written by, for, and about Black Americans—and Shepard considered him "the greatest American playwright." "I don't think there is a playwright in the country," he said of LeRoi Jones, "who speaks with that kind of conviction and intensity."[35]

*La Turista* opened on March 2, 1967, and starred Joyce Aaron and, at Handman's insistence, a lanky twenty-six-year-old fixture in the Off-Broadway scene named Sam Waterston.[36] The play remained three acts until the second week of performances, at which point Shepard accepted the hard truth that the production was "in shambles" from its director, the Open Theater's Jacques Levy, who demanded rewrites for the remaining two acts.[37] "Listen, man, it's too long," Shepard told Handman after talking with Levy. "Let's make it a two-act play."[38]

Shepard actually dropped both the second and third acts, then wrote a new act. The original script is packed with complicated multimedia techniques apparently written to confound audiences and stage technicians alike, with slides on the scrim and recordings playing of earlier scenes until, Shepard wrote in his original stage directions, "they eventually evolve . . . so that the slides and the tape gradually catch up to the play and pass it, the audience then sees and hears the end of the play depicted in the slides and tape before the play itself has ended."[39]

*La Turista*'s plot was inspired by the botched vacation to southern Mexico and opens with two self-involved American tourists named Kent and Salem (after the cigarette brands) who seek medical aid from a Mesopotamian witch doctor and his assistant. In the second act, they are back in New York but in a hotel room, where the same men, this time dressed as folksy Civil War–era soldiers, arrive to provide medical aid, but only to Kent, who is bedridden with a form of sleeping sickness. The doctor prescribes him Benzedrine (amphetamines), which instigates a paranoid delusion in which Kent imagines himself as a splendorous monster while the medic pursues him in the mode of a latter-day Dr. Frankenstein. "It was like a three-ring circus," Shepard said. "Lots of incredible physical feats. Sam Waterston leaping from bed to bed." Kent then bounds down a ramp to the back of the auditorium and madly swings on a rope through the audience, smashing through the upstage wall and "leaving a cut-out silhouette of his body."[40]

Aside from receiving an Obie Award for Distinguished Play, *La Turista* earned Shepard some unwanted notoriety. At one point, the witch doctor sacrifices live chickens; and this, of course, was a requirement for each night, sparking animal rights protests against the theater. Handman consulted his lawyers, who responded that "killing live chickens as a part of a theatrical production, no matter how valid or significant a point is being made," would be a violation of Section 185 of the Penal Law and result in a five-hundred-dollar fine and up to a year in prison. So instead, Levy had the set designers create a fake chicken that spurted out blood from its neck. It fooled the audience all too well: subscription cancellations piled up.[41]

Shepard was thrown by the audience's backlash. Downtown theatergoers were just "people off the street," he said.

> So that was an eye-opener, that suddenly you were held prisoner by this audience of people who were putting their dollar down, and most of them were geriatric. . . . You weren't getting the experience of an audience just coming in raw. This thing of subscriptions is very troubling. I understand why it's a necessity economically, but I just don't like it.[42]

New York's drama critics were eager to gauge the quality of Shepard's first full-length play, but instead of the theater sending out the usual review tickets for the monthlong run, critics were sent brusque notifications to stay away. Even Michael Smith declined to write about it, though he did attend. "Go see it for yourself," he told his readers. "I wish someone would attempt a critic-free playwriting career," he wrote, "and Shepard might be the ideal test case. It might even work—what a catchy publicity gimmick! If it did, it would become legend, and maybe make it harder to take critics too seriously, and maybe release some of the stifling pressure they bring to bear."[43] For promotional purposes, though, the media was a necessary evil, even for avant-garde playwrights, and Shepard consented to give his first interview to the *New York Times*, conducted by drama critic Lewis Funke. "Why should everything be evaluated in terms of success or failure?" Shepard demanded of his interviewer. "If I ever got wealthy enough to produce my own plays," he told him, "I'd never have them reviewed."[44]

Shepard's decrying America's obsession with "success or failure" demonstrates that his 1965 letter to Sam Rogers on the same subject cannot be written off as the cant of a willful child or a momentary drug-induced revelation, but rather a creed, one that made Shepard a sensation in, and a target of, theater columns. "Why," Shepard asked, "have it evaluated by people who first of all aren't writers. . . . I didn't feel like for what we were doing it was necessary to be assessed like that. That wasn't what we were doin' it for."[45]

Shepard's audacious ban on critics naturally made *La Turista* a must-see event among the New York literati. Elizabeth Hardwick, a cofounder of the *New York Review of Books*, got a ticket on her own and, defying Shepard's mandate, wrote up a notice in the *New York Review*. (She and her husband, Robert Lowell, were deeply grateful to Handman for producing Lowell's first play, a sprawling gambit called *The Old Glory*.) Hardwick dubbed Shepard "one of the three or four most gifted playwrights alive," and she called *La Turista* "a dazzling production" of "a work of superlative interest." Professional drama critics, she insisted, didn't yet have the institutional or cultural knowledge to write about contemporary avant-garde theater. It is a fool's errand to assign thematic coherence, Hardwick went on. And like Shepard, she debunked high-minded readings of the plot. She granted it could be a Vietnam allegory, but it could also be "Santo Domingo, racial violence, drop-outs, colonialism."[46]

"It's a *flimsy* situation," Shepard insisted about his plot, "and although it takes place in Mexico and the United States it just as well could take place in Bangkok and Canada. It transcends time and it doesn't correlate to any thesis that I had and worked out afterward. I mean it to be all theatrical event, that's all." In contrast to the ingenious acting and set designs, Hardwick observed, the audience was "for the most part, utterly depressing; middle-aged, middle class, and rather aggressively indifferent: a dead weight of alligators, dozing and grunting before muddily sliding away." "Our new American theater," she pronounced, "cannot play to the old audience; it must have a new one." Joyce Aaron concurred. "Droves of people walked out," she remembered, but for those who remained to witness the show, there was "astonishment."[47]

When Hardwick's review had first arrived, Shepard bristled. Rave though it was, audiences would think they knew what to expect, and that infuriated him. "They need a big finger," he told the reporter Mel Gussow, who later became a drama critic for the *New York Times* and one of Shepard's greatest champions. His contempt for reviews aside, Hardwick reworked hers into an introduction for the book version, which Bobbs-Merrill released in 1968. Mingus designed the cover, a roll of toilet paper unfurling with a Mexican flag as background, and Shepard selected the blurbs: "I'm glad you got out alive." —Barbara Garson. "But an artist is supposed to jerk off." —Bill Hart. "WHOOOOEEE!"—Murray Mednick. "Where do you come from?" —Robert Lowell. "How come we were banned?" —Robert Brustein (drama critic). "I was very surprised anyone could get a handle on it," Shepard told the *Los Angeles Times* in 1979, "but they did."[48]

* * *

Shepard held a jaundiced perspective on his astonishing success as an emerging playwright. "I find words like 'success' and 'popularity' completely meaningless," he'd written to his father from Chicago. "Ernest Hemingway was a success because he thought man was some kind of glorious hero who reveled in making wars and chopping up bulls for the public." But Shepard found Hemingway's brand of success to be gaudy and was infuriated when people asked when he'd publish a book or get a play on Broadway.[49] Shepard's next theatrical work, then, archly tackled the brutally competitive nature around which show business revolved.

His new one-act play had a curious title, *Melodrama Play: A Melodrama with Music*, which opened at La MaMa on May 18, 1967, with an original score by its director, Tom O'Horgan. *Melodrama Play* is about the burdensome edict placed upon successful artists, in this case a rock and roll songwriter named Duke Durgens, to invent *the next big thing*. Duke had stolen his career-making hit song from his brother Drake, and his manager, Floyd, commands him to come up with another, but to no avail. It's notable as the first of Shepard's sequence of "rock plays," dramatic works that incorporate live rock music into the performances.[50]

"Theater is a big bust," Shepard told *Newsweek* for their article on Off-Off-Broadway that May,

> ... so old-fashioned, so steeped in its tradition and its economics. The important things are happening everywhere else. Music is exploding! But the theater is mushy; nobody is really extravagant, like Godard is in films. Nobody is taking big chances. When I see a good rock 'n' roll group like the Mothers of Invention or Lothar and the Hand People, there's something really theatrical about what they do. Nothing in theater is close to that bombardment of the senses.[51]

Shepard's "rock plays" are de facto musicals stripped of any uplift. His lyrics are bleak, and after each song in *Melodrama Play*, the actors ironically applaud the band's somber commentary.

That summer, Joyce Aaron flew to London with the Open Theater to perform in Jean-Claude van Itallie's breakout play, *America Hurrah!* This would be the final time Aaron would abandon Shepard (as he saw it), as she broke up with him before departing. He then called her in London, hoping he could visit, but she said no. In the end, he wrote to his family, "It was good we didn't stay together. There was something about difference in age that would have made it tough later on. For her mostly. She was ready to have a baby and I just wasn't yet. I couldn't see getting that deeply involved when I don't feel completely settled inside myself."[52] "It wasn't because of anybody," Aaron said years later. "It was time. It was right. It had lived itself out."[53]

At the same time, Shepard was preparing for the release of his first book, *Five Plays*, which was scheduled for that December with the publishing house Bobbs-Merrill. The volume included *Chicago*, *Icarus's Mother*, *Red Cross*, *Fourteen Hundred Thousand*, and *Melodrama Play*, with notes on each by Ralph Cook, Michael Smith, Sydney Schubert Walter (of the Firehouse Theater), Jacques Levy, and Shepard. These short introductions are exhilaratingly honest, focusing on the brilliance of the plays but also where the directors believed they had failed them, as in the case of Smith and Walter, who admitted it and explained each play's challenges.

His father was out of touch by the time of *Five Plays*' release, but he was working in a bookstore warehouse when he first spied a copy. His initial response was that the long-haired kid on the cover rakishly flaunting a cigarette in a dark overcoat was an imposter. When Sam Sr. realized it was his "Steve," he wrote his son a barbed note: "I don't understand what the hell you're writing. I can't make hide nor hair of this shit, but I have to congratulate you nevertheless."[54] Shepard signed Jane's copy, "For my Mom, for being extra human in the line of duty," while Aaron's inscribed copy reads, "Whose loving companionship for more than three years molded the shape and content of these five plays. Love, Sam."[55]

CHAPTER 5

# THE ITALIAN JOB

Peter Stampfel's wife at the time, Antonia Duren, couldn't have phrased it better: Sam Shepard was a "sworn enemy of stasis." On June 30, 1967, the Heavy Metal Kid reunited for a blues revue in Woodstock, New York. The following Labor Day weekend, they were back upstate to see the Group Image, a band borne out of an East Village commune of the same name, for what a friend called "a kind of massive shamanistic gathering."[1] The Group Image were playing at the Sound-Out festival on Pan Copeland's farm between Saugerties and Woodstock, the first of two festivals on the farm that inspired Cyril Caster and Coyote Productions to form the Woodstock-Saugerties Sound Festival, popularly known as Woodstock.

Depending on who's telling the story, Shepard was either tripping on acid at Timothy Leary's farm in Millbrook or on crystal meth in a teepee in Woodstock when he met Nancy Mandel of the Group Image.[2] Shepard's romance with Mandel would last from the beginning of September 1967 to March 1969, one of the most pivotal and dramatic periods of his career.

Only a few months younger than Shepard, Mandel hailed from a wealthy family in Queens, and she dropped out of New York University to become a founding member of the Group Image commune; her ex-boyfriend, Jim Rudolf, was one of its founders, making Nancy Mandel, willfully or not, hippie royalty on the East Coast. She was small in stature, with long, thin tresses of sandy blond hair and sharply attractive facial features. Everyone who knew her in the sixties described her in the same terms: she hovered, pixie-like, soft-spoken, and dreamy, among the crowd of die-hard New York hippies, whose milieu she never wholly accepted as her own.

In the best of ways, Mandel was a hard woman to impress, but she phoned her friend Yvette Nachmias multiple times "bursting with enthusiasm," Nachmias recalled, about the playwright and drummer for the Holy Modal Rounders she met upstate. "What is amusing and odd about this," Yvette wrote to a friend at the time, "is that when I finally met her new boyfriend, and I was surprised, nay shocked, to see that her boyfriend is the same silent person I knew only as Sam the drummer." Nachmias had met him at a raucous party at the Group Image's loft on Second Avenue in the East Village, "and thought him very attractive, though almost non-verbal!" That was her impression when he asked to walk her home that night. "I am astonished to learn that he has so much going for him," Nachmias concluded, "aside of good looks and a mysterious silent aura. He certainly hid his lights under a bushel."[3]

* * *

That summer, 1967, a selective group from Theater Genesis occupied a run-down, abandoned farm in East Stroudsburg, Pennsylvania, two hours due west of New York in the Pocono Mountains. They called themselves the Keystone Company after the state's nickname. The farmhouse was in decent shape, but the outlying buildings were falling apart. There was a sizable chicken coop on the far side of a pond that four or five used as sleeping quarters, and they rehearsed in a dilapidated barn at the top of a hill. They wanted an out-of-town location for the development of an improvisational, cooperatively written play on heroin addiction titled *The Hawk*, after an eponymous heroin dealer. Shepard and Nancy Mandel visited them on the farm, and the setting of Shepard's next play, *Forensic & the Navigators*, would be based on the farmhouse's kitchen.[4]

The Keystone Company included a young, dumpling-faced beauty, O-Lan Johnson, so named for the courageous heroine in Pearl S. Buck's 1931 novel *The Good Earth*. O-Lan, her mother, Scarlett, and her younger sister, Kristy, lived in an apartment above Tony Barsha's place across the street from Theater Genesis, and they'd been walk-ins to audition for *The Hawk* at Theater Genesis's rehearsal space, an old municipal courthouse on East Second Street (now home of Anthology Film Archives). They stayed for a month in the Poconos, and Shepard visited for two weekends, ostensibly to visit his cronies from the Heavy Metal Kid, Mednick and Eddie Hicks, who composed the group's music. O-Lan had turned seventeen that May and began dating Tony Barsha, their artistic director. Speculation has circulated that Shepard formed his attachment to O-Lan here. Murray Mednick distinctly remembered, however, that despite Mandel's presence, Shepard had already been infatuated with O-Lan before they'd gathered in Pennsylvania, and he traveled there under various pretenses but was really there to see her.[5]

Shepard had also been working on a play tentatively called "The Marijuana Hoax" when *La Turista* appeared. "I don't know what it is yet," he said at the time, "something to do with having an audience become aware of a kind of prison existence onstage without showing it literally."[6]

*Forensic & the Navigators*, as he retitled it, opened at Theater Genesis on December 29, 1967, followed by a set from the Moray Eels. "This has the effect," Michael Smith wrote about the band in an otherwise rave review, "of driving the entire audience out of the theater." Forensic, a great-sounding word Shepard had to ask a friend the meaning of, is Shepard's character (played by Robert Schlee). He is a knee-jerk, "let's kill 'em all" revolutionary with "long blond hair, a brown cowboy hat, a long red scarf, a black leather vest, jeans, and moccasins." Emmet (Lee Kissman) is based on Murray Mednick, a thoughtful, plotting, less impulsive rebel youth with "long black hair, a green Cherokee headband, beads around his neck, a serape, jeans, and cowboy boots."[7]

The two young men embody America's "Cowboys and Indians" mythos of warring sensibilities. For food, they are served Rice Krispies by a songster named Oolan (named for and played by O-Lan Johnson).[8]

Their goal is to free political prisoners confined by an oppressive authority, represented by two exterminators meant to look like California Highway Patrolmen who carry poison gas tanks to kill rebel agitators. But after one of them falls for Oolan, the theater is engulfed by a colorful cloud of poison gas, courtesy of Johnny Dodd. This was likely "the marijuana hoax" indicated by the original title, as if the audience, primed by the play's apocalyptic vision, would flee screaming when the gas emerged to avoid getting inadvertently stoned.

Part science fiction, part satire of the 1960s youth movement, and part story of the friendship between Shepard and Murray Mednick, *Forensic & the Navigators* depicts an ongoing war of resistance, but from what we don't know. What are these characters' motivations? What is their society like other than an ecology of fear? What are the exterminators guarding? Shepard doesn't say, because it's not the point. There is *something*. "The whole thing may be a smoke dream," Michael Smith wrote, "but the smoke that fills the theatre at the end is real. So are the people, for all their elusiveness as dramatic characters, and so is the paranoia of our times, which Shepard expresses better than anyone else now writing."[9] *Forensic & the Navigators* would win, along with *Melodrama Play*, 1968's Obie Award for Distinguished Play, the same year Shepard was awarded a Guggenheim Fellowship for creative arts.

* * *

Slouched in the cramped St. Mark's theater space, utterly baffled by the weird spectacle of *Forensic & the Navigators*, was a twenty-seven-year-old drifter named Johnny Dark. He was given that name in a Barcelona brothel by a friend of his, who said he dressed like the Tony Curtis character from the movie *Johnny Dark*, and it stuck.[10] Dark was a dyed-in-the-wool beatnik, yet he mostly preferred musicals and romantic comedies to gloomy dramas. He didn't understand why audiences submitted themselves to Shepard's variety of theater. Dark had just started dating Scarlett Johnson, the mother of Shepard's seventeen-year-old lead actress, O-Lan, who moved to New York with O-Lan and her younger daughter, Kristy, after they spent six months living among Mayan Indians in the Yucatán jungle.[11]

Dark only went to *Forensic* to provide moral support. After the play was over, somebody pointed out Shepard, "a scruffy-looking kid in a long overcoat," Dark recalled. The next day, Dark spied Shepard in a pharmacy on St. Mark's Place. He walked up and said, "Hey, I saw your play last night. I was curious what drug you wrote it on."[12]

This was the genesis of an extraordinary friendship, one that would last nearly fifty years. "It was like finding a long-lost kid brother," Dark said. Both were fans of Kerouac and drugs such as Benzedrine and crystal methedrine—"almost any pill that kept us up and going without sleep for days at a time," Shepard recalled. They even shared the childhood ambition of becoming veterinarians. But Shepard and Dark remained like brothers in spite of, or perhaps because of, their differences. For one thing, there was no competition between them. Dark lived hand-to-mouth his entire life, working as a dog walker, a massage therapist, a driver for a rental car company, a deli clerk (his last job), anything that offered a steady paycheck and, most important, left him alone outside of working hours. Unlike for Shepard, fame had no allure for Dark. "But what does seem enjoyable," he said, "is to be the best friend of a famous person, so you could sort of come and go. You could just take some of the benefits of being around a famous person and then leave and not have to drag it with you."[13]

Soon after their first meeting, Johnny Dark moved to San Francisco with Scarlett and Kristy, but he and Shepard would stay in close touch; O-Lan remained behind.

The Keystone's *The Hawk* opened at Theater Genesis on October 13, 1967, after which the play became a new underground theater classic. O-Lan, to Shepard's consternation, soon moved in with Barsha in his new apartment on First Avenue. O-Lan later told Barsha that her school friend Lizette Kocur wanted to join them. "Oh, fine!" Barsha said. "Let's all live together in love and peace." "It's the sixties, and that's the way we did it then," he said, waving it off. Barsha, O-Lan, and Lizette thus initiated a ménage à trois. "Who would say no?" Theater Genesis member Georgia Hadler said. "With these lovely young women, and talented . . . He wasn't just exploiting young women, which both Lizette and O-Lan were when they got together with Tony. . . . They, I think, loved him. Not enough," she said, laughing, "not enough to save him from Sam."[14]

* * *

Meanwhile, in the late fall of 1967, the renowned Italian filmmaker Michelangelo Antonioni was scouting for an American to write a screenplay for his latest movie project, *Zabriskie Point*. Antonioni had gained international notoriety for his two masterworks, 1960's *L'Avventura* and 1966's *Blow-Up*, and the director needed a screenwriter who could capture the disaffected American youth of the sixties and the leftist politics that motivated them. He'd toured the American West and, while there, read about a man who'd been killed attempting to return a stolen aircraft, a scenario that formed the inspiration for his plot. He then read Shepard's book *Five Plays*, and the skywriting sequence in *Icarus's Mother* thrilled him into contacting the "James Dean–like youth with an un-Dean-like intellectual glint in his eyes." The apocalyptic orgy in *Chicago* was also akin to a desert scene he'd envisioned motoring across the Mojave. Add Shepard's rebel mystique to the mix, and Antonioni had found his screenwriter.[15]

The twenty-four-year-old playwright was elated that the cinematic maestro of "modernity and its discontents" wanted to meet, and they had their first sit-down at Caffe Cino to discuss *Zabriskie Point*. Thus, Shepard's life with Hollywood officially began, along with the writer's first real taste of the infringements of commercial moviemaking: Antonioni's distributor, MGM, was paying for his ticket to Italy, and his taking a young unmarried woman with him, Nancy Mandel, prompted grumblings from the studio execs. "MGM was very conservative in those days," Shepard said later.[16] He brought Mandel anyway.

On January 6, 1968, Shepard and his girlfriend sailed for Rome on, ironically enough, the SS *Michelangelo*. Before the ship disembarked,

Johnny and Scarlett, Bill Hart, Barbara Eda-Young, Yvette Nachmias, and others from Theater Genesis and the East Village joined the couple in their first-class cabin, paid in full by MGM, where they drank and toasted Shepard and Mandel's future escapades in Europe. The revelers scuttled off when it was announced the ship was about to set sail, and outside on the deck, the couple waved goodbye to them. The ship set sail for the seven-day voyage to Naples, during which, Shepard wrote home, they ate "pheasant, quail, baked Alaska, steak, the works. By the time we hit Naples we could barely get off the ship."[17]

MGM was to pay Shepard five hundred dollars a week, fifty for living expenses, and all transportation costs. Once they arrived in Naples, they were met by the Italian film producer Carlo Ponti ("Sophia Loren's big love," Shepard bragged), who escorted them to Rome in a chauffeured limousine.[18]

They first stayed at a stylish hotel near Antonioni's apartment in the outskirts of the city, but requested a more central location and were put up at the ritzy Hotel d'Inghilterra near the Spanish Steps. They visited the Vatican and St. Peter's and dined at a historic eatery just around the corner from their hotel, Otello alla Concordia. This was Antonioni's favorite restaurant in Rome and the birthplace of the "Neorealist" cinematic revolution. Otello's embodied la dolce vita of the avant-garde art scene: there you could exchange ideas with openness among high-octane minds such as Antonioni, Pasolini, Fellini, Visconti, and the postmodernist "Andy Warhol of Europe," Mario Schifano. "This trip has really opened my eyes to a lot of things," Shepard wrote to Jane Rogers after a couple of weeks. "I feel much happier outside New York. . . . Here people are really kind to each other and human. There's not all of that selfishness going on all the time."[19]

Most days in Rome, however, were spent hammering out the *Zabriskie Point* script with Antonioni and his *Blow-Up* cowriter Tonino Guerra. Neither Antonioni nor Guerra were capable of writing with an authentic American voice, hence their need for the young phenom.[20] Shepard was dumbfounded by the Italians' impassioned deliberations over the minutest detail. When he'd first met Antonioni and Guerra, he walked in on them embroiled in a screaming match. "Sam, don't worry," Antonioni told him when the smoke cleared. "We are Italian."[21]

Shepard completed his first Hollywood screenplay, a seventy-four-page draft with 156 scenes, by late February.[22] Although this early draft is lost, some unpublished pages still exist and are housed at Antonioni's archive in Ferrara, Italy. There are seven opening scenes that depict many of the graphic acts of violence that actually took place during the 1965 uprising in Watts, California: National Guardsmen and the LAPD fiercely clash with Black rioters in the neighborhood's streets, stores, and private homes. Black snipers, looters, and innocent bystanders are confronted by uniformed men with rifles, pistols, bayonets, machine guns, and a tank, much of which Shepard composed from firsthand accounts in *Newsweek* and the *New York Times*.[23] (Antonioni would ultimately choose a less expensive, less provocative opening for the film, depicting a heated debate among radical youths clashing over the distinction between Black and white activism.)

Shepard included an aria for a rebellious white youth who defends political violence through a lengthy parable about white violence against Native Americans. (This monologue was not included in the script sent to MGM.[24]) In the final version, it was whittled down to a simple decree by a Black agitator: "There's only one way to talk to the Man and that's in his own language. The Man's language is his guns. You talk to him with a gun."[25] Aside from the removal of the Watts riot scenes, the storyline for the film's final cut remained intact.[26]

While Shepard was working daily with the Italian filmmakers, Nancy Mandel was swept under the wing of Antonioni's femme fatale Monica Vitti, who accompanied her on lavish shopping trips and tours of the ancient city. Shepard and Mandel had planned a trip from Rome to Palermo, and from there on a boat to North Africa for a railway tour across Morocco. But an invitation from the Rolling Stones lead guitarist Keith Richards was far too tempting, and they abandoned their plans and would instead travel straight to London to join him.[27]

* * *

Shepard met Keith Richards in Rome through the Living Theatre actor Rufus Collins. They would go to the Piper Club, Shepard remembered, where "Rufus and Keith would take these little decanter-like glasses, drink them down, then throw them against the back wall and watch them splatter. We used to do that for about four hours, stumble out of the place and wander around those piazzas. It was a *lost* time."[28]

They also smoked an inordinate amount of hash with family-sized spliffs wrapped in newspaper. "You took about three tokes off that thing, and you're completely beheaded." But one thing that stuck with him over the years was a massive gathering of Richards's friends at a restaurant. When the evening wound down, Richards strode over to the waiter and paid the obscenely large check. Shepard wanted to be that guy, the one who quietly pays for everyone without a blink.[29]

Also while in Rome, Shepard met the twenty-nine-year-old American filmmaker and jet-set scenester Anthony "Tony" Foutz, a close friend of Richards's. Foutz invited him to his apartment to read an outline he was working on for a Rolling Stones film he'd titled *Maxagasm: A Distorted Western for Soul and Psyche*. Foutz's treatment for *Maxagasm*, short for "maximum orgasm," takes place in a postapocalyptic desert wasteland. The plot revolves around an ultraviolent band of mercenaries called the Skull Squad, described in the screenplay as "a strange mélange of the Japanese Samurai, Tartar warriors, and the Hell's Angels."[30] After reading the treatment over a couple of hours, Shepard turned to Foutz and said, "I want to write the dialogue." "And it was like that," Foutz enthused about the time's unfiltered culture of "connectivity," as yet untethered to the rampant commodification of art in all its forms.[31]

On March 7, Shepard, Mandel, and Foutz checked into the Carlton Tower Hotel in London for a sit-down with Brian Jones, Mick Jagger, and Keith Richards, who were then recording their album *Beggars Banquet*. The Stones knew Foutz well through Richards and his girlfriend at the time, the dazzling German-Italian "It Girl" Anita Pallenberg, and Jagger and Brian Jones were as impressed by Shepard's Off-Off-Broadway pedigree as with his screenwriting collaboration with Michelangelo Antonioni. Carlo Ponti was already on board; it was to be filmed in a

Moroccan desert; and the Rolling Stones willingly agreed to provide the soundtrack and play prominent roles. ("Sympathy for the Devil" was slotted to run during the film's culminating scene.)[32]

Richards was the same age as Shepard and already a rock and roll legend, preposterously wealthy, and reveling in a round-the-clock regimen of snorting purified cocaine to crank himself up, then heroin to ratchet back down. Richards sportingly offered them a writers' retreat to complete the script—Redlands, his fifteenth-century thatch-roofed country manor in the seaside village of West Wittering. For six weeks, Shepard, Mandel, and Foutz hunkered down at the Richards estate. Shepard and Foutz joked over how many typewriters they'd thrown out the window, a competition that Shepard won.[33]

Shepard and Foutz smoked bricks of hashish in Richards's home, which was inspiringly designed by Pallenberg to resemble an opulent sheik's nomadic tent. A wooden "soul bowl" adorned the dining room table where they worked, a prop for the movie's climax, and they read through a pile of reference books on the Aztec, Olmec, and Mayan cultures and shared each other's powerful fascination in the occultist teachings of Aleister Crowley, the prognosticating powers of Nostradamus, and close alien encounters. Shepard adamantly believed in the existence of flying saucers and extraterrestrial life at the time, and Foutz brought a copy of John Michell's recently released book *The Flying Saucer Vision* with him to Redlands.[34]

Shepard was startled awake one morning at Redlands by earthmovers digging a moat, "filled with alligators," he hyperbolized to Andy Warhol's *Interview* magazine. But the relentless moat-digging was real enough. Redlands was a fortress. The Stones were "paranoic," Shepard said, "because they had just been busted."[35] Redlands was in fact the site of an infamous drug raid in February 1967, when Richards, Jagger, and the art dealer Robert "Groovy Bob" Fraser were arrested. After a highly publicized trial, Richards and Jagger were acquitted, but Fraser, caught with heroin, was sentenced to six months of hard labor.

Near the end of their stay at Redlands, Shepard emerged from his and Mandel's room with a poem that Jagger's role of Feelgood would chant during a sacrificial sequence. "Time. Time of life," it reads in part. "Time of death. The waiting is done. . . . In this dust of the Lord of the Dawn we place our celestial man and our celestial woman. . . . Their birth is our death. Their death—our life. . . . Through our communal placement in space—a transcendence shall come. A movement beyond time to a place of no name."[36]

"Wow," said Foutz. "That's the movie."

With two scripts newly written and promises to Tony Foutz to meet in Hollywood to sell their film, on March 12 Shepard and Mandel took the *Queen Elizabeth* from Southampton to New York where Shepard reunited with Antonioni to discuss *Zabriskie Point*'s future. From there, they would drive west to meet the Italian director in California and shoot their movie.[37]

* * *

The Zabriskie Point of the film's title is an isolated desert overlook in California just east of Death Valley. "The feeling of space and time reminds me of the moon," Antonioni said of the location, "and the hills look as if no man has ever walked over them." Over the past two years, Antonioni had met with multiple revolutionary youth groups, was teargassed at the Chicago Democratic Convention, witnessed firsthand the aftermath of the Watts riots, smoked a lot of weed, and attended rock concerts and "love-ins."[38] The director hoped the film would appeal to radical groups such as the Black Panthers and the Weather Underground and thus demanded more political rhetoric than Shepard, now back in California, was willing to deliver; so he hired the writer and activist Fred Gardner (aka Franco Rossetti) to punch up the script with radical speech. The Italian director "wanted to make a political statement about contemporary youth," Shepard said, "write in a lot of Marxist jargon and Black Panther speeches. I couldn't do it. I just wasn't interested." Shepard believed that if the dialogue relied too heavily on politics, it got "stuck in time." Protest art, in his view, simply led to the same old political maneuvering and propaganda.[39]

That summer, Shepard and Mandel arrived in California and reunited with the Holy Modal Rounders in Los Angeles, where they were promoting their new album with Elektra Records, *The Moray Eels Eat the Holy Modal Rounders*. With Shepard on drums, the band played LA rock venues such as Kaleidoscope on Sunset Boulevard and the Cheetah Club in Venice Beach, the venue where they likely opened for Ike and Tina Turner that July, and then drove north to open for Pink Floyd and Crome Syrcus on August 2 at San Francisco's Avalon Ballroom.[40]

On that same promotional tour, Shepard joined the Holy Modal Rounders in a squawking rendition of "You've Got the Right String Baby but the Wrong Yo-Yo" on the popular TV revue *Rowan & Martin's Laugh-In*. Their performance was tolerated by *Laugh-In*'s showrunners for exactly one minute and eighteen seconds, at which point the raunchy comedian Ruth Buzzi interrupted the band and corralled them offstage like a bad vaudeville act. "We were on *Laugh-In*?" Shepard gawks in the documentary film on the band, *The Holy Modal Rounders: Bound to Lose*. "I don't remember any of this! What kind of drugs were we on?"

In early October 1968, Shepard arrived at Zabriskie Point in the Mojave Desert, with Nancy Mandel at his side, and was greeted by Antonioni's publicist, Beverly Walker, herself a product of the New York theater scene. Antonioni consulted with him but, Walker said, he was no longer "on the picture." And yet, she said, "all the sequences relating to [greedy real estate developers] come from the Sam Shepard script and spell out Antonioni's original intention." Walker pointed out that Shepard's disgust over land exploitation and development, which thematically appears in his work as early as *Cowboys*, came "well before ecology became a chic subject."[41]

For *Zabriskie Point*, Antonioni had inveigled a group of Black Panthers, including Kathleen Cleaver, wife of the Black Panther Party's leader, Eldridge Cleaver, to make cameo appearances. According to Shepard, the Italian director had promised them payment in money and guns. "And he gave them some money," he said, "but he didn't give them any guns. And they were a little upset about that." A media storm also erupted over a wild desert "love-in" within the film that the female protagonist imagines while high on marijuana. The notorious scene, a saturnalia of writhing sandy bodies, consisted of about two hundred extras. This was a violation of the Mann Act, the 1910 law forbidding the transportation of females across state lines to perform "immoral" sex acts. (Antonioni faced charges but was never prosecuted.)[42] Most were clothed, however scantily, but one naked threesome would surely have qualified for prosecution under the statute.

While in Hollywood, Shepard composed a two-act play called *Operation Sidewinder* in a house he and Mandel rented in the Hills. The play is a literary collage that blends rock music, science fiction, Westerns, crime drama, and protest literature. Foutz said, correctly, that *Operation Sidewinder* is "the son of *Maxagasm*." But the play also borrows from *Zabriskie Point*: it's set in the Mojave and includes a "flower child" at its center who breaks with the radical youth movement, preaches violent revolution, and has a penchant for seizing airplanes (this time, F-111 fighter jets). There's also a desert sex scene between him and a middle-class woman who happens upon him, as well as combative discourse between Black revolutionaries and white activists, among other borrowings. In other words, Shepard's script for Antonioni, as he might have imagined it at the time, does exist, just under the title *Operation Sidewinder*. He would later turn the script into a full-length play, "a movie for the stage," he said, "the way movies do with time. One scene at 5 in the afternoon. Zap. Another at 3 in the morning."[43]

At one point, Shepard asked MGM whether they would provide him with film stock and cameras to make his own movie, which he considered putting together with friends of Johnny Dodd's from Haight-Ashbury's radical street theater troupe the Diggers. When Antonioni found this out, he bristled, convinced that Shepard was out to steal his idea, and he ordered MGM to shut him down. Antonioni was safe from Shepard's amateur foray with the Diggers, but it was Dennis Hopper's *Easy Rider* in 1969 that would scoop *Zabriskie Point* as the great cinematic achievement of 1960s American counterculture. Shepard would meet Hopper for the first time around then because one of his cowriters on *Easy Rider*, Peter Fonda, happened to hear the Holy Modal Rounders song "If You Want to Be a Bird" (or "The Bird Song") on the radio and thought it would be perfect for the *Easy Rider* soundtrack.[44]

Once it became clear that *Zabriskie Point* was marked for disaster, Shepard downplayed his contribution. "It's mostly [Antonioni's] story, you know, his ideas," he said.[45] Not true, replied Walker, who insisted that the greed of the real estate developers, the culminating factor of the film, was all Shepard's idea. When Walker appeared on location, she expected to see the script, but Antonioni didn't show it to anyone, including Shepard. Instead, an assistant handed her "a short prose treatment by Sam Shepard [about] environmental exploitation by real-estate developers. Vast rural areas had dried up due to water diversion. . . . I found it eloquent. It was just a few pages, but my ignorance was such that I took it for the actual shooting script."[46]

By the time a filmmaker named Harrison Starr was brought on board as line producer (the on-location *capo dei capi*), Antonioni's production was a complete mess. Starr, the cleanup guy, was from Greenwich Village and a champion of Shepard's. He knew something Antonioni couldn't accept: that the success or failure of *Zabriskie Point* would depend on the director's willingness to give Shepard free rein. He didn't. "I put [Shepard] on salary so he could make some money and didn't have to worry," Starr said. "I thought he could be a shadow for Antonioni and perhaps Antonioni would get it right instead of making some romantic Italian nonsense." But Shepard was out, "and that's regrettable," Starr said, "because that picture could have been more significant if Sam had been able [sigh] . . . MGM was very, very conservative. They were the last to wake up to the fact that the motion picture business was changing underneath their feet."[47]

* * *

*Zabriskie Point* opened in February 1970, and one critic described the film as "bad enough to give anti-Americanism a bad name."[48] By then, the film had passed its sell-by date (though it later found a cult audience), as had the countercultural ethos of the sixties as a whole. *Zabriskie*

*Point* was panned by conservatives for its anti-Americanism and by liberals as inaccurate and stilted. The assassinations of Martin Luther King Jr. and Robert F. Kennedy, the police brutality at the 1968 Chicago Democratic Convention, the Manson family murders, the Kent State killings, and the national shock over the escalating number of body bags returning from Vietnam, all had a chilling effect on the film's intended audiences. For many, the sixties had become a bad dream.

Shepard had predicted the film would be "Hollywood's most expensive flop." But a few years later, he wrote Antonioni a heartfelt letter thanking him and wishing he could have done more to help. He went on to apologize for not being the writer Antonioni hoped for and expressed regret over not taking advantage of the opportunity he'd been granted. Regardless of the outcome, he told Antonioni, "you were a great inspiration to me." Beverly Walker, the publicist, read between the lines of this letter: "He sounds almost guilty, as if he might've influenced some of Michelangelo's later choices if he'd paid more attention. And indeed he might've, though we will never know. Luckily for him, he escaped the pundits' wrath, though I am not sure why."[49]

Meanwhile, despite Shepard and Foutz's best efforts, *Maxagasm* faced too many obstacles to get off the ground. Although Shepard's work with Foutz would be abandoned after one more stab in October, it was clear his time on *Maxagasm* wasn't squandered. The experience, Foutz said, "opened thought processes" in him; and soon after writing *Maxagasm*, Shepard produced *Operation Sidewinder*, *The Unseen Hand*, and *The Mad Dog Blues*, each containing Western ultraviolence, cosmic sex, ancient civilizations, and otherworldly powers.[50]

Shepard's time with these Hollywood industry moguls left some permanent scar tissue though. "Sam did not want to be inside those sorts of hierarchies," remembered an old friend, the author and screenwriter Rudy Wurlitzer. "He couldn't wait to get away."[51]

Weighing options for their future, Shepard and Nancy had considered settling in San Francisco at least since Rome. But when they drove up the coast to visit after Shepard finished his work with Antonioni, he found it just as hellish as New York. "I'm really getting these weird 'impending doom' feelings about California," he wrote to Lee Kissman. "In the few days I was up in San Francisco I encountered more guns and bullshit than in my whole life. Armed robbery, stick ups on the street, gas stations, the whole scene." Nevertheless, Shepard's political consciousness had been powerfully affected, however temporarily, by the countercultural revolution he'd witnessed on this trip among the hippies and freaks of LA and San Francisco. *Operation Sidewinder* is about only one thing, he told Mel Gussow, then working at the *New York Times*: "When the shit hits the fan, it will happen out there first." "What shit hits the fan?" Gussow asked him. "The Revolution," he replied.[52]

CHAPTER 6

# SAM AND O-LAN

Once back in New York, Shepard and Mandel moved into a little room off the kitchen of a second-floor apartment in a brick town house at 198 Sixth Avenue, which they shared with the future director and dramaturge Bill Hart. Shepard described Hart as "always brilliant and shining with ideas . . . that seemed to come from far across the known world."[1] Johnny Dark remembered Bill Hart as "a strange guy who used to eat Ravioli and blue cheese and kept a thousand dollars in an attaché case." Hart had inherited $250,000, but spent most of it on amphetamines and a European vacation, staying at the finest hotels and eating at the trendiest restaurants with his boyfriend Stan. By this time, he'd whittled it down to half the original amount, so he needed to invest the balance somewhere and decided to make his own film.[2]

Shepard happily agreed to participate on Hart's project. It would be his first cinematic appearance since *Brand X*, a slapdash celluloid "happening" directed by Win Chamberlain and aimed directly at the throat of American television and political culture. Its cast was a band of countercultural maharishis that included Abbie Hoffman and two of Andy Warhol's superstars, Candy Darling and Ultra Violet. *Brand X* appeared in art cinemas in May 1970, and featured Shepard and the actress Sally Kirkland from Warhol's Factory jumping up and down shouting "USA! USA! USA!" "I know you're an incredible writer," Kirkland told him, "but you should be an actor because you have such charisma." "No, I don't want to be an actor," Shepard replied. "But I don't think you have a choice," she said with remarkable clairvoyance.[3]

Hart conceived of a black-and-white movie in the mode of Norman Mailer's do-it-yourself films, *Wild 90* and *Beyond the Law*, and was prepared to front the entire cost. Along with Shepard, Hart enlisted Charles Mingus, Joyce Aaron, Joe Chaikin, and other Open Theater members. The final product was *Blood*, an off-color work of cinema verité. One scene had Shepard seated in a wooden throne to improvise being interviewed by a reporter. "And I don't know if he was drunk or what or high or whatever," Mingus said, but without getting out of the chair, Shepard somehow folded himself underneath it, "like a Chinese contortionist in a box."[4]

Bill Hart captured, along with pranks and roughhousing, some incendiary scenes as well. One actor had sex with a married woman on camera, who "then sued," and Mingus was filmed ripping the head off a pigeon. Once the shooting was finished, the filmmaker Hilary Harris agreed to facilitate the editing at the Women's Interart Center. After they took the material to be processed, the photo lab, and with it the last of Hart's inheritance, burned to the ground.[5]

Hart had grown up wealthy in California but after this fiasco, he was penniless and descended into heavier drug use. He'd been evicted from his Sixth Avenue apartment and moved into Lee Kissman's place on First Street and Second Avenue, a bustling hub of Off-Off-Broadway activity. As you walked into the storefront space, there would be Hart on a mattress on the floor, wallowing in self-pity and high on something exotic.[6] But Hart would go on to run the Razor Gallery in SoHo, a trailblazing graffiti art space. Later still, he was hired as the literary manager of Joseph Papp's Public Theater, where he worked with Robert De Niro and John Malkovich, and directed Shepard's later plays *The Tooth of Crime (Second Dance)*, *A Lie of the Mind*, *States of Shock*, and *Simpatico*. But what got him off Kissman's mattress in the summer of '69 was a revival of Shepard's latest, *Cowboys #2*, at the Old Reliable Tavern in Alphabet City, a hangout for the OOB crowd that moonlighted as a theater. But whereas Hart's revival succeeded despite his visibly withdrawing from drugs, its world premiere on the West Coast was an abject failure.[7]

*Cowboys #2* was a rewrite from memory of the play that launched Shepard's career in October 1964. He neglected to retain a copy of his first produced play, and in the intervening years it had become a foundational work of the new underground theater, as mythic as the American figures it was named for, and it would only become more so. Much of the dialogue is nearly identical to *Cowboys* but pieced together haphazardly, without the rhythms or power imbalances of the original. Shepard also added the dual dialogue technique (two characters talking over each other) that he'd used in *La Turista* to stunning effect, but again without success.

The play premiered in Los Angeles at the theatrically innovative Center Theatre Group's "New Theatre for Now" series. It was part of a twelve-piece sampler called *The Scene* performed for the premiere season of LA's Mark Taper Forum on October 9, 1967, nearly three years to the day *Cowboys* premiered in New York. This was Shepard's West Coast theatrical debut, and it was panned. *The Scene* contained plays by Off-Off-Broadway's elite: Shepard, John Guare, Terrence McNally, Megan Terry, Lanford Wilson, Jean-Claude van Itallie, and a few other New York underground writers whose reputations, quipped the *Los Angeles Times*, "have been made off-off-Broadway and whose work here is off-off awful."[8]

* * *

It was late March in New York when Shepard reunited with the young actress O-Lan Johnson, a five-foot-tall, brown-eyed teenager with long brown hair parted in the middle. O-Lan grew up outside of Los Angeles, where her father abandoned her family, then lived with her mother and sister across the country as vagabonds. O-Lan did laundry and worked janitorial jobs to help make ends meet, but once her family landed in New York, she dropped out of school at fourteen to pursue a career as a performing artist.

O-Lan adored New York and immersed herself in the avant-garde theater scene happening at St. Mark's Church, right across Second Avenue from the Johnson family's apartment. Now she was eighteen and acting in a new play by Shepard's friend and her boyfriend, Tony Barsha. After *The Hawk*'s success, Barsha was developing another improvisational piece, a play about revolution. At St. Mark's that winter, during improvised rehearsals and acting exercises, Shepard, to the surprise of everyone in the Keystone Company, began showing up and even took on a role he named Slim Shadow. Acting wasn't the draw for Shepard, of course; he was there for O-Lan.[9]

O-Lan's character, given her age, was named "Lo" after the eponymous "nymphet" from Nabokov's *Lolita*. She was as mystified as anyone that Shepard, who was, in her words, "on the magic carpet to success," had joined the Keystone group. During an acting exercise, Shepard deliberately paired off with O-Lan. He pretended he was reaching into a vat of thick taffy, then pulled it up over his head with a snarl. She mirrored him, as the exercise demanded, and "timed it just right," she said, "so that during the little bit of time when we were standing up straight facing each other, in between being bent over and just before the growl, I whispered, 'We can't go on meeting like this!'"[10]

Shepard drove a beige Volvo station wagon at the time, "something you'd find in a suburban driveway," O-Lan remembered. "It was placid and boxy, but he was jagged, vibrant; the air rippled around him." Unbeknownst to Shepard's girlfriend, Nancy Mandel, and O-Lan's boyfriend, Tony Barsha, Shepard and O-Lan began to take meandering road trips together and long nighttime strolls through the perilous streets of the Lower East Side. "What's the worst that can happen?" he'd ask. "We die?"[11]

*Vision: Dead Body/New Body*, as the show was eventually titled, opened on March 14, 1969, at Theater Genesis and ran for four consecutive weekends.[12] It was then that the tumultuous breakups happened to each couple, in a single emotional night.[13]

Shepard and O-Lan convened with the rest of the Keystone group at the iconic nightclub and restaurant Max's Kansas City, made famous by its glam rock and proto-punk acts, including the Velvet Underground, the Stooges, Alice Cooper, and the New York Dolls, along with its clientele of the pop artists Robert Rauschenberg, Andy Warhol, and Roy Lichtenstein.

Murray Mednick had just returned from a trip and joined Shepard and O-Lan at a booth. Shouting over the music, Mednick said, "So what's happening? What's new?" "O-Lan and I are moving in together," Shepard yelled back. This was news to O-Lan, who froze in confusion, but also anger. "I was 18, I wasn't ready," she wrote. "I'd just been playing, glad to have an escape valve from the oppressive world of Tony.... It was a thrill sneaking around with Sam, he was way more fun than Tony, but I didn't have any moving-in plans." Barsha, O-Lan knew, had left his family to be with her and wasn't going to be thrilled about her "moving-in plan" either.[14]

Each night after Barsha's play was performed at St. Mark's, once the lights went down and the audience had exited, Shepard and O-Lan would secretly fool around in the auditorium. Soon enough, Barsha got wind of it, and he and Shepard started fighting in the dark onstage after the curtain went down, with residual audience members hanging back and wondering whether it was part of the show.[15]

O-Lan tried to pull Barsha away from Shepard, pleading, "I want to go home now. I've got to tell you something." "Tell me now," he demanded. "I'll tell you on the way back," she said. During the cab ride, O-Lan announced she was leaving him once the show closed and moving in with Shepard. Barsha seethed in silence for the rest of the ride, and once home, he locked himself in the bedroom. Then he materialized in the doorway and said, "You're moving out tonight. Call him up right now if that's what you're going to do." O-Lan hunted through the director's notes for Shepard's number and made the call. "I'll come and get you as soon as I can," Shepard assured her. "Half an hour or so." Barsha returned to the bedroom. "The wrong move," she knew from experience, "could crack the atmosphere and cause an explosion."[16]

O-Lan finally heard a soft knock on the apartment door, and when she opened it, there Shepard stood in his fur-lined suede jacket, "nervy and excited, and he pulled me out of the apartment and held both my hands. We looked at each other in the stark overhead light of the hallway, jolted by the sudden change in our lives—the laughter bubbled up and we went running down the stairs to his station wagon double-parked in front." She then moved into his apartment on the garden floor of Bill Hart's old building, and Mandel, who'd done O-Lan's astrological chart and even taken flute lessons from her, was heartbroken by the dual betrayals.[17]

Barsha tore up and threw out O-Lan's belongings, then called her and told her she was out of the show (though Shepard, oddly, was still in). He even attempted to seduce Mandel after the breakup. He thought it was a good trade in the spirit of the times, but she didn't want anything to do with it. Mandel was stunned that Shepard would throw her over with no warning after everything they'd been through—New York, Rome, London, Hollywood, and San Francisco, the transatlantic voyages, the cross-country road trips, the love they shared. Tony Barsha awkwardly remained in Shepard's vortex, directing and writing and keeping the lights on at Theater Genesis.[18]

"I didn't shiv him in 1969," Barsha explained, "so he went on to his glory. It was just, 'what the fuck.'"[19]

* * *

Not long after this debacle, O-Lan told Shepard she longed to see Europe, and asked whether he would lend her five hundred dollars. He responded that he would, if he could join her. On May 9, 1969, they took the newly christened *Queen Elizabeth II* to tour London, Amsterdam, France, Germany, and Italy. In London they saw Brecht's *The Resistible Rise of Arturo Ui* in the West End, with Leonard Rossiter as the Adolf Hitler–meets–Al Capone gangster. They also visited Mick Jagger, and O-Lan was starstruck meeting the twenty-five-year-old vocalist. "Just think," she said, "I used to chase Mick Jagger's car, and now I have tea with him." After visiting Stonehenge for her nineteenth birthday, May 23, they took the hovercraft to France. The two fought often, and there were moments where they nearly broke up, but on the voyage home to New York, they discovered that she was pregnant.[20]

Shepard and O-Lan now had some choices to make. Ironically, one of the first friends Shepard phoned for advice was Joyce Aaron, whom they'd met up with that summer in Amsterdam, who counseled that he should marry her. The Theater Genesis playwright Walter Hadler was in St. Mark's with Shepard and Mednick after a board meeting and, having heard from his fiancée, Georgia, that O-Lan was pregnant, invited the two of them to join them in a double wedding. Though everyone in their circle was unwaveringly bohemian, there were still social conventions to be wary of. ("I'm thinking legally here about the unborn child," Hadler said. "What an idiot, but nonetheless I felt that way.") Shepard accepted Hadler's offer at first, though his experience as a child in South Pasadena and Bradbury soured the idea of his raising any kind of normal family. Especially troubling was his terror of his father's bloodline. He questioned his ability to subdue the Rogers "instant animal" on behalf of a family, and he wandered the city streets at night alone, debating whether he wanted to go through with the marriage right up until a few days before the ceremony.[21]

"I've got certain fears about starting a family because of what I went through as a kid with Dad & everything," he wrote to his mother and his sister Roxanne. "But then I began to realize that I have my own choices & my own life I'd live & I can make it whatever I want." He loved O-Lan, and he loved to write, he told them, "and I feel that if I can keep that love alive then everything will work out for the good."[22]

* * *

The wedding guests arrived at St. Mark's on Sunday evening, November 9, 1969, six years, as it happened, to the day Shepard first arrived in New York. There, working the door as greeters, the Holy Modal Rounders sanctified the proceedings with purple tabs of LSD.[23] The church's nave was packed, and everyone aside from Father Allen had dolled themselves up in ironic costumes. Walter Hadler's best man,

Robert Contant (cofounder of the St. Mark's Bookshop) arrived in a drum major's uniform; Hadler himself dressed as a pirate and wore sunglasses; Shepard wore a decorous blue shirt and matching pants, somehow resembling Native American clothing, with O-Lan in a yellow bridal dress and flower crown. Bill Hart was Shepard's best man, and O-Lan's sister, Kristy, was maid of honor. Many of the guests, and some in the wedding party, were tripping.[24]

Michael Allen, whom Shepard characterized to his family in Bradbury as "a far-out Episcopal minister," opened with these remarks: "In a broken world and a polluted land, nothing could be more beautiful than marriage." Eventually, the minister intoned, "Who gives these people to be married to each other?" to which everyone roared back, "We do!" Mel Gussow covered the ceremony for the *New York Times* and noted that Allen encouraged everyone to embrace tenderly, after which "the celebrants began stomping their feet, rapping their pews, clapping their hands, tapping tambourines."[25]

The wedding drew a "mixed crowd," Georgia Hadler said. On the one hand, you had the freaks. "I remember I was shocked at O-Lan's mother, Scarlett," recalled a friend of O-Lan's. "She seemed so young. She was in jeans and had a suede vest with fringe, and I thought to myself, 'Boy! My mother is not like that!'" On the other, there were starchier attendees, including Georgia's mother and blind grandmother, who wore a pink Dior pantsuit. Naturally, few of them understood LSD, and they were, Georgia remembered, "none too pleased when the whole thing broke up without us getting the blessing from the priest."[26]

In fact, as Allen was wrapping up his officiations, "I now pronounce you . . . ," Shepard's best man, Bill Hart, was so drugged up he couldn't hold still, and when Allen asked whether anyone else had something to say, he shouted, "I want to go *outside*!" He then wildly lunged at Shepard to hug him and hand him O-Lan's ring, knocking the groom down, who then knocked the bride down, who knocked the other groom down.[27] "We all crashed to the floor onto the altar," Shepard wrote, "and everyone in the church started clapping again. Then I picked O-Lan up & carried her out of the church in my arms."[28]

While St. Mark's Church reverberated with stomping and cheering, Georgia and her dazed relations never heard Allen's blessing of the nuptials, and a few of them left wondering whether they'd been married at all. "The wedding was incredible," Shepard ended his jubilant letter to his mother back home. "The church felt like it was going to fly up to heaven."[29]

CHAPTER 7

# STRANGERS VS. FRIENDS

Shepard's proliferation of plays was unstoppable through this period. His next one-act was a sci-fi Western farce, *The Unseen Hand*, a play he neatly summarized to the *New York Times* in twenty-one words: "a guy from another planet who used to be a baboon is changed into a human being and returns to Earth."[1] Ellen Stewart took a glance at the script about the extraterrestrial primate and happily accepted it for La MaMa, where it opened on December 26, 1969; it would be moved to the more spacious (and riotous) Astor Place Theatre after a few months.

Then came the autobiographical, phantasmagorical father-and-son one-act titled *The Holy Ghostly*, which premiered on a double bill with *Melodrama Play* at Princeton University's McCarter Theatre on March 8, 1970. The show was produced by Tom O'Horgan's New Troupe, a breakaway company from La MaMa, and O'Horgan widely promoted *The Holy Ghostly* as "a thick weave of symbols and mysticism . . . This play may be the last flashing moment of man dying on the cusp of a new generation, screaming his way into inevitable fire and ice."[2]

Shepard wrote *The Holy Ghostly* after hearing his father had been fired from San Marino High School in the spring of 1969, and it was his most personal play to date. The title likely refers to a time when Shepard went into a reverie while playing drums and felt he'd lost control of his body. "It scared the shit out of me," he recalled. Peter Stampfel reassured him that he was "being visited by the Holy Ghost," Shepard said, "which sounded reasonable enough at the time."[3]

*The Holy Ghostly* is about his tumultuous relationship with the ghost of his own living father, who'd succumbed to alcohol, disillusionment, and regret and cast himself, in his son's eyes, into the spirit world of the undead. In the play, alone in the desert night, the father's haunted by a Chindi, a Navajo spirit that embodies all that had been inharmonious in a dead man's life; and as the "Holy Ghost," he merges the Trinity.

"Jane [Rogers] used to say that I was the most garrulous person in the world and I was the most gregarious and it's true," Sam Sr. wrote in 1974. After his death in 1984, though, Jane penned a psychological sketch titled simply "On Sam Rogers." The sketch has been in the family's hands ever since and is extraordinarily insightful about both Rogers men:

> His mind + spirit had been killed thru events which were due, in part, to his own failure of moral courage + in part to his victimization by forces seemingly beyond his control. He became an accomplice, relentlessly + unknowingly, in his own murder.... Inevitably undone because he could not or would not change himself. Troublesome character traits—His life was like a time bomb waiting to explode.... Seeming disregard for consequences that his actions would have on people who loved him ... disillusionment intensified always from habit + burned out—ambivalent personality fundamental character flaw.[4]

Shepard shared his mother's view that his father's "ambivalent personality" had led him to his hideous fate, the very ambivalence that infused Shepard's own life and thereby supplied the dramatic tension in his plays. He was determined not to let his father's tragic turn happen to himself, however.

A witch in *The Holy Ghostly* attempts to mollify Stanley Moss, as his son renamed his father. She says that only his body remains, and once that's gone, the Chindi (the Navajo spirit acts as a Greek chorus in the play) will take him away to perdition: "It's better this way," the Chindi tells him. "Imagine hanging around for eternity in the state of mind you're in now. Strung out between right and wrong, good and evil, the right and the left, the high and the low, the hot and the cold, the old and the young, the weak and the strong, the body and the spirit. You're a fucking mess." By the end, Moss is reconciled to death and hurls his earthly belongings into the roaring campfire, followed by his own corpse. He looks down on it from the vantage of a disembodied ghost: "BURN! BURN! BURN! BURN! BURN! BURN! BURN! BURN!"[5]

Princeton students roundly panned the evening's two-dollar entertainment at the venerable McCarter. In what may well be the only surviving review of this Off-Off-Broadway ingress into Ivy League minds, the student paper's drama critic Robert Rockwell downright eviscerated the show. O'Horgan's double bill, Rockwell wrote in the *Princetonian*, "was a constant insult to the intelligence and sensitivity of its audience, offering half-baked and overblown allegory as Social Comment, and actors' rehearsal games as Theater."[6]

Two days later, the *Village Voice*'s Ross Wetzsteon offered a downtown perspective, in contradistinction to the Ivy Leaguer of New Jersey's. Wetzsteon declared that *Melodrama Play*'s finale in particular was "the most powerful and disturbing image I have ever seen on stage, and one of the supreme moments in contemporary theater."[7] But another showdown with the Ivy League was in the offing. And like the double bill at Princeton, the incident would also contrast the reception of his work by an Ivy League audience and the "Vanguard of the New Theatre." This time, it would be Yale University, with the script of Shepard's "movie as stage play" *Operation Sidewinder*.

* * *

Shepard considered the full-length *Operation Sidewinder* his first attempt to write a story with a beginning, a middle, and an end, he told Mel Gussow. "I also never wrote in scenes. It's episodic," he went on. "Most plays I've written are in one place. People come to it from the outside."[8]

In the play, a mad scientist has invented a massive computerized sidewinder rattlesnake designed to trace the flight patterns of UFOs under the auspices of the United States Air Force. He believes that if the snake (a sentient AI) were allowed to roam free, it would develop an even higher form of consciousness than humans, and with that, the ability to communicate with alien life-forms. Meanwhile, a character named Young Man, a radical white man who's disillusioned with the youth movement, allies himself with three Black militants and a band of Native Americans led by the historic scout Mickey Free. Each hunts down the creature for their own reasons—the youth to placate the Black militants after a screwup, the militants to use as leverage against the air force, and the Natives to fulfill an ancient prophecy of salvation.

According to the actual Hopi prophecy, World War III will follow the Hopi's deliverance from the evils of the materialistic world, and the United States "will be destroyed, land and people, by atomic bombs and radioactivity." Shepard had read Frank Waters's 1963 *Book of Hopi* to stage the spectacular finale of *Operation Sidewinder*, in which a group of Hopi dancers perform a ceremonial dance with the computerized snake that will usher in the Emergence, or salvation from the end times. "A tremendous bolt of blue light issues from the sidewinder, matched by one in the sky," representing a Star God for the Hopis and a UFO for other audiences, and the band of Hopis, along with Young Man and his lover, disappear into the heavens. "It makes sense," confirmed Louis Mofsie, a Hopi dancer and choreographer of the play, that "relationship" between UFOs and the Blue Star Kachina—a Hopi spirit prophesied to rescue the Hopi tribe before the end of the world. "The Hopi have believed this for many hundreds of years," said Mofsie.[9]

*Operation Sidewinder* was first optioned in late November 1968 for five hundred dollars by the Yale Repertory Theatre, or Yale Rep, though they didn't have the financial means to stage the kind of production Shepard was hoping for (no snake, to give one dispiriting example). Yale Rep's first artistic director, Robert Brustein, needed to recruit Black actors outside the university, since the two students Yale Rep had originally hoped to cast unaccountably turned down the parts. Then, two weeks into rehearsals, in January 1969, six of the seven Black students at the Yale School of Drama wrote a letter to Brustein protesting the script. Their primary issue with the text was Shepard's depiction of the Black militant characters and how he had written their dialect.[10]

In the version of *Operation Sidewinder* used for auditions but never published, the Black militants are more integral to the plot, and more menacing, than in either of the published scripts. Shepard also took far more liberties with street slang—"I can dig it," "tell it sister," "real down cats," "that's cool baby," "outasight," "white boy," and uses of "nigger" and "ofay." [11]

Brustein stood firm against advice from colleagues and some white students and continued to fight for the play, but Shepard had no interest in a public row with Black students. He even fielded a call from a Yale professor and was visited at his apartment by several Black students who convinced him to halt the production. Yale's contract stipulated that Brustein didn't need Shepard's permission to move forward, but Brustein yielded nevertheless. "I realized that I was defeated," he recalled, "and on an issue of supreme importance to me. I had lost the fight for freedom of the stage at Yale." But the outside Black actors they hired wanted to go on with the show. "I have been in jail in Georgia," said one. "I've served time on a chain gang. I've been manacled and beaten and spat on. I would never act in a play against my race. And this play is not against my race." Still, after numerous appeals, Shepard refused to budge. "Mr. Shepard withdrew the play," reads Brustein's press release, "against the will and advice of the school."[12]

When Shepard was asked a few years later why his early one-act *Dog*, from his first show at La MaMa, remained unpublished and unrevived, Shepard answered, "It was about a Black guy—which later I found out it was uncool for a white to write about in America."[13] *Operation Sidewinder* was this self-censoring time in question, and it would be his last play with explicitly identified Black characters.

*Operation Sidewinder* was also the first production of his, thanks to the outcry at Yale, to appear at a Broadway theater, the Vivian Beaumont at the newly built Lincoln Center for the Performing Arts. And this time, Shepard's play was assigned a Black director, Michael A. Schultz, an Obie-winning member of the Negro Ensemble Company.

The Black actors playing the militants (performers with meaningful credits) appeared to have no quarrel with the script. "Everybody was fine about it," said the female lead, Barbara Eda-Young, about Shepard's potentially inflammatory dialect writing.[14]

For Shepard, Broadway was an expediency, since "no one can really afford to do it anyplace else."[15] Even there, they were compelled to devise a round stage that operated like a lazy Susan; after each scene, the prior set would slide into the wings to make way for the next to appear. (It was a technical feat at the time, though later common practice.)[16] But staging a play at Lincoln Center set him on edge; he'd never even seen a play there. The massive arts facility on the Upper West Side was the philanthropic brainchild of the billionaire John D. Rockefeller III, who'd declared that year, 1970, that Lincoln Center had been designed as a "cultural complex that would help fulfill some of the needs of an anxious age [which is] preoccupied with the issues of war and peace, social justice, poverty and pollution."[17] So far so good; Shepard's play checked all those boxes. And to stage a play at the Vivian Beaumont would offer him a colossal leg up in terms of prestige, visibility, and future prospects. He'd be in excellent company too, since the top dramatists Lillian Hellman, William Saroyan, and Tennessee Williams each had recent productions there, but the center attracted uptown audiences who largely preferred the plays of either name-brand American masters like them, or Shakespeare, or Molière. They largely disdained the avant-garde fare produced downtown, and the feeling was entirely mutual.

"I couldn't bring myself to go up there," Shepard informed a reporter. "It's a total bourgeois scene." Shepard preferred the intimacy and relative anonymity of downtown theater, where people knew and encouraged each other. When he met with Jules Irving, Lincoln Center's Repertory director, Shepard looked around and said, "I have to change the image of this fucking place." The dramatist was wearing a floor-length fur coat.[18]

Shepard was forced to make many concessions to Broadway tradition, especially with casting, so neither O-Lan nor Lee Kissman (then Shepard's clear choice for Young Man) were selected despite his entreaties. Irving made it up to Shepard by introducing him to Tennessee

Williams, whose revival of *Camino Real* was just closing at the Vivian Beaumont. The two only connected for a few moments and Shepard wrote to Williams later on, "I really think you're the greatest American playwright ever," hoping to get a sit-down with him. Williams responded somewhat coldly, telling him he'd heard "interesting things" about *Operation Sidewinder* and welcomed him to meet in New York on a date that he'd been informed wouldn't work for Shepard.[19]

The only real fight Shepard won against Irving was casting the lead female role of Honey, a part he specifically wrote for the Theater Genesis actor Barbara Eda-Young. Eda-Young knew he'd campaigned for her and reminisced about a day in the Village when Shepard rode by on a bicycle and asked whether she'd signed the contract for Lincoln Center. Yes, she responded, and they'd also invited her to join their repertory company, so she was cast for two productions before *Operation Sidewinder*, including Williams's *Camino Real*. "Sam moved me uptown," she said of being lifted into "legitimate theater" (shorthand for being paid a decent wage), and she went on to be Theater Genesis's most accomplished actress.[20]

* * *

Shepard's trepidation over the "bourgeois scene" turned out to be more prescient than even he had realized. *Operation Sidewinder* was set to open on March 12, 1970, with the Holy Modal Rounders playing live in the orchestra pit between scenes. A six-week run for an audacious new Shepard play was a major gamble for Lincoln Center. "I'm not worried about the old people," he said, referring to their usual audience. "I'm worried about the young ones." And how did these fledgling middlebrow audiences—whom Lincoln Center's (also young) literary manager, John Lahr, described the night after a preview as "tough—young, mean, and callow"—react when the blond-wigged Honey reaches orgasm as a result of the sidewinder's gyrations?[21] Or when the junkie antihero Young Man ties off his arm with the snake and injects himself with a shot of heroin? Or the UFO-heralding Hopi Snake Dance? Not well, it turned out.

"In the fractious early seventies," Lahr wrote, "it was a shocking thing for the darling of downtown theatre to cross the Maginot Line of Fourteenth Street, and it proved traumatic for all concerned."[22] (Lahr later reported that the show cost them about ten thousand subscriptions.) On the first night of previews, February 27, Lahr wrote in his diary that he took an instant liking to Shepard, who was "funny and playful and affectionate with his wife who is very pregnant." Shepard muttered to Lahr during intermission, "It's not like Theater Genesis. I don't know anybody in the audience." The next day, Jules Irving motioned Lahr into the stage manager's office, where he was shown the audience's livid commentary: "Terrible, terrible, terrible"; "Infantile"; "The artistic director and anyone connected should be fired." A friend of Eda-Young's joked about the "sea of red seats" she'd seen at the Lincoln Center production because so few people had attended, and her aunt was scandalized by her role as Honey. "Did they have to put the snake between your legs?" she huffed.[23]

On the second night of previews, Shepard looked miserable, and Lahr spied him tucking a beer from the lobby bar under his shirt before the show. After being thrown by offensive laughter at the Hopi dance, Shepard was certain the audience was the problem, but Lahr wrote in his diary that "the problem's in the play."[24] Then again, the performers felt that it wasn't so much about the audience or Shepard's writing. "There were too many cooks, that's all," Eda-Young said of the committee that ran Lincoln Center. (For succor, Steve Weber was dealing drugs out of the Holy Modal Rounders' dressing room. "They were always stoned," Eda-Young remembered of the band. "*Always.*")[25]

Shepard was being confronted from all sides. While the Black militant characters no longer appeared to be an issue, after one performance, a Hopi man in his early twenties confronted them about the dance. It was sacred, he asserted, not for public consumption. Shepard was mortified and considered pulling the entire Snake Dance finale.[26]

Louis Mofsie, or Green Rainbow, was listed in the program as an "Indian," along with all the other dancers, but in fact was the uncredited choreographer of the play's Snake Dance. (Shepard dedicated the book to the Hopi tribe and their village Old Oraibi, along with Nancy Mandel and O-Lan, the Rounders and the Rolling Stones, Crazy Horse, and the year 1968.) A Hopi-Winnebago and a founding director of the Thunderbird American Indian Dancers, Mofsie was impressed by Shepard's sincerity about wanting the Hopi scenes as accurate as possible. "What he put in the play was authentic," he said. "It wasn't something he made up." (Mofsie would also supply Shepard with the lyrics and sheet music that appear in the published script.)[27]

Shepard, Irving, Mofsie, and two other Native dancers in the group—Gregory Borst (Long Sword) and his wife, Muriel Miguel (Bright Sun), a founder of the Thunderbird Dancers who knew Shepard from the Open Theater—sat down with the Hopi man who had objected.[28] The only condition for their meeting was that the Hopi's girlfriend, a white activist who Mofsie surmised was the true source of the man's outrage, was forbidden from attending. "I will *not* listen to your girlfriend objecting," Mofsie told him, "because she has *nothing* to do with this." With that, the man acquiesced, and after two days, they had reached an agreement: the Kachina headdress, as a gesture of good faith, would have to go, as would the sprinkling of cornmeal on the participants to consecrate the dance ritual.[29]

In the end, the young Hopi's protest had a powerful effect on Shepard, however minor the concessions he made, and he was now convinced that "putting a real ritual on stage is sacrilegious. The play should change people: It should be the ritual."[30]

The reviews were surprisingly mixed. NBC, for one, considered *Operation Sidewinder* a "glorious piece of pop art." Clive Barnes of the *New York Times* sardonically wrote of the production, "My mind was not so much blown as scattered." Barnes averred that by pitting the American Dream against harsher realities and community activism against realpolitik, Shepard "has written . . . a rather bad play about a rather good subject." Shepard, he concluded on a kindly note, "needs discipline the way a hemophiliac needs blood. Yet you cannot be uninterested. Or at least you cannot be uninterested if you are at all interested in the American theater." Amazingly, the august *Newsday* critic George Oppenheimer (who would hate Shepard's next two plays) thought *Operation*

*Sidewinder* was a vivid example of "total theater": "It is psychedelic and, quite often, psychopathic. It has one foot in science fiction and another in the theater of the absurd, but whatever it has or is, it is never for a moment dull."[31]

Broadway had exactly zero tolerance for a "sea of red seats," however. *Operation Sidewinder* thus has the distinction of being the first and last new Shepard play to premiere on a Broadway stage. The script had been too reactionary for Yale and too radical for Lincoln Center, and in the long run, this was just as well for Shepard. "I don't know who to address on Broadway," he said years later. "I always felt I was writing for people who would understand me. I never had any aspiration to talk to people I don't know. It's a question of strangers versus friends."[32]

* * *

On April Fools' Day 1970, *The Unseen Hand* was revived at the Astor Place Theatre on a double bill with *Forensic & the Navigators*. O-Lan played the pregnant girlfriend, Oolan, again in *Forensic*, but this time she was over seven months pregnant herself. Startled theatergoers were confronted before the performance by La MaMa's Ellen Stewart dancing with abandon in the lobby to the head-splitting chords of the psychedelic rock band Lothar and the Hand People, with Shepard himself banging away on the drums. Abstract landscapes by the painter and performance artist Joey Skaggs lined the walls, and guests were handed pop-art programs by Robert U. Taylor, which were styled by one attendee as an "all-illustrated, all action, if-you-get-bored-with-the-play-grab-the-cartoon program."[33]

From the back of the house on opening night, Shepard, the show's producer, Albert Poland, and its director, Jeff Bleckner, watched the critics disappear into a wall of steam while the fog machine gassed the house for the finale of *Forensic & the Navigators*. "They were looking at each other like, 'I don't know what to do but I guess it would be uncool if I left,'" Poland said. "It was like, for the moment, he won. *They* are vanishing, and *we* have done it." But in the lobby, they heard a commotion, "and there were these dudes in overcoats and violin cases." "'What the fuck is this?'" Poland thought. "And then they grabbed Sam."[34]

Tony Barsha, Joey Skaggs, and a few other pranksters thought the publicity surrounding this production might further inflate Shepard's ego. They decided to rescue him from his own success by kidnapping him and sending him on a one-way bus ticket to Azusa, the town near Bradbury where *The Unseen Hand* takes place. Skaggs was sporting a zoot suit and violin case meant to resemble a 1920s-style tommy gun. When they burst into the lobby, brandishing their fake guns, Shepard started yelling and throwing punches. Barsha had predicted the stunt would backfire, since Shepard was paranoid about having taken O-Lan from him and believed Barsha meant him actual bodily harm. (Luckily, the pregnant O-Lan was still in her dressing room after the performance.) "So the critics walked from a steam-filled theater into a fistfight," Poland said, laughing, after which Skaggs and his band of marauders fled the scene in a getaway car they'd parked on the street outside. Shepard was not amused.[35]

Together with the company, he partied all night until the reviews came in, a customary opening night ritual. But when the morning papers arrived, Peter Stampfel recalled, "Sam got pretty drunk and said bitter things about critics, many of whom had not been treating him very kindly." "I think it was in 'Horsefeathers,'" George Oppenheimer panned in *Newsday*, "that Groucho delivered one of his classic insults to Chico by saying that he had the mind of a child of four but the child wouldn't miss it. After what I have just seen I'm inclined to believe that this applies equally well to Mr. Shepard." Shepard's champions, however, included a range of countercultural bellwethers: The *East Village Other*, a short-lived radical newspaper that promoted the newly named neighborhood's offbeat amusements, said *The Unseen Hand* "is 300% ours and we are its audience." Abbie Hoffman attended only three days after his famous trial with the Chicago Seven and agreed to write an endorsement: "The greatest thing I've seen since *Oklahoma!*," he crowed. "Sam Shepard is Amerika's only yippie playwright. *The Unseen Hand* is the fist of freedom!" "Bored with the Theatre?" Elia Kazan asked in his own blurb. "See Shepard." Andy Warhol thought the show was "wildly hilarious, frenetic, and futuristic," and, more important for his taste, "*The Unseen Hand* has the most beautiful cast in town!"[36]

Clive Barnes of the *New York Times*, who delayed the opening curtain by arriving half an hour late, was more evenhanded than most mainstream critics, while still maintaining a patronizing tone: "Despite my worst instincts I cannot prevent myself from mildly loving the plays of . . . [quoting from Taylor's pop art program] Sam! ack! SHEPARD!" "Mr. Shepard," he went on, "is perhaps the first person to write good disposable plays. He may well go down in history as the man who became to drama what Kleenex was to the handkerchief. And just like Kleenex he may well overcome."[37]

Shepard's Astor Place run lasted for four dispiriting weeks. Nevertheless, one celebrated attendee made the carnivalesque production an unforeseen boon for the playwright: Robert Redford, then basking in the afterglow of his smash hit with Paul Newman, *Butch Cassidy and the Sundance Kid*, saw it with his wife, Lola Van Wagenen. Jeff Bleckner approached the actor about making *The Unseen Hand* into a movie, hoping to direct, and this led to several meetings, during which Redford fed himself grapes with his head tilted back like an emperor, Poland observed, while Shepard "cuddled up to him" and called him Sundance. "And I sat there," Poland said of their final meeting, "while Sam told Redford that he wanted Tony Barsha to direct the movie. It was shocking. . . . Jeff was in shock, and so was I. What kind of loyalty? Jeff was the one who *arranged* this." Shepard invited Barsha to direct the film and write the treatment as a peace offering after the O-Lan fiasco. Barsha then distilled the play into prose and opened it up with the play's protagonists, Willie (the Space Freak) and the Morphan brothers, traveling to planet Nogoland (Shepard's play on the German protectorate Togoland, both lands being oppressed by colonial overlords).[38]

"Sam fucked that up," Barsha said. When the two sat down with Redford at his New York office, Shepard announced that Barsha was going to direct. "No," said Redford. "Tony's gonna do it," Shepard insisted. "He wrote this treatment, and he's in charge." "Not a chance." Shepard wouldn't relent, so they exited the office building with nothing to show. "Why'd you do that?" demanded Barsha on the street. "Why didn't you just say 'yes,' then do what we want to do with it?" "No, I can't do it," Shepard said. "It's not right." Then, Shepard returned to Redford on his own and agreed to write a script himself, and the actor handed him a check for six thousand dollars.[39]

"My appreciation of Sam comes first, as an artist, as a writer," Barsha said between his teeth when first informed about this moment of betrayal. "That comes first. Second, he's the biggest prick I know." Poland likewise regarded him as a dangerous man, "unsafe at any speed."[40]

"Sam worked like hell on the screenplay," Peter Stampfel remembered, but when it didn't live up to expectations, Shepard told him, Redford insisted he keep the money.[41] In fact, Shepard wrote seventy-six pages of the script that still survives but never sent it, after which, Redford told his biographer, "he disappeared to Paris [Nova Scotia, then London] and blew the cash living the émigré life. I didn't see him for a long time, but he eventually apologized and sent the money back."[42]

* * *

In the meantime, following the opening of his double bill, Shepard gushed, "It's getting closer and closer to baby day and we both can hardly wait to see what's inside there. It's like waiting for Christmas when you're a kid or something." He and O-Lan prepared by attending natural childbirth classes, alongside a clutch of expectant middle-class mothers, and Shepard also enlisted in therapy, going twice a week. "I feel a lot freer in some ways," he told his family about the therapy, but added that he longed to extract himself from the tumult of New York City, "just to breathe some fresh air for a change and communicate with nature."[43]

Jesse Mojo Shepard was born on May 25, 1970, just two days shy of his mother's birthday. O-Lan had been in labor for over twenty hours. "I thought I was gonna lose her," Shepard told Barbara Eda-Young. In fact, when the child came out, Shepard fainted, according to their nurse.[44]

He'd strongly considered naming his son Samuel Shepard Rogers, in the family tradition, which flummoxed O-Lan.[45] Why, she asked him, would you name this sweet little baby after such a monster of a man in your life? Instead, the blue-eyed boy was named after the outlaw Jesse James.[46] Mojo was chosen as a middle name as an allusion to voodoo spells (and also street slang for heroin), although some friends had intemperately lobbied for that to be his first name. If Jesse had been a girl, they would have named her after the Hopi spirit Kachina.[47]

* * *

With money left over from Robert Redford's check, combined with funds from a Guggenheim Foundation grant, Shepard bought an off-the-grid summer retreat on the Bay of Fundy in West Advocate, Nova Scotia. He signed the deed for Hill Top Farm, as it's officially known, for twelve thousand dollars in late June.[48]

Desperate to find a place away from the city, he'd been taken to Nova Scotia by a good friend, the writer Rudy Wurlitzer, who owned a summer home there, as did Wurlitzer's friends, the photographer Robert Frank and the composer Philip Glass. Shepard first met Wurlitzer, typically for the downtown literary scene, at a bar on the Lower East Side like the Blue & Gold or the Old Reliable. He would remain a close friend of Shepard's and one of his favorite living authors. "We just connected spontaneously," Wurlitzer said. "A lot was just about how we were going to stay alive and survive in this culture." Together as writers and friends, he added, "we liked to have permission to go off the wall. On the other side of the wall, it's a little claustrophobic, if you know what I mean."[49] Shepard came to abhor the city, Wurlitzer intuited, "because it had become so corporate and so machine-like. I mean, it wasn't personal so much anymore. . . . He wanted to work in a small arena where he could be a part of it in a human, personal way."[50]

The Bay of Fundy's tides are the highest in the world, in some places over fifty feet, and the food was "fresh": "A white goat who gives a quart and 1/2 a day of fresh milk," Shepard reported, "fresh baked oatmeal bread, dandelion wine made by one of the locals, wild strawberries, fresh fillet of Flounder that we caught in the Bay of Fundy, fresh lobster, clams, homemade pie, acres of meadows & virgin forest, miles of beach."[51] Although he had been to Nova Scotia, Shepard bought the farm sight unseen, along with the panoramic view of Advocate Harbour that came with it. The eight-room 1870 farmhouse, constructed by a shipbuilder, had huge wood beams and spacious picture windows. Hill Top Farm was on a forty-five-acre lot and blissfully isolated, and the "Bluenoses" of Nova Scotia warmly welcomed Shepard and his young bohemian family. The village of a hundred and fifty people, with the nearest town thirty miles away, would be an emblematic refuge from what he abhorred about "machine-like" New York.[52]

CHAPTER 8

# THE GOTHIC CROW

On a night in late fall 1970, Shepard was lashing away on his drums on the Village Gate's basement stage with the Holy Modal Rounders, all of them drunk and geared up on speed. In the audience was an émigré from southern New Jersey named Patricia "Patti" Lee Smith, who likened the spectacle to "an Arabian hoedown with a band of psychedelic hillbillies."[1]

Patti Smith recalled that Shepard looked "as if he was on the lam and had slid behind the drums while the cops looked elsewhere," while she gazed at him howling out his proto-punk song "Blind Rage": "I'm gonna get my gun and shoot him and run! *Blind Rage!*"[2] The twenty-three-year-old New Jersey girl was then a budding poet, watching mesmerized as Shepard screamed between drum solos "*Blind Rage!*" "This guy," she thought, "truly embodies the heart and soul of rock and roll." In Smith's telling, she sought him out after his set and offered, "I'm going to write an article about you. I'm gonna make you a star." Then she asked for his name, and he replied, "Slim Shadow."[3]

Patti Smith wrote up this origin story of her and Shepard's relationship in her acclaimed 2010 memoir, *Just Kids*. At the time of its publication, Shepard snickered, "I think she was exaggerating a little."[4] Indeed, Shepard wrote contemporaneously of the same night that amid the audience, he glimpsed "a beautiful chick with hair like Keith Richards." Smith later searched the venue for him, he wrote, but he'd "disappeared into the night" and stumbled home to sleep off a "drunken stupor." The following evening, Shepard continued, O-Lan went alone to the Village Gate for a night off from mothering and bumped into Smith. The two had a long chat, in which Smith told O-Lan that she wanted to interview Shepard. "He's not impressed," Shepard wrote in his journal after hearing this from O-Lan, "but his vanity is tickled."[5]

Shepard phoned Smith the following day, and they agreed to meet at her loft above the Oasis Bar on West Twenty-Third Street, which she shared with her best friend and sometime lover, the photographer Robert Mapplethorpe. Mapplethorpe was then documenting the BDSM scene in Manhattan through a series of black-and-white photos that would shock the world and ensure his name in the pantheon of avant-garde American portrait artists. He also provided the cover art for Smith's debut album, *Horses*, a few years later. Smith would ultimately enshrine her relationships with Mapplethorpe and Shepard in *Just Kids*.

In Shepard's account of the meeting, he refers to himself as "Slim Shadow" and Smith as "Cavale," after a favorite novel of Smith's, *La Cavale* by Albertine Sarrazin.[6] The atmosphere at her tiny loft once he arrived was thick with desire:

> They have an immediate understanding that something bigger than an interview is going to happen—there's a certain nervous tension in the air—Cavale keeps putting on different costumes & parading in front of a mirror—Slim tries to act like a mean cowboy—they leave & go to a Cuban place for rice & beans. As they part, Slim tries to kiss Cavale on the lips but she turns her cheek—he thinks that's weird—they part.[7]

Smith phoned him the next day, according to Shepard's notebook. She already missed him, and he felt the same way. That night, he lied to O-Lan, telling his wife he was going out for orange juice, and then hailed a cab to Smith's place, where he found her in bed with what appeared to be a teenage hustler she'd taken under her wing. Smith threw him out, but Shepard's nerves were rattled, and he kissed her on the forehead before leaving. "He comes home to Lollypop [O-Lan] and Lollypop thinks something's wrong & asks if it's Cavale—Slim admits it—Lollypop starts going downhill—at first she thinks it's an infatuation then when she learns that he's been seeing her on the sly she gets pissed off & says she's going to hurt him bad."[8]

Growing up with Scarlett, though, O-Lan was no stranger to open relationships, and eventually, she told him to forge ahead with Smith. "Me and his wife still even liked each other," Smith told Mapplethorpe's biographer. "I mean, it wasn't like committing adultery in the suburbs or something."[9]

Smith had opened up to Shepard with astonishing candor, "about her life in the New Jersey swamps—how she caught T.B. when she was three—the way she crosses her legs like her mother—that she was insane [and] about the line you cross over from reality to fantasy." In the final line of Shepard's notebook entry, he abandons any pretense of autofiction and concludes that the two of them would "never be able to recognize love until they love themselves first—Patti said that."[10]

Smith's beau at the time was the famed junkie writer Jim Carroll, who took one look at Shepard and gave up: "It was like, 'Okay, *hasta la vista!*'" (In fact, Shepard might have confused the teen hustler he described in his notebook with either Carroll or Mapplethorpe, both of whom were distinctively boyish-looking back then.) Smith was hooked at first sight, body and soul, by this droopy-haired cowboy rocker and the alluring charm of his "coyote laugh."[11] She conducted several interviews with him, ostensibly as a freelancer for *Crawdaddy*, America's first magazine to take rock and roll seriously, although none of the interviews were ever published. If Smith had fallen for him as an embodiment of rock and roll, he soon fell for her unconventional beauty, her gangly legs, her geyser of jet-black hair. "You are like a crow," the Spanish surrealist Salvador Dalí told her in the Hotel Chelsea lobby, "a gothic crow."[12]

* * *

By this time, Shepard had thrown off any lingering affection for Greenwich Village's hippie music scene. The newest rock bands, such as Lou Reed's the Velvet Underground, had vastly more appeal to him than folk or even avant-garde jazz artists.

Shepard became a sought-after commodity in the proto-punk scene, whose twin centers of gravity in New York were Andy Warhol's Factory and Max's Kansas City, where Shepard took Smith for lobster (a meal that would later take on symbolic meaning in their cowritten play). They took their seats at a back-room table reserved for VIPs, and he told the waiter, "Bring her the biggest lobster you have." "When my giant lobster with drawn butter arrived," Smith recalled, it occurred to her that "this handsome hillbilly might not have the money to pay the check." She soon found out, according to her, that he did after meeting a friend in the ladies' room, one of Warhol's "superstars," Jackie Curtis, who informed her that she'd been dining with a downtown prodigy and three-time Obie winner. When dessert arrived, with Smith in a daze, Shepard gently nudged her, "Eat your ice cream, Patti Lee."[13]

Shepard "copped her entire mind," Peter Stampfel recalled of their attraction. "He sure did. And so did she. Cop his entire mind."[14] This period with Shepard had a colossal impact on Smith's artistic career, as she later explained in *Just Kids* and elsewhere. "I was both scattered and stymied, surrounded by unfinished songs and abandoned poems," she wrote of the time before meeting the playwright. "I would go as far as I could and hit a wall, my own imagined limitations. And then I met a fellow who gave me his secret, and it was pretty simple. When you hit a wall, just kick it in."[15]

The couple moved in together, first at her and Mapplethorpe's loft, then, after several months, a few blocks down at the Hotel Chelsea, Smith and Mapplethorpe's old digs.[16]

Towering midblock at 222 West Twenty-Third Street, the Chelsea remains a living museum of redbrick Victorian Gothic architecture that lends the building, and the block itself, a Bourbon Street air. The Chelsea had been refashioned from an apartment building into a boutique hotel with over two hundred rooms, and its cheap long-term housing options promptly established a reputation for its bohemian mise-en-scène, artistic flare, and lax behavioral standards. The hotel boasted a guest list of some of the most illustrious literary, theatrical, and musical talents of the nineteenth and twentieth centuries: Sarah Bernhardt, Mark Twain, O. Henry, Thomas Wolfe, Brendan Behan, William S. Burroughs, Jack Kerouac, Salvador Dalí, Arthur Miller, Bob Dylan, Joni Mitchell, Sid Vicious, the Grateful Dead, Janis Joplin, Jimi Hendrix, and Leonard Cohen are only a smattering of those who stayed and worked there. "It was not part of America," Arthur Miller wrote of the Hotel Chelsea, it "had no vacuum cleaners, no rules, no taste, no shame. . . . The surreal had its citadel in the Chelsea."[17]

If a resident didn't want to leave the building, a door from the Chelsea's lobby led straight into the El Quijote bar and restaurant, where Smith (eventually with Shepard) caroused and talked shop with the Beat writers William S. Burroughs and Allen Ginsberg and the folk rock stars Bobby Neuwirth and Janis Joplin, with occasional sightings of Jimi Hendrix before his and Joplin's deaths in 1970.

Shepard was there when Smith made her debut in the nave of St. Mark's Church, with Gerard Malanga, on February 12, 1971, where she recited a poem cataloging her romantic obsession, "for Sam Shepard."[18] He also was the one to encourage her to team up with the guitarist Lenny Kaye, who was working at the record store Village Oldies on Bleecker Street.[19] Soon, the duo was playing at St. Mark's regularly, with her reading poetry and Kaye accompanying on guitar, and with Mapplethorpe, Andy Warhol, and Lou Reed all looking on from the nave.[20] Smith and Kaye would play with their seminal punk band the Patti Smith Group for over half a century.

Smith's first known press interview took place at the Chelsea, and it appeared in the April 29, 1971, issue of the *New York Flyer*, a supplement to *Rolling Stone*.[21] "I want," she informed the reporter, "to be a big shot." Accompanying the story was a picture of Smith at twenty-four staring into the camera with her street-kid splendor, a look that would not perceptibly change for over fifty years. She clutches a ghoulish-looking plaster of paris doll to her breast. Beneath this disarming snapshot, the caption quotes her declaring, "I'm one of the best poets in rock and roll."

Smith barraged her interviewer with rapid-fire tall tales about herself that echoed the mythically squalid lives of the artists she admired: "I was born in Chicago, in a real slum . . . and was sent to my grandfather, a honky-tonk piano player in Chattanooga. Eventually, I ended up with my parents in South Jersey—my father is an eccentric genius who was a famous tap dancer and used to trace pornography in the Bible and talk Shakespeare and shit, and my mother used to be a stripper and bootlegger." Along with trumped-up stories, she offered him candid facts about her teen years, including having given birth (though she elevates her age): "I never had any boyfriends until I was 19 and then I got pregnant right away but I gave the baby away because I had always wanted to be a performer or an artist and having a child just didn't figure in."[22]

"The root of me," Smith informed the *New York Flyer*, "has always been my heroes." Listed among her idols were Hank Williams, Amedeo Modigliani, Jackson Pollock, Bob Dylan, and Buddy Holly.[23] Shepard instantly joined their ranks and doubled as her artistic mentor. "Everything about Sam is so beautiful and has to do with rhythm," Smith told them. "That's why Sam and I so successfully collaborated. Intuitively he worked with rhythm in his blood. I do it intellectually. He does it from the heart. We were able to establish a deep communion."[24]

When Smith told Shepard about her perpetual hankering to smash her foot through a window, he'd say, "Kick it in, Patti Lee. I'll bail you out." The twosome consummated their bond by asking the Australian artist Vali Myers, also a Hotel Chelsea resident, to give them both tattoos. Shepard chose a crescent "hawk moon" on his left hand between thumb and forefinger, and Smith a lightning bolt on the inside of her left knee (representing the energy of Crazy Horse, whose name she'd stenciled on her T-shirt), while the photographer Sandy Daley, Mapplethorpe's mentor in photography, filmed the whole operation in her room, number 1019.[25] Daley's short film *Patti Having Her Knee Tattooed* reveals the whole ritual, with Shepard appearing for ten seconds as he supports her through the agony. Later, she was recorded for a voice-over narrating the procedure, during which she carefully arranges flowers, locks of hair, her doll, and her stuffed crow, Raymond, then uses spit as an antiseptic. "I started to hate Sam," says her voice-over when he briefly appears. "I don't think I could ever live with him because he could read my mind. . . . He'd shame me constantly because I am a liar. . . . He didn't even care because he was so happy he could read my lie." Throughout the film, Smith is cosplaying as a witch in battle with Vali, another witch, over things like the location of the tattoo and how much pain would be inflicted by Vali. Smith's voice swoons over Shepard's good looks as she observes him bolstering her resolve, then quips, "Yeah, that's one way I beat Vali. She might have done all this to me during the day, but look who I fucked at night."[26]

Another night at the hotel, according to Shepard, they heard a murder take place just outside their door. "I told ya, I told ya," he heard a man shout, and then shoot another with a low-caliber pistol, slamming him against their door. The killer ran, and the corpse fell to the floor, blocking them inside the room. The next day there was a chalk outline on the floor of the man's corpse to protect the evidence, "like Raymond Chandler books," Shepard recalled.[27]

Shepard bought Smith her first guitar for two hundred dollars, a great deal of money at that time. It was a 1931 L-00 Gibson, which Smith called "Bo" (a shortening of the 1939 Gary Cooper movie *Beau Geste*) and cherished for decades. "Bo" would be played by countless rock stars and, most important for Smith, when she wasn't yet savvy with the instrument, tuned by them. Shepard taught Smith her first chords and helped her conquer her initial dread of the stage. "And also, he opened the door that sort of gave me the secret of improvisation. And I carried that my whole life, and it's gotten me out of a lot of jams in front of hundreds of thousands of people."[28]

"It's like drumming," Shepard reassured her about improvising on the fly. "If you miss a beat, you create another."[29]

* * *

After about two weeks of Shepard's absence, O-Lan had abandoned any hope of his return. Still, she gamely accepted the role of Mae West for the premiere of his two-act *The Mad Dog Blues*, a cartoonish pantomime that opened at Theater Genesis on March 4. (Other fabled icons in the play include Paul Bunyan, Marlene Dietrich, Captain Kidd, and Jesse James.)

The plot of *Mad Dog*, a kaleidoscopic "adventure show," depicts the movieland fantasy life of Kosmo (Shepard's character), a highly successful but discontented rock star, and his wayward, heroin-addicted, drug dealer sidekick Yahoodi, based on Murray Mednick. "I became a junkie for a couple of years, and Sam was very upset with me about that," Mednick said. One day, they were walking down the street, and Shepard turned to him and said something like, "You know, you have all this up-front intelligence, and you could do that?" Shepard's hard drug of choice was crystal meth, Mednick went on, but he probably was not an addict. "He was a big drinker more than anything else. He liked his whiskey."[30] Shepard's favorite drug overall was bizarrely the over-the-counter energy supplement Niacin, which he called "my together drug" and encouraged others to take. "It made me wonder if he was a bit schizy or something and this brought him together," said Albert Poland. "It made *my* brain feel like a twisted washrag."[31]

For the production, Shepard was performing on electric guitar, tambourine, and the bongos, and at one *Mad Dog* performance shouted, "Anybody got a kazoo in C?" Nobody did, but one of the other musicians onstage handed an oversized wine bottle to an audience member, gave him a quick lesson on playing the jug, and all of them swung into a country song. *Mad Dog* was directed by Robert "Bob" Glaudini, with whom O-Lan began her own affair. "What's good for the goose is good for the gander," she told Albert Poland. (O-Lan declined to add her matrimonial last name Shepard-Johnson to the cast list, and Shepard listed himself again as Slim Shadow.)[32]

By this time, Shepard's irascibility was common knowledge, and while most at the theater revered him and competed for his attention, others kept their distance. At one rehearsal, with infant Jesse on the stage, the actor Beeson Carroll lumbered in drunk. Stumbling down the aisle, Carroll leapt onto the stage, missing Jesse by a whisker, and loudly started razzing Shepard in front of his jilted wife and baby boy. "Oh, look at that!" Carroll roared. "There's Sammy the actor! *Haw! Haw! Haw!* Sammy the actor!" "Beeson," Shepard warned, "if you don't cut that out, I'm gonna punch you in the mouth." "Oh, Sammy the actor's gonna punch me in the mouth!" he said, spoiling for a fight. "*Haw! Haw! Haw!*" Shepard then slammed his fist into Carroll's jaw, cracking it in two places.[33]

"There was something about him you just didn't want to mess with," Lee Kissman remembered. "I saw him several times be really nasty to people and do really weird things to people, and I just didn't feel comfortable. . . . He felt dangerous to me in all kinds of ways, you know, sexually, physically, intellectually. . . . He could be very charming but he could turn on a dime."[34] If Shepard felt slighted or undermined (true to his nature as a Scorpio, according to one astrologer who knew him at the time), he'd lash out with a wounding insult or worse. "I was a belligerent asshole back then," Shepard ruefully acknowledged. "Really. I mean I was really not a pleasant person to be around."[35]

Roxanne Rogers admitted that all three of Sam Rogers's children grew into rage-aholics like their father. "It's not like other people's anger," she went on. "It's much bigger, much worse, because it has self-hatred in it too."[36] On top of that, Shepard was also eager for attention, and combining that need with his fears and upbringing created combustible reactions.

While Shepard's anger issues had become obvious to his circle, Patti Smith began to manifest her own. She'd turned fiercely possessive, for one. Shepard was so impossibly handsome that strange women on the street would saunter up, with Smith standing right next to him, and brazenly whisper in his ear, "Get rid of the kid."[37] One day, Terry Ork, the future punk impresario, was chatting with Shepard at the Chelsea. He was trying to coax the playwright into allowing him and the exalted cineaste Nicholas Ray (director of *Rebel Without a Cause*) to film *Cowboy Mouth*, a play Shepard and Smith had just written that was then in rehearsals. Smith entered the room and screamed in a jealous fury, "Get the fuck out of here, this is my man!"[38]

On the few occasions Shepard left the Chelsea to visit Jesse and O-Lan, who was provisionally living with a friend in Brooklyn, Smith would wail to Kevin O'Connor, their neighbor down the hall, "*Sam's gone!*" Strangely, no bad blood was spilled between her and O-Lan. Indeed, Georgia Hadler remembered going to a small gathering of women at an apartment in Harlem where two of the attendees were Smith and O-Lan. "I was surprised that Patti was there," Georgia said. If they weren't exactly chummy, they were "perfectly civil."[39]

By then, Shepard was growing resentful of Smith's talent as a poet. He'd been abusing crystal meth too, and a clash of theirs went sideways and ended with his destroying several of her drawings. "Our ways could not be defined or dismissed with a few words describing a careless youth," Smith remembered of their tumultuous romance. "We were friends; good or bad, we were just ourselves."[40]

* * *

The idea for Shepard and Smith's one-act play *Cowboy Mouth* came about after he proposed that they write a drama about their high-wire love affair.[41] While he was out, she jotted down a note to him: "I was messing round trying to think of our play," she wrote. "It's hard cause I don't know how tension stuff is made or how a story goes. But I writ what I was thinking. (Like you call an outline right.)" Her first question to him: "Can I piss onstage?" (The possible titles appear to be "Flash Flood" and "Water.") In Smith's slapdash outline, her character, Cavale, loses conviction and abandons an idea to hold Slim at gunpoint to prevent him from returning to his family. In Cavale's mind, Slim was in control, not she, a power imbalance in their relationship that they largely reversed in the final script. In fact, according to her outline, it was Smith's character, not Shepard's, who had the "cowboy mouth" at first.[42]

Shepard's own outline was just a few sentences long, but it summarizes the eventual plot in one concise line: "Cavale kidnaps Slim with an old .45—she's going to make him a rock & roll star but they fall in love." His working title was "A Long Night's Journey into Day."[43] Smith evidently vetoed this in favor of "The Cowboy Mouth," now referring to Slim's rather than Cavale's mouth, which she originally took from a phrase in Bob Dylan's surreal 1966 blues ballad "Sad Eyed Lady of the Lowlands."[44] (The play was first billed in 1971 as "The Cowboy Mouth," and they only later agreed to drop the article.)

Shepard's stage directions for the setting read like a descriptive poem of their room at the Chelsea, a landfill of hipster Americana. Smith's character, Cavale, is faithfully drawn as "a chick who looks like a crow, dressed in raggedy black," and Shepard's equally faithful Slim is "a cat who looks like a coyote, dressed in scruffy red." "They are both beat to shit," the stage directions read. "We find them after one too many mornings . . . mean as snakes." "We were both so messed up and had a lot of anger in us," Smith told a reporter for the Pop Scene Service that July. "So instead of fighting with each other we sat down at the typewriter and wrote."[45]

They used Shepard's typewriter, sliding it back and forth on their bed. "Say anything," he coaxed her when they began. "You can't make a mistake when you improvise." Once she warmed to the collaborative process, the words of their shared escapades effortlessly filled the pages, and *Cowboy Mouth* was completed over a two-night writing binge. In the play, Smith wrote, "We encoded our love, imagination, and indiscretions."[46]

Before the action begins, Smith's character, Cavale, had kidnapped Shepard's Slim away from his wife and infant boy. She promises to transform him into the musical prophet of their generation, "a rock-and-roll Jesus with a cowboy mouth."[47] Slim charges around in a fit of despair and resists, but he has contracted a strain of Stockholm syndrome and fallen for his kidnapper. The bulk of the ensuing dialogue passionately swells from guilt and rage to love and understanding and back.

Smith would come to regard *Cowboy Mouth* as less a play than a sacrament of their actual love and loss. "We ritualized the end of our adventure," she said, "and created a portal of escape for Sam." Shepard pined for rock and roll glory for a year or two more, but that was a destiny that Smith, not Shepard, was born to fulfill. "You know," he told her, "the dreams you had for me weren't my dreams. . . . Maybe those dreams are meant for you."[48]

* * *

*Cowboy Mouth*'s world premiere was staged, without contractual permission, on April 2, 1971, at the Traverse Theatre in Edinburgh, Scotland (ironically starring an old flame of Shepard's from La MaMa, Brenda Smiley), and ran for four late-night performances. Shepard's agent, Toby Cole, haughtily informed the Traverse Theatre's artistic director, Michael Rudman, that she was "frankly shocked" that they pirated the script.[49]

On April 29, after a few previews, Shepard and Smith performed in the American Place Theatre's New York premiere of *Cowboy Mouth* at St. Clement's Church, with its director, Bob Glaudini, playing the Lobster Man, a restaurant deliveryman in a big red plastic lobster suit. Shepard had contacted Wynn Handman to ask for the American Place, insisting that *Cowboy Mouth* was "the most important thing in my career and I want to act in it." Handman couldn't refuse, though he'd never heard of Patti Smith, and included it as a double bill with *Back Bog Beast Bait*, a surreal one-act that Shepard had written in the fall of 1969, around the time he was married to O-Lan.[50]

Because there was already a Patricia Smith listed in Actors' Equity, and Patti Smith was a theatrical neophyte—"I ain't no actress," she admitted—the union instructed her to change her name, so she listed herself as "Johnny Guitar" (after Nicholas Ray's raucous 1950 New Wave Western starring Joan Crawford).

Shepard wrote a brazen-faced note for the theater's newsletter. "First off let me tell you that I don't want to be a playwright," he started the two-page autobiography, "I want to be a rock and roll star. . . . Writing has become a habit. I like to yodel and dance and fuck a lot. . . . A lot of people think playwrights are some brand of intellectual fruit cake with special answers to special problems that confront the world at large. I think that's a crock of shit."[51]

*Back Bog Beast Bait*, the second play in Shepard's double bill and the one Tony Barsha was scheduled to direct, takes place in a bayou shack, where a cluster of strangers are hiding from a monstrous pig beast in the swamp outside. He was an admirer of the band Credence Clearwater Revival, whose hit song "Born on the Bayou" appeared the same year he wrote *Back Bog Beast Bait*, 1969, and he'd made it clear on numerous occasions that many of his influences derived from his favorite bands. Moreover, around the same time, Shepard wrote a short piece he titled "The Curse of the Raven's Black Feather," in which he writes that he'd always been drawn toward "darkness": "Toward black. Toward death. Toward the South. . . . Away from the quaint North. Away from lobsters and white churches and Civil War graveyards and cracker barrel bazaars. Toward the swamps, the Bayou, the Cajuns, the cotton mouth, the Mardis Gras, the crocodile."[52]

In the one-act play, a swamp gypsy named Gris Gris appears to inform them of the beast and possibly help plan an escape. O-Lan played Gris Gris, who at one point sings Lou Reed and Nico's ethereal song "Wrap Your Troubles in Dreams." (Shepard and the Holy Modal Rounders had opened for the Velvet Underground, with Nico, prior to his writing *Back Bog Beast Bait* in 1969, right around the time he'd first begun pursuing O-Lan.)[53] In that first draft, Gris Gris had been a gentle, sprite-like creature, much like O-Lan. Then Shepard rewrote the dialogue, and suddenly, Tony Barsha fumed, "the sweet little swamp girl turns into Patti Smith!" "And I knew I was in trouble from that point on," Barsha said, "because O-Lan does not do 'evil,' or 'bad,' or whatever you want to call it, which is what it was. It was a dark character."[54]

O-Lan was now, in every respect, miscast in the role of her husband's mistress. It got even messier. She listed herself in the program as O-Lan Johnson-Shepard, though by that time she was romantically involved with Bob Glaudini, *Cowboy Mouth*'s director and costar as the Lobster Man, who replaces Slim in the end, and he was O-Lan's costar as the Preacher in *Back Bog Beast Bait*. O-Lan would stand backstage as Shepard and Smith acted out their love affair to a crowd of strangers, while O-Lan and their director played out another backstage affair to the cast and crew. Barsha was a hapless observer as O-Lan's ex-boyfriend. "I was right in the middle of this whole romantic mess," he said. "It was hard for me. That it was all under the surface made it worse."[55]

But the tension at the theater was its own prowling pig beast, which revealed itself in unanticipated ways during performances. At one preview, they performed for a group of local school kids, a common enough occurrence in theater, though their teachers couldn't have known what they were in for. Smith tenderly thought at the time that the constant disruptions made the children "liberating" collaborators. But Shepard was far less charitable. "Fuck you!" he howled at the kids, then fiercely pounded on his electric guitar strings, bombarding them with sonic distortion.[56]

This group of unruly schoolchildren wound up being some of the timeliest theatergoers of the avant-garde scene. The run was scheduled through June 5, but not even critics got a glance. As the *Village Voice*'s Michael Feingold reported, "Those who hadn't been at the opening night had missed the show." Feingold was heartbroken, as he had tickets for the second night's performance, when, after *Back Bog Beast Bait* was performed, Smith walked out onstage and apologized to the audience. Shepard had gone missing, she explained, and *Cowboy Mouth* was canceled.[57]

One of Shepard's friends heard afterward that *Cowboy Mouth* was "one of the wildest autobiographies he ever produced and one of the most exciting performances they've ever seen—the few that got to see it." Peter Stampfel, who attended a preview, said many years later that it was "psychodrama in that they were acting out their love affair onstage, and it was fucking amazing to see." A couple of years later, when the lore of the short-lived run had captured the popular imagination, Kevin O'Connor joked that a revival of the duo starring in *Cowboy Mouth* could now play Madison Square Garden.[58]

Two close friends who did attend the legendary performance were Georgia and Walter Hadler. In the final scene, they remembered, Slim hands the Lobster Man the gun, smiles, and then, Walter Hadler said, "pauses a moment and turns to look at Cavale. They stare at each other for a moment." Shepard, according to the Hadlers, then peered into the audience, saw them, and broke the fourth wall: "Hey Walt!" "And he walks down to the edge of the stage," Hadler said with a laugh, and Shepard started chatting with him: "Hi, what's goin' on? What's happening?" Right after that, he exited the stage, and the performance ended because Shepard hadn't told anyone where he went.[59]

*Cowboy Mouth* closed after opening night on April 29. There was no replacing Shepard. He abandoned the show and, as abruptly, Smith and O-Lan. The next day, he absconded with the Rounders for a show at Franconia College in New Hampshire. "It didn't work out," he said of the production, "because the thing was too emotionally packed. I suddenly realized I didn't want to exhibit myself like that, playing my life onstage. It was like being in an aquarium."[60]

"The sad part was watching O-Lan and Patti sit there commiserating over Sam's departure," Barsha said. "It was pathetic. . . . They're holding each other and popping Kleenexes under their eyes and all that." Shepard soon after phoned O-Lan and told her he was finished with Patti Smith. If she didn't take him back, he threatened, he might do something "drastic," like move to South America. O-Lan had written him off months before, but eventually assented. "It was Sam's way to dictate to women," Peter Stampfel remembered, "and they tended to go along with it." Smith received a parting gift from her soon-to-be ex-lover (though she didn't realize that's what it was at the time), an envelope full of money to help sustain her while she progressed as a poet-musician. He found out on May 15 that he had been granted a Guggenheim Fellowship for a year, which in all likelihood helped finance his generosity.[61]

Over his last year in New York, Shepard sketched out a batch of short stories, poems, and monologues that would later comprise his slim collection *Hawk Moon*, which he'd dedicate to Patti Smith. *Hawk Moon* is deeply personal, full of violent dreamscapes of inner rage, and the book's panoply of emotions convey the wreckage of his mind in New York. In fact, it was so personal, so eclectic in subject and form, so casual a pastiche, that the book made an inaudible blip on the media's radar, but it swiftly gained a cult following, along with serving as a love letter to Smith.[62]

*Cowboy Mouth*'s final word is "escape." Smith mused to a reporter that they "were only trying to talk about two people that were destined—two big dreamers who came together but were destined to come to a sad end. . . . It was the true story of Sam and I. We knew we couldn't stay together. He was going to go back to his wife . . . and I was gonna go on my way. . . . But even though it was an unhappy love affair," she said, "it was a very happy union. He inspired me to be stronger and make my move." For Shepard, though he did love Smith, his time in New York was an ungodly episode. "Everything," he said, "seemed to be shattering."[63]

# PART II

# 1971–1990

Sam was always taking chances, always being original, somebody who was willing to fail and fail interestingly. And if you're willing to fail interestingly, you tend to succeed interestingly.

—Edward Albee

Sam Shepard is what a star is supposed to be—a ball of fire in a black sky. Brilliant, but very far away.

—Marsha Norman

CHAPTER 9

# THE LONDON FRINGE

Shepard, O-Lan, and Jesse sailed on the *Queen Elizabeth II* to Southampton, England, in October 1971. He'd chosen England in part because it was, in his words, "the rock 'n' roll center of the world," and thus an ideal place to kick-start a music career. England was also home to some of Shepard's favorite bands—the Rolling Stones, the Beatles, the Who, the Kinks, Pink Floyd, and the rest of the phenomenon tabloids back in the States had dubbed "the British Invasion." More important, it was to construct an ocean-sized distance between himself and the emotional turmoil of New York, and, for that reason, to save his marriage. Artistically, he said, "I felt I was drying out. Then there was some trouble with drugs, women. I just wanted an alternative, and I was somewhat lazy because I chose somewhere they spoke English."[1]

But even that far from New York, Shepard still felt emotionally unmoored. One word he used time and again to define his mental state throughout the 1970s was "fractured." He'd created too many "selves" back in New York—country boy, playwright, lover, rocker, husband, father—and each was jockeying for supremacy. Now he was thrust into a new role to grapple with: American. It was only after arriving in his newly adopted land that, like so many expats, Shepard discovered what it actually meant to be an American; and the arrogant notion of American exceptionalism stood out in especially high relief. "Americans get so absorbed inside it, there's a blindness," Shepard told a British reporter. Once he'd moved away, he said, "I realized its isolation, I guess. Its cut-offness. The sense of it being an entity unto itself, not related to the rest of the world. A lot of the inventiveness about America comes from that sense that we're the only beings on the planet."[2]

By the time they landed, small theater groups in London had already revived *La Turista*, *Icarus's Mother*, *Chicago*, *Red Cross*, and *The Holy Ghostly*. And they staged at least a dozen more productions while he was there, including three world premieres. "Everybody was incredibly generous toward me," he said. "Maybe it was the notion of American avant-garde, or whatever you want to call it. I don't know. There was a strange kind of envy about America. Not from the point of view of its power, or of the superficial things. From the point of view of the adventure of it." Shepard Fever was so prevalent in London, in fact, he swiftly relinquished any lingering dream of rock and roll splendor. Rock bands in London were a dime a dozen anyway. Shepard was greeted as a full-blown celebrity as he hobnobbed among the city's theater crowd. He was an avant-garde playwright, the Londoners assured him, and that's what they wanted him to be.[3]

As the British arts critic Jasper Rees wrote about the arrival of the "genius" of Off-Off-Broadway, "His reputation from the New York Underground for courting danger and living on the edge went before him, and the savage immediacy of his plays found a natural home in the small-space houses of the capital." Shepard still soured to the encroachments of fame. His childhood dream had now been realized, more in fact than he'd bargained for, and he found its lack of anonymity emotionally taxing: "Lo and behold it all came true much faster than I'd ever dreamed, and suddenly I was caught in the little nightmare of my own making."[4]

* * *

The theater scene in London that greeted Shepard and O-Lan was radically different from the one they'd left in downtown New York. For one thing, there was almost no alternative theater in London before the late sixties. Everything was relatively conventional until the Americans started coming over—the Living Theatre, the Open Theater, La MaMa Troupe—usually to the Edinburgh Festival, not London, which had few alternative performance spaces as yet. But London's theatrical "fringe," their nascent answer to Off-Off-Broadway, had just begun staging avant-garde dramas at small-capacity houses such as the Royal Court's Theatre Upstairs, the Basement Theatre at King's Head, the Open Space, the Roxy, the SoHo Poly, and the Hampstead Theatre Club, and as with OOB, Shepard's plays would appear in every single one of them.[5]

The London-based director Charles Marowitz helped the family settle in, eventually arranging a hospitable home in a redbrick town house at 62A Pilgrim's Lane. It was a garden flat, and behind it was the sprawling Hampstead Heath with duck ponds for Jesse. "It's a lot like being in the country while still being in a city," Shepard wrote home. There the Shepards settled for three years, sailing back and forth to Nova Scotia each summer.[6]

Their new life in cosmopolitan London was a "flurry of activity," as Shepard described it to his family back in Bradbury: he'd started another rock play, signed up for alto saxophone lessons, stayed off drugs, and indulged in English pursuits such as greyhound racing, watching soccer and boxing, and drinking pints of porter. Despite his relinquishing dreams of rock stardom, Shepard still made sure that drumming was a core part of his life there too, and he played with the bassist Steve Gilmore, and wrote the lyrics for "Song for Marlene," a Velvet Underground–style love ballad dedicated to Marlene Dietrich, by the science fiction and fantasy writer Michael Moorcock's band the Deep Fix. "I much prefer playing music really to theatre," he told the British director Ken Chubb. "Nothing communicates emotions better than music, not even the greatest play in the world."[7] But that wouldn't stop him from trying.

That October, Shepard read *In the Jungle of Cities*, Bertolt Brecht's battle between two obstinate men; and the previous February, he'd attended Heathcote Williams's *AC/DC* at the Brooklyn Academy of Music's Chelsea Theater Center. Williams's apocalyptic vision of media mind-control luxuriates in the kind of warped hipster slang that Shepard adopted for a new full-length rock play. "Not only was the language uncanny but it also had the aura of assault about it," he said about *AC/DC*, and was inspired to write an American version of the two plays combined, using the structure of combat, "somewhere between the old classic Western and rockstar nihilism."[8]

For a month, he wrote a three-act epic called, in a phrase he took from Stéphane Mallarmé's poem "Distress," "The Tooth of Crime." It was a prison drama, but when he finished, he said, "it was a complete piece of shit." So he tossed the script in the sink, burned it, and an hour later started another with the same title. By New Year's Eve, he'd completed *The Tooth of Crime (A Play with Music in Two Acts)*, his most ambitious achievement to date.[9]

*The Tooth of Crime* builds upon *Melodrama Play*'s basic plot—a top-of-the-charts musician is overshadowed by his younger counterpart. But as Anthony Burgess had done ten years before with *A Clockwork Orange*, Shepard devised an operatic rock and roll patois for his characters that refracts reality in a grotesquely exaggerated form. "It seemed to me that rock and roll was beginning to lose its original fire and brass balls," he said of the play's premise.[10]

*The Tooth of Crime* takes place in the futuristic gangland Shepard was certain New York would descend into within thirty or forty years. The play culminates in a lyrical clash between the reigning monarch Hoss (Elvis Presley/Buddy Holly) and his nihilistic challenger Crow (Keith Richards/Lou Reed). Edward Parone, the director for the 1973 West Coast premiere, summed up the plot as "Rock Superstars Battle for Control of the Empire." The play posits what Shepard fervently believed, that an original artist's vision is inevitably commercialized and repackaged for the masses. This is why Shepard rebuffed going commercial: "It turns experimentation into exploitation," he said. "When that happens, you've reached a dead end."[11]

* * *

Despite Shepard's warm welcome and active social life in London's arts community, he and O-Lan were miserable over their first months in

London. The chaos and instability of their New York life—the affairs, the drugs, the sense of feeling lost but with a baby—had all taken their toll, and they wrote to the Darks for help. Johnny and Scarlett Dark's solution for them was a secretive quasireligion founded by the Greco-Armenian leader G. I. Gurdjieff known by its members as the Work. Gurdjieff taught that all of humankind is asleep, and only through the "work" of self-observation do we have a chance of awakening.

At the meetings of London's "system," Shepard felt like a "'bad boy' trying to shape up to my imagination of the 'Conscious Ones'—the real adults." He was terrified of being thrown out for crass behavior, and O-Lan would embarrass him by asking the members hard questions about women's role in the Work. (Gurdjieff's philosophy, however reformist in theory, upheld rigid gender roles among their members.) The required reading for those interested in joining the London system was Gurdjieff's most renowned student and interpreter P. D. Ouspensky's intellectually challenging, often obscure, and highly technical treatise titled *In Search of the Miraculous: Fragments of an Unknown Teaching*, the result of eight years of study under Gurdjieff.[12]

You have to work just to understand Ouspensky's book, and Shepard worked very hard indeed. Above all, the Work was about, as he scribbled in a margin, "letting go": Gurdjieff told Ouspensky, "A man must die, that is, he must free himself from a thousand petty attachments and identifications which hold him in the position in which he is." The "indivisible I" is received in effervescent flashes at first, but with work—and some mystics had reportedly reached this state—the rest disappears "all at once and forever."[13] He admitted in a notebook titled "Fractured" that he had indeed observed his "indivisible I" in spurts, but only momentarily, and only right when he woke up in the morning. And then, he wrote, "I have a suspicion that I'm just a scared kid. Still. Worse. I've disguised so deep I don't even recognize myself."[14]

Members "in the system" were told not to proselytize, but *The Tooth of Crime* broadcasts the Work's impact on Shepard from its opening scene. Like Shepard, Hoss has adopted many guises—cowboy, outlaw, blues man, rocker. But Crow projects faith and courage and trust in his own "indivisible I" for inspiration and success. Accessing the "indivisible I" was an aspirational goal reserved for mystics in the Work, but Shepard had to convince himself, through writing plays and engaging the Work, that his future as an artist would be that of Crow's: "I believe in my mask," Crow proudly sings. "The man I made up is me."[15]

The Work offered his mind a clear path to discipline, but perhaps more important, it was the means to overcome his anger and self-doubt. On a psychological and spiritual level, Roxanne Rogers said, the Work unquestionably helped her brother: "Sam's work with Gurdjieff gave him a path to discipline and allowed him to rise above his own self-pity and human confusion to really stay connected with some universal voice, rather than just sinking into his father's terrible fate."[16]

* * *

That spring, 1972, it was time to get back to the kind of work that paid and take full advantage of his reputation in London's emergent fringe theater movement. At the Royal Court Theatre, O-Lan worked with the American expat director Nancy Meckler, a vanguard of the London fringe who ran an experimental theater company called Freehold. Meckler first knew her as O-Lan Johnson, and often drove her home. When O-Lan referred to her husband, Meckler in time asked his name. "Sam Shepard," she responded. Meckler kept her cool, but inside she was thinking, "Oh my God, Sam Shepard! I adore Sam Shepard!"[17]

It was no accident Meckler hadn't known her friend's husband's name. As an avant-garde theater actor and writer herself, with strong theater credits to her name, O-Lan was ambitious like Shepard, but overshadowed by him. She kept her marriage secret until she felt "established" in a group of people or with a new friend like Meckler. It wasn't easy, she wrote to Roxanne in Bradbury, trying to make a name for oneself in London while married to "the Great Shep."[18]

Meckler owned a copy of *Five Plays*, and through O-Lan, Shepard gave her permission to put on *Icarus's Mother* at a converted garage in Kentish Town they called the Roxy. When *Time Out* magazine asked

Shepard what the play was about, he replied, "I never know what to say when somebody says what are the plays about? They're about the moment of writing." But he offered a more candid response to Meckler before rehearsals started: *Icarus's Mother*, he said, was about "fear of flying." That was all that she needed. For Shepard, Meckler's directing style was a welcome change from the American psychological approach ("all that weird Stanislavski sort of stuff"), and he adored her stripped-down production. "Theatrically," Meckler said, "Sam wanted things to be very simple and very pure. . . . He wanted theater in the raw."[19]

Charles Marowitz, also an American expat, was the founding director of downtown London's newly established Open Space Theatre, and when he first met the greatly overrated, to his mind, Sam Shepard face-to-face, he was utterly disarmed. Marowitz had been resolute in resisting the "Shepard Bandwagon" mentality infusing the London underground theater scene, which he knew emanated directly from Greenwich Village. But the twenty-eight-year-old man before him was "the personification of that conquering charm that is sometimes bred in the southern and western sections of America." Shepard, he said, was "Huckleberry Finn minus the fishing rod," though in rehearsals, Marowitz chided, he was less Huckleberry Finn and more Bela Lugosi.[20]

Marowitz agreed to direct *The Tooth of Crime*, but knew the show would be a slog to sell tickets for. *The Tooth of Crime*, he said, "is the most cynical and dismal forecast of the American future that has yet been written and one has to go back to Pound and Eliot to find a parallel to its pessimism." Like the play's dueling protagonists, the two actual men locked horns throughout the rehearsals. Marowitz accused Shepard of relying on "brow-beating interior probes" without applying stage techniques; Shepard accused Marowitz of destroying an already shaky morale by imposing an "emotional tyranny" on himself and the cast.[21]

Shepard and his family absconded to Nova Scotia before it opened. In spite of the clash of egos during rehearsals, *The Tooth of Crime* eventually premiered at the Open Space on July 17, and the London critics mainly found it a portentous bore. But when the play opened in the United States on November 9, 1972, at the McCarter Theatre in

Princeton, with the future star Frank Langella as Hoss, it was hailed as Shepard's finest play and won him his fourth Obie Award.

* * *

That summer, 1972, Shepard and O-Lan agreed that their old Volvo was in good enough shape for a road trip across the United States. On September 22, they embarked on a barnstorming tour of the West, starting in Reno, Nevada. Then they traveled through Utah, Buffalo Bill's Wyoming, and Little America, where they visited the Wind River Indian Reservation, and on through South Dakota and finally Iowa and Illinois.[22]

Early that October, Shepard, O-Lan, and Jesse arrived in Lombard, Illinois, to visit his grandma Helen and his father, Sam Sr., at the Rogers homestead at 70 North Columbine Lane. The meeting provided the seed, along with previous visits with Joyce Aaron and Nancy Mandel, for his future tour de force *Buried Child*. Grandma Helen (who inspired the character Halie in *Buried Child*) was now in her mideighties, with her son Daniel "Buzz" Rogers living nearby. Shepard couldn't help but remember another of her five sons, his uncle Dick (Bradley in the play), accosting him in Helen's kitchen. "I had long hippy hair and a bad attitude," Shepard recalled, and he "pinned me up against the refrigerator with one of his crutches (the pants leg from his missing limb was waving around like a flag), his blue eyes bore into me with that same maniacal intensity that my old man had and he said to me, 'Don't you ever forget that you are living in the greatest goddamn country in the world!'"[23]

Shepard and his father hadn't spoken for a long while, and Sam Sr.'s life had taken another tragic turn. What happened in the recent past must have been the emotional epicenter of the Lombard house in the summer of 1972.

After divorcing Jane, Sam Sr. had gone on a yearslong drinking bender. He got remarried to a local piano bar performer named Ruth Maxwell, and they lived for almost a year in Ensenada, Mexico, on the

Baja peninsula, in an "idyllic yet funky" trailer on a cliff overlooking the Pacific Ocean. Sam Sr. had also been a repeat offender for vagrancy and spent stints in the California Institution for Men, a minimum-security prison in Chino. Roxanne was the only child left at home, but Ruth wouldn't take her to see him, and it was too painful for her mother to bring her to visit him. As a consolation, Roxanne would take her allowance from Jane and send it to her father in prison.[24]

His incarcerations weren't the worst of it. On November 14, 1971, Sam Sr. was driving through the Cajon Pass on the Mojave Freeway with Ruth and her aunt Mae and uncle George Maxwell when they careened down an embankment, hurling all four passengers from the vehicle. "They rented a car," Sandy recalled. "It was him and his wife and her aunt and uncle in the back seat, and they were driving down to Mexico, and the car lost a wheel. There was a crash, and [Ruth's aunt Mae] was killed. My dad didn't recover from that. He blamed himself, and Ruth blamed him. Everything was terrible, and then they got a divorce."[25]

During the months that followed the lethal car accident, Sam Sr. embarked on another drinking spree, traveled the country aimlessly, and repeatedly found himself on the wrong side of the law. After things had gone completely haywire, he followed the poet Robert Frost's credo, "'Home is the place where, when you have to go there, / They have to take you in,'" and traveled back to Lombard.[26]

By the time his son arrived in Illinois, Sam Sr. was "off the booze for the time being," Shepard wrote, grateful that Sam's vicious side was subdued. "The main thing is his feeling of loneliness I think. At times he seems very distant & silent." Shepard observed in his journal:

> Dad looked really different—his face is fatter & the skin's starting to sag—his mouth looked kind of busted up from his car accident I guess—he seems all broken & defeated by himself—he can't drive a car because he can't get a license on account of the accidents he's had—he can't get a job because of his arrests—Grandma said that the F.B.I. had sent a record of his arrests to Illinois so it's like his past is following him around—it's really pathetic to see him like this—having

to be driven around by his mother & everyone on the lookout to see he doesn't take a drink.[27]

Within a year, Sam Sr. would move from Lombard to Santa Fe, New Mexico, and work piecemeal jobs at factories and as a janitor, just enough work to pay for liquor. Each of his letters to Shepard included a plaintive appeal for him to send money. "You're famous now," came the refrain, "why not lend your old man a hand?" Out of a sense of filial duty, Shepard nearly always did send money.

* * *

The Sheps departed for England on October 3. But their visit in Lombard was hardly an antidote for Shepard's fractured mental state, so upon returning to London, he redoubled his efforts in the Work. On October 19, he and O-Lan reentered London's Work system by driving their Anglia van to attend a "movement," or Work-inspired "sacred dance" at the Gurdjieff Society's house in Bray. (G. I. Gurdjieff, in his travels through Asia and Africa, collected eurythmic "movements" that he believed helped him shed external projections and unlock his true self.) It wasn't a joyful reunion. "First off," Shepard complained to Johnny Dark, "we had to go to Charing Cross & buy some dumb ballet shoes at some fruity ballet store. Then we had to [dance] like little wooden soldiers all in lines to some morbid piano music all in the same rhythm being dictated by some fat little tank of a woman in a long black dress who fancies herself as the reincarnation of George Ivanovich himself."[28]

But still, Shepard clung to the Work, which sternly condemned negative emotions, especially in artists.[29] Consequently, Shepard worked even harder to impose self-discipline: he struggled his way through every recipe in a bestselling French cookbook, read Aeschylus and Sophocles, and on the kitchen fridge he posted a weekly schedule for himself. Monday: Walk, Tuesday: Read, Wednesday: Cook, and so on. "They were trying to live this very pure life," according to Nancy Meckler, "with Gurdjieff and walking and cooking, you know what I mean. Very domestic."[30] Murray Mednick came to visit and was "really impressed," he said. "When I saw Sam I saw that something must be going on that's good because he's no jerk, not stupid, he's not a cult person. So I believed him. And it was Sam, his change made a huge impression, who changed my life." Mednick was trying to break a methadone habit, and soon, thanks to Shepard, he became a lifelong member of the Work.[31] "Sam had a serious search in him," Mednick went on. "He was in search of the truth: What was it like? What are we doing here on Earth? Where are we supposed to be? What am I supposed to do? Who am I?"[32]

London's Gurdjieffian leader Basil Tilley exuded such warmth and reassurance that he became a father figure when Shepard desperately needed one. Celebrating Christmas at Tilley's, he told Dark, he felt like a kid again: "At last I'd found a father. I felt protected and sheltered from the world outside, as though nothing in the world mattered but this experience, this huge family with Mr. Tilley at the head."[33]

London offered him another restful distraction from his dysfunctional family and his theater career: greyhound racing. Shepard grew increasingly infatuated with the sport, and he bought a share of one of the dogs, Crazy Horse, who raced at the White City and Harringay tracks. Then he bought a whole racing dog for himself, an exemplary Irish greyhound called Keywall Spectre. He was a formidable black-gray hound reared in Derry, Northern Ireland, who lived with Shepard and his family as a pet for Jesse on his off-hours between races. "I didn't go to the theater," he said when asked about his London days. "I went to dog racing."[34]

Greyhound racing (using a mechanical hare) and coursing (a real hare) had been a pastime of the British aristocracy for generations, but it was now a working-class and Irish-dominated sport. It was also the most watched sport in England after soccer. Greyhounds, Shepard wrote in his article on the topic, "Less Than Half a Minute," could run up to forty-five miles per hour and leave a Thoroughbred in the dust after four hundred yards. "If you watch [the fastest] close you can see that they're possessed. Something takes them over like a Voodoo god." He soon owned two and a half racing dogs, but his favorite was Keywall Spectre, and the dog would inspire Shepard's one-act *Blue Bitch*, which premiered at Theater Genesis under Murray Mednick's direction on January 19, 1973. The star of the production was Patti Smith.[35]

* * *

Shepard had a solid history of raising and competing well-bred dogs by then, but no matter how many stalls he'd mucked out as a teenager, his upbringing in Bradbury had by no means made him an authentic cowboy. Nevertheless, he felt deeply drawn to cowboy culture, casually drew from it for his plays and personal style, and his road trip with his family out west inspired his next play. He imagined a gangster named Fingers, an urbane tourist describing Buffalo Bill's Cody, Wyoming, the way Shepard himself observed it the previous summer:

> Saloons with rifles tacked up on the walls. Real cowboys with leather chaps. Indians shuffling through the dusty streets. Buffalo Bill's name plastered on everything. And at night. At night it was magical. Like praying. I'd never heard such a silence as that. Nowhere on earth. So vast and lonely. Just the brisk cold night blowing in through the hotel window. And outside, the blue peaks of the Big Horn Mountains. The moon shining on their snowy caps. The prairie stretching out and out like a great ocean. I felt that God was with me then. The earth held me in its arms.[36]

In Shepard's next play, an expansion on *Blue Bitch* called *Geography of a Horse Dreamer: A Mystery in Two Acts*, a Wyoming cowboy named Cody is held captive by two thugs who talk like 1930s-movie-style mobsters, a dialect, Shepard said, he took from the American noir detective novelists Raymond Chandler and Dashiell Hammett. "Just remember the old iron here," threatens one, nodding to his pistol. "She gets very ticklish in a nervous situation."[37]

"Mr. Artistic Cowboy," as one of the gangsters calls Cody, has been shunted around an endless trail of cheap hotels, as he wields a magic power the gangsters greedily hunger after: Cody's imagination is so extraordinary, he can pick winning racehorses in his dreams. The theme of this "atavistic mystery," then, as Shepard announced in his *Time Out* display ad, "is the cannibalism of genius, the manacling of the life force."[38]

*Geography of a Horse Dreamer* would importantly be Shepard's directorial debut, and he'd go on to direct many more. But even by then he had already proven his chops: "In every argument I have ever had with him," Ralph Cook said in 1967, "about staging, use of sound, interpretation, etc., Sam has always been right. He has an instinctive sense of what is theatrically right for his plays that goes beyond rules and preconceptions."[39]

He didn't want to cast the kind of actors he knew in the Village, "throwing themselves against the walls in the name of freedom of expression," but neither did he want English actors "grooved into mannered theatricality." Instead, he got from Meckler's Freehold the young Irish actor Stephen Rea, one of London's most innovative acting talents, to star as the gambling clairvoyant from Wyoming. At first, Shepard thought Rea was "extremely timid," perhaps too timid for his taste. "Then, slowly, he began to bring things out into the open," he said, "and the things he brought were from a deep inner territory that he must have been investigating the whole time. . . . Ever since then I've migrated toward working with actors with this mysterious earmark of inner courage."[40]

Rehearsals at the Royal Court were refreshingly unbuttoned and plainspoken, a stark contrast to the British directors faced by the cast, which included another standout actor with a big future, Bob Hoskins. Shepard was different as a director, Rea reminisced, "in the sense that he removed all the obstacles. . . . He was very clear. I remember thinking after a day and a half of rehearsal that if we'd known the lines, we could have done the play right then. It was remarkable."[41] For guidance, Shepard turned to the theater guru Peter Brook's *The Empty Space* and explained his approach by borrowing from the title. Directing was to imagine, Shepard said,

> a nearly empty space which is the stage where a picture, a sound, a color sneaks in and tells me a certain kind of story. I feel that language

> is a veil hiding demons and angels which the characters are always out of touch with. Their quest in the play is the same as ours in life—to find those forces, to meet them face to face and end the mystery. I'm pulled toward images that shine in the junk.[42]

Stephen Rea was the first shining image audiences would glimpse in the production, manacled to a hotel bed and dangling from the headboard like a drugged-out scarecrow. He wore gigantic mirrored sunglasses, a mass of unkempt black hair, and a plaid cowboy shirt and suspenders like his Wyoming brethren, who would arrive at the motel room, guns blazing, to rescue and corral him back home.[43]

*Geography of a Horse Dreamer* opened on February 21, 1974, at the Royal Court's Theatre Upstairs. Again, the British critics knocked the effort, and the play's autobiographical elements were obvious to anyone who knew anything about Shepard and his work.[44] Ken Chubb, one of Shepard's greatest advocates in London, found an interesting paradox in the play and its rather poor British reception. The problem with much of Shepard's style of drama, Chubb argued, is that the images he manifests onstage are often more filmic than theatrical, "but, their outrageousness is only acceptable in terms of the theater. That may be why he writes for the stage." (This may also be why so many independent filmmakers, especially European ones, became so smitten with his work.) One British reviewer, who otherwise considered Shepard to be the lone savior of American theater, pleaded with him: "Let us hope that the greyhounds will not distract Shepard from filling his house—or at least a few plays—with other comic dreams from America's unconscious into which he has already delved so deeply."[45]

* * *

O-Lan had been having hard luck finding acting work in England, and her friend Dinah Stabb couldn't act because she was seven months pregnant. Stabb was over at the flat one night to commiserate with

O-Lan, when Shepard overheard their grievances, stepped in, and said, "I'll write something for you." "So we all held our breath, crossed our fingers, and waited," said Stabb years later. "It was extraordinary," she exclaimed about his reemergence with a freshly typed script in hand. "It was written by a man, but it didn't feel like that." As O-Lan wrote years later, the play was "a rare excursion into a completely feminine world for Sam."[46]

After the hypermasculine *Geography of a Horse Dreamer* came Shepard's all-women play *Little Ocean*, about the torments and joys of pregnancy, birth, and motherhood. "Little Ocean" refers to the increased water in the womb just prior to birth, when, as O-Lan playing Lo says, "you turn into a little ocean." It also tangentially refers to a young woman's first orgasm: "Like being far away. Way out on the ocean. She said it was like floating. It was like sailing away. She'd never felt anything like it. Ever."[47]

Stephen Rea directed *Little Ocean*, which consists of a series of conversations and role-playing sketches among three women based on O-Lan (with a baby), Dinah Stabb (seven months pregnant), and the British actor Caroline Hutchison (newly pregnant). Shepard wrote the play explicitly for these three struggling actresses confronting motherhood for the first time, but in the process, he spontaneously captured young motherhood with wildly funny role-play and genuine compassion. "He wrote it for a need those women had," Rea said. "Firstly a need to work and also to talk about something so essentially feminine."[48]

*Little Ocean* opened for a late-night, two-week engagement at the Hampstead Theatre Club on March 25, 1974. The critic Peter Ansorge of *Plays and Players* concluded that *Little Ocean*, along with *Cowboy Mouth*'s revival at the SoHo Poly, made Shepard "a revivifying influence on the English fringe." Together, the plays cleared up for Ansorge "the American writer's current high status among the *cognoscenti* of the London underground." It was simply because Shepard's dramas, the critic argued, "brought us nearer to the popular culture of the young than any equivalent entertainment being offered in London."[49]

A few months after *Little Ocean*'s premiere, Roxanne Rogers arrived in London and asked her older brother why he didn't write more parts for women, as he'd done with that play. He told her he simply wasn't good at channeling women. "That is not what I do well," he insisted, despite the play's strong evidence to the contrary. "Other people can do that better."[50]

In January 1974, Shepard next composed his avant-garde tour de force *Action*, a one-act play that would remain high on his list of favorites, and it was the only play for which he spoke each line out loud before committing it to paper. Accordingly, he wrote, "it comes the closest to sounding on stage exactly like it was written."[51] Its four characters were based on himself, O-Lan, Murray Mednick, and his wife, Kathleen Cramer, who'd all gathered together socially in both London and Nova Scotia.

Shepard also applied the Work in *Action* as a foundation upon which to create four fractured souls who've been caught up in a whirl of multiple selves, and the play ultimately became a Gurdjieffian exercise: throughout the ironic inaction of *Action*, Shepard is sorting out his various selves for observation. "The struggle with identification," he wrote in his *Action* notes, "to see myself identified—to know that that's what happens—the outside strikes different notes in me—causes different reactions in me different parts—I am those reactions—to watch this process—to *see* it taking place in me is work toward self-observation each reaction is a different 'I' which I believe is the whole of me, even though it's only a temporary situation."[52]

*Action* portrays the horrors of isolation and captivity when catastrophe strikes (a worldwide pandemic, say) and the humdrum physical and mental "actions" it takes for people to maintain their sanity. Four characters, Jeep (Shepard's character), Lupe (O-Lan's), Shooter (Mednick's), and Liza (Cramer's), are hunkered down during an unspecified apocalyptic event. The group enact a series of mini-diversions in hopes of fending off their existential fear and its attendant emotional boredom—roast a turkey, clean a fish, read a sci-fi novel, string up laundry, smash chairs. They're all searching for their indivisible selves, but especially Jeep. "I look forward to my life," Jeep says in the opening line. "I'm looking forward to uh—me. The way I picture me." It is Christmas, and a small Christmas tree with blinking lights stands upstage. When asked for a teaser, Shepard responded, "It's a surrealistic play about a turkey dinner."[53]

Nancy Meckler was invited by Shepard to direct *Action*'s world premiere on September 15 at the Royal Court Upstairs, with Stephen Rea as Jeep. "Do you want me to tell you what I was thinking about?" Shepard asked her. Meckler admitted she didn't have a clue what the play meant, and he said, "It's about fear of time passing." "Brilliant," she thought, "fear of time passing—of death. That's it. That's all I need. We're off!" With that one clue, like his central theme of "fear of flying" with *Icarus's Mother*, Meckler realized that the characters in *Action* were "doing and saying anything in order to get through it, the fear of time passing. They're not speaking about anything they believe or think or need. They're just trying to find a way through the fear."[54]

Although the reviews for *Action* from the British press were mixed, Meckler also directed the next production of Shepard's minor masterwork and one of the finest one-act plays written by an American. This time, the show would be in New York, at the American Place Theatre, and it was produced there the following year. It would win Shepard another Obie, this time for Best Playwriting.

Whatever Shepard's successes with writing, he told Johnny Dark, the only things keeping him in "boring London" were dog racing and the Work.[55] But soon Shepard learned that he'd be receiving a three-thousand-dollar literary award from the American Academy of Arts and Letters that March, and he knew just how to spend it. The Darks were living near San Francisco, and Shepard wrote to his friend "John," as he called him:

> Let me explain the depth of my dreaming lately: We go through all the pros and cons of buying a house together and we finally settle

for this nifty little ranch somewhere on the outskirts of one of those suburbs. Not too far from all the newsstands and supermarkets yet far enough so that we have a couple of acres or so. . . . We divide the house up evenly between the Sheps and the Darks and sort of float back and forth but each of us has our own special room where we can get obsessive and isolated if we have the inclination. . . . Yessir, we're on our way boy![56]

CHAPTER 10

# CALIFORNIA DREAMING

The Sheps and the Darks reunited in the Bay Area of Northern California in October 1974. "An extraordinary little galaxy of people," Shepard called the collective that included himself, O-Lan, Jesse, Johnny and Scarlett (who married in 1972), and O-Lan's teenage sister, Kristy Johnson. Their rented ranch house in Marin County, at 6 Endeavor Drive, was situated on a winding hillside road in Corte Madera in Mill Valley, north of the Golden Gate Bridge and within driving distance of San Francisco. It was a city Shepard considered "innocent, rich, and a little bit silly," but a much finer place to settle than the "sprawling, demented snake of L.A. to the south. Its fanged mouth wide open, eyes blazing, paralyzed in a lunge of pure paranoia."[1]

Mill Valley lies along a series of peaks, ridges, and canyons that contain six mini-valleys bordered on the north by Mount Tamalpais (Mount Tam), and on the south by Richardson Bay. Now an affluent bedroom community, Mill Valley was then a semirural region locals nicknamed "Nut Hill" for its history of attracting writers, actors, musicians, and countercultural dropouts. Over the twentieth century, Jack London, Dorothea Lange, Jack Kerouac, Gary Snyder, Joyce Maynard, Carlos Santana, and Peter Coyote all lived there or in its vicinity. The house in Corte Madera, Shepard said, was "temporary digs," but Scarlett wrote to reassure Jane Rogers that her son was taking full advantage of the region's natural beauty, "places unspoiled to walk, horse riding, & country stuff that he likes."[2]

* * *

It took Shepard months to find a theater company in the Bay Area that would even perform his work. Unlike in London, his reputation in California was marginal—and his work was mainly known through college and regional performances. Initially, Shepard contacted San Francisco's well-funded American Conservatory Theater (ACT), who were "totally unenthusiastic," Shepard said, and they proposed he use their basement, for workshopping and without the public. "It's like they're asleep, lobotomized over there," he complained to the press.[3]

Then, through a friend, the Beat poet Michael McClure (who wrote the introduction for Shepard's 1972 collection *Mad Dog Blues and Other Plays*), Shepard secured a playwright-in-residence spot, with financing from a Rockefeller grant, at San Francisco's only company dedicated to experimental plays, the Magic Theatre. O-Lan also began acting at the Magic, and she performed that March in *The Death and Life of Jesse James*.[4]

Remarkably, just as it had been with the London fringe and Off-Off-Broadway before that, smaller alternative groups in the Bay Area were in a nascent stage, and the Magic Theatre, first established in Berkeley in 1967, was at the forefront. The Magic, said its artistic director, John Lion, promoted "good writing, new material, good actors—and the willingness to let go."[5] Lion released a statement that *Action* would be directed by Shepard himself at the Magic that spring, along with his newest play, *Killer's Head*, an eight-minute monologue by a fictional ranch hand named Mazon who's blindfolded and strapped into an electric chair. (It was this monologue, said the monologist Eric Bogosian, that made him want to do monologues.) Lion also disabused the press that Shepard was an unknown in California. "Anyone seriously interested in theater who hasn't heard of Sam Shepard," he declared, "was either born before 1930 or after 1970."[6]

Nancy Meckler's production of *Action* and *Killer's Head* at the American Place Theatre was just wrapping up when Shepard's, which he directed, opened at the Magic Theatre on May 2. The Magic had moved from Berkeley to 1618 California Street, "a postage stamp space," Shepard said, "with a few, very hard, bleacher-type seats with no back rests" above a British-style pub called the Rose and Thistle. "Miraculously," he wrote to Lee Kissman, the double bill had "turned into an underground hit here," and the run was extended for two extra weeks.[7]

When the local Corte Madera paper asked him how, at thirty-one, he'd managed to produce over twenty-five plays, an exceptionally rare feat in the theater, he just quipped, "I am prolific because I feel a great urgency. I'm trying to write the one play that will forever keep me from having to write another one." In fact, writing was the only thing holding him together.[8]

* * *

While Shepard was directing *Action* and *Killer's Head* in San Francisco, that spring he wrote "Fractured," an original screenplay primarily dedicated to his obsession with horse racing but that also stands as the most illustrative material of his first year in Mill Valley. The character based on Shepard is Massey Loomis, an actor who makes his living modeling as the Marlboro Man, but he only appears at photo shoots to pay off an Appaloosa racehorse he bought with his friend Leroy Mason (based on the poet Gary Snyder). His wife, Lou-Anne (inspired by O-Lan) is bored but determined, with her five-year-old, Bobby Joe, inhabiting her car seat. She's fed up with her husband's fake "cowboy trip" and with living in the "sticks." "See, it's this kind of scene," she describes Corte Madera and the larger Mill Valley area to a friend. "'Milk goats for sale,' chickens, cow flop, trees and hills. Boring. Not a sidewalk in sight."[9]

Massey, though, belies the simulated nature of his cowboy-ness in a way that indicates Shepard recognized its chicanery himself. His is not an authentic roughneck hero in a pearl-snap embroidered shirt but a poseur, however seriously he might take his assumed role. Shepard, of course, would become a Hollywood Western figure, but lamented in his 1973 prose poem "Hollywood" that

> the cowboy dressed in fringe with buckskin gloves, silk bandana, pale clown white makeup, lipstick, eyes thickly made up and a ten gallon hat, holds the reins of his horse decked out in silver studs. The cowboy squints under hot spotlights. The gaffers all giggle. The cowboy sweats but there's nowhere for the sweat to go. He sinks to his knees and screams: "Forgive me Utah! Forgive me!"[10]

Shepard had now, knowingly, placed all of his fractured selves within a single hardened shell. For him, the identity of the cowboy was the strongest choice—manly, self-assured, tight-lipped, born to nature. In this way, his makeover into an iconic cowboy figure was more an act of psychic self-preservation than artistic self-promotion. Cowboy culture and the West, he admitted later,

> were the type of things that built the idea of who I am. This notion of the cowboy, and of the West, and of this solitary character, this person who was able to fend for himself in spite of everything else, to be self-sufficient—a very important thing which gets more and more lost as we move into our idea of civilization. We don't have that quality any more. We don't have that way of testing ourselves.[11]

Shepard's deliberate cowboy costume, however, wouldn't go unnoticed by the press: "The pale jeans, scuffed boots, Levi shirts and huge-buckle belt are his chosen image," a reporter noted, "not the accident of the [cowboy] trade. And the myths that his presence evokes—loner, maverick, cowboy, someone from the beat generation still miraculously lean and strong—were refined or even invented through books or Hollywood; he embodies dreams." Even Patti Smith described him as "a man playing cowboys." His kick-off play *Cowboys* was about just that—playing cowboys, not being them. He'd only observed them in movies, watching Roy Rogers rear up on Trigger from a distance at the Rose Parade, and on the tour out west two years before. "He thinks he's from the heart of goddamn Wyoming," O-Lan's character says in "Fractured." "Every morning the mail box is full of the *Quarter Horse Journal*, *The Appaloosa News*, *The Western Horseman*. It's driving me nuts."[12]

It was driving Johnny Dark nuts too. "He was presenting himself to the world as a cowboy, like a little kid with a cowboy hat," he said with a laugh. "He just kept it going into adulthood. 'I'm a cowboy! You wanna take a picture of me over by this horse with my lariat?'" When Dark was asked what he believed was the essence of Shepard the man, he responded, "Image. It was so, so important to Sam to project a certain image to the world, even to total strangers."[13]

Most people described in these terms are in self-denial, but Shepard was fully cognizant of how preposterous it might seem to others. Still, he fully embraced cowboy culture: he eschewed jazz and rock and roll music, to a large extent, and transformed into a country-and-western music aficionado; he taught Hollywood actors how to skin a deer and fly-fished in Wyoming; he bought an array of guns; he roped horses and competed in rodeos; he bred racehorses and cattle; he rode on cattle drives; and to the end of his life, he rarely looked back.

"He genuinely became a cowboy," Sandy Rogers said. "He just wasn't *raised* as a cowboy."[14]

The screenplay of "Fractured," which remains unproduced, paints Shepard's new life in Corte Madera as a muted background, but his interior life is luridly drawn. Massey's a gifted man, with Pulitzer Prize–winning poet friends. His father-in-law, Jimmie, based on Johnny Dark, is content to work at a used car lot, as Johnny was, while Massey's consumed with ambition, as Shepard was. During an auction, Massey has an epiphany about himself as the horse: the Appaloosa he wants to buy is being watered down before the sale, and he sees himself reflected in the animal—a natural beauty, a winner, being bought and sold by ugly profiteers, only to be broken.

That April, Shepard drove the script of "Fractured" down to Hollywood. There was interest in making it a TV show, but they wanted the story idea, without Shepard's caustic dialogue and philosophizing allegory. "We want disasters," the movie moguls exhorted, not "character dramas." Hollywood's lust for disaster movies, Shepard said, "kept rebounding in my head over and over again to the point where it felt like the whole town was into that, which isn't so incredible. The place is sort of teetering on the verge of annihilation anyway."[15]

Shepard was also drinking far too much daily, and he knew it. He'd been a heavy drinker since his teenage years and coupled drugs with booze in New York. London had served as a minor reprieve for a few years, though he still drank plenty of stout and tequila. Now, he found himself lost in an alcoholic miasma, a period of misery and introspection that was utterly eroding his faith in the transformational power of literature. "Poets don't even rate an interview in hell," an inner voice taunted him.[16] Then a glimmer of hope landed on Shepard's kitchen table: Bob Dylan had called.

* * *

Shepard and Dark arrived home from an aimless drive around Marin County to find a note left for Shepard on their kitchen table. The timing was spooky: Dark had just been going on about how Dylan's luster was fading. "It's hard to see Dylan ever hitting what he once was back in the sixties," Dark mused. On the note, O-Lan had matter-of-factly scrawled a message: "Sam, Bob Dylan called you + made an offer you might not be able to refuse. I'll tell you details when I get back."[17]

"Something won't compute," Shepard muttered to himself. "Dylan called here? Why would Dylan call? I don't even know him."[18]

Shepard learned from an assistant of Dylan's that he was planning a secret tour of the Northeast. He was calling it the Rolling Thunder Revue, and he was looking for a writer to make a guerrilla film of the tour. Shepard needed to leave for New York right away. "That's how it works, right?" Shepard thought. "Dylan calls you and you drop everything."[19]

Shepard left Mill Valley by train in October 1975 and headed east as the presumptive screenwriter for a film of Dylan's Rolling Thunder

Revue, joining the tour for a leg that would consist of thirty performances in twenty-two cities up and across New England and Canada that ran from October 30 to December 8. "It was a little bit unclear what exactly he wanted me to do," Shepard admitted. His old director Jacques Levy was on Dylan's tour "both as a songwriter and one of the tour's central creative architects," and almost certainly recommended him to Dylan. (Levy was also preparing to stage a new production of *Geography of a Horse Dreamer* that December.) Shepard would soon discover that his presence was a low priority for the music legend. "I was just there for the ride, basically," Shepard said. "Dylan's a gypsy," he added later, "and he thrives on that kind of energy, when nobody knows exactly what's going on." And that was how he would approach the film: "a mystery—a process of uncovering with no hope for a solution."[20]

* * *

On October 24, 1975, Shepard ambled into the coffee shop at the Gramercy Park Hotel sporting an Irish flat cap and plaid-checked wool jacket. He was there to meet Bob Dylan, and one of the tour's female managers, Chris O'Dell, was instantly struck by his fresh-faced, "farm boy look." "His face was smooth and clear," she wrote, "innocent and wide-eyed in a way that you didn't see too often in the rock-and-roll world. He hadn't been traumatized by the lifestyle."[21]

O'Dell was especially awestruck by the way this naive-looking cowboy then plopped himself right down next to Dylan, who rarely talked with anyone but his inner circle on the tour; even more so because Dylan, the great sage of the American counterculture, showed an almost fawning deference to the playwright as a fellow artist: "Do you think we should . . . ," she remembered Dylan mumbling, "leaning toward him and creating a space that included just the two of them, shutting the rest of us out." "Sam's got that special knowledge of the underworld," Dylan said decades later. "How do you write all those plays?" he recalled asking him. "Man," Shepard replied. "It's like I commune with the dead." "Yeah," Dylan said. "You'd have to to write plays like that."[22]

Dylan was riding high from his tour the previous year with the Band—what *New Yorker* editor David Remnick once referred to as "the greatest tour ever."[23] It was Dylan's first tour since 1966, when a devastating motorcycle accident forced him into seclusion. Now he was primed to reclaim his former glory, but in what Shepard described as a "circus atmosphere . . . a dog-and-pony show sort of thing." Dylan compared his traveling revue to a musical version of commedia dell'arte, while Shepard imagined the local audiences being inspired the way Shakespeare had been by traveling theater troupes as a boy: "He grew up in Stratford-on-Avon, you know, where these rivers cross, and it was *way* on the outskirts of London. And these troubadours and vagabonds and carnival people from all over were coming into London to perform. And they would stop at this crossroad, at these rivers, and as a kid, he's seein' this. And then he writes those fuckin plays!" He laughed. "Somebody is charged up like that from something passing through their lives."[24]

The majority of shows were played across small-town New England with little advance notice. The tour kicked off in Plymouth, Massachusetts, a historic but economically defeated town with a population of under twenty thousand. The young local audience there was aghast over its astonishing luck. The Beat poet Allen Ginsberg, who was invited along as a kind of patron saint of the revue, explained that they started in Plymouth because the artists considered themselves analogous to the pilgrims, "pilgrims in the sense of searchers, looking for the kingdom of the nation with maybe a different intention—making America a kingdom of poetry, a nation of poetry."[25]

During the Rolling Thunder Revue, Shepard's mind trailed back to boyhood fantasies of the folk hero Pecos Bill, who could lasso a tornado's neck with a snake and "dug the Rio Grande with his bare hands." Ramblin' Jack Elliott (himself a Jewish boy from Brooklyn) had been pontificating to him on the subject of logging trucks when Shepard's mind first wandered to Pecos Bill. "Small-kid cowboy legend," he wrote, "swimming in his tall white hat, black-and-white pony-hide chaps, burbling cactus legends, coyote prairie dog songs, sailing high off the back of every buckin' horse. A wandering, mythical, true American minstrel." He began to examine his own fascination with cowboys, and not-so-secret desire to be one. (His character in Dylan's movie of the tour was listed as Cowboy.) "About the state of cowboys. About 'real life' and 'fantasy.' About making yourself up from everything that's ever touched you. From Pecos Bill to the Rolling Thunder Revue."[26]

Shepard was thus moved to write a tragicomic operetta, a paean to the "the first cowboy of all time," *The Sad Lament of Pecos Bill on the Eve of Killing His Wife*, for San Francisco's bicentennial celebration the following summer. He perceived a "hunger" in the national psyche, predominantly on the East Coast, for Western folk heroes such as Pecos Bill and Paul Bunyan. Then there were the real ones—Wild Bill Hickok, Jesse James, Billy the Kid, Wyatt Earp, and Buffalo Bill. "Even though they were real guys involved in a real environment," he wrote in a logbook he kept on tour, "their deeds were largely invented to satisfy this growing hunger and intrigue from the opposite coast."[27]

Shepard was determined to feed that hunger, and feed on it. In *The Sad Lament*, Pecos Bill, like his creator, pleads his case to his wife Sluefoot Sue's ghost: "I'm bigger than mountains / I'm bigger than time / I'm written in history pages / They'll find me in writing in two thousand years / They'll find me all down through the ages."[28]

But the day after Shepard's thirty-second birthday, he confessed to Chris O'Dell that he had no clue what his role was on the tour. "It's really weird," he told her. "Bob wants me to do a script for a film, but everything is so disorganized and chaotic."[29] It had become obvious to Shepard that his planned screenplay was never going to make it to fruition. "These musicians aren't about to be knocking themselves out memorizing lines in their spare time," he said. They were busy rehearsing, playing live concerts, jamming together, writing music, and getting loaded until five or six in the morning. "This is truly being transplanted back to the mid-sixties," he wrote during the tour, "when crystal meth was a three-square diet with 'yellow jackets' and 'black beauties' for chasers."[30]

Shepard wrote up a few scenes with archetypal characters such as Wizard, Cowboy, Emperor, and Alchemist, but no screenplay. (Dylan did release the concert film *Renaldo and Clara* in 1978, a bizarre and loosely connected "four-hour fever dream," as one critic called it, but only a scene or two were Shepard's.) There was even talk of bringing in Orson Welles or Francis Ford Coppola to tame the improvisational mayhem. O'Dell reminded him that a few days before, he told her his great ambition was to be a rock and roll star. "Yeah, but I just wanted to play music," he replied, swaying his head in frustration. "I didn't want to do *this*."[31]

Shepard and O'Dell began sleeping together less than a week after his arrival. The casual romance helped them cope on a tour where you were expected to be ever-present but always in the background. As the tour rolled on in a couple of Winnebagos around Massachusetts, Rhode Island, Vermont, New Hampshire, and Connecticut, their ritual was to meet up at the hospitality room where people congregated after the shows, then head up to bed. But after a performance in Niagara Falls on November 15, Shepard never materialized. O'Dell asked around and discovered that he'd gone off with the singer Joni Mitchell, who joined the tour on November 13 in New Haven. O'Dell went up to his room ready for battle; and there he was, lying on the bed, hands behind his head with an innocent smile. Mitchell sashayed from the bathroom right out the front door before O'Dell could catch sight of her. "Sam, who was here?" "No one." "You know what? . . . You're a shit." She didn't bother making a rivalry out of it—this was the dazzling chanteuse Joni Mitchell, after all, no mere groupie.[32]

In fact, in Bangor, Maine, when Shepard caught a ride back to New York for a few days, Mitchell confronted her. "You know I really admire the way you're handling this thing," she said. "You just seem so confident and able to deal with this. . . . I really respect that. I wish I could do the same." O'Dell conveyed her gratitude, only to find herself as a character in a song, "Coyote," that Mitchell wrote on November 25 between Hartford and Augusta, while she was imprisoned in a Winnebago inhaling lines of cocaine northbound on the New England freeways.[33]

"Coyote" is a brilliantly written tell-all about Mitchell's affair with Shepard, and the next night in Augusta, she sang it for the first time before a live audience. She then played it with Dylan at Gordon Lightfoot's house while on the tour, and later recorded it for her album *Hejira*.

Mitchell had no illusions about their romance, and she calls him out in "Coyote" for his wandering eye while they were eating breakfast at a diner. Cocaine was also a significant factor. Nearly everyone but Joan Baez used cocaine on the tour, Mitchell and Shepard included. When the drummer John Guerin told Mitchell about how his grandfather used to own a circus in which the clowns were paid in booze, she responded, "So pay me in cocaine." But there was more than drugs between her and Shepard. "It was like we were twins," Mitchell told her biographer.

> I was born beneath a really powerful sky, and I think he was, too. He's multi-expressive. He's a playwright and a singer and an actor and he's good at all of them. What I think was happening was that I was forming sentences like he would've. Everything was creating an aversion. But for me, on coke, I found him very attractive. He reminded me of the people that I come from, from the region that I come from [the prairie lands of western Canada].[34]

* * *

On December 12, after four nights of recovering from "The Night of the Hurricane," a benefit concert at Madison Square Garden to raise money for the legal bills of the falsely imprisoned professional boxer Rubin "Hurricane" Carter, Bob Dylan and a few members of his band attended the Manhattan Theatre Club's showcase production of *Geography of a Horse Dreamer*. In spite of the creative frustrations of the Rolling Thunder tour for Shepard, he was still in awe of Dylan, and his attendance at this production unnerved and intimidated him; it was also opening night, which upped the ante. "Great," he thought to himself that night, "an audience full of critics and Bob Dylan. Couldn't be worse." As the actor Ethan Hawke said many years later, Shepard had never been "trying to impress New York intellectuals; he's trying to communicate something that he thinks is radical and might impress Bob Dylan."[35]

On one occasion, Shepard shared a monologue with Dylan that he wrote for the singer to perform in their unmade movie. Dylan sat drumming his feet while reading, Shepard recalled, "as though trying to locate the rhythm of it." Dylan glanced up, pointed a finger down, and said, "Is your thought clear on this line?" then darted off to join a hotel party. ("He's the slipperiest guy I ever met," Shepard said. "You try to talk to him and he disappears out the bathroom window.") Even that trifling encounter left him staring at the offending line he'd written in a daze, questioning his own meaning over and over.

> Right then I was faced with the dimension that he works in & I couldn't help seeing the space between his world & mine. Honesty was more than simply telling the truth. It was something that comes long before words. An absolute sincerity in the face of ideas. A responsibility toward the whole line. The position of each word. The words themselves. The rhythm, the color, the tone of it.

Dylan's message to Shepard: Everything counts.[36]

Shepard stood ruminating at the back of the auditorium when Dylan at last made his entrance, sporting a red coat and a gaucho hat, with his wife, Sara, and some of the musicians from Rolling Thunder. None of the critics appeared to be aware of the folk-rock sovereign seated among them. Possibly they thought he was one of them, since he was manically jotting down notes throughout the play with a pencil borrowed from the people seated in front of him.[37]

Shepard stepped outside, just listening to the actors and more deadly silence from the audience. When he peered in, two of the "heavies" had fallen asleep. (Despite what he says he saw from the back of the auditorium, virtually all the critics turned in strong reviews.) Dylan was now standing in the back row, his face contorted. "Wait a minute!" he shouted when the doctor was about to give Cody, the artistic-cowboy horse dreamer, an injection that would enable him to remove Cody's "dreamer's bone" from the back of his neck. "Wait a second! Why's he get the shot? He shouldn't get the shot! The other guy should get it! Give it to the other guy!" Members of Dylan's entourage pleaded with him to sit down and shut up. The ketchup-drenched shootout between Cody's brothers and the gangsters was the final straw, and Dylan stormed out, shouting, "I DON'T HAVE TO WATCH THIS! I DIDN'T COME HERE TO WATCH THIS!"[38]

When Shepard finally arrived back at home in California, Dark eagerly asked Shepard how the tour had gone, and he replied, "Fine," and that was that. To more thoroughly address this question, Shepard had recorded each day in his logbook along the way and typed the notes up as soon as he got home. The final result was *The Rolling Thunder Logbook*, a thumping, Gonzo-style hodgepodge of biographical sketches, dramatic scenes, dialogue, poetry, and photographs from the outlandish tour. "Dylan has invented himself," he concluded of the troubadour. "He made himself up from scratch."[39]

While Shepard was on the other side of the continent touring with Bob Dylan, what remained in California of the Sheps and the Darks had moved into a new home in Mill Valley: the Flying Y Ranch on Mount Tam. The ranch was situated on a sloping twenty acres of overgrazed land with panoramic views of Mill Valley below and came with a rickety two-story house with a mudslide for a front yard. They could easily saddle the five or six horses Shepard owned at the time and ride uphill and over a rise, then down to Muir Beach on the opposite side of their mountain.

The Flying Y also had a lower barn with a hay loft, an upper barn, a feed silo, a goat shack, and a riding arena encircled by cast-off tires stacked up seven or eight high. On hot summer days, the stench of decayed rubber and horse manure saturated the air. And, Shepard grumbled, there was a good deal of work to do: "installing wood-burning stoves, roofing, fencing, foaling corrals, getting ready for the rains."[40] The only way up to the ranch, recalled a former lodger, was "by navigating a steep, unpaved road, a good portion of which turned into a sinkhole in the winter"; another remembered, "It was held together with gum, string, and baling wire." The Flying Y, ramshackle though it was, had "a million dollar view" of Richardson Bay and, on the rare days the fog was cleared, of Berkeley and Oakland on the farthest shore.[41]

It was during his few years at the Flying Y that Shepard, now in his thirties, could indulge his passion for horses and educate himself in riding, breeding, and roping, skills he'd cultivate as a side vocation for forty more years. It's also where Jesse, at five years old, who would grow up to be a movie wrangler and a rancher, first learned how to ride a horse, on an Appaloosa named Cody.[42]

* * *

Growing up outside Los Angeles had trapped Shepard from an early age in what historian and urban theorist Mike Davis has called that city's "ecology of fear." Angelinos were subjected to all sorts of indignities: neighborhoods of poorly constructed buildings demolished by earthquakes, wildfires setting homes ablaze, segregated neighborhoods devastated by bloody race riots, mountain lions appearing in suburban playgrounds, all of which and more had driven generations into varying states of horror. It stands to reason, then, that artists raised amid such an ecological disaster zone would create a singular art form born of this fear.[43]

"It seems like natural disasters sort of correspond to social destruction," Shepard said. "Plagues, holocausts, all that." He was determined to react against this ecological cataclysm, he said simply, "because I grew up there." And each time he was drawn back, he'd reexperience the anger, anxiety, and malaise of his formative years.[44]

Hollywood's rejection of his screenplay "Fractured" was the inspiration for his next play, a takedown of LA's chokingly polluted air and movie-industry pandering titled *Angel City*.[45] Originally subtitled "A Moving Picture Show," it borrows from Raymond Chandler's novels and Nathanael West's *The Day of the Locust* in style and in its contempt for Tinseltown avarice.[46]

*Angel City* is Shepard's most scathing work about Hollywood, and it's also his most environmentalist play. The central irony of the two-act is that the characters are groping for a disaster theme while an actual disaster is taking place outside their window, indicated by a large suspended blue neon rectangle. Shepard's antihero Rabbit Brown (named for the blues guitarist) is a writer who's called into a movie studio to help develop a script. Rabbit's magical bag of tricks proves irrelevant to the film industry, though it was the studio execs who'd summoned him. By the end, the innocent Rabbit transforms into the kind of monstrous studio exec he deplored. "How can I keep my distance from a machine like that?" Rabbit asks. "So I wind up here, in the city of the South. Not knowing a thing but convincing them through mysterious gestures that I'm their main man.... I'm ravenous for power but I have to conceal it."[47]

Shepard was still eager to have one of his screenplays produced, and he wrote a number of them through the 1970s, including "Fractured" and "The Bodyguard" (with the Oscar-winning director Tony Richardson while he was abroad), each of which were doomed by the Hollywood merry-go-round of rewrites and scheduling conflicts. But he still considered live theater his central domain. "Theatre to me is like ... as acoustic rhythm and blues is to electric music, that's what theatre is to movies," he told a reporter. "Theatre just seems more of an immediate thing. It's funkier in a lot of ways because you're dealing with this stripped-down reality. You can't pull so many tricks. In a movie you can trick people all over the place. And you can lose yourself a lot easier in a movie. You can dream, you can just go to sleep."[48]

Hollywood, Shepard admitted decades later, "simply doesn't care what your attitude toward it is. The machinery is too powerful, too awesome. But the seduction of the place is unbelievable, an extraordinary American thing. Like Las Vegas, it's all about winning and losing ... the success and failure and power. Nobody's ever going to turn that system around; this is not a Buddhist culture." But in 1976, the Magic Theatre was Buddhist-adjacent, and *Angel City* opened there on July 2, at which point Shepard told the press, "The play asks: What's actually behind this diet of images we're swallowing every time we step into a deep, dark movie house? Who are the faceless merchandisers, and where does the whole dream originate?"[49] He was about to find this out in person, but this time, he'd be in front of the camera.

* * *

Shepard's friend Rudy Wurlitzer was the first to introduce Shepard to Hollywood as a potential movie star. Wurlitzer was good friends with the film director Terrence Malick, who was looking for someone to play a rich, young farmer in his latest project, *Days of Heaven*, alongside the stars Richard Gere and Brooke Adams. Although Shepard had only performed a few meager parts in indie movies, Wurlitzer knew his pal had "a lot of arrows in his quiver."[50]

Malick met Shepard at the Flying Y, where the director discovered the playwright caked with mud from feeding the forty-odd horses he now housed there. "The movies!" Shepard thought. "I can make lots of money and I won't have to ever again [write grants] or write a play on commission . . . so I can pay the fucking rent to some whacked out landlord." *Days of Heaven* was to be set on the Texas Panhandle in 1916, the thirty-two-year-old director informed him, and they were scheduled to shoot it in Canada that summer.[51]

In early August 1976, Shepard rented a Ford Mustang and headed with his new whippet, Pinto, to Whiskey Gap in the prairielands of Alberta, Canada, and checked into his suite at the Holiday Inn in Lethbridge. What he discovered outside the Alberta town was "extraordinary," he wrote. "Prairie country, very flat. Jack Fisk [their production designer] had constructed this remarkable set in the middle of the plains, out of *plywood*, this house sat there like some Edward Hopper painting. All this wind from the prairie and it somehow stayed in one piece."[52]

Shepard grew to adore and respect Malick, whom he called the "Okie Rhodes Scholar," and he embraced his idiosyncratic process. "Somehow you didn't mind doing things for Terry, as outrageous and ridiculous as some of it was," Shepard observed. "You felt like you were in the presence of somebody who was taking many chances and was kind of a poet." On one shooting day, Shepard was watching the director, impressed by the lyricism of the moment: Malick was setting up an intricate scene when a flock of geese appeared overhead, and he turned the camera away from the set, then pointed it at the sky and onto them.[53]

But by late October, after almost eleven weeks of shooting, Shepard had had enough. "It snowed most of the day & is getting very cold up here," he wrote to Scarlett Dark. "I just can't believe I'm still doing this thing." Off-hours were spent in "orgies of reading then writing then back to reading," binge drinking, and behaving loutishly. "Sam really has a mean streak, especially when he's drunk," said executive producer Jacob Brackman. So did Richard Gere, Brackman said, "and both of them in that macho way when people break furniture and break glass or take a swing at someone."[54]

Late in the shoot, Shepard began a liaison with the film's lead actress, Brooke Adams, who had ended a romance with their costar Richard Gere after seven weeks. This was an uncanny echo in real life of the love triangle that exists in the film. "We were living in this crappy hotel and we would leave the hotel in the morning in this bus that we all were in," Adams recalled. "There was nothing glamorous about it or anything, but it was magic. It was just magic." "I was sort of in love with both of them," she said, "and I think they both felt pretty strongly about me too. So we just kind of used that." O-Lan drove up to visit while Shepard was in the throes of his affair, but there was no trouble. At this point, they had come to an "understanding," as a member of the crew noted.[55] The day the film wrapped, Shepard, after earning six thousand dollars, drove off without so much as a farewell note. This was typical of his behavior throughout the shoot. "Sam notoriously would just *leave* the room when he was finished talking," Adams said. "He'd never say bye or anything."[56]

The first of Shepard's Hollywood roles, *Days of Heaven* launched his reputation as the country's new Gary Cooper. "The shift was so unexpected," remembered the movie critic Gene Seymour, "that many of his fans in the theater thought it had to be somebody else when his name appeared with Richard Gere's and Brooke Adams' in *Days of Heaven*. . . . But his on-screen magnetism was powerful enough to match, if not overpower, Gere's own."[57]

*Days of Heaven* was released in September 1978, at which time Lee Kissman, who'd relocated to the San Gabriel Valley in part to work with Shepard, Murray Mednick and other Off-Off-Broadway émigrés at Mednick's inaugural Padua Hills Writers' Workshop, accompanied Jane and Roxanne Rogers to its first matinee at the Fox Bruin, a Streamline Moderne–style theater in Westwood. After the credits rolled, Kissman was startled to notice Jane appearing "nonplussed." First off, she was disappointed with her son's performance, which, given the film's vaunted painterly visuals, might seem more like posing than acting. Jane was demonstrably more "upset," however, by the shocking resemblance between her handsome young son on the big screen and her wayward ex-husband, Sam Sr. That disturbing reminder of the Rogers heredity cast Jane, Kissman recalled, into "another world."[58]

CHAPTER 11

# BLOOD LINES

The Sheps and the Darks abandoned the tumbledown Flying Y ranch once the lease was up in November 1977. The ranch was too remote and in bad repair, so Shepard bought a white Spanish-style stucco hacienda with terra-cotta roof at 33 Evergreen Avenue in Homestead Valley, a neighborhood of dilapidated summer shacks between Mount Tam and Mill Valley. The house was small for a family of six.

Their next-door neighbor, Jack Suderman, saw Shepard as "just a neighbor, just people," an aloof man but not snobbish. (Johnny Dark was by far the most sociable of the clan, something Shepard grew jealous over.) The local paper described Shepard as "a phantom presence on the streets of Mill Valley." When a reporter arrived to their home, he noted Dark's white Chevy Nova parked out front, which he later discovered matched the description of the car in *Rolling Thunder Logbook*, a book he saw mounted on a wall through a window. At the door, he was rebuffed by O-Lan, then Dark, insisting they didn't know Shepard. They were just fans.[1]

Shepard received piles of fan mail but answered little of it. "He protects his privacy with the militancy of a Salinger," wrote another reporter, "or, for that matter, a Beckett. His friends and colleagues respect those wishes and act as an almost impenetrable first line of defense against attempts by strangers to contact him." Shepard's new literary agent, Lois Berman, also ran interference for him; and if someone persisted, she suggested they write to him at the Magic Theatre. The modern dancer and choreographer Daniel Nagrin, for instance, wanted a monologue for a dance piece and, on Berman's advice, sent his letter of intent to the Magic. To his surprise, Shepard responded, and by July had written *Jacaranda*. "At first, I was dismayed," Nagrin said of the script about a man who feels trapped by his love for a woman. "I circled around it quite a few months but then it became a little like approaching a vortex. The closer I got, the more fiercely involved I became until it poured right out."[2]

Over the winter of 1977–78, Shepard tried his hand at another screenplay, "Koko," about a female gorilla who communicated with simian sign language. "I stepped into the cage," he said after visiting the gorilla at a Stanford University observatory, "and she put her arm around me and kept giving me the sign: 'Tickle me. Chase me.'" And in the Hollywood-Shepard tradition, the script was first accepted, then left to rot on a shelf. But there were other perks, and on one of these trips to LA, Shepard invited Dark. "We can hang out, check the museums, go to movie star parties," he urged. Their first night was spent at a trendy roller disco called Skataway, where the regulars included Ringo Starr, Cher, Jack Nicholson, and Angelica Huston. That night, Shepard brought back Michelle Phillips of the Mamas and the Papas. "Would you walk around Hollywood for about an hour?" Shepard asked when they arrived at the hotel. Dark returned after fifteen minutes and looked in their room's window to behold the lovers. "Good thing I had my camera," Dark said (prefiguring a lurid offstage sequence from Shepard's *Simpatico*).[3]

Their best times together, for both men, were when they got high on weed and tested each other's boundaries for off-the-wall behavior. "I never wanted to be around him when he was drinking because he got to be a nasty drunk," Dark said, "very aggressive. A lot of the anger came out. But when he smoked, it was a transformative experience. It was amazing. He was so accessible, so relaxed, so interested and friendly. All that [rage] dropped away."[4]

Sometimes what the locals call "King Tides" from Richardson Bay would flood the house, during which the two friends would hang out on the ground floor, put their feet on the coffee table, smoke dope, and watch TV while seawater sloshed beneath their legs. When they got stoned, Shepard's "writer's mind" would surface, Dark said, "very funny, sounding very much like his early plays." Years later, after Shepard had long curbed his pot smoking, he wrote to Dark, "I remember only having a good time on it when I was hanging out with you & I think that was because we both shared this preposterous notion that we were seeing things as they really are every time we went into the grocery store or the 7-11. Mostly I remember the great camaraderie & didn't realize at the time how rare that was." After such days, Dark would wake up hoping to be greeted by his pal from the night before, but that person would disappear. In his place sat a "guarded and repressed" grumbler flipping through horse magazines.[5]

Late in life, in fact, Dark had a recurring nightmare that involved Shepard: "We're arguing, and he's shocked that anyone would dare stand up to him. I have a theory that one was not dealing with Sam the father of Jesse, but Sam the son of Sam, and he needed to repair his past by turning around and BEING his father with Jesse and someone like me in a kind of payback that the writing of all those 'Father plays' didn't fully exorcise." Dark took on much of the responsibility of fathering Jesse, who at the time, he wrote, "was just beginning heavy imitations of Sam, slicking his hair back, cowboy boots, sips of beer and that tough-squinty-far-off-expressionless-cowboy-look in his eyes."[6] "I bet I'll win!" Jesse once shouted to him about a coloring contest he'd entered at school, to which Dark replied, "If you're anything like your father you will win and you'll get a film contract out of it too."[7]

Shepard's philandering accelerated in Homestead Valley. "He went to the bars *every single night*," Dark remembered; and every night, he performed the same ludicrous ritual: "Everybody knows he was going to go out, but he had to go through this whole pretense," said Dark. "Anybody want any cigarettes?" he'd say. "I'm going to go to the corner." Then he would head to a downtown rock and blues venue called the Sweetwater Music Hall, where he was a regular. The Sweetwater had pool tables, and it boasted local musicians Carlos Santana, Jerry

Garcia, Elvis Costello, and John Lee Hooker among its musical roster and clientele. "Everybody knew he wasn't gonna come back until the next morning," Dark said, "and it was all about drinking and women." O-Lan, meanwhile, "just buried her head in the sand," he recalled. "She just pretended it wasn't happening."[8]

And then there was Shepard's anger and sense of mental fragmentation. Shepard was keenly aware of his abrasiveness, and he often incorporated his persistent conflicts with Dark into his writing. "I'm not interested in horses," Jimmie, the character based on Dark in "Fractured," says. "I hate horses." "Well, what the hell are ya' interested in then! Hammerin' fuckin' nails in wood!" Shepard's character, Massey, retorts. "Workin' yer fool ass off for used car dealers! Payin' the goddamn rent! Payin' the goddamn bills! WHAT ARE YA' INTERESTED IN!!" "I'm interested," Jimmie replies, "in not going insane."[9]

Unlike most people with serious anger management issues, who often have a difficult time recognizing there's a problem at all, Shepard was seriously trying to heal. He continued to seek help from the Work, which in San Francisco was conducted at a large Spanish-style hacienda on St. Elmo Way, in the Monterey Heights neighborhood, under the tutelage of the Bay Area system's elder statesman, Lord John Pentland. In public life, Lord Pentland was a career politician and businessman; in private, he was a prized pupil of Gurdjieff's and Ouspensky's, and the president of the American Gurdjieff Foundation. Shepard wrote to Roxanne, who was now involved in the Los Angeles system, "With Lord Pentland it's an odd mixture of relief that someone is finally able to see you & extreme discomfort that he may see too much."[10] Everyone at the St. Elmo house, Shepard wrote, "seemed to be in silent slow-motion awaiting the words of the master."[11]

Yet no matter how hard Shepard devoted himself to the Work, a gulf he'd begun to feel in London between his body and mind grew wider still. He was then reading Carlos Castaneda's new book, *The Second Ring of Power*, and the chapter "The Art of Dreaming" helped him confront his "sensation of doubleness, this feeling of separation between my body and 'me.'" This was no poetic flight of fancy, however, or turn of phrase. He actually appeared to himself to be suffering from a mental illness akin to depersonalization-derealization disorder, the terrifying sensation of being detached from one's body and thoughts and even reality itself. "This feeling is only periodic and comes in small flashes but seems to act on me like a sudden insight into another world."[12]

* * *

Shepard had been on the Rolling Thunder tour when he received a call from Joseph Papp of New York's Public Theater offering him a contract for a play. Shepard asked what kind of play he wanted, and the Off-Broadway impresario said, "Oh, a family, two sons, one stays home, one goes off to Viet Nam or anyway to war and gets fucked up."[13]

When Shepard returned home, a letter from his father had arrived, which began, "Hi Steve, As usual, when I write to you I need money." Two months later, another arrived apologizing for not writing sooner to thank him. What follows is a litany of excuses that ends with a frank admission of his own "bullshit." He acknowledged he was only appealing to his son because of his success, "a bad habit for an old, no-good man, who says, 'Oh Boy,' I know where I can go to get bucks."[14]

If Joe Papp wanted a play about family dysfunction, Shepard didn't have far to look to find it. "That play," he said about *Curse of the Starving Class*, "just exploded in front of me."[15]

The time had come, Shepard informed *Newsweek*, to step away from the otherworldly spectacles he was notorious for and begin writing more naturalistic long-form family tragedies in "the style of Eugene O'Neill." He believed he was ready, or at least willing, to enter the heady provinces of *Long Day's Journey Into Night* and its descendants—Tennessee Williams's *The Glass Menagerie*, Arthur Miller's *Death of a Salesman*, and Lorraine Hansberry's *A Raisin in the Sun*.

Shepard acknowledged that critics received avant-garde plays such as *Angel City* and his subsequent play, the avant-garde jazz one-act *Suicide in B♭*, with "bemused condescension or outright indifference."[16] On April 28, 1976, he'd dismissively concluded his acceptance speech at the

Guggenheim Museum for the Brandeis University Creative Arts Award, "I gladly accept this citation not as a token of high achievement but as an indication that experimental theatre and experimental writing in particular is able to be seen as a rejuvenating influence and not merely as a 'promising snot-nosed kid.'" He ruefully mocked, "It's fine if you like that kind of thing, and he certainly has a way with words but when is he going to stop playing around and give us a really MAJOR NEW AMERICAN PLAY?"[17]

Thus, in less than a decade's time, instead of one major new American play, Shepard would churn out five, and they were all stunners—*Curse of the Starving Class*, *Buried Child*, *True West*, *Fool for Love*, and *A Lie of the Mind*. In what came to be called Shepard's "family cycle" of plays, which would later include 2000's *The Late Henry Moss*, he concocted a writerly identity to go with the cowboy—the conscious craftsman, deliberative in plot, character, and setting. Shepard's dramas had arrived at hyperrealism, in which he overlaid the psychological and the imagistic qualities of his early writing onto the everyday realities of dysfunctional American families: "I felt I needed an aim in the work versus just the instinctive stuff, which is very easy for me to do. I started with character, in all its complexities. As I got more and more into it, it led me to the family."[18]

"You've always seen that in the past," Shepard said, "in theater, in melodrama: It's the family. Look at Eugene O'Neill: I mean, I think he wrote one really great play, *Long Day's Journey*. I wish I could write a play that good. When you see *Long Day's Journey*, it's not just the melodrama or the interactions of those people, they cover something else that's going down, happening behind." When *Curse* opened, the critics instantly recognized O'Neill's influence, "that need to track down the family ghosts," as one wrote, "and tell them it's OK."[19]

*Curse of the Starving Class* takes place in a Los Angeles suburb in the kitchen of the Tate family home, based on the Rogers house at 1459 East Lemon Avenue in Bradbury. In the play, Jane Rogers's character, Ella (the nickname of O'Neill's mother), has conspired with a swindling speculator to sell their house and move to Europe, which Jane and Roxanne did in 1974; at the same time, the father has already promised the property to a mobbed-up businessman named Ellis, owner of the Alibi Club, based on an actual bar of that name in Duarte. Neither parent knows the other's plan, but both are victims of the advancing "zombie invasion" of land speculators, lawyers, bankers, and developers, as described by Shepard's character, Wesley Tate:

> There'll be bulldozers crashing through the orchard. There'll be giant steel balls crashing through the walls. There'll be foremen with their sleeves rolled up and blueprints under their arms. There'll be steel girders spanning acres of land. Cement pilings. Prefab walls. Zombie architecture, owned by invisible zombies, built by zombies for the use and convenience of all other zombies. A zombie city! Right here! Right where we're living now.[20]

Everything was a facade. "People are starved for truth," Shepard said, "and when something comes along that even looks like truth, people will latch on to it because everything's so false. People are starved for a way of life—they're hunting for a way to be or to act toward the world."[21] The class of Shepard's title, he admitted, was "the middle class," specifically his own family. "It just deals with a very real situation I went through as a kid."[22]

Sandy Rogers appears as the adolescent tomboy Emma Tate, who wants to escape and is menstruating for the first time—"the curse," her mother Ella calls it. Weston's "curse" is his ancestry, which courses through his blood, he says, like poison: "I never saw my old man's poison until I was much older than you," he informs Wesley. "And then you know how I recognized it?" "How?" "Because I saw myself infected with it. That's how. I saw me carrying it around. His poison in my body." This, of course, is Wesley's curse as well. For Ella, the curse is an invisible and infectious force that perpetuates their captivity: "We spread it. We pass it on. We inherit it and pass it down, and then pass it down again. It goes on and on like that without us."[23]

The Tate family is collectively hungering for something greater out there than their dead-end lives, or at least to have a voice to lend them some agency. California was billed as a promised land of happiness and success, but what the state had wrought for families like the Tates was an accumulation of petty land grabs and get-rich-quick schemes. Wesley pisses on his sister's 4-H project onstage, a controversial bit for any art form, but it's the promise he's pissing on, not the project itself. In the end, starting with donning his father's clothes, he has forsaken all promises.

* * *

Papp eagerly accepted *Curse of the Starving Class* for his 1977–78 season at the Public Theater. Shepard's deviation from his usual black magic theatrics stunned him, and he billed it as the dramatist's "most autobiographical play." Shepard didn't approve of Papp's assigned director, so he contacted his friend Nancy Meckler. Still directing in London, Meckler had an infant and a six-year-old and couldn't see her way to a production in New York, so they decided on the Royal Court, where it opened on April 21, 1977.[24]

Shepard's old nemesis Charles Marowitz gave her production a poor review in the *New York Times*, which chastened Meckler, but otherwise, the world premiere of *Curse* was largely a critical success: "There is an apocalyptic vision in this play," wrote the *Observer*, "held in check by Shepard's truthfulness and Nancy Meckler's understated direction." The *Guardian* wrote that "while the play may lack the wild, imagistic razzamatazz of Shepard's earlier American work, it has a density of texture and echoing resonance that makes it oddly satisfying. It's not perfect but it doesn't short-change the audience and it's palpably the work of a real, complex writer."[25]

*Curse of the Starving Class* then opened at the Public Theater on March 2, 1978, as part of the New York Shakespeare Festival. For a director, Shepard suggested Robert Woodruff, who was then directing at a church basement theater in San Francisco. The play had already been chosen for an Obie the previous year for Best New American Play before it was even staged in New York.

The *Daily News* critic Douglas Watt had Shepard's number: "I have a theory that this astonishingly prolific California playwright has really been writing one long play during the past dozen years, and that he cuts sections from it as needed," Watt wrote. "Though 'Curse of the Starving Class' is better-balanced and more coherent than any of his previous work I've witnessed, it reveals, in common with the rest, a mind crammed with ideas and images both poetic and banal, and an individual talent, however sloppily enjoyed, for treating weighty subjects in pop terms of heightened realism."[26] Most everyone in the press agreed on the stunning performances, especially Olympia Dukakis and James Gammon as the parents, and on Robert Woodruff's exceptional direction.

* * *

When Shepard visited his grandparents' Illinois homestead in the summer of 1972, the family member he truly cared about seeing wasn't his father but his by then deceased grandfather Sam Rogers, who had died in 1968. "Grandpa Sam is the one I loved / Of all the misfit Episcopalians in the family," Shepard wrote in an unpublished poem from May 11, 1971, titled "Long Gone": "Watching himself die was no easy trick / He kissed death in the tit. . . . He wore his baseball cap. . . . His hotel ashtray filled to the brim / His Apple brandy."[27] Shepard's grandmother Helen Rogers was tall and imposing, and after raising six children, five of them boys, she never played the sweet and lovable granny. "Talk about scary people," Sandy said decades after Helen had died.[28]

Roxanne went even further. "I was terrified of her. I mean, you have to be quite a tough woman to bring up so many tough boys, you know?" Roxanne wrote up a lengthy description of the Rogers's marital dynamic, one that forms the roux of what would become the full-length gothic family drama *Buried Child*, Shepard's most acclaimed achievement:

> It was a strange situation in that house as Grandpa was dying (it took forever, poor dear). Even when Grandpa could barely get off the couch (where he lived for months. Maybe years?) Grandma would never

> help him at all. If he needed a glass of water she would ignore him, and he had to struggle to pull himself out of the depths of that old smelly couch and hobble his way all the way into the kitchen, where Helen invariably stood ignoring him, fumble to fill a glass, and shuffle back to the stinky couch. It was so sad. As if they hated each other so much they just agreed to shuffle past each other for all the months it took him to die.

The Rogers living room in Lombard is the setting of *Buried Child*, which he'd begun writing in the summer of 1974 under the title "The Last American Gas Station." Many consider this full-length his greatest tour de force, and it has the distinction of being the first and only play that would win him the Pulitzer Prize. The living room setting, Roxanne wrote, "was so close to my grandparents' dark gloomy house in Lombard. Sam designed that set to look and feel just like their suffocating front room. It was terrifying. Profoundly accurate."[29]

Shepard called his grandfather's character Dodge, Helen's maiden name. His grandson Vincent, Shepard's surrogate, returns with his girlfriend Shelly (based mainly on O-Lan) to the house in Lombard to reconnect with his family, only to find that the disaffected men of his former life, Dodge (Grandpa Sam Rogers), Tilden (Sam Sr.), and his one-legged uncle Bradley (his father's brother Dick Rogers, who also had an amputated leg), have succumbed to a sordid futility. Somehow, despite Vincent's attempt at a suitable reunion, the family can't recognize Vincent either as a relation, initially, or as a symbol of their future. Dodge's wife, Halie (Helen), gripes to her pastor that American youth have turned into nihilistic savages, less focused on what it takes to be a success than on sex, drugs, and violence. "When you see the way things deteriorate before your very eyes," Halie says, "everything running downhill. It's kind of silly to even think about youth."[30]

The family resemblances in the play were not lost on the Rogers clan. After attending a performance in Chicago, one of his cousins told Sandy, "Boy, Sam's lucky that Grandma's not alive!" "All my cousins got to see that play," Sandy said, "and it's all about the . . . real stuff. But a total made-up plot. There was no buried child in the backyard—that was all made up."[31]

*Buried Child* premiered on June 27, 1978, at the Magic Theatre. Robert Woodruff directed, and he recalled that because Shepard was filming *Days of Heaven* during Woodruff's well-received production of *Sad Lament*, and he hadn't bothered to drive to New York to see *Curse of the Starving Class*, "that was the first time we were in a room together."[32]

Shepard heavily revised the script through Woodruff's rehearsals. When asked why he kept editing the dialogue, he responded, "I listened to it, I guess. When you listen intensely to anything you see how it can be improved. It's a rhythmic thing. Like music. You can feel the way that language lifts and turns around itself. The problematic character for me has always been Vince. Because he's closer to autobiography than anything else in the play—everyone else is pieces, figments, fragments."[33]

Shortly after *Buried Child*'s premiere, Shepard, in his self-critical way, dismissed most of the groundbreaking family drama as "verbose and overblown" and "unnecessarily complicated." But one scene stuck in his mind, one "little tiny section" he could "watch over and over and over again." This was the beginning of Act Two, when Vince and his girlfriend, Shelly, arrive at his grandparents' and attempt to ingratiate themselves with a drunken Dodge sprawled on the couch, but despite Vince's entreaties, Dodge can't place him as a member of the family:

DODGE: What are you talking about? Do you know what you're talking about? Are you just talking for the sake of talking? Lubricating the gums?

VINCE: I'm trying to figure out what's going on here!

DODGE: Is that it?

VINCE: Yes. I mean I expected everything to be different.

DODGE: Who are you to expect anything? Who are you supposed to be?

VINCE: I'm Vince! Your grandson!

DODGE: Vince. My grandson.

VINCE: Tilden's son.

DODGE: Tilden's son, Vince.
VINCE: You haven't seen me for a long time.
DODGE: When was the last time?
VINCE: I don't remember.
DODGE: You don't remember?
VINCE: No.
DODGE: You don't remember. How am I supposed to remember if you don't remember?

These rhythmic cadences in *Buried Child* became a touchstone to be emulated in work to come. For a long time, Shepard said, he studied the theory of rhythm under a drummer from Ghana, who taught him the "big revelation" that in African music, "every rhythm is related. You can play 4/4, 5/8, and 6/8 all together at the same time and there's a convergence . . . that rhythm on top of rhythm on top of rhythm always has a meaning. So the same is true on the stage. There are many possible rhythmic structures that an actor can hit, but there's only one true one."[34]

The *Chicago Tribune*'s chief theater critic and culture columnist, Chris Jones, regarded the plot of *Buried Child* as a metaphor "for all the problems in Illinois." It's a regional play, Jones insisted, but with larger elements involved: "It's about economics, it's about addiction; it's about mental health; it's about all the shit the newspapers were talking about for the next twenty years."[35]

"What I wanted to do," Shepard later told a reporter during a revival of the play, "was to destroy the idea of the family drama. It's too psychological. Because this and that happened, you wet the bed? Who cares? Who cares when there's a dead baby in the back yard?" Shepard strongly believed that the impact of the family on the self could never be overcome or treated like a psychic disease for which there might be a cure. The trick was trying not to care: "I think that there is no escape," Shepard said. "People go insane trying to deny what they really are."[36]

Shepard embeds a terrifying actuality in his family play about what one scholar called "historical amnesia," when a group of people unknowingly muddy or repress an unresolved historical event. The buried child of the title, or the "stench of sin" Halie complains has soured her home, is the family secret that Vincent's girlfriend, Shelly, attempts to investigate and reveal. At first Dodge castigates her for trying to "uncover the truth of the matter. Like a detective or something," but in the third act confesses that he killed the baby, "drowned it. Just like the runt of a litter. It made everything we'd accomplished look like it was nothin.' Everything was cancelled out by this one mistake. This one weakness."[37] It was a skeleton in the cupboard so dire the play itself can't tell us definitively, though it's clear enough by the end that the child is the incestuous product of Halie and Tilden's "weakness." But the buried child also mirrors the "stench of sin" on the national narrative that Americans collectively prefer to forget.

*Buried Child* won the Pulitzer Prize for drama in 1979, after its New York premiere at the Theater for the New City and subsequent move to the Theatre de Lys (which, unluckily, closed the day before the Pulitzer announcement); and it also won him an Obie in the category of Playwriting. One critic proposed that the play won a Pulitzer merely "in response to the Committee's delight at finally being able to feel they understood a Shepard drama."[38]

This was Shepard's highest literary accolade, and it was the first Off-Broadway play to win the Pulitzer in the prize's seventy-year history. Shepard self-effacingly considered the award more of an impediment than an inspiration to further his craft, as if he was finished as an artist; the way he described it, winning the Pulitzer Prize was "like receiving the news that you have a terminal illness. You have to get over it. In one way it's nice that there's a kind of recognition, but for the most part you have to get through it, accept it as well as you can and move on."[39]

* * *

These heady days of theatrical prominence corresponded superbly with the arrival of Shepard's similar rise in stature as a film actor. In spite of his mother's ambivalent experience watching the film, *Days of*

*Heaven*'s success whetted directors' appetites for more of this mysterious playwright-performer.

Shepard declined several starring film roles, including Alan Parker's *Shoot the Moon*, which starred Albert Finney, and James Bridges's *Urban Cowboy*, eventually featuring John Travolta. "Who wants to ride a mechanical bull?" he asked of the latter film. "I've ridden real ones, and they're not fun."[40] Warren Beatty also offered him the role of Eugene O'Neill in his historical epic *Reds*, a job that eventually went to Jack Nicholson. (Near the end of his life, Shepard only regretted turning down two parts: one in 1989's *Lonesome Dove* miniseries, which he rejected twice, and Clint Eastwood's 1992 Western *Unforgiven*, where Eastwood asked him to play the villain that became one of Gene Hackman's signature roles and won him an Oscar.)[41]

But early in 1979, he drove to Texas for the second major film role he accepted, playing a preacher's roughneck son named Cal Carpenter, who falls in love with a supernatural healer (Ellen Burstyn) in the Canadian filmmaker Daniel Petrie's *Resurrection*.

Movie audiences loved him in *Resurrection*, especially the press. Shepard, said David Ansen of *Newsweek*, "invests his role with the same sense of lurking psychic violence that permeates his plays. If he wants it, he stands on the brink of an extraordinary new career in the movies."[42] Even Sam Rogers was impressed. "You are a damned good ACTOR," he wrote to his son.[43] The Sheps and the Darks also intuited that he was approaching stardom, and were concerned this could result in domestic upheaval.

Dark wrote Shepard while he was on location in Texas, in which he unsubtly called his friend's attention to the family they had all built: "It was great talking to you tonight (you called). It was like getting a call from someone who was in the civil war and was taking a break to call home. Yes—this house looms large as a hearth of warmth and family activity. It has a real gravity about it—it's a 'center' that we've all created and in it I think we all experience [a] sense of 'being-home. . . .' I'm sure that what's really important is that [Jesse's] growing up and thriving in really healthy soil. He's growing in the midst of the 'results' of all of us being together."[44]

O-Lan wrote him a longing note: "It sure is nice talking to you on the phone except that it reminds me how I'm missing you. It certainly is an experience being apart. Feeling the lack."[45]

* * *

After he briefly returned to Homestead Valley, the rhythm of their marriage contracted again, and in August 1979, Shepard was away house-sitting for his mother at her new condominium at 454 South El Molino Avenue in Pasadena, an attic apartment with a porch with Astroturf off the back, while she was vacationing in Alaska. Shepard had visited his father in New Mexico the previous March on his way home from filming *Resurrection*, a visit that simply proved to him that his father's life was beyond salvation. At Jane's place, he began to think of a plot about two estranged brothers, Lee and Austin, and started to write at once. "I heard the voice of Lee speaking very clearly," he said, "and then I heard Austin's response. The more I listened, the more the voices came."[46]

This is the moment when Shepard wrote *True West*, what he called his play about "double nature," the kind of ambivalence Jane had diagnosed as leading to his father's demise in her psychological profile. "It's a real thing, double nature," he avowed. "I think we're split in a much more devastating way than psychology can ever reveal. It's not so cute. Not some little thing we can get over. It's something we've got to live with." He decided to separate one autobiographical character, like Stu or Kent or Slim or Ice or Cody or Jeep or Rabbit or Wesley or Vince, into a pair of estranged brothers, each possessing fragments of himself. *True West* would strip away the mask of the writer's two most dramatic internalized lives: Austin and Lee, the brothers of the play, form a monodrama of reconciling Shepard's duality—Austin as his Dr. Jekyll and Lee as his Mr. Hyde. "I feel like that's my problem," Shepard said, "that's my major problem. Reconciling."[47]

CHAPTER 12

# THE WOLF AND THE SHEEP

Shepard had made a clear and observable stylistic break from experimental theater with his recent family plays, especially *True West*, but if there was one artist from his past who could reel him back to the avant-garde, even if just as a side angle, it was Joe Chaikin.

Shepard had returned to the Bay Area from Pasadena to write and direct their new piece *Savage/Love* with *Tongues*, their first collaboration from the previous fall. Shepard's were the only collaborations Chaikin would ever allow with a playwright throughout his storied career. As a collaborator, Shepard was deferential to Chaikin and considered himself the elder man's apprentice. Shepard might've been influenced by Samuel Beckett, but Chaikin knew Beckett well. (The Irishman penned his last poem on his deathbed in 1989, "What Is the Word," and dedicated it to Chaikin.) Chaikin, in turn, deeply admired Shepard's ability to transform his abstract notions into poetic dialogue.[1]

With *Tongues*, as with *True West*, Shepard wished to capture the multifarious voices clattering around in his mind, while *Savage/Love* focuses on a man's inner thoughts about the pain and exaltation of romantic love.[2] Chaikin and Shepard shared the stage. "Chaikin remains seated," wrote a local critic, "his legs covered with a Mexican blanket, and recites a stream of consciousness litany on no specific theme. While he talks,

Shepard sits partially concealed behind him, and uses an assortment of primitive musical instruments to punctuate Chaikin's words. He makes percussive sounds with drums, gourds, bells and a cymbal, and his music is skillful, witty and marvelously effective." When the show moved to the Public Theater's Other Stage in New York that fall, under Robert Woodruff's direction, Mel Gussow's *New York Times* review was rapturous: with Shepard's music and Chaikin's "virtuoso performance," the evening was "not only an exquisite piece of performance theater, it is, to a great extent, a consolidation, a précis of the work of these two extraordinary theater artists over a span of 15 years."[3]

The double bill appeared in the Eureka Theater Summer Festival at the Magic Theatre on September 6, 1979, and Roxanne Rogers wrote a congratulatory note to her brother, saying how moved by it she'd been.[4] Shepard responded by citing Chaikin as the "key factor" for its success. "They are the only pieces of theatre I've done that feel totally satisfying," he wrote, despite his recent pivot to the hyperrealism of his family plays. "Always before I've felt pangs of regret & embarrassment about my work. It's never felt whole in the sense of realizing its potential, but these two little pieces really achieve what they set out to."[5]

This was penned, however, before completing the final draft of what he would consider the finest play of his career: *True West*.

* * *

Three days after the opening of Shepard and Chaikin's double bill, Shepard, O-Lan, and Jesse were out on a bicycle ride in Homestead Valley when they heard the high-pitched wail of an ambulance siren in the distance. They thought nothing of it, but on their way home, another ambulance screeched by heading in the opposite direction. A local kid told them there'd been an ambulance at their house. Inside, Scarlett was missing. Shepard frantically called 911 and was soon on the line with the paramedics. Scarlett had passed out in the house, they said, then woke up and called 911. An X-ray revealed she'd suffered a brain aneurism, and the doctor didn't think she would survive surgery.[6]

The Sheps and the Darks were blindsided. When they were back home at the dinner table, Shepard had a strong urge to pray, not to God but to chance, the same unknowable force that had caused Scarlett's ruptured artery in the first place. Eventually, they tracked down "the Wyatt Earp of neurosurgery," as Shepard dubbed him, though Scarlett had to be transferred to San Francisco General Hospital. When the morning of the surgery finally arrived, Scarlett lit a cigarette and, Shepard wrote, "she asked us to promise to keep her with us no matter what. No matter how she turned out. We promised. She said she knew we would bring her back to the world."[7]

After she'd been in the hospital and a therapy center for three months, they decided to take her home. "That night was the beginning of the worst," Shepard wrote. "She began to moan in an agonizing animal voice. We'd ask her what was the matter and she'd just moan. She'd keep it up for hours. Then she'd scream. She said she knew one of us was going to kill her."[8]

Shepard had grown exceedingly close to Scarlett and, to the surprise of the family, devoted enormous amounts of time and energy toward her recovery. "He was very, very tender towards Scarlett," Dark said of Shepard, "almost unrecognizable when he was around her. She had a kind of dignity that he really related to."[9] Scarlett's kind of dignity was Jane's kind, a well-wrought mold of self-reliance and couth, and though Jane and her son were always very close, Scarlett was a proximal mother figure to him. Scarlett never fully recovered and was struck with aphasia, which caused her to disconnect familiar objects from words. She would sometimes whisper about a "traitor" in the family she was sure was plotting to kill her. In fact, the rest of the family began having nightmares that she might murder them.[10]

"Scarlett is taking us all on a profound journey into the unknown," Shepard wrote to Roxanne. "She is totally vulnerable emotionally at this point & the situation is very delicate in terms of finding ways to deal with her. Every day we have to readjust our assumptions about 'where' she is in herself." Her mind would return to her childhood, revert back to the present, then back again. "It's sort of like helping someone through an extended bad trip on acid," Shepard said, recalling his experience with Joyce Aaron, which he'd only recently written up in a story. After a year of astounding teamwork, with Shepard close at hand throughout the ordeal, Scarlett could eventually walk, speak ("in a strange accent"), and eat, but often fell silent and stared into space. "She refers to her past," Shepard wrote, "as the time before she was 'blown away.'"[11]

Many years later, while discussing his wife's harrowing episode, Dark softly disclosed, "I heard Sam wrote a play about a woman that had a brain hemorrhage. But I never saw that play. I don't know anything about it." Just after Scarlett's aneurism, Shepard did write a two-act play called "Knowledge of the Seven Steps" about Scarlett's return home with aphasia—the family's loving ministrations, her attempts at speech, her terror of being killed—which he completed that November. In his opening notes for the play, he lists the dualities that were playing out in her monologues to the family as "Wild-Tame, Dark-Light, Terror-Ecstasy, Savage-Love," and in that play, Scarlett "sees other characters mythologically—they are seen by the audience as she sees them."[12]

Dark's idea of an aphasia play was more likely a reference, however, to a play Shepard wrote several years later, the longest he would ever write. He'd call it *A Lie of the Mind*.

* * *

During Scarlett's recovery that fall, Shepard revised, with significant scene changes, the two-act play *True West* he wrote at Jane's home in Pasadena. He was now writing his plays out in notebooks until almost everything was in place, then he would type out a draft, revising the handwritten draft as he went, then would revise that typed version multiple times over. "Musicians have this terminology—playing in and playing out," he reflected on the composition of *True West*. "Playing out roughly means to improvise, whereas playing in means developing inside a structure. For me, now, it's much more interesting, though more difficult, playing in." *Curse of the Starving Class* and *Buried Child* were his opening salvos into the world of "playing in," but with *True West*, the dialogue was even more finely tuned,

> a mixture of something intended and something just coming out. A line comes out and then you start listening to it and the more you listen to it the more you hear how it's not sounding the way you intended for it to sound. So you ask yourself, what is throwing it off? And it may just be one word. So you take that word out and it brings you closer.[13]

*True West* is set in a small Southern California home on the outskirts of the Mojave Desert owned by a mostly offstage character listed as Mom. Her son Austin, a Hollywood screenwriter and Ivy League college graduate, has agreed to care for her plants while she vacations in Alaska, as Shepard had done when his own mother traveled there. Austin wants to escape the demands of his wife and children "up North" to research a period piece he hopes to sell to his slick movie producer, Saul Kimmer.[14] But his older brother, Lee, a desert-dwelling cat burglar, intrudes on his workspace. Lee is a menace, exuding a bitterness toward his put-together brother with more than a hint of violent intent. But Lee knows that Austin, whom he hasn't seen in five years, has no choice, as the Rogerses hadn't with Sam Sr., but to accept him into their mother's home.

Along with being "played in" and tightly written, *True West* also adheres closely to what Aristotle termed in his *Poetics* a "tragic unity." Tragedies, Aristotle argued, require a concentration of powerful emotions, which call for a "unity of action" that takes place within a limited time frame, restricts the location to one area, and limits the number of characters. In this way, Aristotle argued, the tragedy within a play pressurizes and concentrates, rather than dilutes the emotions by adding extraneous settings, action, and characters. The entirety of *True West*, then, takes place over three days, in Mom's kitchen and breakfast nook, with only two principal characters and two relatively minor ones. In each of the two acts, Shepard's timeline moves forward from daytime (an encounter between two estranged brothers) to nighttime (a sense of mutual doom). The revelations of the characters, as Aristotle observed millennia ago, are revealed through dialogue more than action.

For Shepard, drawing within the lines of classical dramatic structure had been anathema to his earlier quest for "total" theater—in which everything happens simultaneously, and time, space, and character are fluid and transient. The stage directions of the realistic setting also signal Shepard's movement toward unified storylines and stripped-down dialogue. He insists that Mom's kitchen and alcove "should be constructed realistically with no attempt to distort its dimensions, shapes, objects, or colors."[15] The expressionism of his early plays—with their grotesque exaggerations of the outer world and the twisted fantasies of the characters through whom we glimpse that world—is largely absent from *True West*'s staging until the final scene.

Austin and Lee are opposites in both appearance and temperament: Austin is an upright man in his early thirties; Lee is in his early forties with tatty clothes and a rockabilly pompadour. Lee's hostility toward his younger brother crescendos until Saul Kimmer, an archetypal producer, arrives to check on Austin's progress with his film proposal. Lee bullies Kimmer into playing a game of golf, during which Lee bets that if he wins, Kimmer will produce his own film idea about the "true" West. Once Austin is informed of Lee's conquest on the links, their power dynamic reverses along with the brothers' personalities and speech.

Mom returns home early from Alaska to find her home demolished: plates are shattered and beer and liquor bottles are strewn everywhere. Her plants are all dead. Earlier, Lee had promised to accompany Austin out to the desert if Austin wrote his script, but reneged, leaving Austin an infuriated, frantic mess. "There's nothin' real down here, Lee!" he screams. "Least of all me!" Mom, with her eerie affect, personifies contemporary Western culture, and she impassively looks on as Austin strangles Lee with a telephone cord to force him to make good on his promise. Mom scolds them, "There's plenty of room to fight outside. You've got the whole outdoors to fight in."[16] They do not stop fighting, and she exits to find a motel.

Sam Rogers at Morrison Field. "I'm paddling a concrete mixer around with a board," he wrote on the back. "Did you ever see such a pose?" Palm Beach, Florida, April 1942.

Jane Rogers, circa 1962.

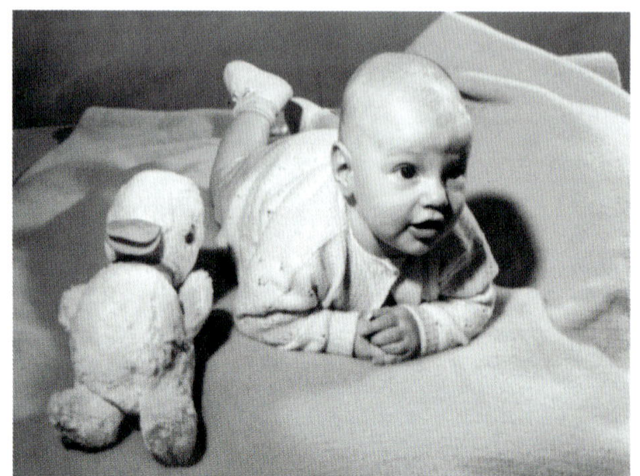

Samuel Shepard "Stevie" Rogers, May 3, 1944.

Shepard and Jane Rogers. Jane, pregnant with Sandy, has a holstered Colt .45 in her lap. "Me on one hip," Shepard wrote, "the pistol on the other." Guam, 1946.

Shepard riding a stuffed bucking bronco at the Riverside County Fair and National Date Festival, used as the cover for *Day out of Days* (2010). Indio, California, circa 1950.

Sam Sr., Shepard, Foxy, Jane, Sandy, and Roxanne Rogers in front of Grace Upton's house, Shepard's first real home. South Pasadena, California, 1957.

Shepard and his first car. "Cars represented everything for a kid," he wrote. "Mine was a '32 Ford Deuce Coup . . . a boss machine." Bradbury, California, summer 1961.

Charles Mingus III. Senior year photo for Duarte High School. Duarte, California, 1962.

Shepard and Joyce Aaron. The chanticleer above the stove was sponge-painted by Shepard the previous night. Bradbury, California, February 1965.

Ralph Cook, founder of Theater Genesis. New York City, 1967.

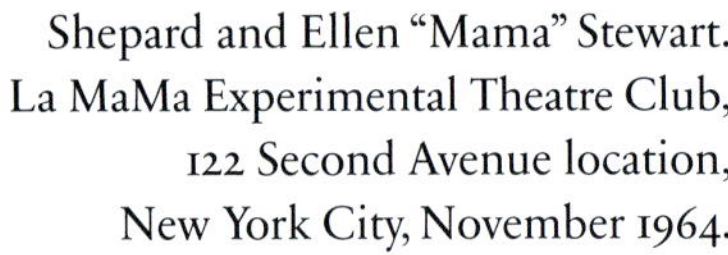

Shepard and Ellen "Mama" Stewart. La MaMa Experimental Theatre Club, 122 Second Avenue location, New York City, November 1964.

The Holy Modal Rounders rehearsing on the set of *Rowan and Martin's Laugh-In*.
From left to right: Peter Stampfel, John Annis, Shepard, Steve Weber, and Richard Tyler.
Burbank, California, October 14, 1968.

Nancy Mandel, Michelangelo Antonioni, and Shepard during the filming of *Zabriskie Point*.
Los Angeles, October 1968.

The wedding party: Bill Hart, Shepard, O-Lan Johnson, Kristy Johnson, and the Rev. Michael Allen. St. Mark's Church in-the-Bowery, New York City, November 9, 1969.

*Operation Sidewinder*. The Holy Modal Rounders (left: Peter Stampfel standing at center, Steve Weber standing at right); snake puppet (center); Robert Phalen (in for Andy Robinson) and Barbara Eda-Young (kneeling); and Louis Mofsie (second from right). Vivian Beaumont Theater, Lincoln Center, New York City, 1970.

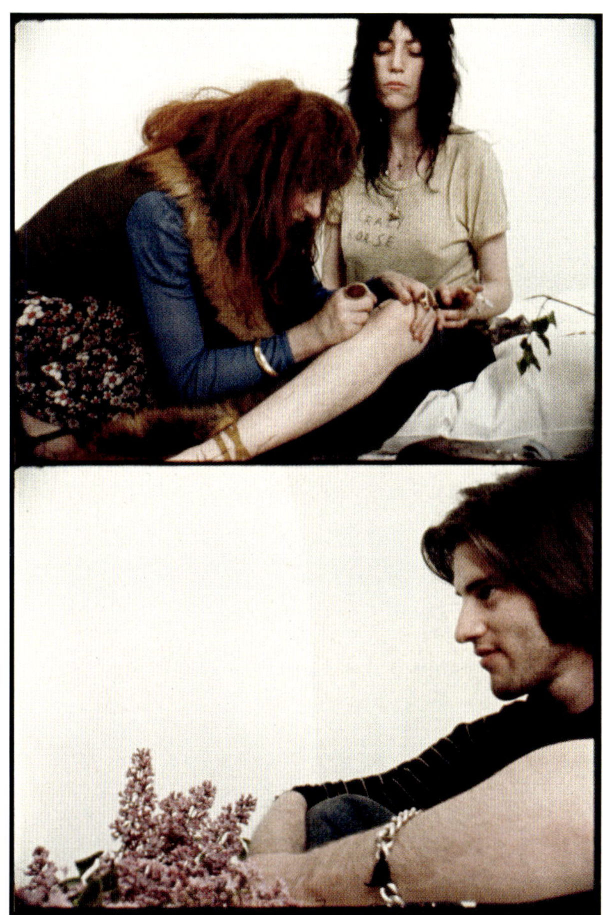

Vali Myers, Patti Smith, and Shepard in scenes from Sandy Daley's *Patti Having Her Knee Tattooed*, later handpicked for this book by Daley. Note the "Crazy Horse" T-shirt Smith is wearing. Hotel Chelsea, New York City, 1971.

Shepard and Patti Smith on the opening night of *Cowboy Mouth*. American Place Theatre, New York City, April 29, 1971.

Shepard and Jesse on Warwick Road. London, November 1971.

Shepard, O-Lan, and Jesse, Mill Valley, California, 1977.

The Sheps and the Darks. Clockwise from top left: Shepard, Scarlett Dark, Johnny Dark, Kristy Johnson, Jesse Shepard, and O-Lan Shepard-Johnson. Hill Top Farm, West Advocate, Nova Scotia, Canada, August 1973.

Shepard meets Bob Dylan at the start of the Rolling Thunder Revue, with visitor Patti Smith in the foreground. New York City, October 1975.

Joseph Chaikin and Shepard performing *Tongues*. The Magic Theatre, San Francisco, California, June 4, 1978.

Shepard, Johnny Dark, and Jesse at the Evergreen Avenue house, Homestead Valley, California, 1980.

Samuel Shepard Rogers III and IV. Bernalillo, New Mexico, April 1982. "He took off his straw Resistol cowboy hat, reached over and placed it on his father's head. It fit perfect." —*Motel Chronicles*

John Malkovich and Gary Sinise in *True West*. Cherry Lane Theatre, New York City, 1982.

Shepard and Brigadier General Chuck Yeager. Hamilton Air Force Base, Novato, California, 1982.

Shepard and Jessica Lange in *Frances*, 1982.

Shepard leaving for Jessica Lange. Homestead Valley, California, March 17, 1983.

*Paris, Texas* movie poster, 1984. Note the tagline: "a place for dreams. a place for heartbreak. a place to pick up the pieces."

Jessica and Shepard at the premiere of *The Natural*. Samuel Goldwyn Theater, Beverly Hills, California, May 9, 1984.

Shepard in Santa Fe, New Mexico, spring 1985.

Shepard on the set of *Voyager*. Mexico, March 1990.

Ethan Hawke as Hamlet and Shepard as the Ghost during the "Remember Me" monologue in *Hamlet*. New York City, October 1998.

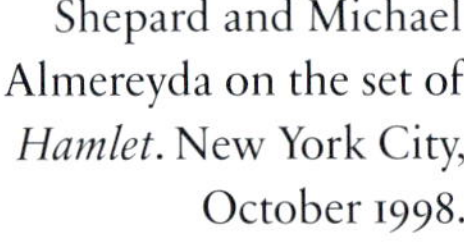

Shepard and Michael Almereyda on the set of *Hamlet*. New York City, October 1998.

Shepard and Wim Wenders on the set of *Don't Come Knocking*. Butte, Montana, summer 2004.

Aleksandra "Shura" Baryshnikov, Jessica Lange, Shepard, Hannah, and Walker when Jessica was honored with a "Gala Tribute" by the Film Society of Lincoln Center. New York City, April 17, 2006.

Stephen Rea as Hobart Struther in *Kicking a Dead Horse*. Peacock Theatre of the Abbey Theatre, Dublin, Ireland, March 12, 2007.

Shepard as Robert Rayburn in *Bloodline*. Islamorada, Florida, 2014.

*True West*, as its title indicates, is about the myth of the Old West, and what, if anything, remained of it by the 1970s. Lee yearns for the "real West," and he refers to the once-blacklisted screenwriter Dalton Trumbo's *Lonely Are the Brave* as his cultural benchmark. *Lonely Are the Brave* parallels *True West* in that it too charts the tale of an ill-fated cowboy, Jack Burns, a staunch individualist who still lives and rides by the cowboy code. On horseback, Jack confronts barbed wire he must cut, junkyards he must avoid, interstates that spook his horse, and teenage hot-rodders who jeer at him from their convertibles. Shepard himself felt a deep kinship with Jack Burns. "I'd rather ride a horse than drive a car," Shepard said. "But that puts you in a very different relationship to the modern world."[17]

The mythology of the Old West—of horses and pioneers, natural wonders and self-reliance—offered Shepard a sense of wholeness. "If I'm at home anywhere, it's in the West," he remarked, "as soon as I cross the Mississippi, I don't feel the same." In Lee's fierce determination not to relinquish his authentic self, he represents the side of Shepard, as the actor John Malkovich once said, "that's always being strangled but never quite killed." In Shepard's Old West versus New, Lee represents the Mojave Desert and Austin the freeway-weary family station wagon. This was the central paradox of Shepard's inner life, but also, he strongly believed, of American men generally. American masculinity always vexed Shepard: "It sounds a little trite," he said, "but there's not a whole lot of men who know what a man is, and I always thought it was weird that American men haven't resolved this; the American male is in conflict, uniquely in conflict in the cultures of the West. You're either a rassler or you're a book guy, and I think they're getting farther and farther apart."[18]

It's well understood that Shepard based Lee and Austin on his own psychic disunion, as he did with many brothers or brother-like roles. But these split selves, a psychodrama he was never able to resolve, can be read as an allegory for America's political divide too—as one critic put it, "between the prosperous, educated, liberal elite and the unlettered, scrounging, embittered working class." Temperamentally, Shepard embraced this second world, Lee's world, if he conceptually agreed with the politics of the left-leaning theatrical world. "He could never decide. I mean, he had such a strong part of him that was conservative and redneck," Dark said, "but then he also had a little too much intelligence to throw himself completely into that. So he had the other side—the artistic side, and the more liberal side. But they both coexisted. Everything with him was two-sided—Was he gonna be sensitive? Was he gonna be macho?"[19] Shepard acknowledged that between them, he affiliated with Lee, but not Lee on his own: "I always identified with the rougher brother," he said, "but it requires the other guy [Austin] in order for him to have a life."[20]

"There's always this battle going on," Shepard said, "between what I am inclined to believe through the influences coming from outside [Austin], and what I sort of instinctively feel myself to be [Lee], which is quite a different creature. And I think this 'split' is where a lot of the violence comes from in the United States. This frustration between imagery and reality." Shepard later came to believe that the brothers' personality split also corresponded to rising political violence across the United States: "America's gotten more dangerous, more polarized, more insane," he said. "Right now it's very, very dangerous. It's volatile. It's ready to explode."[21]

In Shepard's first draft of *True West*, in fact, which he subtitled "Symbiosis," Lee kills Austin with a knife and taunts him while he twists it in. He revised the ending, however. The final version properly ends with a tie: the two brothers murderously facing off with little hope of reconciliation or victory for either combatant. Their resentments are too deep, their history too long, their social and cultural rifts too wide. "Somewhere there's a myth about the wolf and the sheep," Shepard broadly explained to a reporter, "and the man carries both inside him. And the one that wants to devour—the wolf—is the animalistic one, the one that operates on impulse and is pretty insane. The process of keeping alive is trying to have those two cohabit."[22]

Shepard revised the ending while helping Scarlett recover, a time when he was embracing the conscientious Austin aspect of himself. (He explained years later that when he wrote *True West*, Austin was himself from five years before, and Lee was the self he believed he would become in due time.) America's opposing masculine archetypes merge and face off in the finished script, but the conflict between the two poles of masculinity cannot be resolved; the play's curtain of naturalism drops away in the final scene, and audiences exit with a posthypnotic image: "A single coyote heard in the distance," the stage directions read, "lights fade softly into moonlight, the figures of the brothers now appear to be caught in a vast desert-like landscape, they are very still but watchful for the next move, lights go slowly to black as the after-image of the brothers pulses in the dark, coyote fades."[23]

* * *

*True West*'s premiere was scheduled for that summer at the Magic Theatre's new location on a pier at Fort Mason in San Francisco's Marina District. Their two theaters were on the third floor of the century-old army post, a long yellow building with a magnificent view of Mount Tam across the bay. Fort Mason was also, ironically, the marina from which Shepard sailed with his mother to meet his father across the Pacific, first to Honolulu and then to Guam, in October 1946, and they returned there in May 1948. "So," Shepard told a reporter, "it's kind of like coming home for me."[24]

For John Lion and the ensemble of players at the Magic, the idea of Shepard's destiny at their theater was mutual. Robert Woodruff would broaden this sentiment in later years to include all of San Francisco theater culture writ large: "What David Mamet did in Chicago, Sam did in San Francisco," he said. "He gave a kind of viability to everybody working in theater."[25]

Ordinarily, Shepard could only withstand the first few minutes of his plays' productions, then he would flee the auditorium, get drunk somewhere, and arrive back in time for the last scene. "It's like watching yourself being operated on," he told Dark.[26] He infinitely preferred carting his quarter horse to a rodeo in Petaluma behind his Ford pickup to sitting inside in a dark, crowded, judgmental theater. "Most of my inspiration comes from the racetrack," Shepard told a local critic. "I learn more at the race track than from Shakespeare. It's a real situation where the audience has something at stake—namely their own money. I like watching different kinds of audiences. Rodeo audiences—all kinds of audiences. I learn a lot in terms of theater." In fact, Shepard felt that rodeo could do what theater could not: the rodeo, he said, is "not a representation of anything. It's real." "Should theatre be real, and dangerous, in the same way?" he was then asked. "You don't want to hurt anybody," he averred. "But on the emotional level, there can be a comparable experience without hurting anyone."[27]

*True West* was different for Shepard, who was far more of a presence than he'd been at earlier productions of his plays. On *True West*'s opening night at the Magic's new location, July 10, 1980, the playwright could be found slumped into a seat at the back of the house, laughing at his own lines and twirling a red rose while sporting an orange T-shirt, blue jeans, a Navajo belt buckle, cowboy boots, and dark aviator sunglasses. "This is the first one of my plays I've been able to sit through night after night and not have my stomach ball up in knots of embarrassment," he explained to a critic from the *Christian Science Monitor*. "'True West' is the first play I've truly felt hooked up to."[28]

Robert Woodruff directed, and it starred a pair of superbly cast actors from the San Francisco Mime Troupe, Peter Coyote as Austin and Jim Haynie as Lee. The production was such a success that it returned that September by popular demand. If Shepard might've quaked in his boots before prior performances, this time he knew his play was a hit, and a local drama critic noted that the audience did too:

> At intermission and after the final curtain an almost palpable exhilaration permeated the crowd. It's an unmistakable feeling: a theater crowd that believes right down to the toes it is present at, part of, something new and vital—out there at the cutting edge.[29]

*True West* moved to the Public Theater in New York that fall. On the heels of Shepard's Pulitzer Prize the previous year, and soon after the

Obie Award for Sustained Achievement in 1980, *True West* was advertised as the must-see event of the season by "the hottest young playwright in America." (By then, Shepard was second only to Tennessee Williams in terms of plays produced at any given time around the country, at which point Williams scoffed, "I wouldn't cross the street to see a Sam Shepard play.")[30] At the Public, Peter Coyote and Jim Haynie were replaced by Tommy Lee Jones and Peter Boyle. They were highly accomplished film actors who could help sell tickets, but badly miscast. As one critic remarked, they were "too similar in type and temperament."[31]

What followed was a highly publicized theatrical disaster. "I was just appalled," John Lion said after making the trek to New York. "It was lousy. . . . I was really angered because I saw what I consider a terrific piece of writing made mincemeat out of."[32] (Lion then convinced Shepard that they should do a revival at the Magic, which they did the following spring.) Opening night was postponed twice. Woodruff had quit after three weeks of previews, while Shepard was holed up in Maxwell, Texas, where he was filming his next role, *Raggedy Man*, with Sissy Spacek.

If there was ever a time Shepard's fear of flying directly impacted one of his productions, this was it. Everyone needed him there, and he refused despite call after call. "Why doesn't he walk or something?" Papp thought, so he'd phone again: "Sam, you'd better come here."[33] But Shepard's bullheadedness matched Papp's own, which was legendary in the Off-Broadway theater world. "I'm not gonna come!" Papp heard a voice shriek back on his last effort to crack his resolve. "I've never heard a more hysterical voice in my life," Papp recalled later. "High-pitched, completely out of character with Sam's public image as this close-lipped, taciturn Westerner. They don't know he's a screamer, a hysteric of the first water." Shepard's anguish was more likely from guilt than hysteria, and there was no shortage of guilt trips. "I understand Sam doesn't like to ride airplanes," Tommy Lee Jones said, "but hell, you can get to New York City in a pickup truck in two days if you don't waste a lot of time."[34]

After Woodruff fled the production, Shepard testily informed the *Village Voice*'s Michael Feingold that Papp had hijacked their show: "I would like it to be known that the production of my play *True West* at the Public Theater is in no way a representation of my intentions or of Robert Woodruff's." Joe Papp, he went on, had hired movie stars to replace the Magic's original cast. (This was not true; it was Woodruff, not Papp. "I cast the play," Woodruff said. "Nobody twisted my arm.") Shepard still owed Papp two more plays in a contract he'd made with the Public, but swore to refund his advance money, seething, "He'll never see another play of mine."[35]

"He told me he owned my play," Shepard said later. "And he proceeded to do anything he wanted with it, as though it was a used car that I'd sold him."[36]

The two theater giants never spoke again, and by the time *True West* finally opened on December 23, after Shepard had sabotaged the show by phoning in his grievances to the press, Jones and Boyle responded by phoning in lackluster performances. "No wonder the actors were so demoralized," said the critic and future Shepard chronicler Don Shewey. "It must be tough when the author goes around saying publicly you've ruined his work, especially since Shepard never saw the production." Insofar as Papp's hijacking of the play's direction, Frank Rich of the *New York Times* extolled Shepard's masterful script but ridiculed the staging of it: "This play hasn't been misdirected; it really looks as if it hadn't been directed at all." Papp had, in fact, left the show rudderless after Woodruff left. "Of all the versions of that play that were done at that time," Tommy Lee Jones said, "ours was distinguished by being the worst."[37]

Two years after *True West*'s New York implosion, however, Chicago's Steppenwolf Theatre mounted a 1982 revival that was distinguished by being the best—Gary Sinise was its director, Jeff Perry played Austin opposite John Malkovich as Lee, and Laurie Metcalf was Mom. Richard Christiansen of the *Chicago Tribune* hailed this *True West* as one of the most hair-raising, and hilarious, productions he had ever witnessed on a Chicago stage:

> Steppenwolf Theatre tackled—and I mean tackled—Sam Shepard's "True West" in a knockdown, slam-bang, all-out battle to the finish. It

> was a great fight; both Steppenwolf and Shepard won; and the audience, amazingly unscarred from two hours of being slapped around, emerged happily punchdrunk.... John Malkovich, his jaw thrust out in simian style, storms the role of Lee with wild-eyed bursts of intensity, mixed with howling, screaming flights of boorish glee.[38]

Christiansen concluded that *True West* embodied the central theme of Shepard's oeuvre: "the decline and fall of American civilization."[39]

Steppenwolf's production ran for nearly six months, and the *Chicago Tribune* critic Chris Jones later described it as "the most famous production in Chicago theater history." It then transferred for an extended run to Chicago's Apollo Theater Center, then to New York's Cherry Lane Theatre, where Gary Sinise replaced Jeff Perry.[40]

One sparkling instant took place onstage between Sinise and Malkovich that launched, Chris Jones said, "Chicago theater's in-yer-face era ... the so-called Chicago-style acting." At one point in the performance, Malkovich menacingly tapped the steel head of a golf club on Sinise's eyeglasses. ("The tap heard round the world," Ethan Hawke said after performing the role of Lee in *True West*. "I didn't even want to imitate that. It was too iconic.") It was, Jones contended, the most famous ten seconds in Steppenwolf history. After *True West*, he said, all of Steppenwolf's productions circle back around to that tap. "It's impossible to overstate."[41]

The Chicago production of *True West* opened at the Cherry Lane Theatre in New York on October 17 and ran for 762 performances, with Erik Estrada and Jim Belushi and the actual brothers Dennis and Randy Quaid as understudies. It was a must-see theatrical event, and a procession of cultural notables attended—Michelangelo Antonioni, Kurt Vonnegut, Jacqueline Onassis, and David Bowie, among many others. (Shepard did not.) Malkovich was equally contemptuous of long runs and the New York theater scene, but he made a rare exception to hang on for this one. Previously, only diehard Chicago theatergoers knew who he and Sinise were; but after this production, they were bombarded with calls from agents and managers.[42]

During the Cherry Lane Theatre's opening night after-party at Chumley's, a revamped speakeasy in the West Village, the actor who played Saul, Wayne Adams, bellowed out Mel Gussow's *New York Times* review. Malkovich's performance, the critic gushed, was an "acting hole-in-one," and Sinise was "an ideal interpreter of Mr. Shepard; he is finely tuned to a special wavelength." "'True West,' revivified," he wrote, "should now take its rightful place in the company of the best of Shepard."[43]

After Steppenwolf's triumph, arguably the most significant production of Shepard's lifetime, *True West* was nominated for the Pulitzer Prize for 1983.

CHAPTER 13

# THE AVIATOR

In July 1980, O-Lan sat down for an hour-long interview with the *San Francisco Chronicle* for a feature story about her and Shepard titled "A Marriage of Luck and Chemistry." They'd been married for over a decade by then, and the journalist, Ruthe Stein, offered a close account of their contrasts. She was outgoing; he was taciturn. She was dressed all in black like an urban sophisticate; Shepard was dressed like a cowboy out of the Old West. Then, Stein turned to how their mutual love of theater might explain their staying power as a couple. O-Lan cheerfully attributed the length of their marriage to "luck and chemistry and a lot of other things too," and she added how fortunate it was for their son, Jesse, now eleven, to have been raised in a two-parent household.[1]

The timing of this interview was ill-fated, to say the least. The following spring, Shepard agreed to play the male lead, Harry York, a fictional love interest of Frances Farmer, a troubled but independent-minded, studio system–defying Hollywood star who was diagnosed with paranoid schizophrenia and committed to a mental hospital for eight years.

The Australian director Graeme Clifford's biopic *Frances* was to be shot in the fall of 1981, and a who's who of A-listers auditioned for the title role: Meryl Streep, Diane Keaton, Susan Sarandon, Goldie Hawn, Mia Farrow, Natalie Wood, Jane Fonda, Cybill Shepherd, and Sissy Spacek all wanted to play Farmer, a martyr of disaffected actresses beholden to Hollywood's ruthless machinations. Surprisingly, Clifford took a risk on a thirty-two-year-old Frances Farmer look-alike with a comparatively low profile. Her name was Jessica Phyllis Lange.

* * *

The first time Shepard laid his eyes on Jessica Lange was in early 1977, when he and Johnny Dark saw 1976's risible remake of *King Kong*; and in turn, the first time Jessica Lange laid eyes on Shepard was seeing *Resurrection* the previous fall. Her movie, costarring Jeff Bridges, was comprehensively panned, though she won a Golden Globe for New Star of the Year. Shepard didn't care about "the Eighth Wonder of the World" while he was watching this tacky Hollywood disaster movie; he was too entranced by Kong's love interest to notice. "Somehow he knew," Dark said, "if he bided his time, their paths would cross in LA."[2]

Their paths did cross in Los Angeles, in late July 1981, when they met in the office of the director Graeme Clifford, then casting for *Frances*. Clifford set up the meeting independently just to see whether the film's two potential stars would click. "There were three reasons I wanted Sam for *Frances*," he said. "One, I wanted an enigma, which Sam is. Two, I wanted a sexuality that wasn't *acted*, which Sam has. And, three, I thought he and Jessica would get along well together."[3]

Jessica was then leveraging her breakout as a serious dramatic actress, as the Angel of Death in Bob Fosse's 1979 musical drama *All That Jazz*, and then in 1981's *A Postman Always Rings Twice* with Jack Nicholson (who'd archly branded Jessica "a cross between a fawn and a Buick"). Clifford had edited the second film and decided during postproduction that Jessica, despite her relatively short highlight reel, was perfect for the role of Frances Farmer.[4]

Jessica was in the process of divorcing the bohemian Spanish photographer Paco Grande, and she was six years into a relationship with the celebrated Russian ballet dancer and Soviet defector Mikhail Baryshnikov. She and Baryshnikov had a baby girl named Aleksandra "Shura" Baryshnikov, who joined her at the meeting. At first, she and Shepard appeared extremely shy, so Clifford excused himself. When he returned, they were "getting along like a house on fire." Jessica instantly felt a strong connection to Shepard, a rarity for her. "There was something about Sam," she recalled. "I immediately felt I knew something about him, that wildness, that typically American wildness, a no-restraints outlaw quality."[5]

"Movie sets are the most seductive places in the world," she went on, "there's nothing like them for creating an ambience of romance and passion. I had a feeling Sam and I were going to fall in love." They even shared a crescent moon tattoo, Shepard's from the Hotel Chelsea and Lange's from living in Paris at nineteen. "Oh boy," Shepard thought, "this one is going to kill me."[6]

Filming began that October in Seattle, Washington, Frances Farmer's hometown. Playing the role of Farmer was difficult for Jessica. For one thing, Clifford shot the movie out of sequence, forcing her on any given day to conjure different stages in the actress's mental and physical collapse. For another, she was submitted to over eighteen weeks of overshot scenes, according to her, including four days where she played Farmer hiding naked in a hotel bathroom; and there was a distressful series of shooting days in a working mental asylum, where a patient assaulted a member of the crew. Jessica was also compelled to enact emotional scenes with her costar Kim Stanley, who played Farmer's imperious mother, "over and over again, which was quite unnecessarily wearying," Jessica said. "There were times when I got so depressed I burst into tears."[7]

At the hotel in Seattle, Clifford arranged for Shepard and Jessica to be assigned adjacent rooms. "I knew Sam," cast member Darrell Larson reminisced, "and I also knew that they were beginning to get it on." Larson played the role of the gossip columnist Louella Parson's spy, and he noted that Jessica's acting discipline never flagged. "I know Sam!" Larson introduced himself before filming a scene wherein the two clash at a cocktail party. "She just looked at me, stone cold, without shaking my hand." "I'm aware of that," she snapped. Jessica's hostility and its effect on Larson were emotionally perfect for the scene. Weeks later, they met a second time in the makeup room, preparing for their next scene together, which takes place prior to their characters' confrontation; this time, Jessica greeted him warmly, cooing, "Sam says hi!"[8]

Shepard and Jessica's ardent love affair continued to the end of the *Frances* production, then through Jessica's work with Dustin Hoffman on *Tootsie* in the spring and summer of 1982, and for almost thirty years thereafter. "I thought when I first met her that after I got home from L.A. I could forget her," Shepard told Dark. "But I couldn't stop thinking about her. It was ridiculous." He wrote Jessica a long letter, and for her to write back without O-Lan noticing, she sent her reply to a friend in the Bay Area, where Shepard could retrieve it covertly.[9]

Jessica moved from upstate New York, where she and Baryshnikov owned a house, to Los Angeles mainly to be closer to Shepard. He would meet her at the Chateau Marmont, and they would venture out to elite Hollywood canteens such as Ports and Butterfield's. "I've never seen anything like it in a restaurant," a TV producer dining at Butterfield's remembered. "They were literally attached to each other over the top of the table. They kept twisting around, holding hands, then a hand would go up the arm, into Jessica's mouth. I don't think a lot of eating was going on, because her mouth was constantly full of his hand. They were just gorgeous and madly, wildly, passionately involved with each other."[10]

"When we were together we were so wild," Jessica recalled, "drinking, getting into fights, walking down the freeway trying to get away—I mean, just really wild stuff." She gave up on him, and they stopped talking, but friends conspired to ensure their reunion.[11]

Jessica was nominated for an Academy Award for *Frances* and won Best Supporting Actress for *Tootsie* at the 1982 Oscars, making her the first woman in forty years to be nominated for two Oscars in one night. Using money from *King Kong*, she'd built a log cabin in northern Minnesota, where she was raised, but the following year, she wanted to relocate to New Mexico, where she planned a more structured and tranquil existence for herself, perhaps with a new family.[12]

* * *

Once Shepard finished shooting for *Frances* in Los Angeles on November 23, he left Jessica behind and drove north toward San Francisco; but he stopped in Coalinga, a midway point between the cities. He pulled off at the side of the road and walked into a field where he sat down cross-legged and, paralyzed by his indecision with Jessica and guilt over leaving O-Lan and Jesse, wished he could simply remain in the middle of that California field. "A huge hand grabbed him from behind," he wrote in the third person about Jessica's magnetism. It's a passage that carries familiar reverberations of the *King Kong* fable, but with Jessica in the role of the fearsome, lovelorn beast that for Jessica's scenes was played on set by a hydraulic hand:

> A hand without a body. It carried him up, miles above the highway. He didn't fight. He'd lost the fear of falling. The hand went straight through his back and grabbed his heart. It didn't squeeze. It was a grip of pure love. He let his body drop and watched it tumble without hope. His heart stayed high, tucked in the knuckles of a giant fist.[13]

He still had over two hundred miles before he'd reach home.

Shepard recorded this anecdote in a new prose and poetry collection, *Motel Chronicles*. The book was completed under the editorship of the San Francisco–based Beat poet Lawrence Ferlinghetti and was published in May 1982 by Ferlinghetti's famed City Lights Books, with Dark contributing intimate photographs portraying their families' lives together. *Motel Chronicles* contains a farrago of imagistic poems and sketches about his old life in New York contrasted with his vagabond life after moving back to California.[14] In it, Shepard demonstrates his brilliance at employing seemingly minor incidents—imitating Burt Lancaster's smile, watching Jesse dream, Nancy Mandel drawing his astrological chart—and transforming them into crystalline reflections of the conscious mind.

*Motel Chronicles* was in manuscript form under the title "Transfixion" ("trans-fiction") when the forty-year-old director Wim Wenders, a brilliant German filmmaker out of the New German Cinema movement, set up a meeting with Shepard to convince him to write the script for a film on the detective turned mystery writer Dashiell Hammett. At the time, Shepard was refusing to work on studio-funded scripts, but he agreed to play Hammett, a major literary influence of his. After seeing Shepard perform screen tests for the role, Francis Ford Coppola, the film's executive producer, was firmly against casting him.[15] (Shepard would be given another opportunity to play Hammett, in 1999's *Dash and Lilly*, opposite Judy Davis as the playwright Lillian Hellman, which garnered him an Emmy nomination.) But Wenders still wanted to find a way to work with him. He adored *Angel City*, so he next asked Shepard whether he wanted to write a science fiction film along those lines.[16]

Shepard then showed him "Transfixion," and Wenders, sensing its cinematic potential, wrote a draft out of the hodgepodge. But the result, Shepard felt, was too literary. "Rather than adapt them," Shepard advised, "why don't we take some of the essence of the stories in terms of character rather than in terms of making a literal adaptation of the stories?"[17]

The product of this collaboration would evolve, after many drafts, into *Paris, Texas*. Importantly for the film, Shepard included a cover page with the handwritten title "Transfixion" above a photograph of a man in a suit, white shirt, fedora, and no shoes. He's on a set of train tracks scanning the horizon in the middle of a blasted desert, and that is where we find Shepard's eventual antihero, Travis Henderson, in the opening scene of the movie, only the fedora has been replaced by a red baseball cap, the tracks are gone, and he's being followed by a hawk.

One entry in Shepard's manuscript served as the launching point: a tableau of a drifter on a desert highway who fled his home with a battered suitcase full of random belongings: "He drops them all on the pile of rubble. Squats naked in the baking sand. Sets the whole thing up in flame. Then stands. Turns his back on the U.S. Highway 608. Walks straight out into open land."[18]

The finished script of *Paris, Texas*, which took them over a year and a half to develop, revolves around the loneliness of a married man living too deeply in his own fractured mind. There are close parallels in the film to Shepard's abandonment of his own family, but essentially, Shepard said, it is about the "relationship between men and women, the *idea* that each partner has of the other, the idealistic situation that's always at play in the real context of what it's like to be together. These two things are always in juxtaposition with each other; you know, the *idea* of who I'm with, and who I'm actually with." The final scene of abandonment, Shepard explained, posits that when a man is fractured like his character Travis Henderson, "even pulling together the broken pieces of his past isn't enough; what has finally to come about is to bring about the broken pieces in himself. And he has to do it alone."[19]

* * *

It was time for Shepard to step back in front of the camera again, but he was increasingly wary of the effect movie stardom might have on his literary ambitions and his mental well-being. "There was this feeling that my credibility as a writer would go in the toilet if I suddenly became Robert Redford," Shepard said late in life. "I didn't want to be a movie star. I didn't want to have that thing of being an icon. It scared the shit out of me."[20]

Nonetheless, by early 1982, Shepard accepted another role, one that would be the most iconic of his career and ensure a place for him in American film history. The director Philip Kaufman, a relative unknown, aside from his recent remake of *Invasion of the Body Snatchers* followed by an underrated sleeper about Bronx street gangs called *The Wanderers*, was convinced that Shepard would be perfect to play the role of the World War II flying ace and sound barrier–breaking test pilot Chuck Yeager. It was for a screenplay he'd adapted from Tom Wolfe's novel about America's first astronaut program, *The Right Stuff*.

Two years earlier, Kaufman had attended a poetry reading of Shepard's at San Francisco's Intersection for the Arts Theater.[21] His wife, Rose, turned to him while Shepard was reading and said, "That's your guy." "Yeager was a stocky, military general, sort of a Robert Duvall type," Kaufman reflected on the idea. "Duvall was a little bit older than I wanted to cast. But listening to Sam read, I got what she was talking about, because even though Sam was this tall, gangly guy who looked nothing like Yeager, he had that quality, a certain truth, a sort of cowboy feeling." It wasn't until after the film was released that studio executives pretended to have agreed with Kaufman's choice, which they hadn't from the get-go. "Shepard wasn't a magic name in the studio," the director admitted.[22]

When Kaufman first introduced Shepard and the brigadier general in a cafeteria in San Francisco, Yeager didn't think Shepard was up to playing the role, and Shepard agreed with him. But they soon warmed to each other. "The more I talked with him, the more interested I got," Shepard said. "He was the ace of aces. He made all the astronauts shake in their boots. He broke the speed of sound, he flipped planes, he crashed them and he walked away."[23]

Shepard agreed, in the fall of 1982, to get in a plane for the first time since Mexico back in 1965. It would be piloted by Chuck Yeager himself, and he'd give him a tour over the Mojave Desert in a Piper Cub aircraft, "this little thing that he pulled out of the hangar with a hook." "If I was gonna crash," he convinced himself, "I might as well go down with the world's greatest pilot." Yeager assured him that fear of flying was normal. You just have to learn to face the fear. He asked Yeager about the life of an ace pilot, and the West Virginian told him, "Well, by the time I was 12 years old, I'd already killed 26 black bears." But "fearless" would be a misnomer. "He'll be the first to admit he was scared shitless," Shepard said about a test flight depicted in *The Right Stuff* that ends in a ball of flames. "He was crapping in his pants when his plane was flipping upside down. I heard the cockpit tape. I heard the terror in his voice." Shepard next asked Yeager how he was able to shoot down so many planes. "It all came from hunting bears," Yeager replied.[24]

Kaufman's script first appealed to Shepard because of the opening chase scene on horseback, featuring Yeager and his wife, Glennis, riding at a full gallop through the Mojave Desert, "figure-eighting through the cactus and stuff." And his cowboy skills had sharpened admirably. "On set he was often roaming around with a lasso, spinning it around while we'd be talking," recalled Kaufman. "He was really great with it. He'd be hooking chairs while we were having a talk about things."[25]

The woman Shepard would be riding through the saguaros with was the talented Barbara Hershey, who was cast as Yeager's wife, Glennis. When Hershey first heard she was to play opposite Shepard, she thought, "What is a Pulitzer Prize–winning playwright? Is that a human being? Someone I can act with?" Her trepidation faded after their first meeting, though. Interviewed by *Newsweek* soon after the film appeared, Hershey told the reporter, "I loved his looks: one moment he's like a green ear of corn, the next he's a quiet, granite man."[26]

* * *

Shepard had begun work on his next play, *Fool for Love*, the previous spring, 1982. It was a lengthy one-act documenting the emotional price of Shepard's great fortune. The plot was suggested by a visit to Sam Sr. in Bernalillo, New Mexico, in spring 1981, where his father was living, and he has an onstage role as the Old Man. But primarily, he wrote it to hash out his guilt feelings over leaving O-Lan. *Fool for Love*, he said, is about "what it's like to fall victim to love." He was "determined to write some kind of confrontation between a man and a woman, as opposed to just men," he said. "I wanted to try to take this leap into a female character, which I had never really done. I felt obliged to, somehow. But it's hard for a man to say he can speak from the point of view of a woman."[27] To address this problem with *Fool for Love*, Shepard wrote from the perspective of three women whom he knew extremely well.

*Fool for Love* premiered at the Magic on February 9, 1983. Shepard directed the show, starring Kathy Baker, who'd performed in *Curse of the Starving Class*, and Ed Harris, who'd costarred with Shepard in *The Right Stuff*. Shepard's work with these top actors revealed something about the kind of actors he wanted to work with. Fame too often made actors resist direction and shut themselves off, he explained. "Another kind of actor, like Ed Harris, absolutely open—a wide-open actor. Good on the screen but incredible on the stage, because he's continually opening, opening, opening, waiting for any kind of adventure. And Kathy Baker was the same way."[28] The character Eddie uses a lasso, so Shepard invited Harris up to train him, and they became lifelong friends.[29]

*Fool for Love* depicts four characters in a fleabag motel room on the edge of the Mojave Desert. Shepard's persona, Eddie, a wrangler and stunt man, and his sweetheart, May, are trapped in forbidden love—they are half siblings who hadn't been informed they were related until the damage was done. Eddie is based on himself, and May is an unmistakable composite of O-Lan and Sandy Rogers. Shepard said later that May was "probably the most solid female character I've written ... not strong just in the sense of her own willfulness, but as a whole character."[30]

May and Eddie have been together for fifteen years, similar to the length he and O-Lan had been married, and when he asks her to join him at his Wyoming ranch, she responds, O-Lan-like, "Wyoming? Are you crazy?. . . . What's up there? Marlboro Men?" It's true that Shepard was leaving O-Lan for Jessica, which follows the plot, but May's dialogue comes mostly from his actual sister Sandy. "Well, we're a lot alike, too," Sandy said. "It was easy to take himself and become a girl through me." "When you are sister and brother, you have this likeness that you can never find anywhere else," Sandy responded to a reporter about her resemblance to May. "Sam and I have that, but it's not a sexual feeling. You don't have to explain things to each other; you just understand. It comes from having the same chromosomes or something."[31]

Eddie and May's father, the Old Man (played by Will Marchetti), is an apparition, a shared memory between the siblings, "like the old ghost thing in *Our Town*," Shepard said of the character, who sits in a rocking chair watching and sporadically engaging his son over his grievances.[32] The countess, modeled on Jessica, exists offstage. She is a movie star who jealously terrorizes Eddie and May in her black Mercedes outside their motel room. In the final scene, Eddie says he's leaving to check on the horses, but May knows he's leaving her for good. Eddie is, wrote Nancy Scott in a glowing but straight-talking *San Francisco Examiner* review, "a man's man with the heart of a small boy, which is to say, a jerk where women are concerned."[33]

*Fool for Love* moved to New York and opened on May 26 with Harris and Baker in the lead roles. The box office hit ran for a thousand performances, the longest run of Shepard's career. Shepard's script and off-site direction, along with the cast's bravura performance, won Obies for Best New American Play and Direction, and Shepard received his third nomination for the Pulitzer Prize. "Mr. Shepard is the most deeply serious humorist of the American theatre, and a poet with no use whatever for the 'poetic,'" Edith Oliver concluded her *New Yorker* review. "He brings fresh news of love, here and now, in all its potency and deviousness and foolishness, and of many other matters as well." Clive Barnes inserted a proviso for his *New York Post* review, later used as a blurb: "If you don't like this play," he wrote, "I don't like you."[34]

* * *

On St. Patrick's Day, March 17, 1983, Shepard and Dark were eating breakfast in the back of Sam's Pancake House in San Rafael when Shepard abruptly asked, "Where are the women?" Taking French lessons in San Francisco, Dark replied. Shepard told him it was time to go.[35]

They raced home, and Shepard packed a bag and his typewriter, on which he'd just written that morning, "ME—I'M IN THE EYE OF MY OWN HURRICANE." He said to Dark, "I'm going. I'm outta here. Take care of Jesse, and I'll be in touch." Dark documented the event with his tape recorder and camera and captured a photograph of Shepard climbing into his truck, "leaving home forever," Dark said, "abandoning his family, and running off with this other woman."[36]

When O-Lan and Scarlett returned to the Evergreen house, Dark said nothing and fled downtown to San Francisco, where he got drunk on tequila sunrises and went to the movies. After Dark returned home, Shepard called collect from a pay phone in Coalinga, halfway down to Los Angeles. O-Lan begged him to meet her, but he wouldn't. "Sam was frustrated," Sandy Rogers recalled, her voice stricken with a tone of abiding sorrow. "He had a great life, you know? O-Lan is like my best friend, so that destroyed all of us when he took off. I think also he, Sam, was ready to make a change, and then Jessica came along."[37]

*Fool for Love* had gone from autofiction to reality. Each of his lovestruck characters were present. "I walked out of that house into the unknown & it scared the shit out of me," he wrote to Dark soon after,

> but the adventure of hitting life straight on was a thrill I'll never forget. I feel that now—along with the fear. But I see the fear stems from being alone in the world & it has new meaning for me now. You can be alone in the midst of people or you can be alone & join with the other one's aloneness. There can be a real meeting between two people at the point where they always felt marooned. Right at the edge. And that's how it is with me & [Jessica].[38]

That same St. Patrick's Day, *Rolling Stone* published the most comprehensive interview with Jessica Lange to date. "I always go through big cycles," she told the reporter. "Now, I feel a whole period of my life coming to a close and something else opening up."[39]

* * *

Shepard reunited with Jessica at her log cabin in remote northern Minnesota, about half an hour south from the small town of Cloquet, where she attended high school. "It's beautiful," Lange said of her 120-acre sanctuary in the deep woods, where you could find, carefully hidden from the country road, timber wolves and a small lake fed by a stream where otters swiveled through arrangements of flowering lily pads. Jessica was at peace there. Because of her father's itinerancy, the Lange family had moved eighteen times during her childhood, and her parents now lived on a farm near where she was born and a short drive to the cabin. Her mother, Dorothy, was a housewife and her father, Albert, was a history teacher and traveling salesman turned railroad worker. "This gruff old country guy," Shepard noted, "with a black plow horse out back & broken down tractors all sitting around the yard buried in snow."[40]

Up to then, none of the exhilarating turns in Shepard's life had quelled his sense of feeling lost and alienated from himself. His family couldn't help him. His success hadn't helped. The Work didn't help, although he'd continued to attend meetings in San Francisco and New York. Booze and women temporarily abated the dissociative sensation, but afterward, he felt worse. Now he believed that Jessica might save him. He could not stand being without her, nor she without him. "Inside, my world keeps shifting always," he wrote to Dark soon after his arrival in the Land of Ten Thousand Lakes. "I miss the family & Jesse & O-Lan & all of you—sometimes with a terrible sadness that seizes me completely. The thing that hurts me most is knowing I abandoned everyone." He would never get over this guilt, but in his relationship with Jessica, he was struck by an epiphany: "*Guilt* is the opposite of *Acceptance*.... Going further with it I saw that Guilt is always wrapped up with the past & Acceptance can only be arrived at in the present."[41]

O-Lan was livid, mainly with Dark at first. "She was ignoring all of his behavior and everything, even right up to the point when he left," Dark said. She blamed Dark for encouraging Shepard to leave, he said, but he insisted he hadn't. "He was so in love with Jessica. He was so infatuated with her. He couldn't live without her. He was going crazy." O-Lan also believed, according to Dark, that Jane's years of doting on her son had given him a warped view about women.[42]

O-Lan, Shepard wrote to Jane, "tolerated more from me than ten women could have put up with." He'd been out late all the time and drinking too much, he confessed, and O-Lan never much protested about it. But despite his guilt over leaving Jesse, and the fact that O-Lan was furious at him, he was not prepared to leave Jessica. He wrote that his decision wasn't "frivolous," like his affair with Patti Smith, whom he name-checked. "I suffered hard & long & finally, there was nothing to do but go with where my heart took me," he ended his plea for Jane's acceptance of the situation. "I feel like I've found the love of my life, which is like some kind of miracle."[43]

A week later, Shepard and Jessica drove with Shura to Santa Fe, and Shepard got a taste of what it means to travel with a glamorous movie star. "We've only run into the 'star' bullshit once—in Denver," he wrote from Pueblo, Colorado, "but it was a real drag with all the waitresses and customers coming over to get her autograph. I hope it's not going to be a big deal that way in Santa Fe but who knows." Dark's cousin Matthew Schwartzman, owner of the Candyman music store, set them up at a small adobe hideaway on Acequia Madre.[44]

"We knew nobody," Shepard wrote. "We liked it that way. We had no need for anything but each other. . . . Every small event in our lives was filled with sexuality. The kind of sexuality that had total partnership. Total complicity. There was never a moment where one refused the other. Never a moment of doubt or regret. We were never apart. To be out of each other's sight for an hour was pure torture."[45]

But again the outer world impeded his domestic bliss, and this time the trouble was being delivered to his front stoop. In his autofictional description of their first days in Sante Fe, Shepard wrote that after their arrival, an enormous cargo of Shepard's stuff from Mill Valley showed up in a moving van, courtesy of O-Lan: a buffalo rug from Wyoming, a Schwinn bike without a front wheel, back issues of *American Quarter Horse Journal*, mildewed books, all remnants of his former life unloaded in front of their rental home. With this, Jessica's amusement began to cool. "That day forward," he wrote, "I began to sense a change in her."[46]

On June 13, 1983, the couple bought a swank, thirty-three-hundred-square-foot log cabin on Brass Horse Road in the unincorporated district Arroyo Hondo (Deep Brook), which came with five acres of land and a barn across the road that Shepard soon occupied with a few rodeo and jackpot horses and a carpentry workshop. It was only a twenty-minute drive south from downtown Santa Fe. Dark wryly observed that Shepard's effusive letters from Santa Fe sounded like "the further adventures of Huck Finn as written to his friend Tom, in which Huck goes to the American Southwest and begins to get along with himself."[47]

Shepard also took up the sport of polo, which he learned from scratch at the Santa Fe Polo Club. "The game completely monopolized him," wrote Dark. "It was worse than hard drugs." Polo was the most fun he'd had on a horse, Shepard explained to a reporter about his improbable partiality to the tony sport. "It's the toughest sport I ever played," he told another, "you're galloping wide open on a Thoroughbred horse trying to get a little white ball with a hand and stick." It wasn't a matter of getting out of yourself on the polo field, he said, "it's getting into yourself." Similar to writing? "Yeah, it's very similar, but you have to be much more aware on the polo field because you'll get killed," he said with a laugh. "I can't dream on the polo field." He'd find that out the hard way at the Eldorado Polo Club in California, where he was thrown badly. He cracked two vertebrae, which took two weeks to heal, he said, "so I was forced to write."[48]

## CHAPTER 14

# "JUST SAM"

Before Shepard arrived in Minnesota, Jessica had begun working on a film project about the farmer crisis in the Midwest. The idea came to her one day while reading the *Los Angeles Times*, in which she saw a picture of a couple at a farm auction that stopped her dead. "The farm wife was enraged and screaming," she recalled, "trying to disrupt an auction, and the husband, the farmer, was absolutely poleaxed—a term my father used to use. And I thought, *Oh, there's the story.*"[1]

Once they were settled in Santa Fe, Shepard and Lange began developing the project, now titled *Country*, a protest film loosely based on the farmers she grew up with. The Midwest, Shepard said, was in a desperate state: "The cities all have the feeling of communist countries. People are super depressed & very poor. All the small farms are being auctioned off. . . . It's definitely the end of an era." William Wittliff, the writer of *Raggedy Man* (and later, the teleplay for *Lonesome Dove*), finished the screenplay and promised to direct it, then Disney picked it up for their new Touchstone Films, and they had a movie.[2]

*Country* portrays the tenuous relationship of two small farmers, Jewell and Gil Ivy, who are trying to fend off foreclosure on their land in Black Hawk County, Iowa. Jessica and Shepard were to star in the film, and Jessica would coproduce with Wittliff, who would also direct. Later, Shepard, while he was acting, rewrote the screenplay to make the dialogue "tougher," according to him, with "less sentimentality." Two and a half weeks into the shoot, after giving Wittliff's dailies a thumbs-down, Jessica hired Richard Pearce to right the ship. To everyone's relief, Pearce did just that. Several people refused to work before Pearce was hired, including Shepard. "I suppose this move on my part is going to brand me as 'difficult' & 'temperamental' in Tinsel Town," he wrote to Dark. "I really don't give a shit anymore." And some movie competition was also added to Jessica's troubles. "The Texas Movie" with Sally Field, which eventually folded, and *The River* with Sissy Spacek were also under production. But Jessica put on a brave face: "Can't you just see the headlines next fall?" She laughed uneasily. "'New Wave of American Farm Films Finally Arrives!'" The president of the United States, Ronald Reagan, watched *Country* and, as a stalwart defender of Big Ag profits, reduced it to "a blatant propaganda message against our agri programs."[3] Maybe so, and it did poorly at the box office, but it garnered Jessica nominations for both an Oscar and a Golden Globe Award for Best Actress.

For a temporary home, they rented a redbrick mansion in Waterloo, Iowa, with room for their live-in German cook, Gertrude. Filming in Iowa began that October, but winter closed in fast, and by December it turned bitterly cold—subzero for weeks at a time. At one point it got down to twenty-six below. "So cold," Shepard wrote to Joe Chaikin from Waterloo, "the feet of cattle would freeze to the ground."[4]

Shepard's refrain to reporters on set was, "I don't have much to say." When he did finally talk, he refused to discuss Jessica. The crew predictably muttered to reporters, "She doesn't talk to people." Another kind of "talk" had already begun to spread around Hollywood that although Jessica was unquestionably a remarkable talent, she could be "difficult," to use the age-old Hollywood euphemism. "In the old-boy network that is Hollywood," the *American Film* magazine writer Julia Cameron explained, "it is particularly important to be a nice guy—especially if you're a girl."[5]

Meanwhile, O-Lan hired a divorce lawyer, and together they devised a suitable ending to her and Shepard's theatrical marriage: to get at Shepard during the filming of *Country*, which had otherwise proven impossible, the bailiff crashed the set and served him his papers disguised as an extra, and the story was picked up by the press. "Though reclusive," wrote one reporter, "the couple echo almost eerily the 'Misfits' teaming of Marilyn Monroe and playwright Arthur Miller—the blonde screen queen and the rangy intellectual playwright; opposites attracting—and attracting attention."[6] (Shepard and O-Lan's divorce would be finalized on November 9, 1984.)

Shepard and Jessica fought throughout the shoot of *Country*, acting out in real life the unstable fictional marriage depicted in the film. "This was a time when I was desperately in love. I swear," Shepard wrote. "And in this time I did some stupid things which, now, I lay down to this desperate state, but more likely the state gave a good excuse to lose myself in all kinds of physical & emotional abuse which I'd been saving up." Along with the hiring missteps and financial anxieties of producing a feature, they fought over their future visions of life together—she wanted to travel, and he, for the time being, wished to domesticate. Nevertheless, he wrote to Dark, "I'm kidding myself if I think I can live without her."[7]

Arguments often ended with his exploding out of the house and driving off, but his admiration for her talent never flagged: "Jessica has incredible courage in the face of her own emotional territory," he said. "I don't have that particular kind of courage as an actor. I can muster it up as a writer, but as an actor it takes another kind of dimension. Whether it can be nurtured and brought out through more acting I don't know." Shepard was convinced, though, that he was the kind of maladroit actor, who could never achieve the greatness of a Jessica Lange.[8]

"What a saga this life is!" Shepard crowed on December 10, the day after he bought a ring and asked for Jessica's hand in marriage. They were meeting at a motel to watch the dailies, and "I swept her outside into the cold wind & snow & popped the question. We jumped up & down together like little kids, giggling in the snow." As tabloids broadcast over the ensuing decades, they never actually married, although they considered themselves to be. "I think marriage is about your commitment to the other person," Jessica said a few years later. "The legality of it means absolutely nothing to me whatsoever. That's not going to make people live their lives together and be responsible to each other."[9]

* * *

The previous April, just after their arrival to Santa Fe, Shepard got drunk in town at a Zoetrope film festival party with a rumpled character actor named Harry Dean Stanton. They sat next to each other during a screening of *Napoleon*, and Stanton leaned over and said, "Do you realize this thing is four hours long, and it's silent?" They left after ten minutes and headed over to the bar at the La Fonda Hotel, where Sam Sr. had worked as a janitor, then shared a joint outside in the parking lot.[10]

Stanton had just finished his first major film role as a jaded car repossession agent in the punk science fiction movie *Repo Man*, a beloved cult favorite for Generation X punk rockers. "And I told Sam," Stanton recalled, "that I was sick of playing heavies and losers and trash. I wanted to play something with some love and decency to it. Sam just listened." Two weeks later, when Wim Wenders was in Santa Fe working with Shepard on the script of *Paris, Texas*, Stanton's phone rang. "Do you want to play the lead in this film I'm doing?" Shepard asked him. "The guy doesn't talk for the first half hour or so."[11]

*Paris, Texas*, shot over the same period as *Country*, opens with a lengthy sequence of the protagonist, Travis Henderson, tramping through a borderland desert, disheveled and alone, until he stumbles into a bar. Travis being mute, Shepard said, "was a very conscious decision," as it was based on Scarlett's experience "with aphasia, oftentimes the symbolism of language is skewed and the names for things can be swapped around. The person speaking absolutely understands what they mean inside, but they might call a 'door' a 'dog.' It's very easy to lose language—it can be shut off in a second. So, what about a character who can't speak, but has all this stuff going on inside of him? He's feeling, but it's not being expressed. That's where we started."[12]

Travis is otherwise another highly autobiographical character. Harry Dean Stanton summed up his personality in a way that might be applied to any of Shepard's male characters: "He's searching for freedom like everybody . . . freedom from the fear of death. Freedom from facing the void without being afraid. I think everybody's afraid, most people.

It's fear you're gonna lose something. It's attachment. Everybody's attached. . . . That's love when you're not attached. That's real love."[13]

"The character was so much Sam himself," Wim Wenders said at the time. "That's why he didn't want to play it."[14]

Travis has been missing for four years, and he reunites with his brother, Walt (played by Dean Stockwell), and Walt's wife, Anne (Aurore Clément), who have been raising his son, Hunter (Hunter Carson), in his absence. His wife, Jane (the wunderkind Nastassja Kinski), left soon after he did and took a job at a peep show in Houston, Texas. The film's story revolves around Travis piecing together what remains of his family, while the audience is left to piece together what exactly happened prior to the action.

Shepard had to leave the production of *Paris, Texas* to film *Country* with Jessica, and the text of Travis's final monologue was written in a single night, then phoned in from Iowa. From midnight to six in the morning, Shepard read it out loud to Wenders over a long-distance call, reworking the scene as he went. "He wrote it in one night and passed it on to me the following night," Wenders recollected in wonder over his collaborator's imaginative power. For the final monologue, the director said, Shepard "delivered gloriously."[15]

In the speech, Travis recounts his story to Jane in her peep show booth. Jane can't see him behind the obscured one-way window, but she knows his story, because it's hers too. Shepard recognized that ending a feature-length movie with an ambiguous aria, no matter how well written, was unorthodox. "I wanted something arduous and strong," he said, predicting a backlash. "I thought it was worth taking the risk . . . see if language itself can become a kind of character."[16]

Wenders and his crew shot the opening in the West Texas desert, which is later contrasted against the glass and steel high-rises, neon billboards, and clogged freeways of Los Angeles and Houston. When it was completed, Wenders's fascination with roadways and the vast loneliness of the American West was so masterfully executed—with the cinematography of Robby Müller—that the setting became its own character. At one point, in fact, Wenders suggested they set some of the film in Alaska, but Shepard retorted, "Don't bother with that zigzagging. You can find all of America in one state: Texas."[17]

Shepard attributed the film's allure to Wenders's "Europeanness": "There are certain qualities about American culture [that] American directors would totally overlook," he said. "They wouldn't find a neon sign of a stagecoach [all] that fascinating. But because of [Wenders's] European background, I guess, this thing suddenly strikes him as having an obsessive quality about it."[18] It was appropriate, then, that the world premiere of *Paris, Texas* on May 19, 1984, would take place at the Cannes Film Festival in France, where the members of the jury gleefully ignored Hollywood's dismissal of the film and awarded it the Palme d'Or, the world's most prestigious arthouse prize. *Paris, Texas* went on to inspire the postmodern films of Wes Anderson and Sam Mendes, along with rock bands such as U2 (whose 1987 album *The Joshua Tree* was inspired by it); but perhaps most miraculously, the film's gritty charm transformed the Lone Star State into a hip destination, with its roadside bars, neon signs, trailer parks, and desert allure.[19]

* * *

*Country* wrapped in late January 1984, at which point Shepard rented a house in the Beacon Hill district of Boston. He and Chaikin had been hired by Harvard's American Repertory Theater (ART) for a month's residency to workshop a play. In Boston, Shepard discovered that Jessica wasn't the only sought-after movie star. By this time, they were a "celebrity couple" in the mode of Monroe and Miller, which exacerbated his paranoia. "I still haven't gotten over this thing of walking down the street and somebody recognizing you because you've been in a movie," he griped. "There's this illusion that movie stars only exist in movies. And to see one live is like seeing a leopard let out of the zoo."[20]

Boston had worked itself into a lather over this "man with the mind of Kafka and the body of Jimmy Stewart" in their midst. "Did you see him?" joked the *Boston Globe* sarcastically. "Did he smile? Did he look into the sunset with the wind in his hair and a dream of America in his heart?" But the point was well made. "He's absolutely the main character around here," a Beacon Hill resident told the reporter. "All I hear is 'You saw him? What's he like? What's he like?' It's crazy." This was no laughing matter for Shepard. A freelance journalist took a photo of Jessica and baby Shura near their rented house, then asked Shepard for an interview. "If you don't get off this street," Shepard told him, "I'll get a gun and blow your fucking brains all over the street."[21]

Shepard and Chaikin's workshop at Harvard evolved into their next avant-garde collaboration, *The War in Heaven (Angel's Monologue)*, about an angel held in captivity and pleading to be set free. But that spring, Chaikin suffered another heart failure, and on May 7, he had a stroke during his third open-heart surgery. Like Scarlett, Chaikin was struck with aphasia, and it took months for his speaking ability to improve. Shepard visited him in August and interwove his aphasic speech into a monologue with two voices. *The War in Heaven* was recorded in the fall by Chaikin with musical accompaniment by Shepard and broadcast by Free Speech Radio (WBAI) on January 8, 1985. Chaikin would later perform its first live performance at Sushi Gallery in San Diego on December 20, 1985. "For 20 lyrical minutes," crowed the *Los Angeles Times* about the show, "Chaikin held his audience aloft with angel poetry." When a reporter asked him about Shepard, he responded, "Very friends, years and years and close."[22]

* * *

On top of Chaikin's dire health trouble, another of Shepard's mentors, Lord Pentland from the Work, died in February 1984, and his Gurdjieffian maxims haunted Shepard's dreams for years to come. Lord Pentland had urged him not to step on people to move forward in life, to think about his life more philosophically and less "pictorially," and not to rely so much on women to make him feel complete.[23]

A few weeks after Pentland's funeral in New York, he decided to see his actual father, who was still alive, at least technically. His earlier move to Santa Fe was meant in part to be closer to his father in Bernalillo and to get to know him as an adult. "But then Sam never pursued that," Sandy Rogers recalled. "He visited him a couple of times, didn't patch anything up, didn't get to know him any better or anything." In fact, Shepard never informed Sam Sr. that he was living nearby, Roxanne said of her brother's years in Santa Fe. "Sammie had to have really strong boundaries. You can't have Dad in your life; he'd destroy you."[24]

Sam Rogers occupied a small, square adobe house "at the end of a dirt alley," he wrote to Roxanne, called Via Conejo, which was a poor neighborhood, so he only paid ninety dollars a month. On the front door hung a sign that warned MAD DOG in red lettering over a savage bulldog's snarling face. There was no dog. The sign was meant as a warning about its human occupant, whose fridge was strictly filled with bottles of Harveys Bristol Cream, Tiger Rose, and applejack.[25] His son's fame and wealth, Sam Sr. believed, would be his golden ticket out of the desert life. In fact, Shepard had purchased a property in Santa Rosa, California, to stable seven or eight horses, and Sandy was overseeing its management and began breeding cutting horses (quarter horses trained to separate, Shepard said, "the calves from the mama"). The Santa Rosa ranch sat on an idyllic ten-acre spread with rickety barns, a roping arena, and a dilapidated house and garage, all of which required construction work with Sandy as the supervisor. Shepard understood that to rescue his father from destitution, he could put him to work there. But he also knew that his father was beyond saving at this stage, and if given the chance, he would likely, Shepard said, "burn the fuckin' place down."[26]

Sam Sr. had only attended one of his son's plays, the American Conservatory Theater's production of *Buried Child* at the College of Santa Fe in June 1980. Three men were required to navigate him into the theater and get him seated, and throughout the performance, he drunkenly yelled at the actors: "This is not the truth! This is not the way it was!" ("He knew because he was in it," Shepard said, referring to the character Tilden.)[27] Eventually, the ushers escorted Sam Sr. out. But once his identity was revealed as the father of the playwright, Shepard reported, "everyone stood up and gave him a standing ovation. He was in a state of shock."[28]

In Bernalillo, Shepard tried to invent more diplomatic excuses for denying his father a job with Sandy at his ranch in Santa Rosa, but Sam Sr. already heard he wasn't getting it (likely from Sandy; she didn't want him to come either, since she had a teenage daughter), and he considered it a betrayal. In hindsight, Shepard realized his mistake was to try to converse with his father when he was drunk. Every time they drank together, Shepard grimly recalled, "it would always turn, inevitably, on this accusation that there was something wrong and it had to do with me."[29]

Once it was clear the ranch job wasn't going to pan out, Sam Sr. furiously howled at him to get out of his house. When Shepard began backing out of the screen door, with its curtain made of beer can flip-tops, he girded himself against his father's familiar onslaught, coaching himself not to retaliate. "So I just kind of walked away," he said, and that was the last time he saw his father alive.[30]

* * *

Jessica was the first to inform Shepard about his father's death on March 24, 1984. She had answered the call from Steve "Estevan" Sandoval, his father's friend and caretaker who watched over him in his last decade at Via Conejo. She went across Brass Horse Road to the barn, where Shepard was building a tack room, and seeing Jessica standing at the door with a half-smile on her face and a northerly wind whipping at her brown overcoat, he knew something was wrong. She rarely came out there, and after they spoke, he went to the house and called Sandoval.[31]

Estevan Sandoval was a retired insurance salesman who lived across the road from Sam Rogers in a house trailer. He used to cook Sam Sr. black bean soup for sustenance, at which times Sam would shout, "Food is for the living!" "I knew it was the booze causing this devil in him, so I never could take it personally, although it hurt my feelings sometimes," Sandoval told Shepard. "He has a good mind, your father. *Muy listo*."[32]

"His voice," recalled Shepard, "was genuinely heartbroken. I could hear him trying to control the quavering in it."[33] Sandoval related the only known story of what happened to Sam Rogers:

By any measure, even for an unrepentant alcoholic, Sam Rogers's was an ignominious death. After cashing an unexpectedly large VA check, Sam got himself a buzz cut at a shopping mall and a fishing license at a gun shop, then paid for a full hour's cab ride to go trout fishing on the Pecos River. Along the way, he met an Indigenous woman Shepard variously referred to as Matla, Conchalla, or Nuncia, who was rumored to be a witch. For three days, Sam Sr. and the woman fished for trout and drank in the Sangre de Cristo Mountains. When they caught a cab from Pecos back to Bernalillo, they went to Silva's Saloon, and locals subsequently reported a brawl. "They were easy to remember," Shepard wrote, "a very large Indian woman named Matla with bare feet, and a tall, stringy white man with a red beard and a crew cut, both raging drunk."[34]

On March 24, at the tail end of their drinking jag and running out of money at Silva's, Shepard wrote in his mostly unpublished chronicle "Slave of the Camera (An Actor's Notes),"

> a final argument erupted in which Matla demanded that my father prove his innocence to her [she'd accused him of being a demon] by throwing himself in front of the next car that came down the little dirt highway in front of the last cantina in town that would have them. Her reasoning was that if he was truly a mortal man and not a demon then he would be either seriously injured or killed. On the other hand, if he turned out to be a demon, then he would escape unscathed.[35]

Cheered by a crowd of barflies, Sandoval continued, Sam Sr. stumbled off a curb into the middle of Route 66. (Shepard removed Matla's involvement in the published version, likely because either it didn't happen or it positions the blame on the woman rather than where he felt it belonged, squarely on his father's shoulders.) After the first three cars missed him, he was struck, Shepard wrote, by "an oncoming El Camino with neon blue lights silhouetting the lowered chassis. The anonymous driver never stopped." His last words were to a technician asking for his name. "Just Sam," he said, then died.[36]

"Matla rode with him to the hospital," Shepard went on, "kissing his head and weeping the whole time. But she was kissing a dead man." Over the course of Sam's final day, his blood alcohol level had risen to an astonishing .334, a life-threatening level if he hadn't already been run over by a car.[37] The facility that housed the death report burned down, but the medical investigator's report of finding exists, and it states that the crash took place at sunset, 7:45 p.m., after he'd made it across to the northbound lane, and the woman who hit him did stop and told the police, the report reads: "She did not see him until the point of impact. The decedent was struck by the right front of the auto. Both the chrome around the hood and the radio antenna were broken off."[38]

When Estevan finished, Shepard craved the release of forgiveness but wasn't in the mood. "All at once I cursed my father in his miserable contemptible death without even wanting to," he wrote a couple of weeks later. "It took me by surprise—this feeling of total loathing. As though he had purposely gone out of his way to lay a curse on me & all those left in his wake."[39]

Back at his father's house, Shepard found an unsent letter to him, which addressed Shepard's exile from their avocado ranch in Bradbury, what Shepard always considered his "original banishment." In his heartbreaking 1989 autobiographical short story about his father's embarrassing demise titled "See You in My Dreams," Shepard included part of his father's letter to him: "You may think this great calamity that happened, way back when—this so-called disaster between me and your mother—you might actually think that it had something to do with you, but you're dead wrong. Whatever took place between me and her was strictly personal. [Signed] See you in my dreams."[40]

Sam's remains were cremated and the ashes scooped into a small pine box and buried in Santa Fe's National Cemetery on account of his military service. At the funeral, Shepard read his father's favorite Lorca poems and from Ecclesiastes, where he paused in sorrow when he read the words "All is vanity."[41]

Jessica insisted on attending, and Shepard was at first unsettled by that. Then she began weeping over the tombstones of the soldiers, he wrote. "I'd never felt so in love with anyone in my whole life. It was strange to be in love like that and in grief at the same time."[42]

"There's no point in regretting," he said of his lifelong trouble and indecisive efforts to resolve the situation with Sam Sr. "Nothing's clearer to me. You spend a lot of time trying to piece these things together and it still doesn't make any sense. His death brought this whole thing to a head, this yearning for some kind of a resolution which could never be."[43]

Back home at Arroyo Hondo, Shepard fell apart. He stopped shaving, wore the same clothes every day, smoked way too many Old Golds (his father's brand), and tried and failed miserably to stop drinking hard liquor. "I could feel this strange change taking place in me," he wrote, "as though I were slowly taking on the traits of my father." Jessica became despondent over his drunken behavior and depressive episodes, according to his account in "Slave of the Camera," and Shepard reacted by goading her—leaving the seat up when he urinated, firing his .30-30 Winchester rifle from the back porch at oil cans and jackrabbits, "causing the arroyo to boom for hours at a stretch." He hit the bars and returned plastered well into the morning hours. They did not speak for days, and she eventually gave up and went back to Minnesota.[44]

In the decades to follow, Shepard grew to recognize his father's outsized role in his life and, more significantly, in his writing:

> I never knew him as a father. He was a tyrant. I lived under that tyranny as a kid, and I'll never forget it. I'll never forget the fear of it or the terror of it. I don't know how you resolve that. . . . It didn't so much intrude on my life as shape it. If you put a horseshoe down and slam it with a hammer, it's going to have that mark. It certainly shaped my sense of not belonging. And that sense of aloneness formed me as a writer.[45]

CHAPTER 15

# LEGENDS OF LOVE

Shepard was nominated for Best Supporting Actor for *The Right Stuff*, but refused to join the other nominees at the Academy Awards ceremony on April 9, 1984, two weeks after his father's death. Sam Rogers's passing would've been justification enough for his absence, but that he kept private. Instead, he undermined his performance, and the film attached to it, as was his mulish custom when evaluating his own work: "I don't like that performance," he told the press. "It's patchy. I was disappointed with the whole film, to be honest. . . . If I get a nomination, it will be because the Academy membership was persuaded by the press to vote for me."[1]

Shepard also passed on a celebration for his forty-first birthday at La MaMa in early November 1984, where they were staging revivals of *Angel City*, *Back Bog Beast Bait*, and *Suicide in B♭*. More surprisingly, he denied New Mexico's drama groups permission to put on any of his plays while he lived in that state, for reasons of "privacy," according to his agent. He did allow for an appearance on the cover of *American Film* magazine and posed for a fashion layout with Jessica for *Vanity Fair*, but only with the intent of promoting *Country*.[2]

The following year, he agreed to a *Newsweek* interview with Jack Kroll, but forbade a cover story. After the interview, a few days before the issue hit the newsstands, he was told it was going to be a cover story anyway and phoned Kroll in a furor, informing him that he was heading over to his office to smash his furniture. Kroll frantically tried to have it removed but without success. As a result, the close-up of Shepard on a movie set, wearing dark aviator sunglasses and a cowboy hat, appeared under the headline "Sam Shepard: Leading Man, Playwright, Maverick." Though Kroll did his level best to thwart the cover, the photo remains one of Shepard's most iconic portraits.[3]

"I prefer a life that isn't being eaten off of," Shepard explained his aversion to media attention. "It's very easy to be *fed* off of, in a certain way that distorts and actually diminishes you completely, destroys you to the point where you don't have a life anymore." "But then," he admitted, "it's also insidious. There's this whole temptation of . . . here's another project, here's another project."[4] Life as another movie star's partner also tormented Shepard with bouts of bad-tempered insecurity.

Jessica was now pregnant, which exacerbated her lifelong battle with depression. "I get real dark sometimes when I'm pregnant," she told a reporter. "When I'm pregnant I could be like Medea any moment." Jessica just finished filming the part of Patsy Cline in *Sweet Dreams* with Ed Harris, for which she was nominated for another Oscar. But if it was a rocky start between Shepard and Jessica, things only got rockier, especially with their work schedules. The long separations and raising children would be serious challenges for the two traveling film stars.[5]

What happened next is deeply ironic, then, given Shepard's strict code of privacy. His forthcoming venture would widely broadcast his affair with Jessica and abandonment of his wife, albeit in fictionalized form. And it was Shepard who reached out to the film director Robert Altman, who'd directed a series of game-changing films, *M*A*S*H*, *McCabe and Mrs. Miller*, and *Nashville*, to make a film adaptation of *Fool for Love*. Shepard had just seen Altman's adaptation of a play (*Come Back to the 5 & Dime Jimmy Dean, Jimmy Dean*) and proposed to the auteur director that he adapt *Fool for Love* too.

Altman took his time mulling over Shepard's offer, but after meeting with Ed Harris and his wife, Amy Madigan, in Paris, where they discussed the script, he felt he was ready. But first, he needed to talk Shepard into playing the male lead.

Shepard was reluctant at first, as he'd been with *Paris, Texas*, and argued that Ed Harris should reprise the role; but after a couple of days, Altman got his way.[6] Jessica was also supposed to play the role of May until she discovered she was pregnant and was swiftly replaced by Kim Basinger (avoiding another messy casting issue, given that she'd be playing the role of her lover's jilted ex-wife, O-Lan, in the voice of her self-described best friend Sandy Rogers). Harry Dean Stanton was cast as the Old Man, and then Shepard called his sister Sandy.

As a country-and-western singer-songwriter, Sandy Rogers had been sending her brother demo tapes for years, and he'd listened to and kept them all. ("He's always had more confidence in my music than I have," Sandy said.) He played Robert Altman a song from a "funky little cassette I had made" from 1976, without telling him it was his sister, and Altman was entranced. "He told Sam that my voice was real raunchy and nasty," Sandy said with a laugh. "Altman is kind of into that kinky stuff." Altman, though, additionally appeared convinced that the incest between Eddie and May was based on the actual Rogers siblings. "I flew out there, and Altman is a weird dude, I'll tell ya," she remembered. "And I think that he was expecting to find some kind of sexual thing between me and Sam, because of the *Fool for Love* thing, the half-sister thing. . . . I had to make it very clear that this is not our relationship, we are not that way." Sandy was hired to write and perform eight songs for the soundtrack—a big break for someone who mostly considered herself a hobbyist musician.[7]

Shepard also hired Roxanne as an assistant in New York for another project, and it seemed to them that this tri-sibling reunion could only have taken place after their father's death. "We've always been spread around and kind of carefree in our relations," Shepard said. "What happened is we decided to try to put this family back together."

"Sam always needed a family," Sandy added about her brother's return to the fold. "He's always needed a base."[8]

Filmed in Santa Fe and Las Vegas in the spring of 1985, *Fool for Love* was less "opened up" by Shepard's adaptation, the method of expanding settings and action to adapt to the medium of film, than "exploded," he said. And Jessica's visiting him on set invariably ignited Shepard's fuse. Altman recalled a time they were shooting a scene, and the moment she arrived, Shepard performed unexpectedly, he said. "It was aggressive, it was hostile, and really shocked me." Altman gathered that his leading man had been reacting to Jessica and was sure he wouldn't have performed that way had she not appeared in time. He was livid at Shepard's lack of preparation, but when he went to edit the film, it was fantastic. "What I had been watching on the set was his behavior in reality," Altman realized. "I wasn't mistaken in what lit the fuse, but what exploded was real dynamite. Now you couldn't get me to change that scene for anything."[9]

Ultimately, though, both men deemed the movie a failure. *Fool for Love* requires a unified space, not the diluting effects of scene changes and Altman's rapid camera moves; in spite of solid performances, it dropped off the cinematic radar, likely for good. "Onstage it was huge," Shepard said of *Fool for Love*. "It had a frightening physical reality to it. . . . On film it comes across as a kind of quaint little Western tale of two people lost in a motel room."[10]

* * *

Once *Fool for Love* was in postproduction and Shepard was free of his acting responsibilities, he wrote another deeply personal family play titled *A Lie of the Mind*, which gushed out of him, and at three and a half hours' running time, it would be the longest of his career. Writing a three-act epic, he said, "is very difficult . . . because, finally, I'm beginning to see the absolute hopelessness of all forms of negativity—but *hopefully*, this will be some kind of final definitive piece on my age-old themes of father & son, sister, brother, mother, family, etc."[11]

And as Shepard so often did, he unfavorably compared a past play, in this case *Buried Child* and its Pulitzer, to his latest creation. The prize, Shepard declared after presenting his latest to the public, "was given to the wrong play. *Buried Child* is a clumsy, cumbersome play. I think *A Lie of the Mind* is a much better piece of work. It's denser, more intricate, better constructed."[12]

Shepard's certainty that his mind had tricked him into believing lies had appeared in his writing at least since *The Sad Lament of Pecos Bill*, in which Sluefoot Sue forgives Bill for murdering her and gives Shepard his title: "Your crime was invented by lies of the mind / It's a crime when a lie is so true."[13] He wanted to explore the notion of lying, he wrote to Joe Chaikin in 1982, "it's slightly spooky but very interesting—I don't understand it at all. Especially how the lie grows. How the part that originally knew the lie was a lie begins to forget and becomes a conspirator in the lie."[14] More important, he wrote to Chaikin, "lying is *pretending*"[15]: "I know what that acting shit is all about," says his avatar Jake in *A Lie of the Mind*. "They try to 'believe' they're this person. Right? Try to believe so hard they're the person that they actually think they become the person. . . . They start doin' all the same stuff the person does!"[16]

*A Lie of the Mind* could be thought of as a follow-up to *True West* in that it also tackles the struggle between Shepard's dueling selves. But unlike the ending of that play, in *A Lie of the Mind* there is resolution.

Once again there are two brothers: Jake is violent, angry, aggrieved, and selfish like his father, who has died after getting run over by a truck while drunk; his brother, Frankie, based in part on Johnny Dark, is the opposite, a mild, caring soul with no delusions. Caught in the middle is Beth, an accomplished actress married to Jake, whose family lives in the northern wilderness. (In a probable nod to Albert Lange, on whom he based the father-in-law, Baylor, Minnesota was swapped for Montana, since Al Lange had dreamed of owning a ranch there.) Jake has beaten Beth so brutally that he believes she has died. Beth has survived, though, after a hospitalization where she recovered from brain damage and aphasia. When Frankie travels to Montana to investigate his brother's crime, Beth falls in love with him, or, more precisely, with his temperament: "Your [*sic*] other one. You have his same voice. Maybe you could be him. Pretend. Maybe. Just him. Just like him. But soft. With me. Gentle. Like a woman-man. . . . You could be better. Better man. Maybe. Without hate. You could be my sweet man. You could. Pretend to be. Try. My sweetest man."[17]

Shepard made it clear that *A Lie of the Mind* is mainly about male-female relationships, and Beth's mother, Meg, explains that the two are not just distinguished by their sex: The female needs the male, Meg says, but the male "goes off by himself. Leaves. He needs something else. But he doesn't know what it is. He doesn't really know what he needs. So he ends up dead. By himself."[18]

Jake's mother, Lorraine (based on Shepard's mother, Jane Elaine), accompanied by his sister, Sally (Sandy), burns down the family home in Southern California, a symbol of their family's misfortune. Jake goes to Montana to make peace with Beth and her family; after that, he wanders off into the woods, as Travis Henderson walked into the desert in *Paris, Texas*. In the final lines, Meg is looking out from her porch and can somehow see the California house on fire from Montana, a sign that Jake's toxic familial past is incinerated along with his father's cremated remains. "Looks like a fire in the snow," Meg says. "How can that be?"[19]

Shepard wrote *A Lie of the Mind* with country music playing in his head as a kind of soundtrack. Then he heard just the right band for the play's emotional tenor on a college radio station while filming *Country*: the Red Clay Ramblers, a five-piece bluegrass group from North Carolina, whom Shepard instructed his sister Roxanne, now his assistant director, to get on the phone. The Ramblers "left me no doubt," Shepard wrote for the published edition, "that this play needs music. Live music. Music with an American backbone." At the time he wrote it, a British reporter asked him why country music was so sad. "Because more than any other art form I know of in America," he replied, "country and western music speaks of the true relationship between the American male and the American female." "And what is that?" "Terrible and impossible," Shepard chuckled.

In this way, *A Lie of the Mind* replicates the kind of makeup song that pervades country music—it is a promise to Jessica for a better future with their child on the way. "A love ballad, I guess you'd call it," Shepard said. "A little legend about love."[20]

* * *

*A Lie of the Mind* premiered at the Promenade in New York on December 5, 1985, the day after the film of *Fool for Love* was released. Shepard directed, with a good deal of last-minute help from Robert Woodruff. The stellar cast included Harvey Keitel (whose debut theater role was in *Up to Thursday*) as Jake, Aidan Quinn as Frankie, Amanda Plummer as Beth, Geraldine Page as Lorraine, James Gammon as Baylor, Will Patton as Mike, and the inimitable Ann Wedgeworth as Meg.

Frank Rich's notice in the *New York Times* could not have been better. "By turns aching and hilarious," Rich gushed, the play "is the unmistakable expression of a major writer nearing the height of his powers. . . . These four hours pass like a dream, with scene after scene creating a reverberant effect." *A Lie of the Mind*, Rich declared, placed Shepard alongside major American writers such as Eugene O'Neill, Tennessee Williams, Edward Albee, and Mark Twain.[21]

Shepard didn't always respond well to good news, as it tended to be followed soon after by more press. Accordingly, the show's producer, Albert Poland, floated a prediction before the opening-night party. "Tonight there will be fisticuffs thrown" at Sardi's restaurant, the traditional Broadway gathering spot for an opening night party. "If the reviews are bad, it will happen inside the party. If the reviews are good, it will happen outside. And the thrower of fisticuffs will be Sam Shepard."[22]

Shepard spent the party drinking heavily at a corner table with Danny DeVito and other VIPs, and when he walked out onto the street, a paparazzo snapped his picture. Shepard was blackout drunk by then, and he punched him in the face, breaking his glasses. Then he hit him hard in the stomach, rupturing a blood vessel. The way Dark saw these episodes is that the "parasitic press photographers" drove Shepard into "a total inner and sometimes outer rage." This was the main reason Shepard loathed attending celebrity events with Jessica, or even his own Academy Awards ceremony for *The Right Stuff*. The following day, according to Poland, with the box office line around the block, the photographer had a warrant issued for Shepard's arrest.[23]

In the foreground, *A Lie of the Mind* won the Drama Desk Award for Outstanding Play, the Outer Critics Circle Award for Best Off-Broadway

Play, and the New York Drama Critics' Circle Award for Best Play. Miloš Forman, who years before had inadvertently sunk Shepard's screenplay "The Bodyguard," asked whether he could adapt it into a movie. Shepard learned his lesson with Altman, though, and he was now in a position to tell an Oscar-winning director no because, perhaps, as with *Fool for Love*, he felt the play was just too personal for the movies.[24]

* * *

Hannah Jane Shepard, Jessica and Shepard's first child, arrived on January 13, 1986. "I never thought about having a daughter," Shepard mused, "and then I had a daughter and it was a remarkable thing. It was very different from having a son and your response to it. With a son, it's much more complex. And it's probably because of my stuff in the past. With a daughter, I was surprised at how simple it is."[25]

That April, the family moved into a seaside house in Oak Island, North Carolina, where Shepard could drive down to Charleston and play polo at an old slave plantation. The house was located near the set for *Crimes of the Heart*, starring Jessica, Diane Keaton, Sissy Spacek, and Shepard (who played Jessica's love interest). *Crimes of the Heart* wrapped in June, at which point, as recommended by Sissy Spacek, who lived in Virginia with her husband, Jack Fisk (the designer of *Days of Heaven*), they sold their property in Arroyo Hondo and moved to Scottsville, Virginia, in Albemarle County at the base of the Blue Ridge Mountains.[26]

Albemarle County was the heart of Virginia's posh horse breeding, polo, and fox hunting culture. In Scottsville, they bought Totier Creek Farm, a grand country estate with over a hundred acres of rolling hills and a creek running through the center, along with stables and a barn for horses, all of which encircled a stately mansion built in 1799. When Shepard and Jessica wanted to dine out, they did so in relative anonymity at the Boar's Head Inn in nearby Charlottesville. He instructed reporters and theater and film colleagues to meet him there rather than at the farm. The Boar's Head's waitstaff guarded his privacy and arranged for a corner table with Shepard's back to the room and the visitor facing the door. As stories in the press from this period reveal, Shepard's roughneck image took a hit for associating with such high-born surroundings; but the farm allowed him to pursue his passion for horse breeding, as he'd now found himself on a horse farm smack in the center of Thoroughbred country.[27]

Shepard visited with his now sixteen-year-old son Jesse in Hollywood, where Jesse would soon work in the movies as a wrangler.[28] There, in Hollywood Park, Shepard bought his first Thoroughbred: a five-year-old mare sired by a three-figure earner named Upper Nile. This was River Chant, who foaled the stakes winner Ornate, who would have a descendant come in third at the Kentucky Oaks in 2007. Perhaps the best Shepard ever bred was Two Trail Sioux, which he sold in 2002 and went on to win at Churchill Downs, Del Mar, Delaware Park, and Saratoga and earn $664,960. At this point Totier Creek, as he named his breeding business, became extremely lucrative. (In total, his racehorses would eventually earn him around three million dollars.)[29]

The company he kept also went up in status. With Jessica, their closest friends were top-tier celebrities including Sissy Spacek, her husband, Jack Fisk, Diane Keaton, Ed Harris, and Susan Sarandon. Not that they hadn't been strivers, just a different sort than, say, the Theater Genesis cohort who'd transferred to Mednick's Padua Hills Festival in the San Gabriel Valley. Bob Dylan was back on his calendar as well, and for their next collaboration, the songster wouldn't be jumping out bathroom windows.

* * *

On June 5, 1986, a few weeks after Shepard's induction into the American Academy and Institute of Arts and Letters, the playwright drove a rented silver Corvette up the driveway of Bob Dylan's rambling new compound at Point Dume in Malibu, California. The future Nobel laureate had purchased the beachfront spread a few years earlier, prior to the boom, for a proverbial song of about a hundred thousand dollars. The sea-swept redbrick patio off the main house displayed a panoramic view of Santa Monica Bay; a heavy fog had moved in, undulating over the Pacific waves to the accompaniment of a boogie-woogie vinyl record. After the usual pleasantries, Dylan, who was on break from his and Tom Petty's True Confessions tour, got fidgety and turned his attention to his guitar, which he picked and strummed throughout most of the hours-long talk between the two countercultural icons.[30]

Shepard hadn't come to Los Angeles from the East Coast, as has been reported, for this taped interview with Dylan exclusively for an *Esquire* magazine feature; he came because Jane Rogers, at sixty-eight, had undergone open heart surgery at Pasadena's Huntington Hospital. (Hence the Corvette, which he rented to lift his sisters' spirits in the face of potential disaster.)[31] To be with his mother through her surgery and recovery, Shepard flew by commercial airline for the first time in over twenty years. Predictably, Shepard told Dylan, he "hated" the flight. "You don't have any control, right?" Dylan teased him good-naturedly. "I don't like it," Shepard retorted. "I don't like the whole attitude that [the captain and crew] have—like, you know, everything is hunky dory."

Standing guard at each side of Dylan was a pair of oversized English mastiffs. Shepard said that if they had pups, he wanted one, then the interview commenced.

The men taped more than three hours of dialogue on three cassette tapes Shepard brought with him. Their discussion was to be edited by Shepard and published in *Esquire*, with Dylan on the cover. Dylan was then recording *Knocked Out Loaded*, featuring his and Shepard's collaboration "Brownsville Girl," which they wrote over a two-day session together in the spring of 1985, while he was in the midst of filming *Fool for Love*.[32] Shepard arrived at Point Dume with a six-pack of beer, resentful about worrying over the interview upon which they had both somehow agreed. They sound hungover, possibly already tipsy. For the first hour or so, Shepard made a series of feeble attempts to breach Dylan's defenses. Dylan caviled about who was interviewing whom, but Shepard set him straight with a prepared list of topics to cover. Still, Dylan managed to avoid saying anything substantive about everything from angels to the Cold War to Margaret Thatcher, despite Shepard's best efforts.

Round and round they went until something fascinating took place. Shepard continued to flounder, yet Dylan became gradually more alert and attentive to Shepard's line of questioning. About two hours in, Shepard was slowly, unconsciously, exchanging places with Dylan as the interviewee, just as Lee had exchanged places with Austin in *True West* as the conscientious screenwriter. "What I relate to more than anything," Shepard was saying, speaking now about his own writing after nearly exhausting his prepared topics for *Esquire*, "is something that's deeply private—*deeply* private—then suddenly opens out into something that isn't, you know what I mean? It's *so* private it becomes something that's . . . and I don't mean private in a stupid way. ['I know, I know.'] I mean private in the sense that everybody experiences, everybody sees, and it isn't spoken. And one person speaks it [snaps his fingers], and it suddenly becomes like a revelation. It's like this explosion of a moment or something, you know, that widens."

"You make that effect in your plays!" Dylan emphatically agreed. "You take that private thing that goes *way* down deep—that people don't even bring up to the mid-surface—and you deal just on that level." "Hopefully it makes some waves," Shepard sheepishly responded.

At Totier Creek Farm that August, Shepard molded his Dylan interview into a play he titled "Side to Side (Why Fight It?)," an allusion to recurrent themes: Dylan's performance on the guitar in Rolling Thunder, swaying his body to the rhythm "side to side," rather than tapping his feet to keep time; disagreement about political sides, light and dark; and the agreed-upon notion that women function side to side, with compassion, rather than up and down like men, with stubborn resolve. When the script appeared in July 1987, *Esquire* had changed the title to *True Dylan: A One-Act Play as It Really Happened One Afternoon in California*. But they did so without Shepard's permission, and he was furious. His lawyers got involved, insults were exchanged, and still the title remained.[33] Soon after, Shepard had his own cover story appear in *Esquire*. The article was pointedly titled "The Man on the High Horse."

* * *

In December 1986, Woody Allen filmed Shepard as the lead in his latest film, *September*. He was replacing Christopher Walken, but in his turn would be replaced by Sam Waterston. (This exchange happened, reportedly, after Shepard committed the cardinal sin for any actor performing for Woody Allen: he'd used the homespun word "Montana" in an improv exercise.) Nonetheless, soon after the rejection, Shepard shipped the vinyl stacks of his father's Dixieland jazz collection to Allen, himself an accomplished jazz clarinetist. "I was overwhelmed by the sudden arrival of your father's old records," Allen gushed in a thank-you note. "The collection is very eclectic and full of wonderful surprises—a lot of good old-fashioned jazz." But then, Shepard's goodwill dissolved when his *Esquire* interview was released the following year, and the playwright's pull quote read, "Woody Allen and Robert Altman are pisspoor as actors' directors. Each understands zip about acting. Allen knows even less than Altman, which is nothing."[34]

From his dressing room in Queens, Shepard wrote to Johnny Dark after not seeing Jessica for two weeks, "My life is so different without her. When I'm alone I feel lost & stupid & totally useless. I don't know what to do without her. She's my whole world. I never thought I'd be this way with anyone." The holidays were spent at Jessica's cabin in Minnesota, where she was pregnant with their second child and getting restless with the break from work.[35]

Samuel Walker Shepard, their son, was born on June 14, 1987, at Totier Creek Farm. "Yes—another tadpole has sprouted," Shepard crowed, "& a fine lad he is." The household had expanded to three children, Shura, Hannah, and now Walker. "Things are really jumping around here now. Lots of shitty diapers & sleepless nites but a rollicking good time nonetheless. Every once in a while Jessie & I just stare at each other with kids in our arms & break out laughing. Hard to believe a scant 5 years ago we were chasing each other from hotel to motel."[36]

The two began kicking around film ideas, and over the course of Jessica's pregnancy, Shepard wrote the script of *Far North*, a love letter to the Lange family of Minnesota, which they shot in the Duluth area that fall. The film marks his debut as a film director, and it's noticeably softer in tone than anything he'd written before, a change that he credited to Jessica: "I took a tremendous turn in terms of my own vulnerability," Shepard said about this lighter, more sentimental new form. "My relationship with Jessica allowed this vulnerability to show itself."[37]

Jessica performed Kate, a variation on herself, and Ann Wedgeworth played her mother, Amy. Wedgeworth was especially well-suited to the role, as she'd already performed a previous version of Dorothy Lange. (This was Meg in *A Lie of the Mind*; both roles, Shepard said, were "modelled on each other.")[38] In the film, Al Lange's grizzled character, Bertrum, is fussed over by his other daughter, Rita (played by Tess Harper), his granddaughter, Jilly (Rosanna Arquette), and Gramma (Nina Draxten), who is about to celebrate her one hundredth birthday. The women are trying to save the family horse, Mel, after Bertrum swears revenge on the animal, who in the opening sequence bucks and throws him from a horse-drawn wagon and lands him in the hospital.

Shepard made clear that *Far North*, like *Fool for Love* and *A Lie of the Mind*, also presents the issue of intrinsic differences between the sexes. For Shepard, when a man is injured by a horse, he draws a white *X* on its forehead and avenges himself by having it shot; for women, killing the horse for behaving like a horse is "a horrendous, insensitive notion."[39]

Shepard found film directing to be a thrilling departure from acting or even writing. "It's a hundred times more exciting to direct. I'm not a Pacino or a De Niro or a Jessica Lange, and I've never intended to be," he said. "But filmmaking I can get passionate about because it's a natural extension of writing. It's everything you wish writing could be—you can visualize things, and there they are; you can extend shots, change the colors, put wind in when the wind isn't there."[40] Audiences wouldn't dwell on *Far North*'s plot as much as its setting. Shepard's authentic sense of natural wonder leaves the deepest impression on the viewer, and if nothing else, the film is an affectionate portrayal of the magical, snow-packed forests of the Upper Midwest.

That summer, 1988, Shepard confidently wrote to Dark that he was prepared to carry on with his nascent filmmaking career, and he'd begun working on a period Western in black-and-white. "This production company [Alive Films] is very happy with my last film so they say they'll put up the bread for another one. I can't believe I can actually make films now." They wouldn't be happy for long. *Far North* turned out to be a disaster at the box office. It cost five million dollars to make, and when it was released in November 1988, it recouped about a hundred and fifty thousand. "An alternate title," wrote one critic, "could be 'Crimes of the Horse.'" Another chided, "Enter 'Far North' in the Most Malicious Sam Shepard Parody Contest (undergraduate division)." Janet Maslin of the *New York Times* roguishly gave the film's best actor award to the horse that played Mel.[41]

* * *

Once home again in Virginia, Shepard cheerily told Dark, "Mostly now our lives are consumed by raising three little kids. It's a 24-hour task with hardly any let-up. It runs the full gamut of emotions & the rewards & failure are absolutely immediate." Shura was a "tall, elegant" seven-year-old who played violin remarkably well; Hannah, at two, sang and listened rapt to the cowboy songs and tall tales her father told her at bedtime; Walker was cutting teeth and walking, "hence the name;" and Jesse, at eighteen, he boasted, now worked as a ranch hand with Sandy Rogers at Santa Rosa. Beyond that, Shepard continued, "I don't know what to say, except occasionally I do miss those amazing days where we'd get stoned & just wander around through shopping markets or ride bikes or just stare at life & go on mental journeys."[42]

"There was something so great about that time but I guess it's gone," Shepard ended his dispatch to his friend, who still lived amidst their two clans. "Hard to believe things just pass like that but I guess you just go on to the next saga of one's life."[43]

# PART III

# 1990–2017

The urge to create works of art is essentially one of ambition. The ambition behind the urge to create is no different from any other ambition. To kill. To win. To get on top. . . . The ambition to transform valleys into cities. To transform the unknown into the known without really knowing. To make things safe. To beat death. To be victorious in the face of absolute desolation.

—Sam Shepard, *Angel City*, 1976

Careful how you bare your soul
Careful not to bare it all

—Patti Smith, "Cowboy Truths,"
for Sam Shepard, 1992

CHAPTER 16

# "HORRORS OF THE ROAD"

At the start of their romance, according to Shepard, Jessica had been overpoweringly drawn to his "maleness." In the early days, he wrote, she wanted him because "he drives his truck like a real man. (She's been driving with Mercedes men.) He stays at the Motel 6. (She's been staying at the Bel-Air.) He smokes and drinks like a fish. She finds that exotic." After a while together, the novelty of his cocksure machismo wore off, and then, all at once, "she can't stand him 'cause he's such a man. In her eyes he drives his truck like a macho fool."[1]

Jessica granted an interview to *Vanity Fair* in 1989, which was conducted at her cabin hideaway in the woodlands of Minnesota. When asked about Shepard, the film star replied with unusual candor:

> I keep hoping that it settles into a certain dynamic where there'll be no question Sam and I are best friends, which is hard to come by. To me, it hasn't settled in completely. Because of the obsessive nature of our beings, the passionate nature of our coming together—and it's still there, the jealousy, the passion, the insanity—it's hard to let the other thing emerge. When you're in the throes of a love affair, it's about darker emotions.

When next asked what she would do if he left, she just laughed.

> I don't think he ever will. You get inextricable connections with people. . . . Sam actually buried my dad—he dug the grave. I was the one who told him his dad had died. He was with me when I gave birth to two children. . . . I never discard the possibility of anything happening in life, but his leaving would surprise me.[2]

* * *

Soon after Jessica's interview, Shepard typed up a roman à clef in the early fall of 1990 that he intended to publish as "Slave of the Camera (An Actor's Notes)." Many scenes would wend their way into his next two books of stories, *Cruising Paradise* and *Great Dream of Heaven*, but his actual personal dramas with Jessica, as they'd been in *Far North*, were conspicuously removed.

Shepard's unpublished manuscript for "Slave of the Camera" cuts across time, from his youth in California to the present, in which he and Jessica are separated, and he's toggling between a desperation to get her back and his lingering guilt over leaving O-Lan and Jesse. He's behaving erratically throughout, and fueling his misery over being spurned by Jessica was a badly escalating drinking problem. More Bukowski than Beckett, "Slave of the Camera" takes place in the spring of 1990 while he worked in Los Angeles and Mexico on Volker Schlöndorff's *Voyager*, a film the *New York Times* styled as "a modern variation on the Oedipus myth." Shepard was eager to work with a European director again, and his friend Rudy Wurlitzer, as a bonus, had written the screenplay.[3]

While they were filming at their first location, Papantla, Mexico, Shepard would be awakened at six in the morning by an assistant at the Hotel Tajin, where empty Sauza Tequila bottles were strewn about the room. ("Tequila gives you a false sense of courage, if you're susceptible to that kind of thing," Shepard wrote, "and I was at that point.") "Sam Shepard was not an easy person to work with," his costar Julie Delpy sighed. "He was crying sometimes. I don't know what was going on. I was just trying to act and do the best job I could." Shepard, Delpy said about his performance in *Voyager*, "was closing up and closing up and closing up. It was like facing a wall." She correctly intuited that his mood swings were a result of his separation from his family, recalling a scene where their characters were saying goodbye, and he'd fled the set in tears. When she followed after him, he sobbed, "I don't think I could take another goodbye."[4]

Patching things up with Jessica was his first priority, an impossible task to manage from the road. Shepard's hotel room had no phone, and the odds of connecting to her from the lobby, he wrote, were "about one in a thousand." The telephone only made the physical and emotional distance, wherein he couldn't address her accusations, feel even worse anyway.[5]

That June and July, the film production traveled to Europe, where they shot scenes in France, Switzerland, Germany, Italy, Greece, and on the RMS *Queen Mary*. In Wurlitzer's script, there's a monologue on a plane that Shepard, who plays an engineer, delivered faultlessly. He's explaining to the man seated next to him how the aircraft will react if they crash into the desert, which horrifies the passenger as Shepard would've been horrified. Since transatlantic cruises no longer ran, he insisted on taking the high-speed, three-and-a-half-hour flight on the Concorde from New York to Paris to meet them. Cast and crew were then obliged to travel by land or sea to each location because of his refusal to fly.[6]

After four months of shooting, Shepard was back with Jessica and the children. During this time of relative calm, he tried his best to enjoy the fruits of the life of a gentleman farmer at Totier Creek, faithfully reading the *Thoroughbred Times* and overseeing the farm's upkeep and preparing his livestock for sale that summer. "I love sitting on a tractor & plowing or bush-hogging," he wrote to Dark. "It's one of the great pleasures in this life." He was also writing a new play about horse racing, but most important, the family was reunited and the separation was over. "Me & Jessie are in love once again & everything is hunky-dorey."[7]

* * *

Shepard was seated at a bar near Lexington, Kentucky, where he bid for Thoroughbreds at auctions, when it was announced on the TV, January 16, 1991, that the United States had invaded Iraq. "It was stone silence. The TV was on, and these planes were coming in, and suddenly . . . It just seemed like doomsday to me. I could not believe the systematic kind of insensitivity of it. That there was this punitive attitude—we're going to just knock these people off the face of the earth." The Gulf War's combat phase lasted only six weeks, at which point "they've convinced the American public that this was a good deed, that this was in fact a heroic fucking war, and welcome the heroes back. What fucking heroes, man?"[8]

Shepard normally shied away from writing overtly political dramas. If a play came across as too political, he'd said at the outset of his career, when political art was in vogue, it remains "stuck in time." At heart, he'd always been a mugwump. "I'd like to be concerned. To be useful. To put up a good fight," he admitted. "Against what?" a friend asked him. "The forces of evil. Nixon. Capitalism. White supremacy. The profit motive. Somehow I can't give a fuck. I don't give a rat's ass."[9]

Even during the Vietnam War, Shepard's voice was primarily that of an otherworldly absurdist, not a polemicist. But this was the first major military conflict America had undertaken since then. One thing stayed true in America—the country's urge toward intimidation, destruction, and domination. "Aggression is the only answer," says a saber-rattling character, the Colonel, in his next play, *States of Shock*. "A man needs a good hobby. All those horrible long days without the enemy. Longing out the window. Staring at the stupid boredom of peacetime. The dullness of it. The idiot deadness in everyone's eyes." America's thirst for bloodshed needed quenching, Shepard believed, and President George H. W. Bush seemed bent on this national corrective.[10]

With his title, *States of Shock: A Vaudeville Nightmare*, Shepard echoed the "grand tactic" Bush was to impose on Iraq, "Shock and Awe," and during the Second Gulf War, following the attack on 9/11, Shepard clarified: "There is this strange deal—from Lewis and Clark to Iraq. It's very weird that we're continually trying to devour territory. . . . Bush didn't happen out of thin air."[11] The Gulf War became, in short, an effective vehicle to reflect upon the totality of America's history of violence.

Shepard scorned "isms" of any kind, but *States of Shock* is an unalloyed work of dramatic expressionism, a European theater style popularized in America by Eugene O'Neill in the 1920s and characterized by a grotesque theatrical display that projects the tormented psyche of the playwright or filmmaker, and by proxy their characters, onto a stage or big screen. The lead is the Colonel, whose costume is "a strange ensemble of military uniforms and paraphernalia that have no apparent rhyme or reason." In this way, the Colonel is a personified montage of the violent and sustained history of American warfare, Shepard said. "I wanted to create a character of such outrageous, repulsive, military, fascist demonism that the audience would recognize it, and say, 'Oh, this is the essence of the thing.'" His compatriot is Stubbs, a young disabled Gulf War vet who's been temporarily discharged from a veterans hospital. The Colonel insists that Stubbs was present when his son died in combat, but he's in denial, since Stubbs is tacitly revealed to be the son himself, and he'd been injured by friendly fire, not the enemy. "How could we be so victorious and still suffer this terrible loss?" the Colonel asks him. "It was friendly fire that took us out," Stubbs meekly responds.[12]

Shepard wanted the war to become less abstract as the production unfolds, and to achieve this the lighting designers Anne Militello (Johnny Dodd's celebrated apprentice) and Pat Dignan made a strobe light show depicting Stubbs's PTSD and the horrors of mechanized warfare—machine guns, artillery, helicopters, jets, tanks. "We wanted to do a shadow play of chaos and in the simplest symbolism of war shapes," said Militello. "I remember the images of the Iraq War night vision footage of bombs being dropped on the news, and it looked like vertical dots of light dropping from the green sky. . . . Abstract war which would explode on occasion and a quiet menacing presence were the goals."[13]

Bill Hart, Shepard's old roommate, had successfully resuscitated his life with a theater career, as a dramaturge and literary manager for the Public Theater, and he was hired to direct. The casting choice for the

Colonel was known from the start: *True West*'s John Malkovich. Indeed, Shepard was once asked whether he had an ideal "Shepardesque actor," and after some hedging, he arrived at Malkovich. The virtuosic actor was, Shepard said, "extremely intelligent, fearless, and enthusiastic. Just does not give a shit about how this fits into somebody else's idea of what [a scene] should be, just goes for ideas that are completely off the wall." At one point, the Colonel's required to recite a war-mongering aria while eating a banana split. Struggling with this, Malkovich heard Shepard howling with laughter backstage. Afterward, Malkovich chuckled, "He told me that it was the most impressive thing he'd ever seen in the theatre."[14]

*States of Shock* premiered at Wynn Handman's American Place Theatre on May 16, 1991, when American triumphalism over Operation Desert Storm, as the short-lived war plan was called, had reached a fever pitch. But the Gulf War's arrogant brutality flew so far under the media's radar that a few prominent critics assumed Stubbs was a Vietnam vet, not an Iraq vet.[15] Critics expressed delight at Shepard's work coming back to a New York stage for the first time since *A Lie of the Mind* six years before. But not with that play. "Shepard, with a political passion badly needed in American theater," wrote *Newsweek*, "is assailing false pride at this moment of national euphoria. But his voice strains to a pitch of hysteria that numbs all feeling. Like a defective grenade, 'States of Shock' blows itself up."[16]

* * *

It had become Shepard's routine to turn to the bottle for solace after a play of his flopped, and equally routine was Jessica's reaction to this behavior. He wrote a poem titled "Separation (Horrors of the Road)," depicting what he described later as his "big earthquake," above and beyond, to his mind, their past vigorous disagreements and breakups. It was early September 1992, and Jessica was fed up with him. "You're always drunk," he quotes her as telling him before absconding with the children. He was a drunk when they first met, and he was still a drunk. They shared no interests, not even in each other's work. They did nothing together as a couple, or even as friends. "That's basically it," she tells him in the poem after enumerating a list of faults that only grew longer with time, then punctuates her point from the *Vanity Fair* interview about their lack of a "settled" friendship, "I can't live like this."[17]

Two days later, Shepard was driving his pickup truck down Highway 40 West through Tennessee as he wrote, while steering with his knees against the wheel, the first twenty-five pages of a play he was calling "One Last Favor" (later changed to *Simpatico*). "I've always done my best work (i.e. writing) when I'm in the middle of some turbulent change," he wrote to Dark. Once he reached Santa Fe, he'd cooled off sufficiently to phone home. "Hello sweetheart," Dark recalled his apologizing to Jessica. "I'm sorry. And not only am I sorry but I'm in Santa Fe for Christ's sake. I got to drive all the way the fuck back now."[18]

The following month in Los Angeles, Shepard began his next screenplay, *Silent Tongue*, a historical drama about Native Americans. Shepard had witnessed firsthand the abject poverty among the Oglala Sioux at the Pine Ridge Indian Reservation while shooting *Thunderheart*. The movie was a fictionalized account of the American Indian Movement (AIM) and their Wounded Knee protest of 1973. The Oglala at Pine Ridge, Shepard thought, surely had "the most devastated culture in America," with its eighty percent alcoholism rate and crushing poverty.[19]

He worked on *Silent Tongue* over the transcontinental drive back to Virginia, and he was sure his script had a gripping story and broad audience appeal. Getting it funded was going to be problematic, to say the least, since the "money heads," as he called producers, were refusing to take another chance on him after the disastrous financial returns of *Far North*.[20] After several rejections, Shepard reached out to the French company Belbo Films, for $8.5 million. They agreed, making *Silent Tongue* the first American Western ever produced by the French.

In their heyday, AIM had successfully exposed the impoverished conditions at Pine Ridge and other reservations to the white majority, and by the early 1990s, after generations of films distributing distorted images of savage "Injuns," less stereotypical characters played by

Native American actors had begun to appear in big-budget movies—crowd-pleasers such as Kevin Costner's *Dances with Wolves*, Michael Mann's *The Last of the Mohicans*, and Michael Apted's *Thunderheart*, as well as some less extravagantly made films such as Frank Pierson's *Lakota Woman: Siege at Wounded Knee* and Chris Eyre's *Smoke Signals*, which rounded out the decade as the first feature film to be written, directed, acted, and produced by Native Americans.[21]

One vital distinction for Shepard between *Silent Tongue* and "Oscar bait" in the vein of *Dances with Wolves* was a measured tempering of the surge of white guilt that flooded the cultural discourse after Costner's white savior epic was released in 1991. "I wanted to stay away from that," Shepard said, "because, I mean, it's been harped on so much. It's not that it doesn't need to be reiterated—it's just that I feel that that doesn't go anywhere, the guilt. But the possibility of introducing this other element—the ghosts, the intermediaries between the spirit world and the so-called regular one—might be a way of opening up the subject rather than closing it down."[22]

*Silent Tongue* takes place in 1873, while the Kiowa and the Comanche tribes were still warring against American cavalrymen across the Southwest. Shepard shot the film in seven weeks during the spring of 1992, with rattlesnakes and scorpions underfoot along the mesas of Llano Estacado near Roswell, New Mexico. Native characters in the film were played by Native actors, including a Kiowa ghost played by Sheila Tousey, the female lead from *Thunderheart* and a Menominee and Stockbridge-Munsee from Wisconsin.

When Tousey and Shepard performed together in *Thunderheart*, he'd mentioned an offbeat Japanese movie he saw at an arthouse cinema but forgot the title. Based on his description, Tousey found it, the 1962 horror film *Onibaba*, in a video store in New York and sent him the VHS tape. *Onibaba* inspired *Silent Tongue*'s grisly imagery, narrative fragmentation, and brazen-faced camerawork by the Irish cinematographer Jack Conroy.[23] For background, Shepard also read Walter Prescott Webb's two-volume history *The Great Plains*, and in appreciation, he used the author's name, Webb, for parts in *Silent Tongue* and his next play.[24]

The movie opens with the tortured laments of a mentally impaired young man named Talbot Roe, played by River Phoenix, who's overwhelmed with grief after the death during childbirth of his young half-Kiowa wife, Awbonnie (Sheila Tousey). Talbot couldn't bear to set her spirit to rest by letting the vultures eat her corpse, which provokes her ghost to appear before him, demanding to be eaten as carrion and thus set free to roam the spirit world.

*Silent Tongue* premiered at the Sundance Film Festival in January 1993. Though it was well received, the critical response to the opening sequence of River Phoenix mourning his dead wife received enough negative feedback that Shepard cut the scene by eight minutes for wider distribution. He was still working through the editing process in Los Angeles when Phoenix, one of the most iconic heroes of slacker Generation Xers—"a James Dean for the '90s," as *Rolling Stone* called him at the time *Silent Tongue* appeared—died at twenty-three from a drug overdose outside Johnny Depp's Viper Room nightclub on LA's Sunset Strip. The tragedy of such a promising actor cut off in his prime shocked the nation and was international news. As a result, the film's wide release was delayed to avoid accusations that anyone exploited the actor's death.[25]

Shepard's film was critically embraced, but the box office returns would barely have covered his craft services budget. The *New York Times*' Caryn James extolled its audacity, calling it a "gigantic leap" from Shepard's "facile comedy-drama" *Far North*. "Mr. Shepard's vision of the nineteenth-century plains is unlike any other filmmaker's," she declared, and warned against comparing it to other "revisionist westerns" such as *Dances with Wolves* and *Unforgiven*. "Mr. Shepard's imagistic style is daringly different from anything Hollywood might offer," James gushed.[26] The film's finest quality, then, its raw originality, sank its ticket sales.

In the end, Shepard had burned through the French producers' money and given back too little in return. "What do you think of your career as a movie director?" Mel Gussow asked him once the dust settled. "It's finished," Shepard snickered. "I think it's in the pits!"[27]

Neither of his films had made any money, but that was never his main concern. He'd wanted to enjoy the creative possibilities of filmmaking, but direction on a feature level cost the kind of money that necessitated a producer. He'd arrived at the hard certainty that producers were the feckless enemy of artful cinema, and if he met them at a bar or restaurant, he publicly shunned them. In fact, *Silent Tongue* only reconfirmed Shepard's dismal view of the moviemaking racket: "I'd love to direct another film. But I refuse to go through that circle dance they put you through to beg for money, to beg for validity, to keep begging all the way through the process in order to make the thing you want to make. . . . I don't want to be a beggar."[28]

* * *

Shepard resolved that if he was going to work in the movies, it would be to make money, not spend it, so he drove to New Orleans in the spring of 1993 to film a role in the John Grisham thriller *The Pelican Brief*. He described his part, Thomas Callahan, as "a constitutional lawyer having an affair with what's her name, Julia . . . [Roberts]." "It's a pretty extensive character in the book," he carped. "In the film he just sort of kicks the film off. . . . Gets bumped off very early. Blown up . . . in New Orleans, which is a good town to be stuck in, if you have to be stuck."[29]

By late January 1994, he was on another movie set filming *Safe Passage* opposite Susan Sarandon as a father of seven sons. Mel Gussow pointed out to him that in his Off-Off-Broadway days, he preferred the anonymity of Lower East Side churches and cafés. "You believed in the primitive feeling that if they photograph you, your spirit gets stolen," the critic reminded him. "Well, he certainly contradicted himself, didn't he?" Shepard laughed, then his tone got serious. "You know, contradiction is the stuff of life."[30]

Despite Shepard's recent spate of roles in major films, in 1994, it was Jessica who attracted the hot glare of the Hollywood spotlight.

Two years before, she had shot the film *Blue Sky* in Alabama, playing a mentally unstable military wife opposite Tommy Lee Jones. *Blue Sky* was directed by Shepard's old screenwriting partner Tony Richardson, who was then dying of an AIDS-related illness. Richardson passed away soon after the shoot, and by the time his film appeared in 1994, after numerous financial delays, it garnered Jessica, after four prior nominations, her first Academy Award for Best Actress. In her speech, she called her Oscar "a tribute to Tony Richardson" and thanked her children, if neither of their fathers, "who make all of this possible with their love and patience."[31]

"Jessica Lange has not always chosen film roles wisely, but she always performs them well," Caryn James aptly summed up her talent in the *New York Times*. "As a sophisticated city woman or a gritty farm wife, she reaches into characters to suggest the strength of vulnerable women and the vulnerability of the strong."[32] For Shepard, this description could also be fittingly applied to the other most important woman in his life at that time, his mother, Jane Rogers.

Shepard was wrapping up his work on *Safe Passage* when, on March 10, Jane passed away from ovarian cancer. The night before her death, a full thirteen years after she'd been diagnosed, there was a small line of people and a dog waiting outside her bedroom for their turn to say goodbye. Jane's obituary in the *Pasadena Star-News* begins, "Jane Schook Rogers was a woman you liked even when she was mad at you—and 25 years of Pasadena Polytechnic students benefited from her zest for life."[33]

They buried her in the Schook family plot in Baileys Harbor, Wisconsin, where generations of Schooks had summered at the "Schook Shack," Pop Schook's cabin overlooking Lake Michigan. Right after she passed, a hawk, an animal of mystical stature for Shepard, alighted outside his window and returned to the same perch for a few days. He was certain this was an omen, perhaps his mother returning as a shape-shifter to comfort him, or send a warning.[34]

* * *

With Jane Rogers buried up north and Jessica a newly minted Oscar winner, Shepard traveled solo to New York to confirm a venue for his full-length thriller *Simpatico*.

*Simpatico* tells a sordid tale about horse racing and the dark human instincts Shepard witnessed among the stables, paddocks, and racetracks he'd worked at as a kid and his horses now inhabited. "It's a rivalry between two close friends that have known each other their whole lives," Shepard said, "and it involves women and horses and all kinds of stuff, gambling, deceit, envy, jealousy, rage."[35]

The play had been accepted by Broadway Alliance, the Promenade, and Variety Arts, but each in turn ran out of funding for it.[36] Now, after nearly two years, he'd found it a home.

Over the prior decade, the *True West* debacle had kept Shepard away from the Public Theater, but in the wake of Joe Papp's death and with some help from Bill Hart, he and the Public were reunited. The celebrated company's new leader was George C. Wolfe—the Broadway director of Tony Kushner's *Angels in America* and his own *Jelly's Last Jam*—who had one great advantage over his predecessor, wrote the *Los Angeles Times*: "He can get along with Sam Shepard."[37] The opening was scheduled for November 14, 1994, and on October 1, Shepard moved to Manhattan to direct rehearsals with a few friends he had in mind while writing to play the characters—Ed Harris, Fred Ward, and James Gammon—along with Beverly D'Angelo and Marcia Gay Harden for the female leads.

A three-act mystery play that aspires to the noir detective plots of James M. Cain's *Double Indemnity* and Dashiell Hammett's *The Maltese Falcon*, Shepard's drama follows the star-crossed machinations of a trio of former hustlers trying and failing to get on with their lives. Fifteen years before the action, Vinnie Webb (played by Ward), his wife, Rosie (D'Angelo), and Lyle Carter (Harris) were small-time gamblers who switched near identical racehorses to make a score, but the Commissioner of Racing, Darrel P. Simms (Gammon), had caught them in the act. The three hatch a plot to protect themselves by disgracing Simms (for their method of blackmail, think of Dark outside a hotel window photographing Shepard and Michelle Phillips in the act); after this, Carter and Rosie abandon Vinnie in California to start a family and lord over a Thoroughbred horse farm in Kentucky.[38] After nearly a decade, Shepard had once again returned to the theme of brotherhood and karmic reversal.

On the surface, Lyle Carter bears a close personal resemblance to Shepard: he has risen above his lowly station in the San Gabriel Valley to horse breeding; he lives with a beautiful wife and kids on a country estate on which he breeds Thoroughbreds, and he has abandoned his best friend, leaving the friend to live a hand-to-mouth existence in California. But it's Simms who acts as Shepard's civic mouthpiece: "All in the genes," he says, expanding on the notion of blood-horse research and human temperament. "We've got nothing to do with it. It was all decided generations ago. Faceless ancestors." He rails against the supremacy of the digital age, the litigious ruthlessness of "lawyer types," the City of Los Angeles ("the Golden Land of high purses and racial conflict"), and horse-racing industry tycoons ("Bushwhackers and Backstabbers").[39]

"The great god so what is the nemesis of all playwrights," *Newsweek*'s Jack Kroll wrote of *Simpatico*. "Dialogue may crackle, actors may soar, but if suddenly the audience thinks 'So what?' all is lost. . . . Shepard's plays used to burst with revelation, but here he's sticking messages all over the play like Post-it notes." The cowboy-poet was there with his lyrical wiles, but he'd lost himself in the plot. Audiences were too busy straining to understand his tentacular storyline to allow for a true Shepardian experience. (Once *Simpatico* was adapted for the screen by the British director Michael Warchus, with Jeff Bridges, Nick Nolte, and Sharon Stone, the plot was given more room to breathe.)[40]

Storylines were never Shepard's strength, anyway. He was always more attuned to the moment, which was why he revered writers such as the future Nobel Prize–winning Austrian novelist and playwright Peter Handke, a man who specialized in dazzlingly accosting his audiences with rapid "flare-ups" of consciousness. "I hate fucking storylines," Shepard grumbled a decade on, adding notes of the Work. "Either the material suggests a storyline or there isn't one. . . . The storyline is inside the experience of doing it. It's not something outside to conform to."[41]

* * *

Shepard acted in two Westerns back-to-back in the summer of 1994 and early spring 1995: the telefilm *The Good Old Boys*, Tommy Lee Jones's directorial debut, and the TV miniseries of Larry McMurtry's *Streets of Laredo*, both shot on location in Texas. *The Good Old Boys* was filmed at the Alamo Village in San Antonio and across the arid Trans-Pecos region. Indeed, it was by now a Hollywood axiom that if you want Sam Shepard in your movie, tell him it'll be shot in Texas. (His next, *The Only Thrill* with Diane Keaton, would be shot in Texas the following winter.) He felt he belonged in Texas, but by mid-March, filming *Streets of Laredo*, with Jesse as a stunt rider, he wrote to Dark from a Best Western in Del Rio, "Me & Jesse have been in Texas now for months & it's time to spring for home and greener pastures."[42]

Totier Creek Farm, at least, wouldn't be his pasture for much longer. In his poem "Separation," Shepard makes clear that Jessica had been desperate to move away from Virginia for several years. The place was driving her crazy—the people, the humidity—it didn't matter where they went, as long as it wasn't there. "She wanders the farm & removes herself."[43]

Hence, in June 1995, the family relocated to Stillwater, Minnesota, next door to Jessica's widowed mother, Dorothy Lange. Their new home, a former bed-and-breakfast, was a Victorian mansion situated on a grassy hillock in an oak-lined residential neighborhood a short walk from town, with a broad front yard with old maple trees, a white picket fence, and sweeping views of the St. Croix River. Jessica discovered a talent for landscaping in the Twin Cities suburb, and Shepard kept up with his horse breeding, retaining the name Totier Creek Farm for his business. He also took over a sizable ranch in Kinnickinnic, Wisconsin, across the St. Croix, where he could let his horses run free on fifty open acres that would soon include a herd of cattle.[44] There, he set up a writing hideaway in an old one-room oak cabin that came with the land and was perched on a limestone bluff, "with a typewriter, a piano, some photographs and old drawings. Lots of junk and old books."[45]

Shepard and Jessica were having coffee one September morning when she confessed that "she was suddenly profoundly depressed about returning to the land of her childhood & that everything she'd imagined about being here in Minnesota was a total fantasy." After their upbringings marked by alcoholic fathers and their wayfaring lives, their sense of place had been irreparably distorted. "Neither one of us know where we want to live & call 'home.'" They'd already tried three principal American mythologies—Hollywood, the West, and the Old South—and now it was Main Street USA, but in the end, he said, "where we ought to be is together & so far, that's holding. The beat goes on."[46]

CHAPTER 17

# THOSE SO-CALLED DISASTERS

Even by Minnesota standards, the winter of 1996 was brutally cold, the coldest temperatures ever measured in that state. On February 2, it was thirty-nine below in Stillwater, so Shepard and Jessica decided to pack up their children and travel to the seaside resort of Tulum, Mexico, on the Yucatán Peninsula. To join them, Shepard would have to fly four hours down to Cancún, and he spent days wrestling over whether to brave the trip. Then Jessica produced a secret weapon: Xanax. "It really works!" he wrote to Dark. "I almost feel cocky now about climbing on board and nestling into one of those blue seats with the little pillow and the blanket all laid out for you."[1]

"Sun, Spanish, palm trees, blue Caribbean," he trumpeted from the luxurious thatched retreat Casa Violeta. "I couldn't believe I might have missed this out of some old, idiotic mind-habit about not flying." After that, the family made an annual trek to Tulum each spring, and in 1998, they bought a blissfully remote sanctuary in the Sian Ka'an Biosphere Reserve.[2]

Shepard published a short story about this trip titled "Land of the Living," in which Jessica's character accuses him of having an affair. On the drive to Tulum from the airport, she informs him that she answered his cell phone back in Minnesota, and an unfamiliar woman was on the line, evidently not expecting Jessica's voice. For the remainder of the trip, Shepard's character haplessly denies an affair and claims he was too old for that. "Lots of young women are attracted to that these days," she counters. "It's become chic or something." "Attracted to what?" "Older men. Men of influence." Throughout the first-person narrative, there is little doubt of his guilt. "He couldn't *not* cheat on his wife," Dark said.

> It was exactly who he was. He had no control over it, and with all his accomplishments and his good looks, women were throwing themselves at him anyway. He literally stepped into Ali Baba's cave, won a Pulitzer Prize, became a famous playwright and movie star living with one of the most glamorous blonde Hollywood actresses of the day. Wouldn't you want to meet him? I don't know if he even hesitated stepping into that world. Would you? Success was like a tide that came crashing through his front door.

* * *

In the fall of 1995, Shepard was asked whether he had any movie roles on the horizon. "Not if I can help it," he said. Instead, in 1996, he gave up acting and went to New York to attempt to reclaim his role as America's leading playwright, and he did so with an astonishing head of steam.[3]

In April 1996, Alfred A. Knopf, the most prestigious publisher yet for his work, released *Cruising Paradise*, Shepard's intimately revealing volume of forty autobiographical tales interspersed with raw dialogue, a freeing minimalism that's hard to pull off in staged plays "without any stage directions or any indication where the characters are or who they are."[4] Chicago's Steppenwolf, moreover, launched a revival of his Pulitzer-winning play, *Buried Child*, directed by Gary Sinise, first in Chicago in 1995, then Broadway in 1996, making that production, incredibly, Shepard's debut on the Great White Way.

Also that April, New York's Signature Theatre Company, who specialize in repackaging one living playwright's work per season, announced that Shepard was their pick for 1996–97. "At fifty-two, Sam

Shepard has come to look like one of his own solitary characters," the *New Yorker* greeted the occasion that April, "reemerging after long exile from some blasted American Nowhere—the desert, the badlands, the bewildering plains. And, indeed, Shepard seems to have been away for a while." The *New York Times* announced, "Atlanta may have the Olympics this year, but New York has Sam Shepard."[5]

When Gary Sinise first proposed his revival of *Buried Child* at Steppenwolf in Chicago, Shepard agreed, but on the condition that they use an updated script. The main revision he had in mind was rounding out Vince, the character based on himself, who in the first version had seemed too wooden. "In many of my plays," Shepard explained, "there was a kind of autobiographical character, in the form of a son or young man. The purpose of it, of course, was to write about myself. That character was always the least fully realized. Eighteen years later, you realize, 'That's what he was about.'"[6]

In the face of this promising resurgence, Shepard became more devoted to the bottle than ever. During the Chicago run, the actor-comedian Nick Offerman (*Parks and Recreation*) was an understudy for Ethan Hawke as Vince, and before a rehearsal, "Sam Shepard corralled me, slipped me $40, and told me to go get him a bottle of Marker's Mark." "It was like King Arthur handing me a sword and saying, 'Please have this sharpened so I can go into battle with Excalibur,'" Offerman wrote. "It wouldn't have been half as cool if he'd asked for something else, like, 'Hey, can you get me a two-liter bottle of Sprite?'" Jessica was expected any minute, so the bottle of whiskey was needed posthaste and with discretion. "In hindsight," Offerman continued, "acquiring intoxicants for your playwright before rehearsal begins is probably not ever a good idea." Once Jessica arrived as expected, the actor wrote, "her mood didn't seem great, and there was some quiet but stern talking happening, and it dawned on me that maybe the reason he surreptitiously sent the gofer kid out for booze was because he wasn't supposed to be having it."[7]

Another day before the opening, Hawke was off for lunch when Shepard turned to him and said, "Do you want to get a drink?" Hawke muttered that technically, he was still in rehearsal. "Pussy," Shepard retorted, then absconded from the production for a ten-day bender.[8]

Hawke considered Shepard an artistic mentor and a father figure, similar to how Shepard considered Joe Chaikin at such a crucial time in his career, but Hawke's work with Shepard over several decades, he said, was always like those rehearsals in Chicago:

> Clouded with his relationship to alcohol and how that was at any given moment. You could meet him and have wonderful, inspiring conversations about human relationships and humor and fishing and romance and life and Sophocles. . . . And then there's another part of him. Later that night he'd just be shit-faced and impossible and incorrigible. . . . It was so *incongruous* with the other part of him . . . and how sensitive and caring and interested he could be—and curious, you know, wanting to know about David Foster Wallace, or whatever else it was. So the bipolar nature that's reflected in his work was very much represented in the man. This was a person that was writing from a very truthful space.

Hawke made it clear that alcohol was a major cause for Shepard's conduct, though not an excuse. He also believed it was of paramount importance to see his faults as part and parcel of what made his writing stand out. "A lot of the issues that his characters have are issues that he was struggling with in a daily way," Hawke said. "I think to understand the writer, alcoholism is a huge part of his demons." When Shepard was sober, Hawke recalled, "it was really exciting to have him there. He would watch and make changes . . . changing the delivery and sharpening the edges."[9]

In New York, Shepard's substantial rewrite of *Buried Child*—nearly half the dialogue, if not the plot, was revised—led Sinise to argue that the Tony Awards committee could nominate it for Best New Play as opposed to Best Revival, at which point Shepard told Sinise, "O.K., enter the S.O.B." The bid was successful, and it was nominated for five Tonys, including one for Shepard and one for Sinise (neither won).

Shepard's response to his name in lights on a Broadway marquee was typically blasé. "It's a tourist deal," he told a group of college students. "'Cats' on one side of the street, 'Phantom' on the other. There's nothing wrong with that. But I don't see where my play fits in."[10] Terry Kinney, who played Tilden, put it more bluntly: "I don't think [Broadway] is the place for Sam," and as Kinney carried the corpse of the dead child onstage in the final scene, he was thinking, "What the hell are we doing on Broadway?"[11]

With *Buried Child* on Broadway and the Signature's Shepard festival in full swing, along came the inevitable wave of unwanted media attention, and reporters were quick to point out Shepard's churlish demand for privacy. Passing through a blockade of hand-wringing assistants referring to "Mr. You Know Who," the reporter Patti Hartigan teased, "He's the Greta Garbo of the American theater. He simply vants to be alone."[12] Another likened him to "a rancher who's been roused at 4 a.m. on his only day off to tow a neighbor's truck out of a ditch: It's got to be done so let's get on with it."[13] After *Far North*, he'd guarded himself closely against interviews. "It was like I'd volunteered for my own hanging," he told Ben Brantley (in an interview).[14]

Shepard's contempt for interviews led him and Chaikin to write their two-hander *When the World Was Green (A Chef's Fable)*, about an aged chef on death row after he killed a man as a result of a seven-generations-long feud over a poisoned mule. He is being interviewed in his cell by a reporter whose father may or may not have been his innocent victim, killed in a case of mistaken identity. "She thinks there's some secret I'm keeping, but I have no secret," the chef repeatedly insists. "You're like all the rest of the press. Fabricate anything just to sell a story. It's shameless! Make a story out of nothing! . . . I just want to be left alone."[15]

Chaikin, who riffed on ideas such as love with *Savage/Love* or voices with *Tongues*, wanted to explore, as he described it, "vengeance. The devil."[16] Who better than a reporter? *World* was also meant to evoke the blood revenge and ethnic cleansing then taking place in Bosnia. The chef recounts a time soldiers arrived at his village laughing and firing their rifles over a bucket of their enemies' testicles, an actual scenario Shepard borrowed from Elma Softić's account of the Bosnian War, *Sarajevo Days, Sarajevo Nights*. "It stunned me—the power of it," he said of the book. "It devastated me that this is not the Nazis or the distant past. This is happening right now."[17]

*When the World Was Green*, under Chaikin's direction and starring Alvin Epstein and Amie Quigley, opened on July 19 at the Olympics Arts Festival in Atlanta. Soon after, on July 27, a bomb exploded at Centennial Olympic Park, plunging the Arts Festival into a darkness of half-empty houses and vacant art exhibitions. "All a woman has to do is remove the scarf from her head and wave it in the air and all bloodshed must stop," the chef tells the interviewer. "She has the power to give birth, so only she can stop death."[18]

"The play's stunning final moment provides a wonderful final metaphor for the Games and the Arts Festival," wrote Patti Hartigan of the final scene, in which the interviewer takes off her headscarf and waves it while singing a soulful tune, "offering not so much a symbol of surrender as a sign of hope."[19]

Shepard's rewrite, *Tooth of Crime (Second Dance)*, starring Vincent D'Onofrio as Hoss, opened at Greenwich Village's Lucille Lortel Theatre on December 15. Shepard had reworked *Tooth of Crime* many times over to make it sound less dated and sentimental, but went no further than this. The reviews were terrible. He thought it might have been his bickering producers, or his friend Bill Hart's direction. "Maybe it's better if the director isn't a friend," he reflected, then brushed it off as plain bad luck. "Maybe the play's snakebit."[20]

One consolation, perhaps the sole one for this play, was that his music was replaced with an original score by Joseph Henry "T Bone" Burnett. T Bone Burnett had first met Shepard when he was playing guitar for Bob Dylan on Rolling Thunder, and he equated working with Shepard to a musical partnership: "Sam Shepard is an incredible drummer, among other things," he said. "If you take rhythm out of his plays, there's nothing left. His dialogue is very much like drum solos. When I started working with Sam, I saw that what we were doing was storytelling. When a certain song gets played in one town in the jungle, the next village over knows what's happening. It's about music as a vehicle for communication."[21]

* * *

From New York, Shepard flew to London in January 1997 to see Jessica reprise her role as Blanche DuBois in a West End production of *A Streetcar Named Desire*, then independently took the children on a barnstorming tour of Ireland. Despite the Xanax, Shepard never completely got over his phobia, and the casting agent Boaty Boatwright, a friend of Jessica's who knew about his fear of flying, once asked him how he'd flown a transatlantic flight. "I got myself very, very, very drunk," he replied, "and rolled up into a little ball, and put myself on a plane."[22]

When he arrived in London, he stopped drinking for the first time since the brief cessation Stephen Rea reported in that same city twenty-five years before. It was a dry period that would last nearly four years. His relationship with his family was also in the balance, so he joined Alcoholics Anonymous (AA) while he was in Los Angeles, then New York. "Don't put me in with Elton John or anything," he told his LA sponsor. "Just throw me to the lions."[23]

"Alcoholism is an insidious disease," Shepard admitted. "Until I confronted it, I wasn't aware that it was creeping up on me." He confessed to Dark, after attending AA meetings in Los Angeles and New York,

> I came very close to destroying just about everything that really meant something to me—my relationship with Jessica, my kids most of all. . . . I'm amazed I lived through it actually: blackouts on the road doing ninety miles an hour, winding up sleeping in ditches; fist fights with Marines; hangovers that went on through half the day and were only remedied by more booze, strange women who could have been carrying anything; pool games til the crack of dawn with Italian Mafioso types where I lost hundreds of dollars; terrible fights with the ones I loved; the shakes, vomiting, shitting my pants on the

street. . . . I thought the world was fucked up and I was just reacting like some kind of underground hero.

Because of drunkenness or not, Shepard's stream of acting jobs abruptly ground to a halt in the fall of 1997. "I've been running this 'acting' scam for twenty-two years," he said, "never even imagining that one day the well would run dry." And suddenly, no prospects. "I feel like I'm a much better actor now, and yet I don't have any work," he told a reporter. "Maybe I pissed off too many people."[24]

During this respite from the acting "scam," Shepard was invited by his buddy Bobby Miller, a Thoroughbred horse breeder he knew from Lexington, Kentucky, to take part in a cattle drive across the plains of Texas, and he gladly accepted. Over three days, he rode horseback across "huge open country," he wrote, "big campfires under the stars & cooking with Dutch ovens, cowboy style." That epic way of life would soon vanish, he knew, and he resolved to join Miller's annual cattle drives until the nation's cowboy heritage had completely disappeared into legend.[25]

He also worked on an adaptation of another writer's fiction for the first time—a gift from his father's grave. Sam Sr. had passed down myriad bad habits, but there were good ones too, like his *afición* for Spanish literature and language, which Shepard was teaching himself, and, as a result, his son devoured the works of Octavio Paz, Pablo Neruda, Jorge Luis Borges, Federico García Lorca, Gabriel García Márquez, César Aira, and Roberto Bolaño.

The story that drew Shepard's attention was Octavio Paz's work of flash fiction "The Blue Bouquet," about a man who's accosted by a bandit armed with a machete. The brigand is collecting a bouquet of blue eyeballs from *Mexicanos blancos* for his whimsical girlfriend. Shepard transformed this one-page fable into a two-act autobiographical play titled *Eyes for Consuela (From the Story "The Blue Bouquet" by Octavio Paz)*. That summer, he sent a rough draft to Steppenwolf's Terry Kinney, who agreed to direct the full-length at the Manhattan Theatre Club in New York. It opened on February 10, 1998, with David Strathairn as the playwright's antiheroic avatar Henry, a tourist in his fifties self-exiled in a jungle village in Mexico.

Shepard completed *Eyes for Consuela* on his fifty-fourth birthday, likely his first play ever written in a state of daily sobriety. The occasion led to a clear-eyed view of his personal life as it stood and how his behavior had badly affected his loved ones:

> I kept having little glimmers of the truth (that's all I hope for now) of how incredibly selfish I've lived my whole life—everything geared toward what I might gain out of it—even in my relationships with family & those I think I'm closest to.... It's sickening & yet this amazing truth of 'seeing' comes on now with a force far greater than I ever felt it during those periods when I was "In the Work."[26]

The Irish critic Fintan O'Toole equated *Eyes for Consuela* with "a mixture of humor and terror of the sort that might emerge from Edgar Allan Poe's re-writing of 'The Odd Couple.'" In it, the bandit Amado (played by Daniel Faraldo) and Henry shift to a verbal exchange about love, exile, and America. Henry's sure his wife only loved him at the start of their relationship: "One day—it was—just gone. She became cold. Indifferent. As soon as—the children—I mean, as soon as she became pregnant, really. I couldn't believe it. . . . By now we'd grown hard against each other. Contempt. We despised each other's presence. We were enemies of the heart." "Your mind is American," Amado responds. "Like a scorpion. Love is outside your language."[27]

Henry had been consumed by ambition before he met his wife, but once he did, he came to recognize his own egocentric urges. Her faith in herself and her identity infuriated him. Over time, he says, vanquishing her integrated sense of self became "my new ambition."[28] To many around him, Shepard, like Henry before his epiphany, seemed incapable of empathy. "He did not believe in any type of compromise," Dark said. "He was unable to extend himself out to feel what other people might be feeling. He was just so incredibly self-involved and self-centered. I just accepted that, you know? When I was with him, I was more like a sidekick."[29] Shepard understood this about himself too. The proof is in his plays. But unlike his father, he was uncommonly articulate expressing guilt, and he also had a tendency to cry. "He was a good crier," Sandy affirmed. "He was very in touch with his emotions and had no qualms about crying if he wanted to cry."[30]

Vincent Canby's review in the *New York Times* is in the running for the most blistering Shepard ever received: "The suspicion is that it's something that might only be fixed by starting over," Canby opined. "From scratch. That is, by rewriting from beginning to end."[31]

The play's topic, in the end, was simply too deeply personal for most drama critics or regular theatergoers to fully comprehend or appreciate. "Most men who talk that way would probably go to a marriage counselor," wrote Ben Brantley. "Henry, being a creation of Mr. Shepard, flees to a decrepit boarding house in the deepest jungles of Mexico." In fact, as Brantley goes on to write, "he finds a kind of marriage counselor anyway," in the literary form of the fictional Amado.[32]

* * *

Terry Kinney had asked Shepard during their first run-through, "Why are we doing this to ourselves? We could be making movies." "Yeah, movies," he replied. "I know about movies. But this is fun." By this time, Shepard had acted in over twenty films, and he'd gleaned a distinct pattern: "You just don't find any characters, you find these formulas," he told the radio host Terry Gross in a *Fresh Air* interview that March. "You find these sort of Hollywood rituals going on, but you don't find characters. Many, many of the characters don't even feel human. They feel computerized or faxed or, you know, somebody's mailed it in. And they all kind of sound like . . . they come from the same person. I don't know if it's a secretary out there who's doing it or what." However, his latest film, *Snow Falling on Cedars*, which he was then filming in Vancouver, was, thankfully for him, an outlier with "actual human beings in it."[33]

Shepard was in the Pacific Northwest acting in *Snow Falling on Cedars* when his fellow cast member Ethan Hawke, who played his son, informed him that the indie filmmaker Michael Almereyda was preparing a postmodern remake of *Hamlet*. It was to be set in turn-of-the-millennium corporate Manhattan, with Hawke cast as Hamlet, and Shepard was their first choice for his father's ghost.[34] (Almereyda's ensemble would also include Julia Stiles, Liev Schreiber, Kyle MacLachlan, and Bill Murray.) "I saw *Days of Heaven* when it first opened, twice in one sitting, then I chased down Sam's books and became a fan," Almereyda said.[35] Shepard called Almereyda, whom he'd played pool with in South Dakota while working on *Thunderheart*, and confirmed his interest in the role. Once the director started filming, Shepard confessed that the ghost's soliloquy was the most challenging acting work he had ever done, but he nailed it. "I can report," Almereyda wrote later, "that I never saw the ghost played with such an electrifying sense of reality."[36]

Hawke recalled that after Shepard finished what he considered his best take of the "Remember Me" monologue, he discovered that the cameraman had "botched the focus." Shepard flew into a rage, only to reconvene the company to apologize, "blaming his outburst on his own mediocrity as an actor."[37] When he wasn't lashing out, Hawke said, "it was awesome, and the reverence and respect that he had for every word choice, he was so interested in it. So whenever he said he wasn't interested in this playwright or, you know, this cowboy tough guy talk that he wasn't well read. This guy could flip out over Sophocles and really inspire you."[38]

Shepard's familiarity with the Bard had been limited to reciting "To be, or not to be" to himself on lonesome cross-country treks, but he was surprised to find that Almereyda's film had brought him to tears outside on the street.[39] "I've never really studied Shakespeare and confess to a very superficial familiarity with *Hamlet*," he wrote to the director, "but this was the first time I felt I really 'got it.'" Shepard praised Hawke's ability to express Hamlet's "vulnerability and deep hurt," feelings that overwhelmed him after the death of Sam Sr., and like the Danish prince, Shepard had mourned by embodying many of his father's traits—his obsession over past grievances, his self-importance, his difficulty in forming meaningful relationships.[40]

Mainly, though, he shared the prince's compulsion for revenge: "I guess the most important thing that dawned on me," he told Almereyda, "was how this revenge was not a question of choice for Hamlet but one of absolute destiny. There's no escaping it." His role conjured "many new ideas for what might be possible" about the return of his own father's ghost for a new play. "I've always been fascinated by fathers and sons and by this thing about revenge," he told his local paper in Minnesota. "In a way, the film makes clearer than anything I've ever seen this idea about trying to rectify a wrong from the past through violence. The violence gathers force in the play, and nobody can see how they are getting swept up in this brushfire, in this death."[41]

* * *

During the first month of the new millennium, Shepard overhauled a script he'd started fifteen years earlier about the ghost of his own father. It was called "Sangre de Cristo" (alternatively, "The Original Liar" and "A Drowned Man"), and he'd given it to his archive at Texas State University, San Marcos, then promptly forgot about it. But the Signature's James Houghton dug it up when they'd worked together, and he and Joe Chaikin strongly urged him to finish it.[42]

The play was a tragicomic portrait of his relationship to Sam Rogers that he retitled *The Late Henry Moss*.[43] Once more, Shepard split himself in two, the brothers Earl and Ray Moss. ("Brothers again," he informed Dark, "what a surprise!") Meanwhile, the already famous brothers, Lee and Austin, were being showcased by Philip Seymour Hoffman and John C. Reilly in the Broadway debut of *True West*, which opened on March 9 at the Circle in the Square Theatre, twenty years after its world premiere. The show was a mythic triumph of theatrical skill, wherein they flipped a coin on the first night to see which role they would play, then alternated roles every few nights (not every night, as often reported) to underscore the dual nature of each of their characters. Switching roles, Shepard said, "was a dangerous idea. It could be dangerously kitschy to do that, but the actors were so good that they succeeded." It was only his third Broadway show, and it turned out to be "a smash hit," he swaggered. "The sucker is sold out and got the best, across-the-board reviews I've ever had in my life. I'm in a state of shock."[44]

Long before he'd even completed *The Late Henry Moss*, Shepard had already lined up an all-star cast: Nick Nolte and Sean Penn as the brothers Earl and Ray, James Gammon as the titular father, Woody Harrelson as the luckless Taxi, Cheech Marin as Esteban, and Sheila Tousey as the father's mystical Indigenous girlfriend, Conchalla. What was especially gratifying about having such a vibrant cast of movie actors was that the audience who turned out was markedly younger than usual. Shepard conceded that the star power helped draw them in, but on the street outside the theater, he also witnessed a group of twentysomethings yelling out his lines the way the mod Londoners roared out the lyrics to "Pinball Wizard" when he saw the Who back in his London days. "One of the great things about kids coming to the theatre," he said, "is that they are directly involved with the question of identity, of who they are.... Anything that speaks to that question of identity calls the kids' attention."[45]

Shepard took the new play's title from Frank O'Connor's 1931 short story "The Late Henry Conran," which he'd read in Ireland in 1997. The Irish writer's tale has many parallels with Shepard's play, scenes that are funny but dark, including an overbearing father in the story "who had the biggest appetite for liquor of any man.... You could honestly say [Conran] would drink porter out of a sore heel." Conran's son, Aloysius, dismisses his father as dead and grouses that "all he ever had his eye on was the main chance. And grander and grander he was getting in himself."[46]

The elder sibling, Earl, in *The Late Henry Moss* is tortured by his father's emotional legacy, while Ray is hell-bent on extracting facts, with his fists if necessary, from Esteban and Taxi. All the while, Henry's corpse lies on the bed. But as in *Fool for Love*, his ghost, often in flashbacks on the night of his death, haunts the adobe dwelling set in Bernalillo, New Mexico.

"It's an amazing dilemma when one begins to discover that you are living your life as a somnambulist," Shepard said, discussing his autobiographical theme in terms he'd learned from the Work. "When that occurs, there's a kind of amazing thing that takes place. One is despair. And the other is a sudden awakening, you know? There's another way of seeing. And the character Henry Moss, of course, realizes that he's in fact dead, although he's walking around. But there's nothing he can do about it. He's a walking dead man. And that's the tragedy."[47]

Shepard directed *The Late Henry Moss* with Anne Militello as the lighting designer and live background music by T Bone Burnett and Jerry Hannan. For a premiere, he settled on the Magic Theatre in late 2000.[48] The Magic had held a "SamFest" from April 30 to May 3, 1998, during which they produced ten of his plays, Chaikin read *War in Heaven*, Shepard read from *Cruising Paradise*, and the Magic renamed their Southside Theatre the Sam Shepard Theatre.

But Shepard mainly chose San Francisco, he said, because Sean Penn, whom he'd recently worked with on Penn's neo-noir movie *The Pledge*, "was pretty much stationed here and he didn't really want to leave the area." Nick Nolte was Penn's idea, and Woody Harrelson agreed because he was, in his words, "a huge Sam Shepard fan," having acted in college productions of *Chicago* and *Icarus's Mother*. Those early roles, Harrelson told a reporter, "were definitely some of my best experiences in acting. There's only a handful of writers who can do dialogue like Sam. It just lifts off the page and spins out into orbit—and you don't know where it's going." None of them did it for the money, as they each worked for scale at seven hundred dollars a week.[49]

Shepard had been running ideas about *The Late Henry Moss* by James Gammon for over a year, and it was Gammon who suggested they cast the comic actor Cheech Marin as Esteban. ("You're going to get a lot more laughs from this thing because I'm doing it," Marin warned Shepard. "Not because I'm necessarily funny. . . . It's just that I have a history, people expect comedy to come out of me.")[50] Shepard had been struck dumb when he first saw Gammon in Los Angeles play Sam Rogers as Weston Tate in *Curse of the Starving Class*. "I wanted him to be in every play I wrote," he said after seeing him that first time, with his mountain man gruffness, whiskey-and-smoke-ravaged speech, and squinting eyes evoking a defense against the sun and a suspicion of humanity. (By the time Gammon was cast as the latest Sam Rogers character, Henry Moss, he'd already appeared as Weston in *Curse*, Baylor in *A Lie of the Mind*, Simms in *Simpatico*, and Dodge in *Buried Child*.) "You know, I've heard a lot of the New York press say that Sam doesn't scare us like he used to," Gammon told *San Francisco* magazine. "They miss the fear that scattered them, that left them on the outside." *The Late Henry Moss*, the actor said, "is frightening in its own way. I don't know if I should run around using the word *frightening*, because the play has more to it than that. But there are certainly frightening aspects here. . . . There's a great depth to Sam in every aspect—massive amounts of mystery—and great auras created from the plays."[51]

Once the play was cast, Shepard phoned Michael Almereyda, the director of *Hamlet*. "[Shepard] had been writing and directing plays that left no trace and wanted a record of this new production," Almereyda recalled of the conversation. Rehearsals started October 3 in Fort Mason's newly appointed Sam Shepard Theatre, but a couple of the actors balked at the idea of a camera filming them for 140 hours. Additionally, through Almereyda and with Shepard's blessing, the author of *Jesus' Son*, Denis Johnson, himself an aspiring playwright, sat in on rehearsals taking notes on the process, but Sean Penn registered a complaint, and the affronted novelist was banished from the theater.[52]

"And why not?" Almereyda said of the actors' reluctance to be filmed rehearsing. "It wasn't hard, on reflection, to fathom why you have to look far and wide before finding a previous example of high-profile actors allowing themselves to be filmed in rehearsal—under pressure, searching, fumbling, EXPOSED. . . . For a brief spell, I considered resorting to half-whispered narration—like what you'd get in a nature program about lemurs in Madagascar, tracking the elusive creatures in their natural habitat." Almereyda's film, *This So-Called Disaster*, titled after the line Sam Sr. had used for the upheaval that sent Shepard packing as a late teen, captured all of this. "It's common for theatre to evaporate like snow," Almereyda said. "I think Sam knew he'd assembled a once-in-a-lifetime cast. He didn't want the experience to vanish without a trace."[53]

The much-heralded opening of *The Late Henry Moss* took place on November 14, 2000, at the Theatre on the Square for a seven-week, sold-out run. Larry Eilenberg, the Magic's otherwise humble artistic director, told the press that "this collection of stars is unprecedented in American theater," and tickets were scalped on the street for nine hundred dollars.[54] The national media dispatched critics to cover one of the biggest theater events of the year. TV crews set up in the lobby as celebrities, including Penn's wife, Robin Wright, Geoffrey Rush, Don Johnson, and Jerry Brown, glad-handed around the theater before settling in for the three-hour performance.

Like much of Shepard's late work, *The Late Henry Moss* was the kind of play only a biographer (and the odd actor and director) could truly love, because it was Shepard's attempt, at long last, to reconcile his lifelong fixation with his father. The only problem was, there had been no reconciliation after Sam Rogers's death, nor, this play tells us, would there ever be. "To me my father was deeply mysterious," Shepard admitted to Mel Gussow a couple of years later. "There is a mystery about him that still exasperates me, that still intrigues me." "I think he was a mystery to himself," he said. Then he laughed, realizing he'd provided a rather accurate self-description. Gussow asked whether he learned much about himself writing autobiographically. "It's given me an avenue to express certain areas that probably would have gone dormant if I hadn't found a form," he replied. "Whether or not I've *learned* more about myself, I don't know."[55]

With his newest family play, *The Late Henry Moss*, nearly all the drama critics surmised as a chorus, Shepard had expanded a script from the old days of the family dramas, and it showed. "As hard as Penn, Nolte and Gammon work," wrote the San Francisco critic Robert Hurwitt, "you feel that they're trying to invest their characters with a depth the playwright hasn't provided, as if he'd visited these figures so often that they've become icons rather than people." It was déjà vu from his Magic Theatre days, Hurwitt wrote, "almost to the point of self-parody."[56]

Because it was a montage of Shepardian elements drawn from his family plays over the years in this way, *The Late Henry Moss* comes as close as he'd be emotionally capable of to his own *Long Day's Journey Into Night*, which Eugene O'Neill had also written after many earlier plays based on his family. Like O'Neill's towering masterpiece, *The Late Henry Moss* marked a culmination of Shepard's family oeuvre, with a shocking view into the origins of his fear. But O'Neill had written *Long Day's Journey*, in his words, "with deep pity and understanding and forgiveness." His play was a profound act of reconciliation with a grievously flawed family.[57]

Shepard just wasn't there yet, not really even close. "In the final analysis," wrote the San Franciscan writer Hal Gelb, who otherwise revered the playwright and exalted his legacy in the city, "Shepard is extremely hard on his characters, father and sons. You might say unforgiving."[58]

## CHAPTER 18

# TRIGGER WORDS

Once *The Late Henry Moss* completed its run, Shepard was devastated by its reception and stopped to see Johnny Dark in Deming, New Mexico, where he and Scarlett had eventually settled, to commiserate, then on to Santa Fe to a favorite eatery of his and Jessica's called the Pink Adobe. On the wall there hung a portrait of Jessica and Walker, and as he stared at it, a powerful wave of loneliness washed through his soul. "So I decided I would get good and drunk," he told Dark. "I hadn't had that thought in over three and a half years—totally dry—not one single drip of liquor and now, suddenly, I know without a doubt that I am going off with the full intention of getting absolutely smashed."[1]

Shepard's first drink was a large glass of Cabernet from Healdsburg, California, where Jesse now lived. Then he strolled back to the plaza and the La Fonda Hotel, where Sam Rogers had worked as a custodian, and downed another large glass of wine. Then he moved on to yet another bar out on the street and eventually, he wrote, got himself "good and sloshed." "I start feeling very sorry for myself," he continued, "and conjure up all this stuff about my father and the play I just finished up in San Francisco which deals with his death and all that stuff and the whole thing just becomes a god-awful drunken mess of emotional indulgence in the past!!!"[2]

In the meantime, Jessica was reveling in well-deserved accolades for her superb interpretation of Mary Tyrone in a West End revival of *Long Day's Journey Into Night*, which opened two weeks after *The Late*

*Henry Moss*. "The top, the absolute top of anything I've ever done," she enthused about the role. "I think it's the most powerful part ever written, but that's just me."[3]

Shepard braved the transatlantic flight to see it, and on Christmas Day in London, the couple went for a leisurely stroll, arm in arm through the byways of the St. John's Wood neighborhood. In a short piece he wrote the day after Christmas titled "At Home," Shepard describes himself and Jessica during their stroll conferring over where to move next, since they both agreed that Minnesota, where they'd heard it was then twenty-five below freezing, was too cold. (After Hollywood, the West, the Old South, and Main Street USA had played themselves out, they really had only one archetype left—New York, New York—and that's where they would go.) It's unclear whether he told her about drinking again, but on that walk, he wrote, they "just felt easy in each other's company. After all these years, they finally felt at home with each other."[4]

As they strolled past a newsstand, Shepard was thinking how "remote" American politics felt when a *USA Today* wafted into his field of vision with the ominous headline "Bush Names Cabinet." If George W. Bush was anything like his father, his election might well lead to another war, especially with Cheney, Rumsfeld, Wolfowitz, Rice, and the rest of the neoconservative "Bushies." The previous March, in fact, Shepard had flown to Rabat, Morocco, to act in Ridley Scott's film about the 1993 Battle of Mogadishu, *Black Hawk Down*, based on the bestselling book by Mark Bowden. Shepard was cast as the commander of the ill-fated mission, Major General William F. Garrison, whose decision to extract the Somali warlord Mohamed Farrah Aidid led to the death of twenty-one soldiers, one captured, and nearly a hundred wounded.

"I remember very clearly my strong, emotional reaction to [pilot] Mike Durant's battered face in the photograph released by the Somalis when he was captured, as well as the bodies of the dead Americans being dragged through the streets. These were very disturbing from the American point of view." Indeed, the militiamen who defeated Delta Force and the Rangers were reportedly trained by an Al Qaeda leader soon on every American mind: Osama bin Laden.[5]

* * *

On that sunny Tuesday morning of September 11, 2001, Shepard was halfway to the New York opening of *The Late Henry Moss* when he heard on the radio that the World Trade Center and the Pentagon had been attacked, whereupon he turned his truck straight around and went back to his Wisconsin cabin. Exactly nine years later, Shepard was listening to the car radio when 9/11's anniversary was announced and got lost in a reverie about "how beautifully clear & bright that fall day was. Not a cloud in the sky, the horrible contrast of the perfect weather & the ghastly destruction. Watching it all unfold on T.V. like some Orson Welles science fiction. The actual sensation of terror in the chest. The sudden vulnerability."[6]

One of Shepard's most heartbreaking memories of the day, he wrote, was driving up to his Wisconsin ranch and spying his neighbor, a farmer, "sitting on his tractor in the middle of a lush soybean field with the engine cut off—staring up at the sky. Not a phone anywhere. Absolute silence."[7]

That night, when most theaters in New York had gone dark, cast and crew debated about whether to go forward with the evening's performance of *The Late Henry Moss* at the Signature Theatre. Previews for it had started on September 5, and Joe Chaikin, who was directing the show, stood firm that no matter the horrific circumstances, "the show must go on." Half of the cast and crew thought it was "disrespectful" to the thousands of victims consumed by fire and rubble. It was also potentially dangerous, given that the United States was under attack. "Who the hell wants to see a play about a couple of sons who can't get along with their father when there's a war going on?," Ethan Hawke, who played Ray, recalled the dispute. In Hawke's telling, Chaikin called the company together and told them, through his aphasia:

> Imagination is reality. *Thought! Action! Thought! Action!* Sons and fathers love each other. Buildings don't fall down. Buildings fell down a long time ago. Imagination is real—it's *real*. Play *must* go on. Fathers *must*

> love sons. Sons *must* forgive fathers. Or buildings *keep* coming down. We *must* do play![8]

Hawke said that about ninety percent of the audience didn't show, but "we had eight walk-ins of people who were just desperate for somewhere to be. . . . I held on to it as an example of why what we do matters . . . that imagination is extremely real and that often what we imagine becomes reality. We have to be careful what we imagine."[9]

The opening was delayed to September 24, and New York's critics, most of whom revered Shepard, Chaikin, and the cast, were even more merciless than San Francisco's, calling *The Late Henry Moss* "half-shaped, wobbly," "Shepard lite, pallid and perfunctory," "unable to find its form or convey its meaning," "torpid and repetitive," "long, plodding," and "a moss-gatherer."[10] Hawke closely observed Shepard, his ostensible mentor, hoping to find an explanation for the playwright's lackluster performance at the typewriter. "It is true that his writing kind of reached a plateau and hung out there," the actor reflected later.

> You really see a grown-up man trying to grow up. And he can't quite do it. I think he's so scared that growing up, like his talent and his pain were so connected that I think he was, in his mind—I'm speculating now—I think he was worried that healing as a man might rob him of his gift. You know, the place that he wrote from was so painful. And I've seen this in other artists. The fear is very real.[11]

Along with his potentially faltering artistic ambition, Shepard had also, when he was a new father, been fearful of the possibility that his children, especially his sons, might get infected by the "poison" of the Rogers line. But over time, his anxiety abated. He'd developed genuine feelings of admiration for his three children as they'd grown into adults, mainly because they betrayed so few characteristics of his own. Fatherhood seemed to call up his better angels in a way to which nothing else was comparable.[12]

Jesse was perhaps the most like himself, a horseman and a drifter, which made sense being raised by the Sheps and the Darks. Jesse was even coming out with his own book of short fiction, *Jubilee King*, much of it based on his experiences as a horseman. Jesse urgently wanted his father's approval. He wanted to be like him, while at the same time prove his mettle and stand proud of his own identity, despite his father's fame and prodigious talents. "I wanted," he wrote, "all the things that sons of men have wanted." Shepard was asked about Jesse's publication of *Jubilee King* when it was released. "Like father like son?" "He's really good, and he's worked very hard at it," came the response. "I like his stuff."[13]

Shepard was preparing a new volume of writing that dealt directly with his family. He'd cultivated a notion of a story's "simple core" from reading, along with Frank O'Connor's short stories, Denis Johnson's *Jesus' Son*, Tim O'Brien's *The Things They Carried*, and Dante's *Inferno*. But it was Graham Greene's collected stories that left him "stunned totally by his ability to go so cleanly and directly to the heart of the matter—the core event—the 'burning center,' as Frank O'Connor put it."[14] This was the standard he aspired to while cobbling together his slim volume of eighteen stories, sketches, and raw-form dialogues under the expansive title *Great Dream of Heaven*.

The stories in the new volume were works of compression, tightly wrought vignettes that favor images over words, brevity over bombast. His children and Shura have several cameos, and he takes their side against a father (himself) who's a loving man but behaves erratically and is woefully disconnected from teenage concerns. The story "Berlin Wall Piece" is written from Walker's point of view when he was a seventh grader working on a short homework assignment. He's been asked to write about the 1980s, but found consulting his father was no help. "I tell him I need stuff about style and fads and what was going on in the country at the time," Walker's character says, "and he says none of that has anything to do with reality; that reality is an 'internal affair' and all the rest of that stuff is just superficial and a lie—like the news. . . . My dad's fucking crazy. He is. I didn't realize it for a long time but he is."[15]

*Great Dream of Heaven* was released in the fall of 2002, and its cover displays a haunting picture that Jessica, now an accomplished photographer, had taken of Shepard and Walker fishing off a wood-planked pier at an "ancient lake" while on vacation in Mexico. Though Jessica is with them, the men look blissfully remote: a man with his son staring ahead, a thin black stripe of land on the horizon separating the dark water from the azure sky. "I don't think anything compares to the love you have for your children," Shepard said. "That's the deal. It goes way beyond the love you have for their mother or the women you've had in your life or your dog or your horses or anything else. . . . You can't compare it to any other affection."[16]

* * *

Early on, Shepard and Jessica made a pact not to be away from the children at the same time, but now that Walker had gone off to college, they were free to work whenever and wherever they chose. The timing was right, then, to develop a second film with Wim Wenders, which they'd committed to do several years before at a chance meeting at a Lou Reed concert. "I think we both decided that enough water had flowed under the bridges of the Mississippi River that we could work together again," Wenders said.[17]

Wenders flew to the Upper Midwest, and the two men settled into a regular work routine: each morning they ate breakfast at the Oasis Cafe in Stillwater, then drove over the bridge to the Wisconsin cabin and hunkered down to write, Wenders on his computer and Shepard on his old electric typewriter. It was to be a black comedy with the working title "Phantom of the West" (later *Don't Come Knocking*). They worked like this, intermittently, for three years.[18]

"I thought we were going to be finished in one year," Wenders joked about the extraordinary time it took, "and so I saw the river freeze and unfreeze. And then I saw it freeze two more times." They might spend weeks developing a scene, then throw it out and start over again. The story revolved around the commercialization of Hollywood and the feeling of exile that propelled Shepard's self-destructive behavior along. Wenders wanted him to star as their aging antihero, Howard Spence, a washed-up actor of popular Westerns, but instead of asking directly, he told his collaborator he'd already tried Jack Nicholson. Shepard stopped typing and shot back, "Jack can't ride a horse anymore." And at that instant, Wenders knew he'd bagged his leading man.[19]

The following summer, 2003, Shepard lost one of his dearest friends and collaborators when Joe Chaikin died as a result of congenital heart failure at age sixty-seven. Hearing this news was a terrible blow to Shepard, and his strongest reminder of mortality since his father's death nearly two decades earlier. It came as no surprise, as Chaikin contracted a chronic heart condition from a bout of childhood scarlet fever that plagued him throughout his life, and Shepard had comforted him through open heart surgeries and his aphasia for almost twenty years now. Ethan Hawke attended the funeral with Shepard. "I remember with all Sam's tough guy posing and stuff," he said, "watching him read poetry at Joe Chaikin's memorial and just sobbing through tears—he just loved that man."[20]

"I don't know how long it's going to take to get over the loss of Joe," Shepard told a friend, the actor Clark Middleton, who was also at the funeral. "Maybe never."[21]

* * *

Shepard believed his terror of flying had at last played itself out. "Oh, I'm flying now," he told a British reporter in 2004 who was worried his phobia might prevent him from visits to London. "I'm over that hump. I've never tried to examine the phobia, but for some reason it's gone." Still, in January of that year, when Shepard flew to Sydney, Australia, to film the thriller *Stealth*, he was "armed with Xanax, Tylenol PM, Dramamine, & every other over-the-counter pain killer I could lay my hands on," to go with his plane-sized glass bottles of red wine and a huge bundle of books.[22]

Sydney to Shepard was "an exotic San Francisco without the fog & rain," and he taught himself to play a didgeridoo on his hotel balcony. He also drove out to the famed Outback destination Alice Springs. Mostly, though, he was acting in front of computer monitors on the soundstage of a "monster studio." "It's very tough," he carped. "I'm having a relationship with a television. It's horrible. I don't ever want to do it again."[23] This degrading work was under the *Fast and Furious* director Robert Cohen, who had "an earring & tattoos of green & red dragon fish running up & down his forearms . . . the kind of short guy you love to immediately detest on meeting & then slowly grow to admire for his sheer bravado & odd intellect."[24]

Once Shepard returned stateside, he shot a film that mattered a good deal more to him, *Don't Come Knocking*, with the script he and Wenders had worked on for three years. Shepard had long fixated on Elko, Nevada, "a kind of stop-over cowboy/gambling town," so that's where they began shooting. Wenders was equally fascinated by Butte, Montana, the "Poisonville" of Dashiell Hammett's *Red Harvest*, Wenders's favorite American novel. "So, that's where we took the story," Shepard wrote of the two western cities. "We followed our yearnings like a couple of hitch-hikers just wanting to roam the country for a while and see what we'd run into."[25]

Shepard played Howard Spence, a sixty-year-old narcissist, alcohol and drug abuser, and actor in big-budget Westerns. He is sick of his job, and of his pointless existence. But Howard discovers he has a son, then a daughter, whom he was never told about. Wenders worried about Shepard playing the complexities of this character. "Do you think you can handle this?" he asked. "I can't promise you because I've never done it," Shepard replied. "But that's why I'm writing it, because nobody would ever offer it to me, so I gotta write it for myself."[26]

And yet, like in all of Shepard's dramas, no matter how desperate a situation becomes, he found the laughs. "As we were writing," Wenders said, "we realized that Howard would be unbearable if he took himself too seriously. So slowly, the script became . . . not quite a comedy, but a farce, it became very farcical."[27] In the final scene, Howard rears up his horse like the Lone Ranger and Roy Rogers did, as Shepard had dreamed of doing at six years old when he ran away from home as a boy and saw *The Lone Ranger* on TV. Wenders disapproved of this gratuitous nod to American kitsch, but the scene survived the cutting room floor.[28]

*Don't Come Knocking* opens with Howard awakening from a night of debauchery in his trailer on a Western movie set in Moab, Utah. After a few irksome reminders of his responsibilities as an actor on the picture, he leaps onto a horse and rides off at a gallop to visit his mother (played by Eva Marie Saint) in his hometown of Elko, Nevada. Howard hasn't been home in thirty years, and his mother informs him that a woman contacted her twenty-five years before to tell her she'd given birth to his child.

The boy was the product of a fling he'd had with a waitress named Doreen at a coffeehouse in Butte while he was shooting his breakout role. Howard then leaves for Butte to reunite with Doreen and meet their son, Earl (Gabriel Mann), a local musician who fiercely rejects any attempt at reconciliation. Then, Howard discovers he has another love child, Sky (Sarah Polley), from another tryst during the same fateful shoot that spawned both a career and two offspring.

It took some doing, but in time Shepard persuaded the generally reticent Jessica to play Doreen, a waitress and mother to his long-lost son. Working with Jessica, Shepard said, was "a little bit scary, because of the emotional territory of it. It's something I don't think you can do every day." For her part, Jessica sounded cheery about working with her ne'er-do-well partner:

> I know some couples don't like to work together, but I've always found it easy working with Sam. And in this case it's a little different than just working with your partner because he also wrote it, so I'm speaking his words. As soon as you start saying those trigger words, like "son," suddenly when you're looking at the father of your son and you say, "son," it brings up a whole well of emotion that you're not even aware that you're going to touch on. Something there makes it richer.[29]

Jessica suggested they not rehearse for the first encounter between Howard and Doreen, so the scene would feel more genuine. The cast and crew gathered at a café in Butte for the shoot, and when Wenders yelled "Action!" Jessica slapped Shepard hard across the face. He was so stunned by the blow, he neglected to follow the script's cue to walk away. Following his return from Australia, in fact, Shepard knew he'd behaved poorly and deserved a good slapping. "I don't know what's wrong with me," he wrote that April.

> That's the hard part. I don't know why I keep returning to these horrible bouts of drinking & bad behavior. I've ruined an amazing relationship just out of a callous disregard for anyone else's feelings & the worst part of it is that I don't know how it all happened. Anyhow, she's finally come to the end of her rope with me. The pathetic part is I don't know what to do now. I know that if I can't stop drinking I'm really finished.

They decided to "soldier on" separately until all three children had gone off on their own.[30] And that is when, late in the summer of 2004, they started filming with Wim Wenders.

"The story is about so many things," Shepard said of *Don't Come Knocking*. "It's about estrangement more than anything. It's about this strange, American sadness that I find, the alone-ness they feel. We don't know each other in America, we don't even know who we are, we just don't. I'm haunted by that American character, and that strange, strange lack of identity."[31]

Critics found the film to be purposeless, and they attacked what they saw as Shepard's now tired cowboy mystique, the bland voyeurism of an epic Western manqué, lazy acting styles, and the cliché of the Old West versus the New (a cliché that was cliché, it was reluctantly implied, because of Shepard himself). "Ms. Lange's Doreen spits fire," complained Stephen Holden of the *New York Times*, "but the actress can't sort through her character's sudden changes in attitude, and because the upper half of Ms. Lange's face appears immobilized by cosmetic work, she is only able to give half a performance." (Jessica had been "conflicted," she acknowledged, about getting a facelift, and said Shepard thought it was "insane." "*Never touch your face*," he demanded, apparently without success.) What she wanted was to act in a Shepard *play*. "You would think maybe at some point he might write a play that would have a part in it for me," she said. "But, see, when I say things like this then he gets really pissed off. He says, 'I've written a lot of parts you could have played.' I would love to do one of his pieces and be directed by him onstage."[32]

* * *

The intensely private nature of Shepard's work was placed on hold for Shepard's next play. Historical forces again encroached on his imagination, as they had during the previous Bush administration's Operation Desert Storm. Shepard still had never voted in a presidential election before, but he understood that the stakes involved in the 2004 race between the incumbent, George W. Bush, and Senator John Kerry of Massachusetts went beyond political partisanship. And so, after Bush's post-9/11 abuses of power, torturing the enemy and bombarding civilian populations with thousands of tons of explosives, he responded with a one-act political farce, *The God of Hell*, which competes only with *States of Shock* as Shepard's most overtly political work.[33]

He'd already finished a draft of *The God of Hell*, under the working title "Pax Americana," in November 2003, but by the spring of 2004, shocking photographs of abused Iraqi prisoners at Abu Ghraib prison appeared in the press. Prisoners were strung up hooded with electrodes hooked up to their genitals, then forced to pile on top of each other naked while American soldiers, some of them women, jeered and hammed it up for the camera. Such a national disgrace was too much for even the politically ambivalent Shepard, and he rewrote the play to reflect the news.[34]

*The God of Hell*, Shepard declared, in a highly circulated word of protest, was "a takeoff on Republican fascism." He also scheduled a conspicuously political time and venue: previews to begin October 29, 2004, four days prior to the election, at Greenwich Village's progressive New School university. "I kind of wanted to get it done in New York before the election," he told a reporter. "I'm not sure it matters, but I figured I'd get it out there."[35]

Preferring what he called "the politics of feeling" to dogma, Shepard still believed that artists had a responsibility to "convert" the time in which they lived to reflect their own lived experience.[36] What Americans saw at that time was a flood of propagandistic messages under the guise of patriotism, he argued. But statements he'd made on the politics of the sixties were as historically relevant in the twenty-first century as they ever were. "We're being sold a brand-new idea of patriotism," he scoffed in 2004. "It never occurred to me that patriotism had to be advertised. Patriotism is something you deeply felt." Don Shewey, the author of Shepard's first substantial biography, pushed him further in a magazine interview. "What is that show-your-colors mentality about?" "Fear," the dramatist replied.

> The sides are being divided now. It's very obvious. So if you're on the other side of the fence, you're suddenly anti-American. It's breeding fear of being on the wrong side. Democracy's a very fragile thing. You have to take care of democracy. As soon as you stop being responsible to it and allow it to turn into scare tactics, it's no longer democracy, is it? It's something else. It may be an inch away from totalitarianism.[37]

Shepard insisted that the so-called red state–blue state divide was all "media manipulation." Instead of picking one side, he usually applied his "redneck" logic to his inner political turmoil, one that gripped the nation as a whole: "For George W. to be construed as a cowboy," Shepard fumed, "is about as far from the truth as you can possibly get. It's ruined the reputation of Texas, which actually has more authenticity than many, many states." Then, he'd turn it on progressive politicians such as Hillary Clinton, "riding around in trucks and talking about how she's a blue-collar girl."[38]

George W. Bush's "War on Terror" was in full swing when Election Day arrived, however, and Shepard, voting in a presidential election for the first time, pulled the lever for John Kerry.[39] Kerry was defeated, of course, which had an unnerving effect on the play's audience. Before the election, according to the production's director, Lou Jacob, "the audience was more reticent. They were holding their breath more. Now it's a reality and they're gasping with horror." Shepard agreed that "in a terrible way, the election has caused the play to have more bite."[40]

*The God of Hell* alludes to Pluto, the Greek god of the underworld, which leads us to plutonium, the radioactive chemical element in nuclear weapons. The protagonists, Frank and Emma, are Wisconsin dairy farmers hosting a visitor, Frank's old friend Graig (rhymes with "Ghraib") Haynes. Graig's work is top secret, so his job is unknown to Frank, though he's let slip that he arrived from Rocky Buttes, Colorado (a portmanteau of Rocky Flats, Colorado, and Butte, Montana, which hosts a nuclear weapons facility that leaked plutonium). When Frank slouches off to tend to his heifers, a man named Welch arrives at the door. "The notion of somebody coming from out of nowhere and disturbing the peace," Shepard said of Welch. "It fit perfectly with the Republican invasion. The whole storm that built up after 9/11. The Welch character came in last. I wanted him to be like something out of Brecht's clown plays. Tim [Roth] plays him with the perfect tone: the demon clown." Like Bush and his hawkish spokesmen, Welch wears the uniform of a neocon Republican male politico of the twenty-first century: "Dark suit with American flag pin in his lapel, short cropped hair, crisp white shirt, red tie."[41]

Welch impersonates a door-to-door salesman hawking patriotic gear of the sort that adorned many American homes following 9/11 and its aftermath. Eventually, we learn that Graig has fled his post at Rocky Buttes, and Welch is a government agent tasked with his capture and "reprogramming."[42]

"His fanaticism really drives the play," Shepard remarked of his American-born monster. "I've always been interested in the innocent versus the depraved and how that corruption takes place, insidiously, inch by inch, and how the corrupter is always full of self-confidence compared to the innocent." When he showed Tim Roth the script, Shepard informed him, as he had with his actors for *The Late Henry Moss*, "There's no money, no board, and you'll have to do it pretty much for free."[43] Roth agreed, and the play enticed a marquee cast to perform Off-Broadway, with minimal pay and no frills, at the New School's Actors Studio Drama School Theatre: Roth as Welch, Randy Quaid as Frank, J. Smith-Cameron as Emma, and Frank Wood as the beleaguered Graig Haynes, all led by the highly regarded Off-Broadway director Lou Jacob.

The notices were indulgent, though largely depended on the critic's political stance and sense of humor. "What a deliriously entertaining and deeply scary message has arrived from Shepard," wrote Linda Winer of *Newsday*. "Better late than never," she mused of his timing the production right before Bush claimed victory in the election, "but too late all the same." Meanwhile, Terry Teachout of the conservative *Wall Street Journal* regarded *The God of Hell* as "a smug, oafish fantasy." Ben Brantley of the *New York Times* went right down the middle and called the ending, when the men exit in lockstep with Welch's marching orders, "pretty standard agitprop," yet the play makes up for it by satirically poking fun "at its own righteous self as well as its broad political targets."[44]

At the same time, Shepard made the decision to act on the stage, for the first time since *Cowboy Mouth*, in the avant-garde British dramatist Caryl Churchill's *A Number*. Previews for the two-month run took place on November 16 at the New York Theatre Workshop, across the street from La MaMa. Shepard read *A Number* in one rapt sitting while filming *Stealth* in Sydney, and he soon pronounced it to be the most brilliant play he had read since *Waiting for Godot*. "It's a short play, but I couldn't believe how powerful it was. It's a major, major contemporary play. I think it will go down as a classic." Shepard next contacted its New York director, James Macdonald from the Royal Court in London, about the lead role, but Nick Nolte had already been cast. "People have been trying to get me to be in plays for 30 years," Shepard said with a laugh, "and the first time I said yes, I had to wait for Nick to turn it down."[45]

A deeply personal chord was struck by Churchill's play: Shepard played Salter, a rueful alcoholic who abandoned his son Bernard, as

Shepard always felt he had done with Jesse, then cloned him to retry fatherhood. "His taste as an actor is towards minimalism, which is exactly right for the piece," said Macdonald, who'd directed three of Shepard's own plays. "It doesn't need a lot of external huffing and puffing. Just do the thing as simply as you can with the greatest truth you can muster." During the run, Shepard bumped into the playwright Horton Foote at the Jane Street Tavern, where Foote asked him what it was like to tread the boards after all those years. "Very scary!" Shepard replied. "He was super vulnerable," Macdonald concurred. "He was terrified and the audience was right on top of him [because of its vaulted staging], so that didn't help." Shepard's performance after over thirty years off the stage, Ben Brantley enthused, was "terrific . . . magnetic." "Mr. Shepard turns out to be an ideal interpreter of Ms. Churchill's disjunctive prose. Her fragmented dialogue flows from him like blood from an opened vein."[46]

* * *

While Shepard was juggling *The God of Hell* and *A Number*, and Jessica was preparing for a Broadway revival of Tennessee Williams's *The Glass Menagerie*, they put the Stillwater house and the ranch in Wisconsin on the market. "When we first moved to Stillwater it felt like a real place," Jessica told a reporter. "It had a downtown with a hardware store, a furniture store, a clothing store. Now it's all gift shops and these terrible condominiums. It was a little town with a great deal of character. Everything gets yuppified, I guess." They settled in Greenwich Village, with views of Washington Square Park and the now gentrified environs where Shepard had first made his mark.[47]

Around this time, Shepard and Jessica were walking down the street one day, and there was Patti Smith. Now the adulated Godmother of Punk, Smith had been walking in the opposite direction and reacted at seeing Shepard with something like, "Oh, my God, you're still alive!" Smith meant this literally, since many close friends of hers had been dying off, including Robert Mapplethorpe, who died of AIDS-related complications in 1989, and her husband, Fred "Sonic" Smith of the proto-punk band the MC5, who died of a heart attack in 1994. Then or soon after, she invited Shepard to record a version of Nirvana's grunge anthem "Smells like Teen Spirit." Shepard agreed, and he brought Walker along. Walker had become the musician his father once wistfully hoped he might have been. "He really admired Walker's dedication to music," Roxanne Rogers said. "He was really blown away." They both played on Smith's track, Shepard on the six-string guitjo and Walker on banjo.[48]

Shepard started a play that December called "Sway," a family drama set at Christmastime in their new Greenwich Village apartment. In this confessional play, Shepard demonstrates a keen awareness of the impact his absenteeism had on his family, and he acknowledges his children's dissatisfaction with leaving Minnesota, along with their untethered existence as the wayfaring children of celebrities. Hannah's character, Hattie Vale, protests to Jessica's, named J, "We've *never* been all together. Never ever." "The house-moving," Hattie continues, "being here—not having a home—never having a real home—never being somewhere permanent—never knowing from one moment to the next whether we're here or someplace else."[49] Shepard's avatar eventually appears: Hollis, a Civil War reenactor who's wearing dust-covered cowboy gear after a three-day drive from Texas. "Forged his way across the Appalachians through the driving snow," his wife quips. "Down through the mighty Shenandoah, dodging flaming arrows the whole way." This was Hollis's first visit to their new apartment, and he's oblivious to major events in their lives.[50]

After typing up sixty-four pages, Shepard abandoned "Sway," which was to be a kind of treatise on "stories, the *influence* of stories." But he lost the drive to complete such an ambitious project. "There is this aura that a three-act play is the important one," he griped after abandoning the work. "It's the one that you do to win the Pulitzer. Some part of you falls for that, and then after a while you don't fall for that. . . . At this point, I'm writing for me." Ethan Hawke believed that he'd become fearful of literary ambition. "I don't think it's a legit fear," Hawke said:

> When we were working on *Lie of the Mind* together [later, in 2010], he was very critical of how ambitious that play was—he liked his newer

> plays better because they were less ambitious. And I just felt, that's the alcohol talking buddy. I wish you were still trying to write a play this good. *Lie of the Mind* is a masterpiece, and I felt him actually afraid of the playwright he had been twenty years earlier. The talent, you know, those big plays, *Curse*, *Lie of the Mind*, *Buried Child*, *True West* . . . They are masterpieces, and he was afraid of them.[51]

Shepard admitted that at this time in his writing career, "the stigma of 'greatness' is . . . very haunting. I keep thinking I'm past that but it rears its head now & then. How to simply write for oneself—like Salinger was talking about:—'There's a great peace in not being published.'"[52]

* * *

Once *A Number*'s run was finished, Shepard left the family behind in New York and headed straight to Kentucky. He was taking a long break. Back on August 28, 2003, Shepard signed the deed for three parcels of about 150 acres of farmland, which he'd already been promised several years earlier, near the amiable hamlet of Midway. The property came with a whitewashed brick house built in 1808 and was once inhabited by the gunslinger Jesse James's mother.[53] (Shepard was soon going to play James's brother, Frank, opposite Brad Pitt's Jesse, in the 2007 film *The Assassination of Jesse James by the Coward Robert Ford*.)

Lexington, Kentucky, had been the nerve center of Thoroughbred horse racing for two centuries, and its surrounding farmland was some of the most coveted in the world. Shepard bought the farm in nearby Midway for just under a million dollars, and he filled its outlying meadows with quarter horses, about six at a time, and thirty or forty head of cattle, but his broodmares would be stabled and foaled at Midway's Nuckols Farm. He refused to build a gate, because he didn't want any landmark that might indicate where he lived and attract nosy outsiders. It took years for Shepard's new friend Phil Gerrow, a master renovator of old Kentucky homes, to make the tumbledown brick house habitable. At the start, it even had a tree growing through its roof, so he briefly rented a house large enough to accommodate his family on North Winter Street, then an apartment in downtown Midway, where the character Simms's office is located in *Simpatico*.[54]

Prized as the farmland around Midway was, and thus as affluent as most of its residents were, it was still a haven away from the pretensions of New York, Los Angeles, and even Santa Fe. Shepard and Jessica were far and away Midway's most famous residents, where the town's motto was "Your business is our business." But the Queen of England sometimes stayed down the road, so the residents were well schooled in protecting their celebrities' privacy. Jessica was nonchalant and unpretentious when she visited Midway, but for her, the quaint southern town represented everything she disliked about her partner's Wild West routine. Though Jessica visited on occasion, she never settled there. Each time he drove down from New York or Minnesota, she would act, Shepard said, "as though I'm abandoning her or something. Like a jealous lover."[55]

Only fifteen miles from the Keeneland Race Course, where Shepard had attended horse auctions since the 1980s, Midway retains the historic authenticity of its mid-nineteenth-century years as a railroad depot that went back to Daniel Boone. During the few months out of the year when he was not in New York, Los Angeles, or on a film set, he would contentedly relax at Midway. He was also a short drive away from the Kentucky Derby, which he described, after his fourth time there, as an "absolute piece of American madness—more than 100,000 drunks in fancy clothes—ladies in big straw hats—men in 3 piece suits & all the peasants in the in-field tattooed, 1/2 naked, rolling in mud, screaming profanities at the wealthy. It's all very medieval."[56]

Whenever a tourist mustered the audacity to take Shepard's picture without his permission, a local friend of his recalled, he

> would remind them that he wasn't some animal in a zoo. Knowing that he couldn't very well take their cameras away, he would warn them that he had better not see or hear about the picture appearing on Facebook or anywhere else. The violators would apologize, duck their head, and disappear as fast as they could.[57]

He ate dinner and drank red wine and Patrón tequila at Heirloom, a local restaurant, four or five nights a week, and when they saw his head down at the back table, reading or scribbling away in his notebooks, the local patrons knew to leave him alone. He soon befriended Heirloom's owner, Henry "Buzz" Wombles, who acted as his personal sentinel. For a time, waitresses were forbidden to make even the friendliest banter with Shepard, a tall order for a happy-go-lucky Kentucky waitstaff. One night, Governor Steven Beshear and his wife, Jane, arrived at Heirloom, and she asked their waiter to call Shepard over. He was loaded but agreed, a friend recalled, but "you could see wheels turnin' in his head, and he tried to get up, and he slipped, and that was the end of it." He routinely drank so much that he couldn't stand, or grew combative when someone offered him a ride home. He was kicked out of Midway bars more than once, and a local estimated that he'd totaled at least two cars. Asked whether this was true, Phil Gerrow shrugged: "Naw, he never totaled a car. He just ran into a lot of shit."[58]

Shepard came to Midway to get away from obligations, but he was also, as Gerrow testified, "estranged from everybody" important to him by the time he got there. Women would come and go from his house, but he mainly focused on his horses. "The axiom goes: 'No man with a promising two-year-old ever committed suicide,'" Shepard rhapsodized over a colt.

> He sips on his hot chocolate and coffee mix and feels like a genius for breeding this blistering-fast colt. The whole rest of his life is a catastrophe; his marriage, his family, his dying friends, his lost opportunities. But this colt—even in the dark, as he flashes by—rippling sorrel muscle—the rhythmic blasts from the nostrils—this colt lights up what's left of the man's mind. That part that still lies vulnerable to brilliance and courage. It lifts him up like a love affair or the great ball of sun just now cracking over the backstretch.[59]

## CHAPTER 19

# AT HOME AT THE ABBEY

In Kentucky, Shepard had adopted the role of the country Irish gentleman, so the timing of his next prospect was auspicious. In the fall of 2006, Shepard had a breakfast meeting at Pastis, a favorite restaurant of his in Manhattan's Meatpacking District. There he met Fiach Mac Conghail, the artistic director of Dublin's Abbey Theatre, a historic playhouse established by Lady Gregory and W. B. Yeats in 1904. They wanted to hire him, according to Mac Conghail, because the Abbey, Ireland's national theater, was in decline and needed help to revive itself. "I was quaking in my boots," the Irishman remembered of this exchange with Shepard. "I mean, you're meeting theater history, right?"[1]

Mac Conghail had a working relationship with Shepard's old friend from London Stephen Rea, his "calling card to Sam," the Irishman said. When Mac Conghail first asked Rea to return to the Abbey after an eighteen-year absence, the actor said no. But once Mac Conghail floated Shepard's name as the playwright who might help transform the Abbey, and hopefully inject some life into Shepard's work, Rea changed his tune.[2]

Mac Conghail was there to pitch a major survey of Shepard's plays at the Abbey, like the Signature had done in 1996. He sought Shepard because he hoped to engage a foreign playwright for the Abbey who might inspire eager young actors, directors, and dramatists then coming up in Ireland. And when Shepard informed him that his greatest influences were Samuel Beckett and Little Richard, he knew he'd found his man. Shepard was impressed by the Abbey's mission too, Mac Conghail recalled, "a political theater engaging with ideas of nationhood, engaging with the idea of identity, always trying to unpack all those things."[3]

Mac Conghail also chose Shepard, he told the *Boston Globe*, because "his plays have a resonance here—dysfunctional families, globalization, these are issues we in Ireland struggle with." Shepard, Mac Conghail remarked on the playwright's recent string of bad luck on American stages, "was out of step" with the neorealist direction American theater seemed to be taking, "or maybe the U.S. was out of step with him." He thought the Abbey Theatre might serve him well in terms of commissioning and promoting his work.[4] This was the start of an impactful collaboration with the Irish, which would last to the end of his career and form what the *Irish Times* would call "Shepard's Irish renaissance."[5]

In Stephen Rea's view, the three greatest dramatists of the late twentieth century were an Irishman, an Englishman, and an American: Beckett, Pinter, and Shepard. Rea had been directed by each of the three playwrights. "All three," he said, "are engaged in a theater that is beyond the mere traffic with, in Yeats' phrase, 'the sensation of an external reality.'" Shepard objected, telling Rea, "You shouldn't include me in that company," but Rea insisted. Each of these writers, the actor wrote, create for the stage "his own unique yet universally recognizable world."[6]

"I might have something," Shepard told Mac Conghail at Pastis, with Rea in mind. Back in Kentucky, he dug up a play idea called "Dead Horse," set in the Civil War, and reworked it into a one-act about a Western art dealer in his twilight years named Hobart Struther.[7] Hobart ruminates over his lifelong "quest for 'AUTHENTICITY,'" a term Shepard capitalizes sardonically, while he's stuck on a Nebraskan prairie digging a grave for the carcass of his overworked horse.[8] Shepard described Hobart as a man, like him, who "had a past in which there was some semblance of a connection with the land, which he abandoned for this art-world thing. And now he's trying to retrace it, get back to it, but it's impossible."[9]

Within a month of their first meeting, the play was accepted and scheduled for March under the title *Kicking a Dead Horse*, with Shepard to direct. The timing was fortuitous, as Hannah was attending graduate school in Ireland at the University of Galway, and Jessica was acting close by in the West End revival of *The Glass Menagerie*. But if the women were greeted in the Land of Saints and Scholars with typical Irish warmth, the reception of Shepard's arrival to their shores was mixed: "The Abbey has lost its soul," protested the writer Ulick O'Connor, who thought putting on an American play was ill-conceived at best. "Bringing Sam Shepard in is hardly going to revitalize Irish theatre," he grumbled. All the same, the comedian Colin Murphy countered, "Stephen Rea's return to the Abbey stage is unmissable, even if Sam Shepard's vehicle for him is more obscure than your average work in the Irish canon."[10]

For Shepard, Mac Conghail said, "the Abbey was a place to hide, to recuperate artistically, and maybe emotionally. . . . He felt a part of the Abbey Theatre family . . . and we gave him a home."[11]

* * *

The Irish drama and culture critic Fintan O'Toole was taken aback by Shepard's appearance when he arrived for an interview in Dublin with the *Irish Times*. O'Toole wrote that at sixty-three, the American dramatist was "still lithe, rangy, and almost boyish. He still has the chiseled, angular features of a movie star and the easy self-possession of a rock star. . . . But he is warm and unfussy, speaks in a deep drawling western accent and laughs a lot with a gleeful cackle that betrays no hint of cynicism or world-weariness."[12]

Shepard informed O'Toole that he believed that, unlike his own countrymen, the Irish knew who they were. He then cited a number of Irish writers he'd discovered over the years: Beckett, of course, but also older writers such as John Millington Synge and Frank O'Connor, his contemporary Tom Murphy, and younger writers such as Conor McPherson and Martin McDonagh, whose *The Beauty Queen of Leenane* Shepard saw several times on Broadway in 1998. McDonagh had borrowed from *True West* for his 1997 play about two combative brothers, *The Lonesome West*, and actually wrote an apologetic letter to Shepard about this, but Shepard said no harm had been done: "The idea of conflicts between brothers goes back to Cain and Abel."[13]

Rea described the one-act *Kicking a Dead Horse* as "like *King Lear*, except you have to play the Fool as well." Indeed, from the opening lines, Shepard notes in his stage directions, Hobart should mimic the movements of "the classic clown." Rea was one of the few actors Shepard knew who had the range and ability to blend Lear and the Fool into one hilariously doomed character.[14]

Rea was more political than Shepard ever was, and he perceived strong parallels between American imperial might, especially as seen in Iraq, and the history of Irish subjugation to the British Empire. As a result, Rea's reading of the play was more political too. "It's about advanced capitalism," he said of *Kicking a Dead Horse*, "about using up resources as fast as you can. And to sustain the lifestyle, you're then moving on to invade sovereign nations."[15] Hobart, for one, believes Lewis might have shot himself after he and Clark finished their expedition across the Louisiana Purchase because he prophesied how his country was going to behave "after opening up all that great expanse of country." Crazy Horse is "a true American Hero," Hobart reasons. There should be a National Day of Rest for such "a man of his people."[16]

Rehearsals started on February 7, and the play opened at the Abbey's Peacock Stage on March 12, 2007. "The dead horse should be as realistic as possible," Shepard insisted. "In fact, it should actually be a dead horse." So the Abbey made a cast from an actual dead horse and wrapped it in the same horse's hide.[17]

For Dubliners, a Shepard play at the Abbey was a major cultural event, and a sizable contingent of Irish playwrights attended: Conor McPherson, Tom Murphy, Billy Roche, Thomas Kilroy, Sebastian Barry, Bernard Farrell, and Michael West. "Braitheas an-bhrodúil go raibh Sam Shepard agus Stephen Rea ar stáitse na Mainistreach," Fiach Mac Conghail beamed in his native tongue: "It was a very proud feeling to have Sam Shepard and Stephen Rea together on the Abbey stage." Shepard's fly-fishing buddy, the fiction writer Richard Ford, was there too. "It seemed like the stage was full of people," he said of the one-man show. "It was full up with emotion, language, movement."[18] This was high praise for any play from the Pulitzer Prize–winning novelist, who later disclosed, "I don't enjoy the theatre, never go to plays, don't read plays, and while I'm in touch with Sam's theatrical work . . . when we tried to talk about my writing, or his writing, we quickly discovered we had different aesthetics, different vocabularies . . . just complementary sensibilities."[19]

Overall, the notices for the Abbey's *Kicking a Dead Horse* were mixed, and the critical reception foreshadowed that of the New York premiere in 2008 at the Public Theater. Still, the play had its fans. *The New Yorker*'s Hilton Als praised it for "some of the most poetic and metaphysical writing Shepard has produced since the seventies."[20] For other critics, the title aroused suspicion: "The legend simply protests too much," wrote Karen Fricker in *Variety*. "If Shepard really wanted to 'make a clean break' from the dead-horse weight that is his cowboy-playwright image, then why write another cowboy play?" He was asked about this by the *Guardian* that June, to which Shepard curtly responded, "Fuck it. If you don't understand it, I'll just write another one."[21]

Shepard completed his next work, *Ages of the Moon*, which was also written for the Abbey Theatre, in early 2008. Johnny Dark, who was the basis for the character Byron, called it Shepard's "two-old-guys-on-a-porch-play." And that's precisely what it was. "Ames and Byron are talking to each other in the same way as we talked to each other," Dark told Shepard after reading the one-act script, "except with Byron and Ames, it's just you talking to yourself."[22]

*Ages of the Moon* takes place the previous August 27, 2007, the night of a total eclipse, on the back porch of Shepard's house in Midway. The whitewashed brick structure should appear, he said, "hovering in space," and there's a malfunctioning electric fan whirring above.[23] Ames and Byron are two old friends. The former, based on Shepard, is in exile after his wife found a note on a fishing map from a much younger woman. He believes his marriage is over, and he's called his old friend Byron to help him through the crisis. "Drinking and young snatch," Byron scolds.

"At your age." "You'd think love would change all that, wouldn't you?," Ames scoffs about his life spent "on the run." "All that . . . wandering. Desolation. Motels. Love."[24]

Their conversation invokes the back-and-forth prattle of Laurel and Hardy, if the comedians were obsessively neurotic and blotto on thimblefuls of Woodford Reserve. Dark told Shepard that he was reminded by his portrait in the script of "how not so wonderful I am or ever was. It's not enough for a man to be a miracle simply by being alive. He wants to be wonderful as well. I think that's probably why I joined The Work. I wanted to be even more wonderful than I already thought I was. Because I have trouble facing my own degree of wonderfulness."[25]

* * *

Shepard supervised the Public Theater's rehearsals for the American premiere of *Kicking a Dead Horse*, then dug through decades-old notebooks for his next book, *Day out of Days*, and paid the bills by acting in a few fly-by-night films. But mainly he spent long stretches in Kentucky, writing his next play and avoiding New York City. "Sometimes I'll talk to Jessica on the phone," he wrote to Dark, "and she's in the fucking city, which I absolutely can't stand anymore and she's got the Grandkids [Shura's two girls] and is very busy with all kinds of big city doings like museums and parks and exhibitions and meetings and seems happy enough to be consumed by that all the time but all I want to do anymore is just sit on my back porch, sip coffee and stare at the birds."[26]

Shepard knew he was also "drinking way too much and too often," as he put it. He was disenchanted with the Work, his usual path to mental stability, mainly because it hadn't worked: "I really don't have any real notion of where I stand in respect to knowing & understanding myself at all," he wrote to Dark.

> I certainly see many aspects which I can hardly bear: my anger—my judgement of others—my arrogance—my ignorance—my jealousy—etc. etc. . . . I feel a long way away from total acceptance, though. I know

> that much. . . . Can't seem to ever learn the lesson of it, whatever that is—other than total abstinence. Total anything never seems to work.[27]

The "lesson of it" would arrive sooner than expected. Shepard was driving his Chevy Tahoe home after visiting Jessica in Minnesota when he stopped at a Bloomington, Illinois, tavern and cigar club called Fat Jack's, where he routinely stopped on the route. Fat Jack's had Warhol-esque murals of Jack Nicholson (for whom the bar was named) as the Joker grinning down at the patrons, and a bottle of Woodford Reserve bourbon signed by Shepard. On that night, January 2, 2009, he sat down with two guys he'd met a year before who were military helicopter pilots during the actual Black Hawk Down incident. Just before two in the following morning, and many drinks later, Shepard headed for a Best Western and was pulled over in Normal for going sixteen miles per hour over the speed limit. Shepard blew 0.175 on his Breathalyzer test, more than twice the state limit.[28]

The police arrested Shepard, he wrote to Dark soon after, "for the terrible offense of driving blind drunk (which I've been doing for 50 years & just now got caught)," and he was brought to the McLean County Jail. Shepard recorded his time in the "drunk-tank lockup" with a confessional sketch called "Normal (Highway 39 South)," which he wrote in his jail cell on toilet paper and would soon publish in *Day out of Days*. In it, Shepard studies the cinder-block walls of the holding cell long and hard. Surprisingly, there was no graffiti, "not even a lover's name or a racial slur. No pictographs of genitalia even. Just random gashes" across the cell window's steel frame. He wondered how the gashes got there. Must have been a zipper, he thought, but the acrobatics would have been implausible given the watchful eyes of the cops. The rage implicit in the marks was a puzzle: "He no longer had it in him, he realized. The fight. The hate. The energy. That was mainly it." All a man behind bars could feel was "exhaustion and dismay."[29]

A prominent local lawyer named Hal Jennings advised Shepard that his crime might be expunged if he provided character statements to the judge. For that, Shepard phoned LuAnn Walther, his editor at

Alfred A. Knopf. Walther's first response on the phone was to burst out laughing, but she regretted this in hindsight: "I feel I should apologize for laughing on the phone.... I guess the notion of having to write a reference letter for someone of your stature just struck me as absurd." In her letter, Walther testified to Shepard's brilliance as an author, adding that he was "of remarkable character: genuinely kind, unfailingly polite and unpretentious, a person of strong values and sound judgement."[30]

This was Shepard's first DUI charge, but he'd also been pulled over for reckless driving in Virginia six weeks earlier. (He did not show at the court date and was found guilty in absentia.) "It's a constant struggle," Shepard said of relapsing after his long dry period:

> It's such a knucklehead disease because you refuse to see it.... It's like being a junkie. I think I have a sort of thing in my blood, in my psyche. I can become addicted very easily, although the curious thing is that I have two sisters who are not.... Maybe it's just a toss of the dice.[31]

Shepard's arrest was widely covered in the press, where it was often accompanied by a humiliating mugshot. "Great! A laughingstock—at my age when I should be revered & honored," he carped after apologizing to Hannah for missing her birthday, to which she responded, like LuAnn Walther, by laughing "hysterically."[32]

On his way to the courthouse, a couple of local reporters were taking pictures of him, but it was raining hard, and he pulled his raincoat over his head, thinking, "Hell, man, I've dodged Italian paparazzi with Brad Pitt! This is nothing—This is Normal fucking Illinois!" His lawyer trained him in advance, Shepard said, to show Judge Casey Costigan "how I'm the nicest, most polite citizen on earth & how I've learned my lesson & never ever again will I even think about stepping into a vehicle of any kind having had even a swallow of beer."[33]

In the end, the judge ordered Shepard to pay a fine of six hundred dollars, serve a hundred hours of community service, and complete twenty-two and a half hours of an alcohol treatment program in New

York. For community service, Shepard elected to help students with theater and writing projects at New York University's Tisch School of the Arts. He also had to show up twice a week at an alcohol counseling center for urine samples, talk-therapy sessions with groups of other addicts, and anger management counseling.[34]

Shepard was genuinely altered by this DUI episode, and he sobered up a few weeks later. "I must admit I like getting drunk," he told Dark. "I like the feeling that comes over me. The numbness. The moving into a different state . . . I could make a good case for wine being a low-end substitute for smack. It goes straight to your blood."[35] Nonetheless, he went on to say, "My drunken days are definitely over, far as I can tell. To go back to drinking would be a kind of suicide, which never appealed to me & I don't have the guts for."[36]

* * *

Within a couple of weeks of the arrest, Shepard flew to Dublin for the rehearsals of *Ages of the Moon* with Stephen Rea as Ames and Sean McGinley as Byron, at the Abbey's Peacock Theatre. (This time, though, Shepard handed the director's chair to the Abbey veteran Jimmy Fay.) "Somewhere on the north side of Dublin," Shepard wrote home, "across the River Liffey, where Joyce & Beckett & Yeats used to stroll there's a small dark room on the 2nd floor of a Protestant church where 2 actors are sitting down at a table to read my new play. How amazing is that? Somehow, miraculously, I'm connected to a lineage of literature in the 21st century."[37]

*Ages of the Moon* opened on March 3, 2009, and, as with *Kicking a Dead Horse*, numerous Irish cultural luminaries gathered to attend the event, including the actor Brendan Gleeson, the filmmaker Jim Sheridan, and the Dublin-based novelist Roddy Doyle, who singled out Shepard's unstructured narratives as his greatest strength. "His characters at one level seem to be very inarticulate but they're very clear about what they eventually want to say," Doyle told the press on opening night. "So that is a story in itself. . . . I love that and admire that."[38]

Once again, reviewers couldn't help but link the play to their native son Samuel Beckett, specifically Ames and Byron as twenty-first-century American versions of *Waiting for Godot*'s comically forlorn pair Estragon and Vladimir. Indeed, Stephen Rea had already published an earnest promotional piece titled "Waiting for the New Beckett Is Over" in the *Irish Times*. "Shepard's plays," Rea wrote about his venerable American friend, "more than any since Beckett's, feel like musical experiences. . . . Sam Shepard is creating a theatre more distinctive and complete than anyone since the other Sam. That is why he demands our attention."[39]

* * *

Back in the United States, Johnny Dark stole, as was his longtime habit, a months-old issue of the *New Yorker* from his doctor's office. This one contained his friend's story "Land of the Living," about the botched family trip to Tulum and his philandering ways.[40] "I love it when you write about yourself, denying your guilt," he teased.[41]

The story was reprinted in *Day out of Days*, Shepard's autobiographical collection of short stories, flash fiction, lyrics, and dialogues, which was released on January 12, 2010, a month before *Ages of the Moon* and a revival of *A Lie of the Mind*, directed by Ethan Hawke, appeared in New York. "Working on this new book has actually shown me aspects of myself I'd never really seen before," he told Dark. "Most of my life, I now realize, has been consumed by flight. I guess, initially, from the nightmare of my father's wrath which I never understood & still don't. . . . The frantic futility of constantly searching for a new place; a new life, a new partner. As though change itself were some kind of elixir."[42]

Ethan Hawke's New Group revival of *A Lie of the Mind* opened on February 18, 2010, at the Off-Broadway Acorn Theatre. It wasn't helpful that Shepard, as he'd done with Joe Papp during the New York premiere of *True West*, discouraged people from attending. The weekend before opening night, Shepard informed the *New York Times* that if readers wanted to see one of his plays, it should be *Ages of the Moon*, which was playing concurrently. "I have to admit, with this experience with

*Lie of the Mind*, I've come to see it as a bit of an awkward play. It's like an old, broken-down Buick that you kind of hold together to just get down the road. . . . Whereas this new play, *Ages*, is like a Porsche. It's sleek, it does exactly what you want it to do, and it can speed up but also shows off great brakes."[43]

Shepard and Hawke already had a terrible falling-out after a blow-out during rehearsals, and Shepard's comments to the press seemed personal. "About the hardest thing I ever had to do as a human being was to try to stand up to him because I admired him so much," Hawke recounted the hurtful experience. "But I didn't think he was being fair or kind or constructive." Shepard stormed out in a huff, and Hawke never heard from him about it again—that is, until the show opened and the rave reviews started pouring in. He called Hawke from the highway and said, "I bet you're feeling pretty high on yourself, aren't you? When are we gonna move to Broadway?"[44]

Sometime later, Hawke asked Shepard whether he could direct *The Late Henry Moss*, and Shepard told him that they would need to work more closely together, which Hawke saw as the core dispute over *A Lie of the Mind*. "I don't think we'll have any better of a time because I don't see myself changing," Hawke said, "and I don't really imagine you changing, so I feel like you need to set me free or we should agree not to do this." "Well, I guess we just agreed." "To what?" "Not to do it." On another occasion, Hawke invited the actors Martha Plimpton and Marin Ireland to his house to read *True West*. "I swear to God it was the funniest, most moving two hours of my life," he remembered. So again he called Shepard for permission. All that was needed was to change the pronouns, he assured him. "I think that play is the war between the masculine and feminine inside the self," Hawke reasoned. "That's true of women as well. There's no reason why they couldn't be sisters—and it's actually funny as shit to have them stealing toasters and stuff." "You are a weird dude," Shepard said, and ended the discussion.[45]

* * *

Shepard abstained from booze for just over a year but fell off the wagon hard, and this time for good. It was then that he broke up with Jessica, parting ways after nearly twenty-eight years, in the summer of 2009. He was staying at a hotel near their old house in Minnesota that December when the magnitude of the breakup truly hit home: he imagined the previous summer, when he and Walker were fishing for pike on the St. Croix River. It was then, he wrote, "I knew without a doubt that it would be the very last summer we would spend together like this." This grim realization, he went on, "came to me that day like a clean knife blade." He observed his son, mercifully oblivious and having a grand old time reeling fish into the boat. It was a cold emotion, though, "a sinking feeling, a feeling of falling away in time."[46]

After he met with Jessica on March 5, 2010, they wouldn't see each other again for many months. (Remarkably, they were both able to hide their breakup from the paparazzi until late 2011.) "I suppose I'll always think of her as the 'love of my life,'" Shepard wrote to Dark. "I just can't live with her any more. That much is clear." After writing so much about transforming into Sam Sr., Shepard believed it was now his reality. "You think about it, talk about it, analyze it, and then all of a sudden you have become the thing that you were most vehement against. It's very Greek. They invented this shit. Or at least gave it a name."[47]

In April 2010, Shepard traveled to Bolivia to film *Blackthorn*, costarring his friend Stephen Rea. In it, Shepard plays the outlaw Butch Cassidy, living under the assumed name of James Blackthorn twenty years after his presumed death at the hands of the Bolivian army in *Butch Cassidy and the Sundance Kid*. Shepard grew a full gray beard for the role of Blackthorn, and at sixty-six, he genuinely felt his age. All his life, he was fit enough to do almost anything athletic he wanted, so despite his years, he chose to perform his own riding in the high altitude of the Andes Mountains, fifteen thousand feet above sea level. The final scene, a reckoning between Shepard's and Rea's characters on a desert plateau, was shot on Salar de Uyuni, the world's largest salt flat. It was a brutal test of physical endurance, and the cast slept in whichever accommodations the nearby villages had available.[48]

For the rest of the summer, Shepard licked his wounds in Midway, obsessively talked through his own inexorable demise with friends, and wrote a play, *Evanescence, or Shakespeare in the Alley*. It was the first he composed, in August, after breaking up with Jessica. Many of its lines are near identical to his thoughts expressed in private about Jessica—the frenzied passion of their first years together, their mutual bonding of identities, their growing apart, their foreseeable breakup and its aftermath.[49]

*Evanescence*, a monologue for a woman, is spoken by an elegantly dressed, beautiful middle-aged blonde called Woman, but with strong overtones of his own masculine feelings. "Out of the blue, you've suddenly both had enough," Woman says in the fittingly titled play. "But . . . the thing's been building up over time. Together for decades, maybe; births, deaths, children, homes, careers, then—POW! Apart, like that. Completely apart. . . . You might start thinking, how is this going to be now—just me—alone—me, by myself? What am I going to do now?"[50] Shepard's surrogate Roscoe says in his next play, *Heartless*, "I didn't see it coming. In a moment everything comes unraveled. Years and years—kids—schools—peanut butter sandwiches—then—your whole life turns upside down. Just like that. It's devastating."[51]

*Evanescence* opened on June 15, 2011, in the three-part festival "10 × 25," a series of ten-minute plays by twenty-five top-shelf playwrights that also included works by David Auburn, Annie Baker, John Guare, and David Mamet at the Atlantic Theater Company's Stage 2 in New York. The Atlantic had just presented *Ages of the Moon*, and although *Evanescence* received no press then, and little to no attention since, it's an arresting gender reversal from *Ages of the Moon*, a play about the unstoppable disintegration of his and Jessica's romance from a female perspective.

At last, he had written a moving part for Jessica, even if she would never play it. Woman ends with an ardent cry of hopefulness for a lasting bond between them: "It *is* good to feel you in the world, though. To know you're there. Somewhere. To know there's a connection. (*Pause.*) We are connected, aren't we? Always. In that way—I mean. We are—always. Aren't we?"[52]

"I can't imagine what it would be like if Jessica died before me—even though we've split up," he wrote to Dark the following month. That fall, after Scarlett had died of natural causes at age seventy-six, Dark shared with Shepard a manuscript he wrote about her. "Your memories and reminiscences of Scarlett are achingly sad," Shepard replied.

> I sometimes have similar recollections of my life with Jessica and she's still alive. I don't know why impermanence is so hard to swallow when there's evidence of it all around us, every day. I do fall victim to loneliness and self-pity and sometimes long for a steady companion but I suppose it's a bit too late for that. My myriad girlfriends are all somehow disappointing. My only solace seems to be in writing.[53]

* * *

The only problem with writing plays, Shepard asserted, was that "you can't make a living as a playwright." "One movie," he said, "and I don't have to work for a year—then I can feed some horses."[54] At the same time, he deplored press junkets, but it was difficult to sidestep the film industry's on-set interviews for what they call electronic press kits (EPKs).

On April 2, 2009, he was interviewed for an EPK while filming *Fair Game*, about the Bush administration's vengeful outing of the CIA officer Valerie Plame (played by Naomi Watts) as payback after her husband, Joseph Wilson (Sean Penn), exposed the administration's lies about Iraq harboring weapons of mass destruction. Shepard, who played Plame's father, was interviewed by the aspiring documentarian Treva Wurmfeld, who described it as "a collaborative happening of sorts—it felt like we were riffing off the moment."[55]

Wurmfeld later wrote him a letter in the summer of 2010. Would he be interested in a documentary based on his life? Shepard remembered her well and thought of her as charming, smart, savvy, and exceedingly attractive, so he agreed, inviting her to film a reading for his most recent book, *Day out of Days*, in Santa Fe on September 23. He also, offhandedly, told her about his collaboration with Johnny Dark: they were compiling their correspondence (about a thousand letters over a forty-five-year period) for William Wittliff's Western culture archive at Texas State University, San Marcos, and they planned to edit a book with them.[56]

After the reading, Wurmfeld and Shepard went down to visit Dark in Deming, New Mexico, where he was working at the deli counter in Peppers Supermarket. Deming is one of those small Western towns, Dark later said, where the residents are Trump fanatics, and "everyone wears a cross around their necks, or the electric chair, or however [Jesus] died." It was at a Mexican restaurant in Deming that Wurmfeld concocted the idea of a documentary about their friendship. Wurmfeld saw that this odd pairing of deli clerk and world-famous playwright would make a great movie. And Dark was a truly American character who must be captured on film—a surviving beatnik, perhaps the last, who talked and sang like Al Jolson if he were drugged up and looking for work. "I was the catalyst for that film," Dark insisted.[57]

Wurmfeld's documentary, *Shepard & Dark*, became a portrait of a long fraternal bond and its heartrending breakup. "I followed the whole storyline," Jesse wrote to Dark after viewing the film when it was released in 2012, "and found it intriguing as a study of two men who in many ways weren't any longer able to tolerate each other in person but only in writing." ("Wow," Jesse also mused, "Johnny is stoned in every single scene.")[58]

Late that December, a couple of months after Wurmfeld started shooting, Shepard began a fellowship at the Santa Fe Institute (SFI), a not-for-profit, state-of-the-art research and educational facility for studying a range of the most complicated aspects of human endeavor. Serving preeminent scientists, theoretical mathematicians, data analysts, and political cognoscenti, SFI's Cowan Campus is nestled high in the desert hills outside of Santa Fe and offered refuge for an eclectic group of masterminds whom Shepard described as "a think tank trying to find if there's an inner dialogue between different pursuits: science and art and within science itself, anthropology and quantum physics and mathematics and all that."[59]

Shepard was endorsed for the fellowship by Valerie Plame after they met during *Fair Game*. The novelist Cormac McCarthy, an SFI fellow and author of *All the Pretty Horses*, which was adapted to film in 2000 with Shepard in the cast, wrote the official invitation. "Science was never [Shepard's] core interest," wrote SFI's president, David Krakauer, "but the deeper mysteries of existence, the anguish of conscious life, and our attempts to express natural beauty through language and mathematics captivated him." Shepard asked Krakauer to write down a line for him by the Scottish biologist D'Arcy Wentworth Thompson that indicates a crossover between scientific discovery and the transmogrification of everyday objects one so often finds in Shepard's own writing: "It behooves us always to remember that in physics it has taken great men to discover simple things. They are very great names indeed which we couple with the path of a stone, the droop of a chain, the tints of a bubble, the shadows in a cup."[60]

The work environment at the Sante Fe Institute was ideally suited to Shepard, since in Kentucky he was preoccupied with horseback riding, breeding, womanizing, and cavorting with his Midway pals. His unrelenting acting career still required driving to locations across North America, and he used the institute as a base. (He acted in nearly a dozen films and two television series, *Klondike* and *Bloodline*, in the United States and Canada during the five-year period he spent at SFI.) Shepard would arrive at nine in the morning, write at a desk in the library on his Olympia SM9 typewriter until the fellows' communal lunch at noon, and then end the day at three or four. "It does have a formality about it," he said. "I get quite a bit done, whereas if I stay home I can write, but I don't have that exterior, enforced discipline."[61]

At night, he cruised cantinas such as Harry's Roadhouse and the Coyote Cafe, and he downed Silver Coin Margaritas at the Pink Adobe's Dragon Room with its owner, Rosalea Murphy, who served everyone from Shepard and Jessica to Robert Redford and Georgia O'Keeffe. Locals considered him "reserved yet available for conversation," and his closer Santa Fe acquaintances remembered "a playful, generous" man who encouraged the young would-be writers in town.[62]

* * *

By late January 2011, Shepard had largely abandoned his writing to focus on his book of letters with Johnny Dark, which they now called *Two Prospectors* (a title they'd saved for a play idea about their friendship). The two settled in at SFI to compile their correspondence into a collection of approximately a thousand letters that spanned the forty-five-year period from London in the 1970s to Kentucky in the 2010s. Shepard assured Dark that they could "eliminate [letters] that may be deemed too pornographic, too personal or whatever. . . . I just started realizing what a great lifetime we've both had & how rare it must be in this age that full-grown (well that may be going too far) men still carry on the ancient art of letter writing & over such a span of time."[63]

Dark arrived at SFI in early February to assist Shepard with the letters and be filmed by Wurmfeld. On his first day, he was struck dumb by the number of romantic relationships Shepard had been juggling: a married actor who, he recalled, was "dressed to kill—absurdly so"; a woman in New York, and another from Kentucky. Yet another, a young woman whom Shepard had just met at a bar, arrived to the library and told Dark, "I've read all his plays and they changed my life." "Sam is in his glory," Dark wrote. "I find his need for attention and adulation rather embarrassing." Wurmfeld was under the impression she was meant to film all this. "I probably should have," she said later. "Perhaps it would have been like watching a Shepard play unfolding in real time, but I felt sorry for the women and left."[64]

The next night, the two men took some Xanax, and Shepard told Dark that instead of joining him in Deming, as they had planned, he was going to drive back to Kentucky to sell some horses; then up to New York to visit his kids and Jessica and see Patti Smith; down to Georgia to act in the film *Savannah*; and finally back to Santa Fe, where he would meet up with Jesse.[65]

This was enough for Dark, who at this point was finding it increasingly difficult to get past their differences (a rift laid bare at the end of Wurmfeld's film). Dark was incensed by Shepard's "rudeness, insensitivity, alcoholism and general grumbling scoffing negativity." At three o'clock one morning in mid-February, he slumped into his Chevy Nova and returned to Deming. After a month, a pile of FedEx packages arrived on his doorstep. They contained all the letters and photographs he'd sent Shepard over forty years time, along with a note:

> Here are all the letters of yours back. I've just realized that I have come to the end of this obsession & long to be free of it. I'm no longer interested in poring over the past—re-making the past—goofing on the past—reminiscing about the past or re-writing the past. I need to move on to my own stuff & leave this behind. It may be some emotional territory I'm going thru that has prompted this—in the same way as leaving Jessica but in any case this whole phase of things is over & done with, for me. Finished.

He went on to say that Dark had full editorial control—he could arrange the letters, edit them, change them, whatever he wanted to do. "I don't care—be my guest. Take it away, Johnny & good luck!" For a time, he refused to take Dark's calls or answer his letters.[66]

Wurmfeld stayed on with Shepard after he abandoned the letters project. "Filming with Sam was complicated," she told *Filmmaker* magazine. "No amount of filming could truly capture all the layers at play that existed somewhere in the space between his work, his character, me, and the tension that comes from having head-to-head creative agendas."[67]

Before *Shepard & Dark*, a film Wurmfeld had been working on for five years lost its financing and was shelved. It chronicled a team of Texan surgeons who invented a new type of artificial heart, and its working title, not incidentally, was *Texas Heart*.[68] "I had this notion of the heart transplant," Shepard said later about how he came up with his next play idea, *Heartless*, "and I desperately wanted to write something more substantial than *Evanescence* featuring women, which I haven't done before. And so those were the essential elements that I started with."[69]

When Wurmfeld's documentary was released in 2012, Dark attended both openings, in Toronto and New York, but Shepard was nowhere to be found. As far as anyone seems to know, he never saw it.[70] This is too bad, if true, as the film is a gimlet-eyed view of the devolution of this charmed friendship. But if Wurmfeld felt she'd missed out on filming a Shepard play, with those women making a jealous fuss over him, she would find herself a character in precisely that position.

* * *

Shepard was visiting a girlfriend in the Hollywood Hills in the summer of 2011 when he formed the setting and characters for *Heartless*, his first play since *Little Ocean* with a female-dominated cast, and the only one that he published aside from *Evanescence*. "I thought I had gone as far as I wanted to go with male characters," he said. "They were beginning to decay and I needed to rejuvenate them. And it was kind of exciting suddenly having female characters. The only man in the play is lost in this whirlwind of indecision, and confusion, and lostness, and doesn't know where to go and finds himself in the midst of females. And a kind of madness ensues."[71]

*Heartless* is a full-length autobiographical play that portrays Shepard's anguish over leaving Jessica, along with his ongoing romantic relationships. The action revolves around Roscoe, a sixty-five-year-old Cervantes scholar who lives alone in Kentucky and has just broken up with his wife and alienated his children. Roscoe is having a consolatory affair with a documentary filmmaker in her early thirties named Sally, who first interviewed him for TV and is now making a film about his life. Wurmfeld asked Shepard point-blank whether Sally was based on her, to which he brusquely responded, "You're not the only documentary filmmaker I know." "Which was true," Wurmfeld said. "He often stayed with another one in the Hollywood Hills when he was in L.A."[72]

This other filmmaker was Sophie Huber, a Swiss director who interviewed him for *Partly Fiction*, her 2012 documentary on Harry Dean Stanton. Shepard had made advances toward the winsome Huber but soon discovered she was openly gay, so it surprised him when she called soon after their interview. More important, he attested after a few minor romances were fading that "Sophie is still my number one. She's always great to be with—always happy to see her. She makes me feel good, which can't be said about the rest of them." Huber was the likely model for the heartbreak in *Heartless*, but it was understandable that Wurmfeld, with whom he'd also purportedly had a brief romance, questioned the source of the character Sally, since she shared the character's age, appearance, manner of speaking, and most recent film project, but not, it turns out, her heart.[73]

In the play, Roscoe and Sally visit her family at a mansion overlooking the endless sprawl of Los Angeles, and Roscoe finds himself in the middle of a shadowy family drama, intriguingly making him, like Henry in *Eyes for Consuela*, both interloper and protagonist. "You know nothing about us, do you?" shouts Sally's mother. "An utter stranger—waltzing into our lives as though—Who are you, anyway? Some vagabond, homeless wretch! Spawn of the air force!"[74]

There's a scar on Sally's chest caused by a heart transplant, and the ghost of the heart's original owner, Liz (for "lust," he wrote in his original notes for the play), is introduced as the mother's caretaker. Liz is influenced by Huber, as we're told she's also "tall, elegant, beautiful, young," and, when she speaks, has a "lovely, lilting" Scandinavian accent (a slight feint, since Huber was Swiss).[75] The setting was inspired by Huber's bungalow on Lookout Mountain in the Hollywood Hills, in which she said James Dean had lived before he became famous.[76] "I was spending some time with a friend of mine in LA," Shepard replied when asked why he set the play in a city that he regularly attacked. "Usually I'm kind of down in the city, so it gave me this incredible vantage point that I'd never seen before, and it started in places like that, where the main character, the old woman, sort of looks out over the 'abyss' as she calls it [laughs]."[77]

While Shepard was acting in the Arkansas Delta along the Mississippi River (what would be one of his finest performances, in the 2012 film *Mud*), he put down the central theme of *Heartless* in a poem. In it, he accepts blame for breaking up with a girlfriend, and for the rage he unleashed on her in the fallout. "The truth is," Sally informs her mother in *Heartless*, "he never loved me. I can see that now." Roscoe protests, "I did—at one point in time—."[78]

*Heartless* opened August 7, 2012, at the Signature Theatre's new home on Forty-Second Street, an ultramodern three-theater complex designed by Frank Gehry. Nancy Meckler's son Daniel Aukin carried on the family tradition as Shepard's director, but direction aside, the production was an oddity, especially for the cast. Shepard arrived at the first reading with only the typescript and no copies (a frantic intern took the pages and ran off to the copy machine), and during rehearsals, they were forbidden to ask him questions because, Betty Gilpin (who played Liz) quipped years later, "that wouldn't have been avant-garde." As a result, the actors were baffled by their own characters, along with the play's meaning, and critics felt the same way. "The audiences seem to dig it," Shepard said with a laugh. "The critics didn't get it, but that's OK."[79]

Back on June 27, 2011, while on Lookout Mountain, Shepard sketched out ideas for a second play titled *A Particle of Dread (Oedipus Variations)*. He would expand his feelings over specific lovers that we find in *Heartless* to incorporate the whole puzzle of what he considered his various crimes of womanizing and drinking, his inability to remain with Jessica, and his hit-or-miss style of child-rearing. "OEDIPUS believed himself INNOCENT right up to the moment JOCASTE hangs herself," he wrote in his notebook. "The REALIZATION of GUILT."[80]

* * *

Shepard bought a Beverley Spears–designed house in Santa Fe in November 2011. Home was still Midway, but this was his base until his Sante Fe Institute fellowship ended. The property, a fifteen-minute drive from downtown, included five acres of desert and scrub brush, with panoramic views of the desert environs and the distant Sandia and Ortiz Mountains. Over the winter and early spring of 2012 in Santa Fe, he completed his full-length play, *A Particle of Dread*, writing being, he told Dark, "my last resort of consolation for a wandering, meaningless life."[81]

The line for Shepard's title appears early in Sophocles's play, when Oedipus demands to know his father's killer, and the chorus leader tells him, "If the killer can feel a particle of dread, / Your curse will bring him out of hiding!"[82]

"This destiny is somehow written," Shepard eventually wrote of the play, "forecast, like the weather."

> No matter how we might acquire and connive and manipulate, there's no way we can get out of it. A typhoon is coming and it will engulf us completely. Can we come to terms with this life no matter how terrible the truth of it might be? Can we become something completely ourselves even while wishing we were something else? The denial or refusal of this predicament seems to me what might be called "Tragic."[83]

Back in 1983, a month after Shepard left O-Lan for Jessica, he'd arrived at the revelation that guilt was "probably the single most powerful negative influence in my life & it's ruled me in one way or another for years—going back to my early childhood. . . . Guilt obviously produces tension. . . . The energy is locked off. There's no flow or interaction between the parts—so everything gets messed up." The play he composed thirty years later, *A Particle of Dread*, was written to release that pent-up, guilt-born tension. But as he wrote in *Day out of Days*, you never learn "how to protect others from your own manifestations of cruelty and malice which you've learned so insidiously through skin and blood and find impossible to shake free from no matter how much you'd like to be thought of as a decent, wholesome person."[84]

Shepard's first page of notes for *A Particle of Dread* contains the heading "Yet ANOTHER Stab at Oedipus (from what we can recall)." Earlier in his career, he'd avoided the ancient Greeks because, he said, "I didn't think I was bright enough to get it. I was intimidated by it." But Joe Chaikin encouraged him to give them another try. He did, in London during one of the rare dry spells in his writing, and was stunned by "how simple, how direct and to the bone it was—the language, the ideas, the audacity of it, it's quite incredible."[85]

Shepard's previous "Stab at Oedipus," "Guilt," is a full-length unproduced and unpublished play written in London in the early 1970s.[86] But he'd convinced himself that a modern adaptation was impossible, he said, "because nobody knows what that religious culture was like back then, and it seemed stupid to try and imitate it." (He envisioned the characters in *Oedipus Rex* ludicrously wearing suits, ties, and dark glasses, "like the Blues Brothers doing the Greeks.")[87] Then, on a trip to Utah in 2009, he revisited *Oedipus Rex*, and then *The Iliad* and *The Odyssey*, and found them "astounding." He was now determined, after being haunted by guilt for over sixty years, to try his hand at an adaptation on the themes, plot, and characters of *Oedipus Rex*.[88]

*A Particle of Dread* is the product of this determination, a ghoulish pastiche with fragments of dialogue that form part whodunit detective story, part Greek myth, and part literary confession. At the outset, Shepard was not interested in the Freudian complex, but rather the unstoppable force of fate: the son will kill the father and destroy his city, no matter who or what intervenes.

* * *

After his breakup with Jessica, then Sophie Huber, and, in a way, Wurmfeld, he resolved to concentrate on the one thing that, in the end, truly mattered to him—his writing. And for that, since *Heartless* exacerbated the chilling effect of American theaters' willingness to put on his plays, he'd return again to Ireland, but not with the Abbey Theatre, and not in the Republic.

When Shepard was asked at the time to name a few of his favorite contemporary playwrights, he replied, "I like the Irish the best. I think the Irish are doing the most interesting stuff. There's a bunch of them who are heads and shoulders above us in terms of modern writers." On December 7, 2012, the Irish returned the compliment, bestowing upon him an honorary Doctor in Letters from Trinity College, Dublin (an honor New York's elite performing arts conservatory, the Juilliard School, also conferred to him in 2007). "He was often embarrassed by accolades," Patti Smith remarked, "but embraced this one, coming from the same institution where Samuel Beckett walked and studied."[89]

On the night before the ceremony, Shepard performed a reading at Trinity. He then introduced Patti Smith, who'd just wrapped up a tour with Neil Young & Crazy Horse. At the Trinity reading, she read scenes from *Cowboy Mouth* and then joined Shepard in a duet of Patsy Cline's rendition of "Side by Side," "our theme song," Smith told the audience. To round out the evening, Shepard took up a guitar and sang Richard "Rabbit" Brown's "James Alley Blues."[90]

After receiving his doctorate, "our own Irish Playwright," as Trinity's Professor Nicholas Grene dubbed him, headed to the city of Derry in Northern Ireland to confer with Stephen Rea's newly reopened Field Day Theatre Company about putting on *A Particle of Dread*. Shepard hadn't written the script yet, and asked Rea whether he was looking for a specific theme or "balls out." "Oh," replied Rea, "I think 'balls out.'"[91]

Nancy Meckler was hired to direct but was flummoxed by the material and took Shepard aside. "Sam, do you remember when I used to be doing your plays, you used to come and you used to tell me what it was about?" "*Did I?*" he said, aghast. "He started out trying to write a modern version of *Oedipus Rex*," Meckler said of the improvisational rehearsals, "and when he was halfway through writing a lot of the scenes, he suddenly thought, 'Sophocles did it brilliantly. Why am I even trying to do this?'" But then, Shepard said on adapting *Oedipus Rex*,

> The play has so many submerged and overt themes that have to do with family, fathers and sons, and murder. All of these thematic things in it speak to themselves in a way, and they're very ancient. If you strip away in a certain way it's very American. It's very much about murder and rape and pillage—it's not a pretty play—but it certainly speaks to the horror of contemporary life. And that's what I was trying to get at, improvisationally.[92]

Derry was the site of Northern Ireland's Bloody Sunday (January 30, 1972), when British soldiers opened fire on unarmed Catholic protestors, shooting twenty-six civilians, thirteen of whom died. Rehearsals were held near the walls that look down upon the Bogside neighborhood, where the massacre took place. The murals depicting the slaughter, its leaders, and the Troubles became a tourist attraction, which riled some locals. "We should be forgetting the past," a group told Meckler. "We want to focus on peace now." When Meckler shared this with Shepard, he replied, with reference to the Oedipus riffs they'd been working on, "Everybody wants to forget the past but you can't." Shepard acknowledged the play's connection with the Irish Troubles, but Rea had lived them, and he'd been married twenty years to Dolours Price, a notorious IRA soldier from Belfast, so he had the context to explain it: "It's very hard to imagine [the Troubles] never happened," he told a reporter. "But that's what people are trying to do. They are trying to ignore the legacy of thirty, forty years of murder and political turmoil rather than dealing with it. Sam is such a great writer, he couldn't be in a place and have that not enter the play."[93]

During one of Meckler's workshops, Shepard decided that both the ancient and the modern Oedipus roles should be doubled by Rea. "And finally," she said, "it became about killing the father. So it became personal." Shepard, who believed "fate" to be the Greek myth's thematic engine, had unwittingly stumbled into Freud's Oedipal complex anyway: in the end, Meckler continued, the play became more about "killing the father and never getting over it. He didn't say that, but that's what happened." Of course, he'd already killed off Sam Sr. in *The Holy Ghostly*, *A Lie of the Mind*, and *The Late Henry Moss*, but the feelings remained. It was Shepard's father inside him, that carnality and furious temperament, he was trying to kill off.[94]

*A Particle of Dread*'s world premiere took place at the Playhouse in Derry on November 28, 2013, with a set by Tom Conroy of a blood-splashed abattoir with gore-soaked rags dangling from a clothesline. "It went over well in Ireland," Shepard said of its reception. "The Irish loved it," but, he said, "I don't know how well it will go over in New York." He was right on both counts. Peter Crawley for the *Irish Times* raved, "His fractured, briskly episodic take on Oedipus is fascinating for its arch transposition, individual focus and wry updating. . . . He pulls the Oedipus legend up by its roots, fits it with earthy new poetry, straddles it between comedy and tragedy, and splinters characters and time frames to construct an eternal dilemma."[95]

When it moved to New York's Signature Theatre, however, opening on November 23, 2014, Shepard gave strict instructions not to change the Derry production, at a cost. As Shepard foretold in Derry, Americans didn't like it. The *Hollywood Reporter* called it an "oblique intellectual enterprise" in which "Shepard's willful self-indulgence smacks more of an overeager university drama student than a seasoned playwright."[96] Ben Brantley's analogy was as "an antic intellectual puzzle, suggesting a Rubik's cube being twisted every which way by a highly precocious kid."[97]

*A Particle of Dread* was the last new play of Shepard's fully produced in his lifetime. Two years later, in his final press interview, the *New York Times* culture critic Alexis Soloski remarked to Shepard how he was often considered "the greatest living American playwright." She then asked, "Do you feel you've achieved something substantial?" "Yes and no," he replied. "If you include the short stories and all the other books and you mash them up with some plays and stuff, then, yes, I've come at least close to what I'm shooting for. In one individual piece, I'd say no. There are certainly some plays I like better than others, but none that measure up."[98]

CHAPTER 20

# "COYOTE FADES"

In 2014, at seventy years old, Shepard found himself unable to muster the steam to do laps in the pool—the first instance he knew something was wrong with his body. He was on location for the Netflix series *Bloodline*, in Islamorada, Florida, in the Florida Keys. "I do a crippled version of the Australian crawl and barely accomplish a lap," he wrote, "then prop both elbows in the green drain, panting like a scalded dog. What is this? Adrift. Adrift between lives?"[1]

Shepard was more angry than frightened over the debilitating sensation in his arms at first. He'd been looking forward to his new life in the wake of Jessica, and senescence was not on his bucket list. "But there it is," he'd written to Dark about the demoralizing process of aging. "As Mr. B[eckett] says: 'You're on Earth—There's no cure for that.'"[2]

That October, he met Dark in Deming. It was the first time they'd reunited since the fallout portrayed in *Shepard & Dark*. Shepard was about to drive to New York to celebrate his seventy-first birthday, and in the winter months to follow, he was slotted to shoot a film and check in on *A Particle of Dread* before its New York premiere at the Signature. But he'd stopped going on his annual cattle drive with his friend from Kentucky Bobby Miller. "I've finally realized I don't want to be a cowboy," he told Dark. "I realized that when I was down in Texas at my friend's ranch helping him brand cattle—all these guys standing around pretending to be cowboys. It was just bullshit. Also

I was having trouble breathing and moving my arms." Shepard also told him something Dark hadn't fully understood about his friend's volatile nature, a surprise for him at this stage in their relationship, and a substantially instructive one, as Dark explained later:

> When he was writing and the writing was going well, he felt connected to something in life and it was a wonderful feeling. But when the writing was not rolling itself out or when there was no writing at all, he wandered through life like a dazed vagrant, not belonging anywhere, an outcast, feeling disconnected and miserable until the writing connected him again to some reason for being alive.[3]

* * *

Shepard had committed to writing a debut novel that summer in Santa Fe, under the working title "Stacked," because, Shepard wrote in his notebook, it was intended to be consumed "like a movie, only different," stacking "one image on top of another." Still, long-form prose never came easily to him. He believed that writing for the theater was vastly different from any other literary form, "because what you write is eventually going to be spoken. That's why I think so many really powerful novelists can't write a play—because they don't understand that it's spoken, that it hits the air."[4] Though he'd tried with "Slave of the Camera," Shepard was reluctant to write a book-length narrative, a hesitancy that began as far back as 1972: "I like a good story as well as the next guy," he'd said. "But I like it short & sweet. A story that hangs on you. Doesn't beat around the bush. Nothing in my life ever acted like a story. Nothing ever began, evolved & ended. I never saw a 'character' out of a book. I never saw a plot."[5]

Shepard's life and work were, like his mind, fragmented and compartmentalized into plays and sketches and stories and poems and songs. It stands to reason that his novels wouldn't be novelistic either. As Shepard told a reporter, "Hopefully it's a novel, but I have the hardest time sustaining prose. I feel like I'm a natural-born playwright but the prose thing has always mystified me. How to keep it going? How do people do it, for years and years?"[6]

Preparing for his next movie shoot, Camille Thoman's *Never Here*, wherein he played the elderly lover of a much younger artist, Shepard reread Nabokov's *Lolita* and eagerly devoured Bruno Schulz's short story collection *Sanatorium Under the Sign of the Hourglass*.[7] In one of Schulz's bizarre tales, the Polish Jewish writer describes an eccentric character named Dodo, "an outsider, a passive observer of other people's social intercourse." He suffered brain damage as a child, with the result that as an adult, "Dodo's mind did not register anything but the present." One night, Dodo is heard sobbing uncontrollably in his bed. When his mother rushes to his bedside and asks what's wrong, he says, "It is not I, it's he . . ." "Which he?" his mother asks him. "The one inside . . ." Dodo doesn't explain it further, but the narrator already had in a way that resonated with Shepard: the one inside is, Schulz wrote, "his unlived life . . . In Dodo's body, the body of a half-wit, somebody was growing old, although he had not lived, so, somebody was maturing to a death that had no meaning at all."[8] Shepard had found his title.

*The One Inside* is a roman à clef that chronicles its author's vertiginously complicated love life as he approaches his own death. It opens in the spring of 2012, with a character based on Shepard dolefully rising from bed and tugging on a pair of blue thermal socks he'd swiped from a film set. The socks, like a madeleine, send his mind wandering back over all of the movie characters he'd played: "They've come and gone, these characters, like brief, violent love affairs: trailers—honey wagons—morning burritos—craft service tents—phony limousines—hot towels—4 a.m. calls. Forty some years of it."[9]

His first storyline concerns a nightmare Shepard had about a "tiny man," the inner demon his father implanted inside him, he said, but "why or how he was shrunken inside those various dreams and apparitions is beyond me." It was another dream of patricide, like *A Particle of Dread*, killing off Sam Sr. with his writing to purge himself of the prevailing mania of his life—the sins of the father perpetuated by the son. "Now I'm seeing things," he tells a young lover in *The One Inside*.

"My father, for instance. I see my father in everything. He just pops up. In miniature sometimes. I see him in my walk—my whistle. I see him flying planes. Bombing villages. Fires far below. For no good reason."[10]

In the book, he concedes that the tiny man is glaringly Oedipal. It's possible, he writes, "that I'm dreaming him like that—tiny—because it's a way of distancing myself—but that's a bit Freudian, don't you think? As though there were some kind of outside intelligence driving all this—the subconscious or some such bullshit like that."[11] And yet, another Oedipal storyline involves Shepard as an adolescent, observing his father having sex with a fourteen-year-old girl named Felicity Parks. At thirteen, he replaces his father as the girl's lover, and his father is arrested for statutory rape. Shepard might not have placed much credence in Freud's Oedipus complex, but the story is Freudian nonetheless. *A Particle of Dread* was supposed to be about fate and destiny, but it turned into a play about killing Sam Rogers.[12] Here, in *The One Inside*, Shepard becomes his father. He is no longer afraid of this, he insists, but fears his own suffering and the suffering he imposes on others.

Shepard interweaves other storylines in *The One Inside*, all of which concern his latest romantic dealings, and none of them are strictly fictional. These girlfriends include the Canadian actor and activist Mia Kirshner, who'd played the ghost of his character's daughter in *Bloodline* and lived with him for a time (the book recounts their actual, excruciating breakup); the filmmaker Sophie Huber, who "always talked with that thick accent of hers from a faraway mountain country where Rousseau used to hide out" (Switzerland); and even Jessica, "a long relationship of insipid stalemate," who hunkers down with him to read Graham Greene novels and books on the North Pole, then binge-watch *Breaking Bad*.[13]

But *The One Inside* principally concerns an intense romantic interlude in Santa Fe with a twenty-year-old technology whiz and live-in assistant he refers to as Blackmail Girl. In real life, he called her Manuscript Girl. Their romance lasted at least through the fall of 2012, and they remained on friendly terms as late as 2015. In the book, she accompanies him to a film shoot in "Whippoorwill, Oklahoma" (the town in which his character lives in 2013's *August: Osage County*) where everyone gaped at them, "befuddled and judgmental."[14]

"I really like this girl," Shepard told his friends about Manuscript Girl. "She's pretty and young and incredibly smart. She's got it all—and I am really hung up on her. I know it's crazy." At first, they made a "pact not to have sex of any kind," but that didn't last long. In the book, her character has been taping their phone conversations, and she informs Shepard's incensed stand-in that she plans to publish them as a book, a real situation that he dramatized as the controlling plotline of *The One Inside*. Ironically, as presented in the story, the skill Shepard carefully cultivated over his writing career had been turned against him. Although they remained friends, Manuscript Girl ended the love affair. "I'm only beginning to realize how I've ruined every relationship with women in exactly the same pattern & that booze is always the centerfold."[15]

* * *

Miraculously, that December 2014, Shepard met a thirty-three-year-old photographer named Carey Gough at the Grey Goose restaurant in Midway. He'd rarely felt so at ease in the company of a woman, so he told her about his malady and offered her a job as his caretaker and amanuensis. There was no romance, but with Gough, Roxanne said, "he could be himself. He could unpuff all the sails and float." Along with helping Phil Gerrow with daily chores on the farm, Gough wheeled him in his wheelchair, fed him, helped with tasks around the house, and massaged coconut oil into his swollen arms and hands to reduce the swelling. She also kept his spirits up and greeted him each morning as she walked in, "*Hola, guapo*!"[16]

While Shepard continued to work on *The One Inside* throughout 2015, he settled into a mode of living, with the help of Carey Gough, that he experienced only intermittently as an adult since he'd first joined the Work in London: a daily routine. His life by now was shaped by the agonizing battle between body and mind. His labored breathing was caused by emphysema from smoking, but his lungs were weakening badly, and he lugged an oxygen tank around with him at all times. The sensation in his arms was also getting worse.

At first he had to support his hands with pillows to type, but soon they shook too violently to use a typewriter at all. His coordination was so bad, he could barely slide his credit card into a gas pump, and getting dressed became a struggle. Shepard hated going to the doctor, but on February 4, 2015, he went out for breakfast in Santa Fe and accidentally trapped himself in the bathroom. The can opener on his Swiss Army knife barely saved him from calling for help, so he went to a hardware store for better tools. Whatever this illness was, it was advancing fast.[17]

"I wish they hadn't told me I have only 3 to 5 yrs left to live," he wrote in his notebook on February 10 after an appointment at the Mayo Clinic. He'd been tested for Lyme disease and other ailments, but the results were negative. Whatever it was, the doctors were sure his symptoms betrayed a fatal prognosis. It's a chief concern with unusual neurodegenerative diseases: by the time the symptoms have arrived, it's too late for much palliative care.[18]

Then in September, a plainspoken Kentucky physician ended the mystery and informed him that he had progressive muscular atrophy (PMA), a condition characterized by the degeneration of neurons in the spinal cord. It was widely reported before his passing that he was struck down by ALS, or "Lou Gehrig's disease," since Shepard himself had told people that's what it was. (He thought it was better to die of a disease named for the New York Yankees slugger.) The disease had affected his hands first and his legs were relatively stable, which ruled out ALS. Roxanne explained the medical confusion:

> They never diagnosed him with full ALS because he was asymptomatic, because his legs were still working pretty well. Not perfect, but well. And it was his hands that gave out as the neurons to his arms and hands closed down. And his feet were pretty good. Basically. I mean, see his legs, they weren't top notch. But he was still walking, even the day he died he was walking.[19]

Little was known about PMA, the doctor said, other than that it was irreversible and there was no cure. "I mean I wish I hadn't implied that I wanted to know. I wanted to know what I had—what was wrong with me—the name of it, but I didn't necessarily want to know when it would do me in. They told me anyhow. They told me the air would eventually go out of me. That I would struggle." Shepard was also perplexed about his final few years. "What are you going to do," he asked himself in his notebook, "now that you've done everything you've wanted?"[20]

* * *

"There are only three people in the world I could turn to that I trust," Shepard wrote to Dark, disregarding their feud. "You, Patti, and Jessica. But Patti and Jessica are both very ambitious and always on the move, and they have their careers. They could never stay long in one place. So I thought maybe you could help me." His meaning was clear enough: Shepard wanted Dark to care for him at his bedside as he died of his debilitating brain disease. Dark responded that he required medical care he couldn't provide, but Shepard was insistent.[21]

In the end, Dark conclusively refused. When a friend later asked Shepard how Dark was doing, he scoffed, "Aw, fuck him." Dark had arrived at the same conclusion. "As for Sam, fuck him," he said years after.[22] They remained in contact, but their best times together, Shepard always said, took place back in their Mill Valley days: "It was all a dazzling whirl of activity & philosophizing about it & writing plays about it & riding motorcycles & conversations about Kerouac—I can't think of any different or more exciting way to live."[23]

One day at the racetrack that spring, his cell phone rang, and it was Stephen Rea. The Irishman asked whether he'd play Beckett's blind master Hamm in *Endgame*, with Rea as Hamm's adopted son, Clov. It would be the first time the two of them would act onstage together, in a Beckett play no less. Shepard seriously considered the offer, thinking it might be a fine way to die, onstage as the domineering, physically hobbled

Hamm, but declined. He no longer trusted himself to remember lines, especially not the European-inflected phrasings of "the other Sam."[24]

Michael Almereyda also called to ask him to play Mark Twain in his film about the inventor Nikola Tesla, *Tesla*, starring Ethan Hawke. "I figured Sam's caustic frontier fatalism could fuse with Twain's and provide an interior ripple within the film's nervous system," but that too was out of the question.[25] Soon after that, Gough brought him to Dynamix Productions, a sound studio in Lexington, to record a voice-over for a documentary about NASA and space flight in the 1960s. The director kept asking for a stronger voice, but Shepard didn't have one to deliver, and the struggle brought him to tears. Aside from one last scene with his costar Ben Mendelsohn for *Bloodline*, filmed at a restaurant in New York that fall, his acting days were now over.[26]

* * *

May 25, 2015, was Jesse's forty-fifth birthday, the same luckless day that Shepard was arrested for a second time on drunk driving charges. He'd been eating tacos and drinking margaritas at La Choza Restaurant in Santa Fe when a parking lot attendant called the police as they watched him haltingly attempt to drive off in his blue Toyota pickup. He'd been on the phone with a girlfriend when he pulled over a couple of blocks away, and he refused to take a Breathalyzer. Then he failed the field sobriety test. Each time the police asked for his driver's license and registration, he handed them his social security card. A woman from the restaurant ran out to offer to drive him home, and several others volunteered to be character witnesses, but he was charged with aggravated driving while intoxicated and booked at the Santa Fe County Jail.[27]

Shepard was arraigned the following day with thirty other inmates, each of them outfitted in red jumpsuits and handcuffed to chains around their waists, with the judge presiding in absentia on a big video monitor. "It was like some Orwellian nightmare," he fumed. After a friend of his paid the five-hundred-dollar bond, he made the four-hour drive to Deming to commiserate with his semi-estranged friend Johnny

Dark, the one person he knew from experience he could count on in such circumstances, no matter their recent dustups. Dark walked into Denny's at eight thirty that night, took one look at his ailing friend, and said, "When we sat talking on that stoop on 11th Street in New York nearly fifty years ago, I didn't realize you'd still be hanging around."[28]

Shepard swore up and down to anyone who'd listen that he only drank two margaritas at La Choza, and that one of the restaurant's employees assumed he was drunk because of his wobbly gait from his illness. In addition, the police gave him the wrong sobriety test: standing on one leg was no longer a trick he could perform, and that was how his lawyer got him acquitted. If there's one sure thing about this unfortunate DUI episode, however, it's that at this stage of his disease, his hands were no longer able to respond to mental commands, so he was only able to steer a car with his knees, wrists, and elbows. Yet he continued to drive, both drunk and sober, and his family were desperate to get him rehabilitated and turn his life around. "They think I'm just going to become this Dad who sits by the fire and smokes his pipe all day," he groused, "but it's never going to happen. Just go to rehab and everything will be O.K. It pisses me off. And what really got me was that Jessica kept saying, 'What a waste. What a waste.'"[29]

Other than Dark and Gough, few people knew about his illness, and, wanting to keep it that way, he never went public. But after the DUI, he suspected that despite his acquittal, the folks at SFI wanted him out, and Santa Fe's thin, high-altitude air was no longer tenable given his emphysema. It was time to return to Kentucky for good. He shouldn't have been driving, of course, but he did, and he stopped in Deming again to see Dark. It was fitting for him to visit his longtime muse for the last time on what would be his final solo long-distance drive.[30]

* * *

Patti Smith arrived on September 11, 2015, and stayed for several days to help him through his initial edits on *The One Inside*.[31] Smith was one of the few people he'd informed about his illness by then, as he didn't want anyone's pity or pestering get-well wishes. But by December, he called his sister Roxanne. They decided not to notify Sandy until February ("'cause she's only gonna worry," Sandy chided her siblings). He also had lunch with O-Lan in New York; he didn't tell her about the disease, but she watched him awkwardly drop a fork and knew something was wrong.[32]

Shepard had set ideas, images, and dialogue down on paper over the past six months, but his writing needed help, since he'd largely lost the ability to type or edit his work by hand. He and Smith did little else but work, as he was desperate to complete the book while he could. On one of her several visits to help with his writing, they were seated at the kitchen table eating peanut butter on toast with coffee when Shepard looked up and caught her eye. "And it was like we had the same thought," Smith said later. "Patti Lee," Shepard observed, "we've become a Beckett play. . . . Yep, a Beckett play." "But he loves Beckett," Smith said, "so I figured that's a good thing." Together they removed many of his impressionistic sketches to give more novelistic heft to the chapters involving the tiny man, Felicity, and the Blackmail Girl.[33]

When *The One Inside* eventually arrived in stores in early 2017, there was little publicity and no fanfare. "There was no talk about it," Gough said. "There was no press. He didn't do any interviews." The *New Yorker* published the sections on his father, and there was a smattering of mediocre reviews, but that was it. This might've been cause for concern, but Shepard was just thrilled to hold the new volume in his incapacitated hands. Ed Harris called it "the most intimate thing he wrote. Read that and it's like you're holding the essence of Sam in your hands." Johnny Dark was struck by its candor but baffled by its difficulty: "The book had been interesting to me because much of it was a retelling of stories he had told me on the phone, although there was a lot of abstract writing mixed in with the rest of which I could not make heads nor tails."[34]

One troublesome question has since remained unaddressed: with Shepard's well-known proclivity for autobiographical writing in mind, why would the author have invited potential blowback—at a time when the #MeToo movement was just revving its engine—by publishing a book about an affair he'd conducted with a woman fifty years his junior? On the surface, preemption seems the likeliest rationale—if Manuscript Girl was to publish their story, he'd get it out there first. "There's a wry poetic justice in the spectacle of a writer, that scavenger of others' lives, helplessly furnishing material for another," jibed the *New York Times* when the book first appeared. "The voyeur voyeured."[35]

But a more likely explanation for Shepard's act of literary self-exposure, almost to the point of performance art, is that he'd been writing about his innermost secrets all along. His work had always served to reify socially unacceptable behavior by laying it out for the world to see, but on his terms. Patti Smith, who helped arrange the manuscript (after which her section was cut), explained the impulse grandiloquently: "We travel the coils of his prismatic mind, his weary heart," she wrote, "not through confession, but a potent honesty, a fascination for not caring. The truth is that he may be changing, yet he remains unchanged, the running boy, the empowered adolescent, the seething man whose muscles betray him."[36]

When Gough had balked at the book's content, Shepard urged her to call Dark. "I'm so worried about what people are gonna say about Sam after they read this," she said. Dark replied, with less tact than Smith, "We all have a hungry old man inside us. He's just being honest about it."[37]

* * *

The fall after Smith's visit, hoping to avoid the Kentucky winter, Shepard relocated to the "little zocalo town" of Healdsburg, California, where Jesse and his wife, Maura Harrington, lived, and he rented a house near Maura's popular café, Flying Goat Coffee.[38] Despite his declining health, he next traveled to Minnesota to spend his last Christmas at Jessica's cabin, then on to New York to assist Ed Harris and Amy Madigan in a revival of *Buried Child* at the Signature Theatre. "He was ailing, and he came to rehearsal every day," said the grateful New Group director of *Buried Child*, Scott Elliott. "It was a beautiful thing to watch him collaborate with the cast."[39]

While in New York, Shepard passed Harris a ten-page typescript he'd just written as a kind of theatrical companion piece to his last works of prose. He wanted his friend to give it a staged reading, which Michael Almereyda recorded on video at the Signature on March 31, 2016.[40] But Shepard never titled the piece, and as a result, with the camera running, Harris misconstrued the word "Signature" at the top of the first page as the play's title rather than the theater in which it was to be staged, so that's what he called it.[41]

Almereyda offers the only known statement about Shepard's intention with the work: "Sam had originally, with a sense of urgency, told me and Patti that he envisioned the piece as a collaboration, a group effort to be filmed in some self-contained way. But his illness advanced more quickly than anticipated and the idea was taken off the table." Harris's poignant rendering of this text, delivered from a stool parked before the otherwise empty living room set of *Buried Child*, was performed before a handful of witnesses—Almereyda, his cameraman Pablo Tapia-Plá, Amy Madigan, Patti Smith, Scott Elliott, and a few stragglers. It was the playwright's last new play to be staged in his lifetime, though its existence was never made public.[42]

"Signature," for lack of any other title, still holds a vital place in Shepard's late works. He'd chosen an epigraph for *The One Inside*, which appeared that February, 2017, by an author about whom he'd spoken in hushed tones, David Foster Wallace. (Shepard compared him to Lou Reed, "the kind of writer who comes from an angle no one else would think of.")[43] His epigraph isn't from Wallace's most famous novel, *Infinite Jest*, but rather from a monologue in his later book *Brief Interviews with Hideous Men* entitled "On His Deathbed, Holding Your Hand, the Acclaimed New Young Off-Broadway Playwright's Father Begs a Boon," and it reads, "Why does no one take you aside and tell you what is coming?"[44]

"Signature" consists of a forty-five-minute monologue modeled on Wallace's *Brief Interviews with Hideous Men*—a collection of remorseless confessions by men who haven't grasped or accepted the pain they've brought down upon others. In Shepard's play, an elderly wheelchair-bound gentleman calling himself Ben Jones (which is meant to sound generic, but was also, notably, the last name O-Lan chose for herself after their divorce). Jones speaks directly to the audience but insists he wasn't responsible for mass atrocities he may or may not have carried out as a secret agent or mercenary, though he'd been forced into exile in an unnamed seaside "brown village," attended to by a lone female "protector" (no doubt a salute to Carey Gough) who mops the floor as he talks. He's even had facial reconstruction surgery to blend in, and people stared at his bandaged visage with fear, "afraid of what I might become. Something hidden. The eyes. They saw my eyes. I saw them seeing me. I could tell they knew. The monster underneath. I would become that monster underneath."[45]

Like Oedipus, Ben Jones has created an epic misery for those under his purview, but unlike the Greek king, Jones harbors no remorse. He admits to being a spy—too many fake passports (the play's only specified props) and stripped identities to ignore. But he insists he'd never carried out the atrocities he's charged with, "something in the past that violated all decency." Rather than confronting the past, a futile task, or stabbing his eyes out from guilt like Oedipus, Jones wishes only to shed the totality of his past identities and settle into his final days quietly, to abide as "a fixture in the neighborhood" if ultimately to escape into "the dropping off place to other worlds." The final lines are translated from Guillaume Apollinaire's poem "Le Pont Mirabeau": "Let the hours chime / the light wanes / The days go away / I remain."[46]

* * *

Back in Healdsburg, Shepard knew his time was running short, so he redoubled his efforts on a new book he'd started in Midway, its chapters now toggling between the Healdsburg house and the Midway farm. He no longer had control over his arms or hands, and his symptoms worsened rapidly in Healdsburg, so he submitted to the vagaries of dictation. "They won't take direction—won't be dictated to—the arms, legs, feet, hands," Shepard wrote of his condition in *The One Inside*. "The brain isn't even sending signals."[47]

That February, Roxanne arrived in Healdsburg from Southern California, where she was working a part-time teaching job, to help out with her brother's convalescence after his return from Minnesota and New York, and to replace Gough as his literary transcriber.[48]

Knopf positioned his latest book, *Spy of the First Person*, as a "novel," though Shepard strongly argued against that categorization. In truth, aside from a few name changes, it was a memoir, but he didn't want that either. "Why does anybody need a label? . . . I don't know what the fuck it is. It's just rambling."[49] (Calling it a "novel," at bottom, had to contend with the fact that the book's only truly fictional section is the boilerplate disclaimer: "Any resemblance to actual persons, living or dead, events, or locales is entirely coincidental.")

Lyrically composed in a voice of wry observational humor and stoic resignation, *Spy of the First Person* is another autobiographical work, this time charting his physical and mental struggles with muscular atrophy. And this time, unlike with *The One Inside*, which he'd written while still living independently, he kept a lid on some of the more incendiary tales of his life as a septuagenarian. "I'm quite sure that that book would have been totally different if he had been able to handwrite it," Roxanne noted after his death.

> I think that he would have loved to cut loose, but he was so nervous about his sisters and his daughter being in the process, I think it curtailed stuff that he might have wanted to say. All this hot, saucy stuff that his sisters and his daughter are going to transcribe? Parameters, you know? But it ended up being really sweet for us, because we got to very calmly work with him. Jesus, I mean, who gets that opportunity?[50]

The family hired a hospice worker to provide palliative care in Healdsburg, and that March, the care worker told them that if they wanted to take him back to Kentucky by Luxury RV as planned, they'd better take him soon because his lungs were about to fail. "We practically killed him going across the Continental Divide," Roxanne said, who joined Jesse, Walker, and Shepard to help out, "but he wanted to do one last road trip with his sons."[51]

Most mornings over the following spring in Kentucky, Shepard was rolled outside in a wheelchair and transferred to an Adirondack chair, where he dictated his book into a tape recorder Hannah bought him. "Recording was a very different experience for him than the physical act of writing, and he found it somewhat disorienting," Hannah reported later, but he got the hang of it. When he took a break, either sister would transcribe it onto a computer file. Then they would bring the pages back for him to read over.[52] "He's a writer so he needed to write every day to be himself," Sandy said, "and that was our mission, to help him be as close to normal as possible."[53]

Two of his personas observe and speculate over the other in *Spy of the First Person*, a psychic division that had a history with him. He'd told Chaikin about an inner division back in the seventies, that "sensation of doubleness, this feeling of separation between my body and 'me'" that he believed had given him access to "another world." Before, the sensation only came in "flashes," but now it was a perpetual state. There are two Shepards here too, a doubleness we find memorialized in *True West*, but rather than Austin and Lee, there's an ambulatory observer and an immobile one being cared for by his family. Neither fully recognizes the other as his double. "I'm not normally a suspicious person," he writes in *Spy*. "I don't go around looking over my shoulder for surprises. But I have the sense—I can't help having the sense—that someone is watching me."[54]

That someone, of course, was himself. But it was also perhaps, to his mind at least, a manifestation of his long sought after state from the Work, his "indivisible I."

The fragments of the past interwoven into *Spy of the First Person* are tenderly, even proudly rendered: Jesse's life with Maura in Healdsburg, and the immigrant laborers there for whom Maura, an activist, had dedicated her life to providing refuge; Scarlett and Dark's move to New Mexico and Scarlett's death; his youth in California and New York, and a final chapter that describes departing the El Farolito restaurant in Healdsburg after a family meal. Shepard couldn't recall what they discussed at the restaurant, he wrote, "Probably Trump, the country in a Mexican standoff." Within these final pages, he uncharacteristically names the actual people he dined with, Roxanne, Sandy, Jesse, Maura, Walker, and Hannah. "Perhaps naming everyone just lets us exist in that one moment together," Roxanne said. "Or perhaps it is just a 'thank you.'"[55]

Shepard censored himself admirably in the book, but couldn't seem to hold back one fact that might have attracted some repercussions. In that final scene, Jesse and Walker are wheeling their father down the streets of Healdsburg. He names each and describes them as "my two sons" but then corrects himself, "two of my sons." Again, no one seemed to notice after the book's release, but it leaves open the strong possibility that Shepard's fictional son, Earl, in *Don't Come Knocking* was based on an actual son, which also leaves open the possibility that Howard Spence's estranged daughter, Sky, also exists. ("It's about estrangement more than anything else," he'd said about his film with Wim Wenders.)[56] If true, in this culminating scene of Shepard's final book that he'd dictated about genuine filial love, this self-correction can only be read as an affectionate gesture to the living son.

* * *

Despite his physical infirmities, Shepard was plucky in his final days in Midway and observed his death head-on. He also, astonishingly, completed his edits on *Spy of the First Person* just a week before his death. "The way he went through the world was as a writer," Hannah said of her father's remarkable determination to complete his last book. "That drive and desire was never going to diminish."[57]

Those terrible insecurities that fueled Shepard's work but ravaged his inner life appeared to vanish. He tried to stay alert and upbeat with his family, coaxing them into driving him to Whole Foods, watching horse races on the streaming service the women rigged up (Shepard never had a TV in the house, nor did he have clocks or wear a watch), making peanut butter sandwiches and root beer floats with his sisters like in the old Bradbury days. When he got bored, he'd supervise a rearrangement of the library. "He'd just sit there in his wheelchair and guide me through it," Roxanne said with a laugh. He'd begun Proust's *In Search of Lost Time* but gave up the struggle, so Roxanne read it to him out loud. Once he caught pneumonia, "the old man's friend," it was only a matter of memories and time.[58]

Shepard knew that rainy Thursday, July 27, 2017, would be his last day alive. His three children and two sisters lovingly gathered around his bed, where a copy of Beckett's *Endgame* was placed on his bedside table. Perhaps somewhere in his oxygen-starved thoughts, he conjured his favorite line from Brecht: "A man can make a fresh start with his last breath." Early that afternoon, at two twenty, Shepard's breathing stopped. The family sent his body to the funeral home, where, three days later, they cremated him. This was a Native American ritual Shepard had read about, to wait three days and allow the family to commune with the resting spirit while it contemplates its final destination.[59]

"Everybody dies," Shepard told Patti Smith on her last visit. "But I'm all right with it. I've lived my life the way I wanted."[60]

EPILOGUE

# A PULSE IN THE DARK

Shepard's family made the announcement on the day of his cremation, and on August 2, at 7:45 p.m., the lights of Broadway were dimmed for a full minute to observe his passing. His theater colleagues then gave a raft of heartfelt interviews about Sam Shepard's impact on American theater.

An early tribute to his legacy came from his fellow Southern Californian dramatist Matthew Paul Olmos, who recalled "the rather countless conversations I've had over the years with other playwrights about how Sam Shepard was also their one playwright that inspired them to even be a playwright. The common phrase in these conversations was often some version of 'Sam Shepard showed me that theatre could be *cool*.'" One such playwright was a former student of Shepard's from the Bay Area, the Pulitzer-winning author of *M. Butterfly*, David Henry Hwang: "I think of Sam as America's great rock 'n' roll playwright," Hwang testified. "Of the theatre creators who came of age during the rise of rock, Sam is the dramatist whose work lives on."[1]

Charles McNulty, chief theater critic of the *Los Angeles Times*, doubled down on Shepard's astonishing influence on young writers: "If Samuel Beckett has been the god of modern theater, Shepard has been the more accessible demigod who has inspired more young talents in the last few decades than any other." Lynn Nottage, the only woman to win the Pulitzer Prize for Drama twice, recounted a time when she'd been performing her monologue *Welcoming Gerte* at a bar in Utah.[2] This was in 1994, well before Nottage emerged as a dramatic force, and she acted out the times she'd been called the N-word. The only person of color there, she recounted how petrified she was, sweating profusely, and afterward went to the bar for a drink. "Can I give you a piece of advice?" a man beside her asked. "And I was like, Oh shit! It's Sam Shepard—of course you can give me a piece of advice!" "Fuck these people," he told her. "This is your writing. Next time you do it, you have to live every single moment and own all of your words. And not be intimidated, not be scared." "I've always clung to that advice," Nottage wrote.[3]

The playwright Carson Kreitzer went as far back as her teenage years, when she bought her first pair of cowboy boots after reading Shepard's collected volume *Fool for Love and Other Plays*. "That was when I got the boots," Kreitzer wrote. "That was when I figured out how to stride through the world. How to take up more room than was apportioned to me, as a girl."[4]

Actors, directors, and critics joined in the chorus of grief and appreciation. John Malkovich called him "super American, incredibly authentic, free of bullshit, quick to laugh, horse crazy, and with a humility that was very charming." Philip Kaufman wrote of his leading man in *The Right Stuff*, "He was not a writer of what you could call articulate literature but more of a writer of the streets. He had this divining rod that he held over words and behavior, and if it quivered at a certain rare time, he knew it was right." Michael Feingold of the *Village Voice* praised Shepard's "questing, reflective, poetically visionary mind, steeped in art, literature, and philosophy." Memorials were soon scheduled for Shepard at La MaMa in New York, the Bootleg Theater in Los Angeles, and the Royal Court in London, where the actress Ronkẹ Adékọluẹ́jọ́ rounded out the evening with a nontraditional haiku as his portrait was lowered from the flies above the stage: "A Renaissance prince / with a coyote howling / in the distance."[5]

Ethan Hawke sat down with the British director James Macdonald only a couple of days after Shepard's death to discuss a Broadway revival of *True West*. Neither of them had any idea he was already gone, since the family hadn't announced his death until after the cremation.[6] Not long before he passed, Shepard told Hawke that he wanted to see one last great revival of *True West*. He envisioned Hawke starring as Lee and James Macdonald, who'd gained his respect directing him in Caryl Churchill's *A Number*, to direct. They staged the play on Broadway, with performances beginning in December 2018 and adding Paul Dano as Austin. It was received as a splendid send-off for its author.

Patti Smith got the call from Roxanne on the afternoon of Shepard's passing. She was in Paris playing with U2, and she burst into tears. "We'd all been prepared," Roxanne said about the call, "but you're never prepared." Soon after, Smith remembered a letter he sent her many years before, in which he described a recurrent dream of his. "He dreams of horses," she told the Lion of Lucerne, a sculpted memorial carved into a Swiss cliff that seemed to her like a messenger from the afterworld. She hoped that her friend might have a horse where he was going. "Fix it for him, will you? . . . He won't need a saddle, he won't need anything."[7]

Jessica had arranged to travel to Midway on July 28, having just returned home from Galway, Ireland. They'd sustained a warm friendship after all they went through. Somehow, he even managed while in New York to see her Tony Award–winning performance as Mary Tyrone in *Long Day's Journey Into Night*. "I miss him every single day of my life," Jessica said.[8]

Hannah sent out invitations for a memorial at the farm in Midway on September 2, which she and her siblings titled "Sam Shepard: A Great Recognition." In lieu of flowers, they asked invitees to donate money in his name to the Cherry Lane Theatre's Mentor Project, a program for budding playwrights in New York City. By all accounts, the send-off was as Shepardian as it could've been without his actually being there, singing, strumming his ukulele, yipping like a coyote. "In fact he would have preferred you have the memorial service while he was still alive," Johnny Dark responded to Jesse's description of their plans for the gathering.[9]

Dark bought his plane ticket, reserved a hotel room near the Midway farm, packed his bags, and kenneled his dog. But on the road to the airport, he turned back. Hurricane Harvey delayed his flight and airports were shutting down; thus, the storm provided him with the excuse he needed to stay home. "I am trying not to think of Sam," Dark wrote about his estranged best friend's death, "and at the same time I'm wondering why I can't bring myself to talk about any of his good qualities, his unusual gifts, his charm, his generosity. And I think it's because those things weren't what I found so attractive about him. No, it was his sense of lostness, his angers, frustrations, and consuming appetites that reminded me so much of myself."[10]

Shepard's private memorial at his Midway farm was like the post-hypnotic spells his fractured imagination once conjured so readily. An eclectic cast of over a hundred and fifty mourners traveled there, wept over him, celebrated his career, drank bourbon, did drugs, made music, and enacted familial dramas of the kind that inevitably erupt when a patriarch falls.[11] Peter Stampfel, Stephen Rea, Michael Almereyda, Lois Smith, T Bone Burnett, Ed Harris, Sissy Spacek, Diane Keaton, and others from the astonishing cast of characters in Shepard's life made their way to central Kentucky to pay their respects. His local cohort also attended—Carey Gough, Phil Gerrow, the University of Kentucky professor Richard Schein, the Nuckolses, along with cowboys, musicians, and restauranteurs who lived nearby. Even Shepard's boyhood chum Ernie Earnshaw from South Pasadena made the trek.

O-Lan spoke first, and she teasingly opened her speech by declaring, "First again!" Jessica, the second, read his dialogue "Repeat," a candid conversation between the two of them in *Cruising Paradise*. ("Now, repeat. Let's get it in our head: 'I am a man, not to be trusted.' Let's repeat.")[12] Jesse gave a fittingly hilarious and heart-wrenching eulogy in which he marveled at the incredible blessing of being born the child of such a man. Hannah read his short story about Walker, "Berlin Wall Piece" from *Great Dream of Heaven*, and a story she wrote about her father's superstition, derived from Native American lore about hawks in flight. "There are superstitions that I still hold to," Shepard once said. "For instance, hawks, the flight of hawks. Hawks passing from right to left in front of you are good luck, left to right in front of you are bad luck." (The running family joke was that each time Shepard brought it up, he changed the sides—left to right, right to left.)[13]

Ed Harris, soon after his brilliant turn playing Dodge in *Buried Child*, with his wife, Amy Madigan, as Halie, reportedly hopped up on a table and belted out a monologue from that play, high on euphoria.[14] "As a really private guy, Sam didn't talk a lot about his feelings," Harris said later. "When he found out he was seriously ill, he became more open and accessible. A kindness crept into him. It allowed me to feel the nature of our friendship, and I'd like to think it was the same for him."[15] Stephen Rea made a speech about how he was going to miss the "madness" of time spent with Shepard, and he joined Walker's band, the Down Hill Strugglers, in a rendition of "Oh, Didn't He Ramble" from *Kicking a Dead Horse*, then Walker, Stampfel, and John Cohen of the New Lost City Ramblers played into the early hours of the morning.[16]

Sandy delivered an inspiring speech at the Los Angeles tribute held for him at the Bootleg Theater. In it, she told a story about how Jane would send her newspaper articles and reviews, writing, "Look! Steve's doing this, and Steve's doing that!" Then she described going to a performance of her brother's breakout hit *Chicago* from 1965 with a couple of friends at her college, the University of California at Davis, where Shepard briefly taught. Sandy had no knowledge of theater, as such, and the whole thing seemed like a weird psychedelic trip. Then she told him, "You know, these kids here think you're a god." "Well, I am," he replied matter-of-factly. "But so are you, and so are they."[17]

Shepard reflected at the time of his father's passing that there were two main roads to death: "You either die like a dog or you die like a man. And if you die like a dog, you just go back to dust. All that stuff in the Bible is absolutely true. Dust to dust." He had chosen to broadcast his fears and insecurities to the world, but when he died, he did so surrounded by a supportive, loving family. He had suffered stoically for so many months on that Kentucky farm, while ushering into print *The One Inside* and *Spy of the First Person*, which was released that December. Meanwhile, Shepard's greatest fear, the bedeviling curse of his bloodline, might never come to an end. And yet he was once asked whether "there's a Steve Rogers still out in the Mojave, living an alternative life." "Spinnin' his wheels," Shepard said with a chuckle. "Yeah. I'm sure there is."[18]

# ACKNOWLEDGMENTS

This book is dedicated to my mother, Janet B. Kellock, who first sparked my interest in literature, theater, Sam Shepard, and Eugene O'Neill. She passed during the worst days of the Covid disaster, on July 4, 2020, and intuited that when her prognosis arrived, I'd dedicate this book to her instead of my friend Jackson R. Bryer, whom I'd originally intended. But I say, why not both? Jackson, an authority on American drama, is my longtime mentor and coeditor, including, with his inimitable wife, Mary C. Hartig, our book *Conversations with Sam Shepard*. I am deeply fortunate to have had the honor of being mentored so closely, and for so many years, by such a rigorous scholar and endlessly supportive friend. I would also like to thank my sisters, Susanne Magee and Elisa K. Olds, who helped me with transcriptions and drafts through these nearly eight years, God help you both. My daughter, Mairéad Dowling, was equally long-suffering over my fixations. Love you, kiddo.

Next, I would like to thank my school, Central Connecticut State University, along with my colleagues in the English Department, for their abiding support. The course releases, research grants, and travel funds CCSU has offered me over the years made this book possible. Importantly, I'd also like to thank my two exemplary graduate assistants, James Harlow and Griffin Pickett, who graciously typed up vast amounts of interviews and bibliographic material for this book.

My first agent, Geri Thoma at Writers House, has been an unwavering supporter of mine, and I miss her expert guidance now that she's retired. Geri's replacement was the nonpareil Susan Golomb. When I texted a friend to tell her Susan was my new agent, the response came back in a single true line: "Susan Golomb is the best literary agent alive." In my experience, Susan has hit that high mark and then some. Peggy Boulos Smith, my agent for the UK, is an old friend. What a joy that we can share this experience together too. Indeed, this kind of research and writing is often described as terribly lonely, but thanks to my beloved community of compañeros, including, along with my wonderful nieces and nephews, Adam Kroshus, Kamal John Iskander, Derron Wood, Alex Smith, Shiyan Xu, Sun Dong, Sara Duffy, Rob Cowan, Sheila Power, Joey Bothwell, Jon and Laura Heller, Chris LaSalle, Eric Michaelian, Tim Raycroft, Art Cox, Tom Cerasulo, Burl Barr, Chris Francescani, Samantha Doucette, Jefferson Singer, Joanne and Mickey Williston, Herman Farrell, Alex Pettit, Mark Charney, and so many others, I never once felt the stab of loneliness.

This book required not one but five editors: Valerie Steiker, my undaunted acquisitions editor at Scribner; Heidi Pitlor of Heidi Pitlor Editorials; Scribner's executive editor, Chris Richards, and their copy editor Jane Elias and production editor Mark LaFlaur. It was a terrific honor to work with editors of such well-earned stature. But most effusively my gratitude goes to Chris, who knew how far to push me to access my most effective writerly self and thereby restrain my completist impulses. His editorial assistants, Joie Asuquo and Madison Thân, made my transition to the trades as smooth as could be—many thanks to you both.

*Coyote* is based on over a hundred interviews, most of which were conducted with Shepard's close friends, family, colleagues, and other more innocent passersby in the arc of his career, and thus American theater history. I'll just list these remarkable people alphabetically, and their impact will be clear from the narrative: Joyce Aaron, Michael Almereyda, Nancy Lee Andrews, Tony Barsha, Boaty Boatwright, Tom Bratigan, Barbara Bright, Sandy Daley and Josh Lawson, Johnny Dark,

Julie Delpy, Walter Romanus Donati, Barbara Eda-Young, Herman D. Farrell III, Richard Ford, Anthony Foutz, Carole Friedman, Jeremy Gerard, Phil Gerrow, Steve Gomer, Carey Gough, Joe Grifasi, Georgia and Walter Hadler, Dawn Hall, Ethan Hawke, David Henry Hwang, Chris Jones, O-Lan Jones (who, when I asked her why she doesn't give interviews about Shepard, responded with an amused grin, "I'm writing my own book," and I very much look forward to that), Lee Kissman, Henry A. Lewis, Fiach Mac Conghail, John McDaniel, Nancy Meckler, Murray Mednick, Clark Middleton and Elissa Meyers, Anne Militello, Charles Mingus III, Louis Mofsie (Green Rainbow), Bill Mohr, Yvette Nachmias-Baeu, Andee Nathanson, Ciarán O'Reilly, Albert Poland, Philip Rhodes, Roxanne Rogers, Sandy Rogers, Aaron Ryder, Lucy Sante, Richard H. Schein, Theodore Shank, Michael Smith, Peter Stampfel, Harrison Starr, Richard Strand, Jack Suderman, Beverly Walker, George C. White, Laura Wolfrom, Henry Wombles, Rudy Wurlitzer, Treva Wurmfeld, Bradley M. Zamczyk and Cassidy Chivers, and Guy Zimmerman. It was an honor to work with such an inspiring and talented cohort. My deepest gratitude to you all for allowing Shepard's life and work to spring to life in this book.

*Coyote* is also based on hundreds of notebooks, unpublished manuscripts, letters, and other correspondences and literary material, along with the multitudinous press interviews Shepard conducted from 1965 to 2016, many of which can be found in *Conversations with Sam Shepard*. As such, I'd like to express my gratitude to the archivists at Shepard's major depositories: Jane Parr and Laura Russo at Boston University's Howard Gotlieb Archival Research Center; Katie Salzmann at the William Wittliff Collections at Texas State University, San Marcos (who also helped ensure a remarkably generous travel grant and sort out Johnny Dark's photos); and Eric Colleary at the Harry Ransom Center at the University of Texas, Austin. I will include here, for her many hours spent on this project, Sarah White of the Elihu Burritt Library at Central Connecticut State University. (Thank you, Sarah!)

Along with those larger collections, my sincere gratitude to Jeremy Megraw and Nailah Holmes of the New York Public Library's Billy

Rose Theatre Division at Lincoln Center; the University of California at Davis Special Collections; the University of Virginia's Special Collections Department of the Alderman Library; Kate Medicus of Kent State University's Special Collections; Ozzie Rodriguez and Kylie Goetze of La MaMa Archive; the Archivio Michelangelo Antonioni; New York University's Fales Library; Barry Houlihan and Geraldine Curtin of the University of Galway's Archives & Special Collections; the Mt. San Antonio College Library; the University of Michigan Special Collections Research Center; the University of Delaware's Morris Library of Special Collections; the Chalmer Davee Library at the University of Wisconsin, River Falls; Princeton University Library Special Collections; Jennifer Wilson, of Emerson College's Archives and Special Collections; the Bancroft Library of the University of California at Berkeley; Caroline Seigel of the Santa Fe Institute Library; Charlie Weaver of *Minnesota Daily*; Jordanna Enrich of the Insitute of International Education; the San Francisco Performing Arts Library and Museum; Phil Rhodes and Cathy Solomon of the Mill Valley Public Library; Carol Acquaviva and Anne T. Kent of the Marin County Free Library; Rebecca Murray of the Library and Archives of Canada; the National Library Scotland; Ann Quach of San Marino's Crowell Public Library; Alejandro Aragonez of the New Mexico Office of the Medical Investigator; and Amy Gerretson of Ripon College. Thank you all so very much.

# CHRONOLOGY OF SHEPARD'S WORLD PREMIERES

*Productions in New York City, unless otherwise noted.*

*Cowboys*—October 10, 1964, Theater Genesis
*The Rock Garden*—October 10, 1964, Theater Genesis
*Up to Thursday*—November 23, 1964, Village South Theatre
*Dog*—February 10, 1965, La MaMa Experimental Theatre Club
*The Rocking Chair*—February 10, 1965, La MaMa Experimental Theatre Club
*Chicago*—April 16, 1965, Theater Genesis
*4-H Club*—September 9, 1965, Village South Theatre
*Icarus's Mother*—November 16, 1965, Caffe Cino
*Red Cross*—January 20, 1966, Judson Poets' Theatre
*Fourteen Hundred Thousand*—March 11, 1966, Firehouse Theater, Minneapolis, MN
*La Turista*—March 2, 1967, American Place Theatre
*Melodrama Play*—May 18, 1967, La MaMa Experimental Theatre Club
*Cowboys #2*—October 9, 1967, Mark Taper Forum, Los Angeles, CA
*Forensic & the Navigators*—December 29, 1967, Theater Genesis
*The Unseen Hand*—December 26, 1969, La MaMa Experimental Theatre Club

*The Holy Ghostly*—March 8, 1970, McCarter Theatre, Princeton, NJ
*Operation Sidewinder*—March 12, 1970, Vivian Beaumont Theater, Lincoln Center
*Shaved Splits*—July 27, 1970, La MaMa Experimental Theatre Club
*The Mad Dog Blues*—March 4, 1971, Theater Genesis
*Cowboy Mouth*—April 2, 1971, Traverse Theatre, Edinburgh, Scotland, UK
*Back Dog Beast Bait*—April 29, 1971, American Place Theatre
*The Tooth of Crime*—July 17, 1972, Open Space Theatre, London, UK
*Blue Bitch*—January 19, 1973, Theater Genesis
*Geography of a Horse Dreamer*—February 21, 1974, Royal Court Theatre Upstairs, London, UK
*Little Ocean*—April 4, 1974, Hampstead Theatre Club, London, UK
*Action*—September 15, 1974, Royal Court Theatre Upstairs, London, UK
*Killer's Head*—April 15, 1975, American Place Theatre
*Angel City*—July 2, 1976, Magic Theatre, San Francisco, CA
*Suicide in* $B^{\flat}$—October 15, 1976, Magic Theatre, San Francisco, CA
*The Sad Lament of Pecos Bill on the Eve of Killing His Wife*—October 23, 1976, Bay Area Playwrights Festival, San Francisco
*Inacoma*—March 18, 1977, Magic Theatre, San Francisco, CA
*Curse of the Starving Class*—April 21, 1977, Royal Court Theatre, London, UK
*Seduced*—April 21, 1978, Lederer Theater, Providence, RI
*Tongues*—June 7, 1978, Magic Theatre, San Francisco, CA (with Joseph Chaikin)
*Buried Child*—June 27, 1978, Magic Theatre, San Francisco, CA
*Red Woman*—July 30, 1978, La Verne University, La Verne, CA
*Jacaranda*—June 7, 1979, American Place Theatre
*Savage/Love*—September 6, 1979, Magic Theatre, San Francisco, CA (with Joseph Chaikin)
*True West*—July 10, 1980, Magic Theatre, San Francisco, CA
*Superstitions*—July 3, 1981, Intersection for the Arts Theater, San Francisco, CA
*Fool for Love*—February 9, 1983, Magic Theatre, San Francisco, CA
*The War in Heaven*—December 20, 1985, Sushi Gallery, San Diego, CA (with Joseph Chaikin)

*A Lie of the Mind*—December 5, 1985, Promenade Theatre
*States of Shock*—May 16, 1991, American Place Theatre
*Simpatico*—November 14, 1994, Public Theater
*When the World Was Green*—July 19, 1996, Fourteenth Street Playhouse Mainstage, Atlanta, GA (with Joseph Chaikin)
*Tooth of Crime (Second Dance)*—December 15, 1996, Lucille Lortel Theatre
*Eyes for Consuela*—February 10, 1998, Manhattan Theatre Club
*The Late Henry Moss*—November 14, 2000, Magic Theatre, San Francisco, CA
*The God of Hell*—November 16, 2004, Actors Studio Drama School Theatre
*Kicking a Dead Horse*—March 15, 2007, Abbey Theatre, Dublin, Ireland
*Ages of the Moon*—March 3, 2009, Abbey Theatre, Dublin, Ireland
*Evanescence, or Shakespeare in the Alley*—June 15, 2011, Atlantic Stage 2
*Heartless*—August 7, 2012, Signature Theatre
*A Particle of Dread*—November 28, 2013, Derry Playhouse, Derry, Northern Ireland
*The Mildew*—February 13, 2018, Mt. SAC Studio Theater, Walnut, CA

# SOURCES, ARCHIVES, AND WORKS CITED

**Note:** Interviews conducted by the author include follow-up correspondence and are cited with the subject's name followed by the date of the interview or correspondence. Unless indicated otherwise, letters, emails, and texts were sent to the author. Letters, interviews, photographs, and other material without an indicated location are unarchived and in private hands.

## ABBREVIATIONS OF WORKS CITED

### WORKS BY SAM SHEPARD


**AC:** Sam Shepard, *Angel City, Curse of the Starving Class, and Other Plays* (*Killer's Head, Action, The Mad Dog Blues, Cowboy Mouth, The Rock Garden, Cowboys #2*) with a preface by Jack Gelber and a poem by Patti Smith, "Sam Shepard: 9 Random Years [7+2]" (New York: Urizen Books, 1976).

**CP:** Sam Shepard, *Cruising Paradise* (New York: Alfred A. Knopf, 1996; repr., New York: Vintage, 1997). Citations refer to the Vintage edition.

**DD:** Sam Shepard, *Day out of Days: Stories* (New York: Alfred A. Knopf, 2010; repr., New York: Vintage, 2011). Citations refer to the Vintage edition.

**FFL:** Sam Shepard, *Fool for Love and Other Plays* (*Angel City, Geography of a Horse Dreamer, Action, Cowboy Mouth, Melodrama Play, Seduced, Suicide in B*$^{\flat}$), with an introduction by Ross Wetzsteon (New York: Bantam, 1984).

**FO:** Sam Shepard, *Fifteen One-Act Plays* (*Ages of the Moon*; *Evanescence, or Shakespeare in the Alley*; *Short Life of Trouble*; *The Unseen Hand*; *The Rock Garden*; *Chicago*; *Icarus's Mother*; *4-H Club*; *Fourteen Hundred Thousand*; *Red Cross*; *Cowboys #2*; *Forensic & the Navigators*; *Holy Ghostly*; *Back Bog Beast Bait*; *Killer's Head*) (New York: Vintage, 2012).

**GDH:** Sam Shepard, *Great Dream of Heaven* (2002; New York: Vintage, 2003).

**HM:** Sam Shepard, *Hawk Moon: Short Stories, Poems, Monologues* (Los Angeles: Black Sparrow, 1973; repr., New York: PAJ, 1981). Citations refer to the PAJ edition.

**LHM:** Sam Shepard, *The Late Henry Moss, Eyes for Consuela, When the World Was Green: Three Plays* (New York: Vintage, 2002).

**LM:** Sam Shepard, *A Lie of the Mind* (New York: New American Library, 1987).

**MC:** Sam Shepard, *Motel Chronicles* (San Francisco: City Lights, 1982; repr. as *Motel Chronicles & Hawk Moon*, London: Faber & Faber, 2018). Citations refer to the City Lights edition.

**OI:** Sam Shepard, *The One Inside,* with a foreword by Patti Smith (New York: Alfred A. Knopf, 2017).

**PK:** Sam Shepard, "Paper King" notebook, 1970–1971, Box 26, Folder 9, HGC.

**PR:** "Sam Shepard," 1997, in *The Paris Review: Playwrights at Work*, ed. George Plimpton, with an introduction by John Lahr (New York: Modern Library, 2000), 329–45.

**RT:** Sam Shepard, *Rolling Thunder Logbook* (New York: Viking, 1977; repr., with new preface by Shepard and new foreword by T-Bone Burnett, Cambridge, MA: Da Capo Press, 2004). Citations refer to the Da Capo edition.

**SFS:** Sam Shepard, *States of Shock, Far North, Silent Tongue: A Play and Two Screenplays* (New York: Vintage, 1993).

**SP:** Sam Shepard, *Seven Plays* (*Buried Child, Curse of the Starving Class, The Tooth of Crime, La Turista, Tongues, Savage/Love, True West*), with an introduction by Richard Gilman (New York: Bantam, 1981; repr., Dial Press, 1984; reissued as *Sam Shepard Plays: 2*, London: Faber & Faber, 1997). Citations refer to the Dial Press edition.

**UH:** Sam Shepard, *The Unseen Hand and Other Plays* (*Forensic & the Navigators*, *The Holy Ghostly*, *Back Bog Beast Bait*, *Shaved Splits*, and *4-H Club*) (Indianapolis, IN: Bobbs-Merrill, 1972; repr., New York: Urizen Books, 1981; repr., New York: Vintage Books, 1996). Citations refer to the Vintage edition.

## SOURCES

**AD:** *American Dreams: The Imagination of Sam Shepard*, ed. Bonnie Marranca (New York: PAJ Publications, 1981).

**AL:** Amy Lippman, "A Conversation with Sam Shepard," *Harvard Advocate*, March 1983, 2–6, 44–46; reprinted in part as "Rhythm and Truths: An Interview with Sam Shepard," *American Theatre* 1 (April 1984), 9–13, 40–41; reprinted in part as "An Interview with Playwright Sam Shepard," *Dialogue*, April 1985, 50, 58–59; reprinted in BDH: 68-84. Citations refer to the *Harvard Advocate* printing.

**BB:** Blanche McCrary Boyd, "The Natural," *American Film: Magazine of the Film and Television Arts*, October 1984, 22–26, 91–92.

**BDH:** *Conversations with Sam Shepard*, edited by Jackson R. Bryer, Robert M. Dowling, and Mary C. Hartig (University Press of Mississippi, 2021).

**CC:** *The Cambridge Companion to Sam Shepard*, ed. Matthew Roudané (Cambridge, UK: Cambridge University Press, 2002); reprinted in BDH: 185–200. Citations refer to the *Cambridge Companion*.

**CR:** Carol Rosen, "'Silent Tongues': Sam Shepard's Explorations of Emotional Territory," *Village Voice*, August 4, 1992, 32–42; reprinted in BDH: 126–149. Citations refer to the *Village Voice.*

**CS:** Joseph Chaikin and Sam Shepard, ed. Barry V. Daniels, *Joseph Chaikin & Sam Shepard: Letters and Texts, 1972–1984* (New York: Theatre Communications Group, 1994).

**DS:** Don Shewey, *Sam Shepard* (1985; updated ed., New York: Da Capo Press, 1997).

**EO:** Ellen Oumano, *Sam Shepard: The Life and Work of an American Dreamer* (New York: St. Martin's Press, 1986).

**JA:** Jennifer Allen, "The Man on the High Horse: On the Trail of Sam Shepard," *Esquire*, November 1988, 141–44, 146, 148, 150–51.

**JD:** Johnny Dark, "Sam Shepard: A biography based on letters, phone calls, and conversations with Johnny Dark," typescript with no page numbers, Johnny Dark Accession 2017–131, Box 3693, WC/SD.

**JW:** John J. Winters, *Sam Shepard: A Life* (Berkeley, CA: Counterpoint, 2017).

**KC:** Kenneth Chubb, "Fruitful Difficulties of Directing Sam Shepard," *Theatre Quarterly* IV, no. 15 (August–October 1974), 17–27.

**KT:** Kenneth Turan and Joseph Papp, *Free for All: Joe Papp, the Public, and the Greatest Theater Story Ever Told* (New York: Anchor Books, 2010).

**MG, 1969:** Sam Shepard, transcript of interview by Mel Gussow, November 7, 1969, Series II, Container 139.1–5, Mel Gussow Papers 1933–2005, HRC; reprinted in BDH: 3–4. Citations refer to the original transcript.

**MG, 1993:** Sam Shepard, transcript of interview by Mel Gussow, December 14, 1993, Series II, Container 139.1–5, Mel Gussow Collection, HRC. Published as "As a Play Lies Fallow a Writer Moonlights," *New York Times*, December 27, 1993, C11; reprinted in BDH: 150–165. Citations refer to the original transcript.

**MG, 1997:** Sam Shepard, transcript of interview by Mel Gussow, September 27, 1997, HRC/MG.

**MG, 2002:** Sam Shepard, transcript of interview by Mel Gussow, September 27, 2002, Series II, Container 59, Mel Gussow Collection, HRC. For article "From Plays to Fiction: Thanks, Dad; Sam Shepard's Rascals Are Inspired by Memories of a Mysterious Father," *New York Times*, October 15, 2002, E1; reprinted in BDH: 201–224. Citations refer to the original transcript.

**NC:** Nancy Collins, "Full-Tilt Jessica," *Vanity Fair*, October 1991, 182–86, 228–38.

**PH:** Pete Hamill, "The New American Hero," *New York*, December 5, 1983: 75–102; reprinted in BDH: 85–97. Citations refer to *New York.*

**PR:** Mona Simpson, Jeanne McCullock, and Benjamin Howe, "Sam Shepard: The Art of Theatre XII," *Paris Review*, Spring 1997, reprinted in *The Paris Review: Playwrights at Work*, ed. George Plimpton, with an introduction by John Lahr (New York:

Modern Library, 2000), 329–345; reprinted in BDH: 173–184. Citations refer to the Modern Library edition.

**PRLA:** Paul Rosenfield, "Rough Country," *Los Angeles Times*, January 29 1984, 22.

**RG:** Robert Greenfield, *True West: Sam Shepard's Life, Work, and Times* (New York: Crown, 2023).

**SA:** Soren Agenoux, "Sam Shepard," *Interview* 3, no. 1, January 1970, 6–7, 28.

**SB:** Stephen J. Bottoms, *The Theatre of Sam Shepard: States of Crisis* (Cambridge, UK: Cambridge University Press, 2000).

**SD:** *Shepard & Dark*, directed by Treva Wurmfeld, Music Box Films, 2013.

**SGF:** Samuel G. Freedman, "Sam Shepard's Mythic Vision of the Family," *New York Times,* Arts and Leisure, December 1, 1985, 1, 20.

**SM:** Stewart McBride, "Sam Shepard," *Christian Science Monitor*, December 26, 1980, B3; reprinted in BDH: 52–58. Citations refer to *CSM.*

**SOC:** Sam Shepard, "Slave of the Camera (An Actor's Notes)," partial early draft with photographs, August 1990, Series I, Container 25.1, Sam Shepard Papers 1965–2011, HRC.

**TP:** *Two Prospectors: The Letters of Sam Shepard and Johnny Dark*, ed. Chad Hammett (Austin, TX: University of Texas Press, 2013).

**TSD:** *This So-Called Disaster*, directed by Michael Almereyda (IFC Productions, 2003).

**TW:** *Tangents: From the Making of* Shepard & Dark, ed. Treva Wurmfeld (Brooklyn, NY: Oscilloscope Laboratories, 2022).

## ARCHIVES

**HGC:** Sam Shepard Collection 1943–2017, Boston University Libraries, Howard Gotlieb Archival Research Center, Boston University.

**HRC:** Sam Shepard Papers 1965–2009, Harry Ransom Center, University of Texas at Austin Libraries.

**HRC/MG:** Mel Gussow Papers 1933–2005, Harry Ransom Center, University of Texas at Austin Libraries.

**KS:** Joseph Chaikin Papers, Kent State University Special Collections and Archives, Kent State University.

**NYPL:** Billy Rose Library, New York Public Library. New York, NY.

**UCD:** Toby Cole Archives D-055 (1950–1979), Department of Special Collections, General Library, University of California, Davis.

**WC:** Sam Shepard Papers 1980–1999, The Wittliff Collections, Texas State University.

**WC/SD:** Sam Shepard and Johnny Dark Collection 1972–2011, The Wittliff Collections, Texas State University.

# NOTES

## PROLOGUE EXILE

1 MG, 1969.

2 HM, 71; Sam Shepard, "Azusa Is a Real Place: Sam Shepard Writes a Special Preface to *The Unseen Hand*," *Plays and Players* 20, no. 8 (May 1973), 1.

3 Shepard, "Azusa Is a Real Place," special insert (centerfold), 1.

4 Roxanne Rogers, March 18, 2025; Steve Rogers to Helen Dodge Rogers, August 1961, HGC.

5 Sam Shepard to Jane Rogers, January 26, 1968.

6 Shepard, "Azusa Is a Real Place," 1.

7 SD.

8 Sam Shepard, notebook, April 2008–February 2009, box 17, folder 1, HRC.

9 Sam Shepard, "Snake Eyes," 1974, box 22, folder 4, Sam Shepard Collection 1943–2017, HGC; Jane Elaine Schook Rogers, "Notes from Jane=," n.d.

10 Johnny Dark to Lee Kissman, March 25, 2017; Roxanne Rogers, September 27, 2024.

11 SP, 169; Sam Shepard, "Machismo Sagas," August 1978, HRC.

12 Sam Shepard, "Snake Eyes," 1974, box 22, folder 4, Sam Shepard Collection 1943–2017, HGC.

13 Charles Mingus III, December 8, 2024; quoted in KC, 3; Sandy Rogers, July 28, 2023.

14 Quoted in PH, 86; HM, 58; PM, 86; HM, 58.

15 Sam Shepard, "Wisconsin Wilderness," DD, 271; notebook, October 1979, HRC.

16 Military, Compiled Service Records. World War II. Rogers, Samuel Shepard. Army of the United States, First Lieutenant. Record Group 36 047 789. U.S. Air Force Reserve, Captain. World War II. Record Group 810 030. National Personnel Records Center, St. Louis, MO.

17 Quoted in "Sam Shepard," interview by Terry Gross, *Fresh Air*, March 31, 1998; Sam Sr. had the scar since he was a baby, when Grandpa Sam Rogers jokingly threw a hairbrush at Helen; she ducked and it hit the back of Sam's neck, leaving a deep and permanent scar. MC, 118; "Notes from Jane."
18 Sandy Rogers, July 28, 2023; Roxanne Rogers, text message, February 11, 2025.
19 Quoted in "Sam Shepard," interview by Terry Gross, *Fresh Air*, March 31, 1998; FO, 24; Sam Shepard, "Sangre de Cristo" (unfinished), spiral notebook, August 25, 1989, WC; Sam Shepard, "Snake Eyes," 1974, box 22, folder 4, HGC; "See You in My Dreams," CP, 146.
20 Sam Shepard, notebook, April 2008–February 2009, box 17, folder 1, HRC; Roxanne Rogers, February 9, 2018; Sam Shepard, "Sangre de Cristo" (unfinished), spiral notebook, August 25, 1989, WC.
21 LHM, 112.
22 "One Night in the Long-Ago," DD, 21, 22.
23 Sandy Rogers, July 28, 2023.
24 Steve Rogers to Grandma (Amy Schook), August 1961, HGC; Sandy Rogers, July 28, 2023; Sam Shepard, "Snake Eyes," 1974, box 22, folder 4, Sam Shepard Collection 1943–2017, HGC.
25 Notebook, October 1979, HRC.
26 Notebook, July 24, 1980, HRC.
27 Sandy Rogers, July 28, 2023.
28 Sam Shepard, "My First Year in New York; 1963," *New York Times Magazine*, September 17, 2000, online.

## INTRODUCTION **THE SIDEWINDER'S HEAD**

1 Quoted in Colin Dwyer, "Sam Shepard, 'Poet Laureate of America's Emotional Badlands,' Dies at 73," NPR: The Two-Way, July 31, 2017, online.
2 Eleanor Lester, "The Pass-the-Hat Theater Circuit," *New York Times*, December 5, 1965, 100.
3 Sam Shepard, "Snake Eyes," 1974, box 22, folder 4, Sam Shepard Collection 1943–2017, HGC.
4 Notebook entry, January 23, 2001, HRC; quoted in Jonathan Cott, "The Rolling Stone Interview: Sam Shepard," *Rolling Stone*, December 18, 1986–January 1, 1987, 166–72, 198, 200.
5 Quoted in John O'Mahony, "The Write Stuff," *Guardian*, October 10, 2003, online.
6 Quoted in Laura Barton, "Sam Shepard: 'America Is on Its Way Out as a Culture,'" *Guardian* (UK), September 7, 2014, online.
7 Charles Mingus III, November 2, 2019.
8 Patti Smith, "Flash Flood. Water," PK; FFL, 145.
9 Sam Shepard, "Instant Animal," HM, 69.
10 OI, 138, 165. The movie Shepard was working on was *August: Osage County* (2013).

11 Sam Shepard, UH, xi.

12 John Lion, "Rock 'n' Roll Jesus with a Cowboy Mouth: Sam Shepard Is the Inkblot of the '80s," *American Theatre*, April 1984, 7.

13 Quoted in TSD; quoted in AL, 44–45.

14 Quoted in *Great Performances*, season 26, episode 17, "Sam Shepard: Stalking Himself," directed by Oren Jacoby, aired July 8, 1998; Clive Barnes, "Theater: A Sam Shepard Double Bill: Dramatic Cartoons Are Displayed in the Village," *New York Times*, April 2, 1970, 43; Joyce Aaron, "Clues in Memory," AD, 172.

15 Quoted in Stephen Schiff, "Showcase: Shepard on Broadway," *New Yorker*, April 22, 1996, 84–86.

16 Quoted in Patrick Healy, "Getting Faster with Age: Sam Shepard's New Velocity," *New York Times*, February 12, 2010, C1 (L).

17 Quoted in Eileen Blumenthal, "Sam Shepard and Joseph Chaikin: Speaking in Tongues," AD, 145.

18 Quoted in Dan Hulbert, "World Awaits 'Green': Shepard-Chaikin Team Has the Right Stuff for High Drama," *Atlanta Journal-Constitution*, July 19, 1996, 45.

19 Robert Mazzocco, "Heading for the Last Roundup," *New York Review of Books*, May 9, 1985.

20 Quoted in Joe Penhall, "The Outsider," *Guardian* (UK), June 14, 2006, Culture, 20.

21 Jack Kroll, "Desert Apocalypse," *Newsweek*, March 23, 1970, 69.

22 Jacques le Sourd, "Sam Shepard: California Playwright Puts the Bite on the Big Apple," *Burlington (VT) Free Press*, March 25, 1979.

23 Samuel G. Freedman, "Leaving His Imprint on Broadway," *New York Times*, November 22, 1987, A38; Ben Brantley, "Sam Shepard of Today, and of Many Days Ago," *New York Times*, November 8, 1996, C1.

24 David J. DeRose, *Sam Shepard* (New York: Twayne Publishers, 1992), 139, 140.

25 Quoted in Michael Almereyda, "Sam Shepard: The All-American Cultural Icon at 50," *Arena* (May/June 1994), 66.

26 Quoted in Kevin Sessums, "Digitized Dialogues: Sam Shepard," 1988, online.

27 TP, 171.

28 Joyce Aaron, August 2, 2022.

29 Nancy Meckler, May 10, 2023.

30 TP, 171.

31 Sam Shepard, notebook, May 18, 1980, and April 30–July 1980, HRC.

32 Quoted in Jonathan Cott, "Strong Words: An Interview with Sam Shepard by Jonathan Cott," *Vogue*, September 1988, 681, 756.

33 Quoted in Jack Gelber, "Sam Shepard: The Playwright as Shaman," AC, 2–3.

34 Roxanne Rogers, December 29, 2020.

35 Susanna Massie Thomas, August 3, 2019.

36 Quoted in Sean Elder, "Bringing It All Back Home," *San Francisco* 45, no. 4 (April 1998), 48. Their friend, the actor Kim Stanley, also used to refer to him as "Old Horse

Eyes." "Interview with Jessica Lange," *WTF with Marc Maron* (podcast), November 11, 2024.

37 Quoted in Patrick Healy, "Getting Faster with Age: Sam Shepard's New Velocity," *New York Times*, February 12, 2010, C1.

38 Quoted in Michiko Kakutani, "Myths, Dreams, Realities: Sam Shepard's America," *New York Times*, January 29, 1984, B26.

39 Quoted in Eric Killelea, "Sam in Santa Fe: From the Mailbox of a Great American Playwright," *Santa Fe Reporter*, August 29–30, 2017, online.

40 Johnny Dark, July 25, 2020.

41 Quoted in Michael Almereyda, "Sam Shepard: The All-American Cultural Icon at 50," *Arena* (May/June 1994), 66.

42 Quoted in ibid., 69.

43 Sam Shepard, foreword, in *Seen and Heard: Teenagers Talk About Their Lives*, ed. Mary Motley Kalergis (New York: Stewart, Tabori & Chang, 1998), 6–7.

44 Quoted in Michael Ross, "Made of the Write Stuff," *Sunday Times* (UK), March 11, 2007, Eire Culture, 4.

45 Quoted in Patrick Healy, "Getting Faster with Age: Sam Shepard's New Velocity," *New York Times*, February 12, 2010, C1.

46 TW, 156.

47 Ethan Hawke, December 28, 2021.

48 Quoted in Katie Roiphe, "The Naked and the Conflicted," *New York Times*, December 31, 2009, online.

49 Quoted in NC, 228.

50 Quoted in Alistair McKay, "Hollywood Got Rid of Me but I Feel Loved in London," *Evening Standard* (UK), February 16, 2007, online.

51 JD.

52 Quoted in Sylvaine Gold, "Harried Child," *New York Times*, April 18, 2004, online.

53 Sam Shepard, *Motel Chronicles* notebook, April 1981, HRC.

54 Quoted in KC, 20.

55 Quoted in MG, 2002.

56 Quoted in Samantha Weinberg, "Pale Writer," *Harpers & Queen* (UK), December 1996, 153.

57 Ben Brantley, "Sam Shepard, Storyteller," *New York Times*, November 13, 1994, Arts and Leisure, 26.

58 Roxanne Rogers, January 25, 2023.

59 O-Lan and I conducted this discussion in the lobby of La MaMa after the final show of her opera *Iceland* on April 2, 2023.

60 Sandy Rogers, July 28, 2023.

61 Johnny Dark to Lee Kissman, May 22, 2017; Johnny Dark, *People I May Know: The Uncollected Essays, Photographs, Letters, Notebooks, Commentaries and Tales of Johnny Dark* (New York: Little Bear Press, 2006); JD.

62 Quoted in Gwynne Watkins, "Sam Shepard Gives a Rare Interview, Thinks Safe House Could've Been Better," *GQ*, June 11, 2012, online.

63 Richard Gilman, "Introduction," in SP, xvii.

64 Quoted in Fintan O'Toole, "A Nod from One Sam to Another," *Irish Times*, February 24, 2007, Arts, 1.

65 Sam Shepard, *Operation Sidewinder*, 1970, UH, 273.

## CHAPTER 1 SON OF SAM

1 MC, 52–53.

2 Jane Rogers to Sam Shepard, November 2, 1988, GRC; Sam Shepard, *Drifter (Rage of Unknown Origin)*, October–December 1978, GRC, box 9, folder 17.

3 *Halconado '61*, Duarte High School Yearbook, 38.

4 "Notes from Jane"; National Personnel Records Center, National Archives, "Samuel Shepard Rogers."

5 Amy Gerretsen (Ripon College), email, August 27, 2024; Jane Rogers, "Notes from Jane." Shepard believed it was Texas. (Laura Barton, "Sam Shepard: 'America Is on Its Way Out as a Culture,'" *Guardian*, September 7, 2014, online; UH, 318.)

6 Jane Rogers to Sam Shepard, November 2, 1988, GRC; National Personnel Records Center, National Archives, "Samuel Shepard Rogers."

7 TP, 276; Joe Penhall, "The Outsider," *Guardian* (UK), June 14, 2006, Culture, 18.

8 TP, 277.

9 Sue Allan (Susanna White's biographer), email, November 4, 2023.

10 FamilySearch.org, the Church of Jesus Christ of Latter-day Saints, "International Genealogical Index (IGI)," database, online.

11 Sam Shepard, *Heartless* (New York: Vintage, 2013), 61; quoted in Jamie Brisick, "Day of Days: Sam Shepard's Long Ride," *Wrestling Elephants*, December 11, 2013, online.

12 Sam Shepard, "The Seventh Son," typed draft, July 4, 1977, HGC, box 10, folder 9. An early version of *Curse of the Starving Class*.

13 SP, 194.

14 Sam Shepard, "I Wonder What I'm Doing Here," August 14, 1977, HGC, box 3, folder 3; "Orange Grove in My Past," DD, 172.

15 National Personnel Records Center, National Archives, "Samuel Shepard Rogers"; TP, 223; Robert Coe, "Saga of Sam Shepard," *New York Times Magazine*, November 23, 1980, 56; "Notes from Jane."

16 Quoted in PH, 80; quoted in KC, 3.

17 National Personnel Records Center, National Archives, "Samuel Shepard Rogers"; Bill Mohr, January 4, 2019.

18 Sam Shepard, *Spy of the First Person* (New York: Alfred A. Knopf, 2017), 8; "184 Freshman . . . " *San Marino Tribune*, September 4, 1952; *Titanian 1960*, San Marino

High School yearbook. Shepard's first real home, Auntie Grace Upton's house, was located at 710 Adelaine Avenue in South Pasadena.

19 Quoted in Andrea R. Vaucher, "The Secret of Indie Success," *Washington Post*, July 23, 2000, online.

20 "Notes from Jane"; MC, 29. Shepard reports in the story that he was ten years old, but Jane noted he was six and in the second grade in "Notes from Jane."

21 Sandy Rogers, July 28, 2023.

22 Roxanne Rogers, September 27, 2024.

23 MC, 31.

24 TP, 231.

25 Roxanne Rogers, text message, September 30, 2024.

26 "The Real Gabby Hayes," CP, 10; MG, 2002; "The Real Gabby Hayes," CP, 10, 11.

27 JW, 12; Sandy Rogers, July 28, 2023.

28 Sandy Rogers, Ibid.

29 For eighth grade, Shepard attended the Royal Oaks Grammar School. Duarte High's school grounds, however, weren't ready to open in September, and Shepard was required to attend Monrovia-Duarte High School for about three months. Geri Houlihan, "Duarte High 50 Year Reunion of the 1st Graduating Class," *Duarte View*, September–October 2011, 8.

30 Quoted in Harriet Shapiro, "Sam Shepard Has Enough Horse Sense to Corral His Talented Sisters into His Dramatic Stable," *People*, January 6, 1986, online.

31 Roxanne Rogers, July 6, 2024.

32 Roxanne Rogers, December 29, 2019.

33 Clark Middleton, January 2, 2019; James Ellroy, *My Dark Places: An L.A. Crime Memoir* (New York: Vintage Books, 1997), 22–23, 24.

34 Roxanne Rogers, December 29, 2019.

35 Sandy Rogers, July 28, 2023.

36 UH, 320.

37 OI, 165.

38 UH, 214.

39 UH, 214; HM, 63; Jonathan Cott, transcript for interview, "The Rolling Stone Interview: Sam Shepard," December 18, 1986–January 1, 1987, HRC, 166–72, 198, 200; Nat's Cats included Nat Henkins on clarinet, Mitchell Chaney on slide trombone, and Shepard on drums; Sam Shepard, "Slave of the Camera," August 1990, HRC, 61; JD.

40 "Units of Duarte H.S. Dedicated," *Daily News-Post* (Monrovia, CA), May 15, 1958, 1; "Doubles in Brass: Duarte Councilman Lauded for Work as an Orchestra Leader," *Daily News-Post* (Monrovia, CA), January 17, 1958, 7.

41 Roxanne Rogers, email, August 10, 2019.

42 Sam Shepard, "Snake Eyes," 1974, box 22, folder 4, Sam Shepard Collection 1943–2017, HGC.

43 Roxanne Rogers, December 29, 2020.

44 Sam Shepard to Sam Rogers, May 26, 1965.

45 Quoted in Harriet Shapiro, "Sam Shepard Has Enough Horse Sense to Corral His Talented Sisters into His Dramatic Stable," *People*, January 6, 1986, online.

46 Comision Para Intercambio Educativo to Mr. Samuel S. Rogers, March 22, 1961. Sam Rogers resided in Colombia from July 8 to August 25, 1961. Previous biographers have reported that he won a "Fulbright Linguistic Scholarship," but there is no such award. JW, 20; RG, 41.

47 Quoted in Kevin Sessums, "Digitized Dialogues: Sam Shepard," 1988, online.

48 Notebook, January 23, 2001, HRC; Jonathan Cott, transcript for interview, "The Rolling Stone Interview: Sam Shepard," December 18, 1986–January 1, 1987, HRC, 166–72, 198, 200.

49 Quoted in Harriet Shapiro, "Sam Shepard Has Enough Horse Sense to Corral His Talented Sisters into His Dramatic Stable," *People*, January 6, 1986, online.

50 Sandy Rogers, July 28, 2023.

51 Carole Cadwalladr, "Sam Shepard Opens Up," *Guardian*, March 20, 2010, online.

52 Sandy Rogers, July 28, 2023.

53 Roxanne Rogers, email, August 10, 2019.

54 JD; quoted in Harriet Shapiro, "Sam Shepard Has Enough Horse Sense to Corral His Talented Sisters into His Dramatic Stable," *People*, January 6, 1986, online; Roxanne Rogers, email, January 31, 2020; quoted in TW, 32.

55 Quoted in Jack Kroll, "Who's That Tall, Dark Stranger?," *Newsweek*, November 11, 1985, 70; quoted in "Sam Shepard," interview by Terry Gross, *Fresh Air*, March 31, 1998; Murray Mednick, March 13, 2019; DD, 166–67.

56 Quoted in Laura Barton, "Sam Shepard: 'America Is on Its Way Out as a Culture,'" *Guardian*, September 7, 2014, online.

57 Quoted in Michael Ross, "Made of the Write Stuff," *Sunday Times* (UK), March 11, 2007, Eire Culture, 4.

58 Roxanne Rogers, July 22, 2020.

59 MC, 93; "Enters Sheep," *Independent Star-News* (Pasadena, CA), November 9, 1958, online; Sam Shepard, "Snake Eyes," 1974, box 22, folder 4, Sam Shepard Collection 1943–2017, HGC; PK.

60 Quoted in Jack Kroll, "Who's That Tall, Dark Stranger?," *Newsweek*, November 11, 1985, 70.

61 Quoted in Harriet Shapiro, "Sam Shepard Has Enough Horse Sense to Corral His Talented Sisters into His Dramatic Stable," *People*, January 6, 1986, 80.

62 "Arabian Horse Show Plans," *Pasadena Independent*, April 6, 1961, 11; Sam Shepard to Jane Rogers, January 26, 1968; JD. In 1975, Ellsworth was also discovered to be fatally neglectful, and the Chino ranch was shut down ("Ellsworth's Horses Are Starved," *New York Times*, January 22, 1975, online).

63 "A Man's Man," CP, 31; quoted in "Q&A: Sam Shepard," interview by Rosanna Greenstreet, *Guardian* (UK), June 21, 2014, online; "A Man's Man," CP, 28, 32.

64 Ibid., 32; quoted in TW, 106.
65 "A Man's Man," CP, 32–33.
66 "And So Does Your Mother," HM, 58.

## CHAPTER 2 FISHING IN THE DARK

1 Sam Shepard, "Art House," manuscript, n.d., from "Works, Fragments, 1978–2008 and Undated," series I, container 14.2–4, Sam Shepard Papers 1965–2011, HRC.
2 Quoted in "Sam Shepard," interview by Terry Gross, *Fresh Air*, March 31, 1998.
3 "Favorites," notebook, 1993–1996, WC.
4 Charles Mingus III, October 8, 2019.
5 *Halconado '61*, Duarte High School Yearbook, 148.
6 "DHS Produces 'Rainbow,'" *Daily News-Post* (Monrovia, CA), March 18, 1961, 12.
7 "Sam Shepard Briefly Went to Mt. San Antonio College, May Have Written First Play as Student," *San Gabriel Valley Tribune*, July 31, 2017; 4-H Club Record, 1960, box 29, folder 3, HGC.
8 John O'Mahony, "The Write Stuff," *Guardian*, October 10, 2003, 22.
9 Ibid., 22.
10 Quoted in Boris Kachka, "How the West Was Lost: Sam Shepard Takes on Cowboy Poseurs—and His Own Iconhood," *New York*, June 22, 2008, online.
11 Fintan O'Toole, "A Nod from One Sam to Another," *Irish Times*, February 24, 2007, Arts, 1.
12 Quoted in Michael Ross, "Made of the Write Stuff," *Sunday Times* (UK), March 11, 2007, Eire Culture, 4.
13 Quoted in PH, 86.
14 Quoted in Brian Case, "Slay 'Em Again, Sam," *Time Out* (London), no. 1350 (July 3–10, 1996), 26.
15 *The Mildew*, with a cast of ten and a fifteen-minute running time, was first performed at Mt. SAC in a triple bill along with Rebecca Prichard's *Dream Pill* and Robert Anderson's *I'm Herbert* on February 13, 14, and 15, 2018.
16 Steve Rogers (Sam Shepard), *The Mildew: A One-Act Comedy*, *MoSAiC*, 1961, 9, 16; Sandy Rogers, July 28, 2023.
17 JD.
18 Arthur and Barbara Gelb, *O'Neill* (New York: Harper and Brothers, 1962), 191, 268. Sam Shepard's copy.
19 Arthur and Barbara Gelb, *O'Neill* (New York: Harper & Brothers, 1962), 350. Sam Shepard's copy; quoted in Alexis Soloski, "An Urban Cowboy Returns to Broadway," *New York Times*, January 31, 2016, AR5.
20 "Sam Shepard," interview by Michael Almereyda, *Interview*, September 24, 2011, online.
21 Sam Shepard, notebook, October 1979, HRC; Michael VerMeulen, "Sam Shepard: Yes, Yes, Yes," *Esquire*, February 1980, 80; "Sam Shepard Briefly Went to Mt. San Antonio

College, May Have Written First Play as Student," *San Gabriel Valley Tribune*, July 31, 2017.

22 "Players to Stage Satire," *Pasadena Independent*, May 2, 1963, 21.

23 Roxanne Rogers, July 6, 2024; Charles Mingus III, November 5, 2019.

24 Roxanne Rogers, July 9, 2024.

25 Quoted in Ellen Oumano, *Sam Shepard: The Life and Work of an American Dreamer* (New York: St. Martin's Press, 1986), 18–19.

26 Charles Mingus III, October 8, 2019 and January 9, 2025; "Players to Stage Satire," *Pasadena Independent*, May 2, 1963, 21.

27 "Christopher Fry Play at Presbyterian Church," *Signal*, January 3, 1963, 4; Wayne A. Clarke, "America's First Repertory Company Prepares to Note 10th Anniversary," May 2, 1963, 39.

28 Quoted in Michael White, "Underground Landscapes," *Guardian*, February 20, 1972, 8.

29 Wayne Clark, "The Bishop's Company: Good Shepherd Chancel Was Setting for Strong Plea for Understanding," *Arcadia Tribune*, December 26, 1963, 8.

30 "Sam Shepard: The Art of Theatre XII," interview by Mona Simpson, Jeanne McCullock, and Benjamin Howe, *Paris Review* (Spring 1997), reprinted in *The Paris Review: Playwrights at Work*, ed. George Plimpton, with an introduction by John Lahr (New York: Modern Library, 2000), 335.

31 The tour's repertoire also included dramatizations, aside from Christopher Fry's plays, of Alan Paton's novel *Cry, the Beloved Country* (1948), Christopher Fry's *The Boy with a Cart* (1945) and *A Sleep of Prisoners* (1951), A. A. Milne's *Winnie-the-Pooh* (1926; dramatized by Kirsten Sergel, 1957), C. S. Lewis's *The Great Divorce* (1945), and Rumer Godden's *An Episode of Sparrows* (1955).

32 Quoted in Wayne Clark, "The Bishop's Company: Good Shepherd Chancel Was Setting for Strong Plea for Understanding," *Arcadia Tribune*, December 26, 1963, 8.

33 Jamie Brisick, "Day of Days: Sam Shepard's Long Ride," *Wrestling Elephants*, December 11, 2013, online.

34 Steve Rogers to Sam and Jane Rogers, July 18, 1963.

35 Steve Rogers to Sam and Jane Rogers, August 11, 1963.

36 W. Lester Trauch, "Bishop's Company Deft in Church Performance," *Daily Intelligencer* (Doylestown, PA), October 18, 1963, 1–2. See also JW, 51–52.

37 Alexis Soloski, "True East: American Icon Sam Shepard Returns to New York," *Village Voice*, June 25–July 1, 2008, 27.

38 Steve Rogers to Jane Elaine Rogers, October 29, 1963.

39 Sam Shepard, "My First Year in New York; 1963," *New York Times Magazine*, September 17, 2000, online; Steve Rogers to Jane Rogers, November 10, 1963. Shepard's first apartment in New York was located at 353 West Forty-Fourth Street, Apt. 4A.

40 Steve Rogers to Jane Rogers, November 28, 1963.

41 Steve Rogers to Jane Rogers, December 9, 1963.

42 Charles McHarry, "On the Town: 'Golden' Girl Search Narrows," *Daily News*, January 27, 1964, 34.

43 EO, 21. In Charles Mingus III's interview with Ellen Oumano, Mingus said it might have been in Hedda Hopper's column, but her column was adjacent to McHarry's and doesn't mention him.

44 Charles Mingus III, November 2, 2019.

45 Charles Mingus III's apartment was located at 146 Avenue C, Apt. 2A, and the building's lot was later demolished and replaced by the more hospitable Ninth Street Community Garden. Shepard's letters indicate that he paid, unless he was lying to his mother, which is possible, fifteen dollars a month in rent (Charles Mingus III, November 5, 2019; *Jump Cuts*, directed by Christopher Lukas, December 31, 2011). Steve Rogers to Jane Elaine Rogers, March 7, 1964, and February 18, 1965; JD.

46 *Great Performances*, season 26, episode 17, "Sam Shepard: Stalking Himself," directed by Oren Jacoby, aired July 8, 1998.

47 JD.

48 Lee Kissman, November 24, 2024. As Kissman pointed out to me, the East Village wouldn't be assigned that name until around the time the *East Village Other* magazine appeared in 1965.

49 MC, 75.

50 Charles Mingus III, December 8, 2024.

51 Patti Smith, "Sam Shepard: 9 Random Years [7+2]," AC, 244.

52 Charles Mingus III, January 9, 2025; Georgia and Walter Hadler, October 19, 2019. This apartment and its inhabitants would inform the setting for Shepard's 1965 one-act play *4-H*.

53 Steve Rogers to Jane S. Rogers, August 9, 1964.

54 Steve Rogers to Jane S. Rogers, May 8, 1964.

55 Ibid.

56 "Drama to Be Given Sunday," *Madison (NJ) Eagle*, March 12, 1964, 4.

57 PH, 86.

58 Lee Kissman, "50 Years On: Theater Genesis and Sam Shepard," *Contemporary Theatre Review* 25, no. 4 (2015), 576, 580.

59 Quoted in EO, 22.

60 Steve Rogers to the Rogers Family, March 7, 1964.

61 Ibid.

62 Quoted in Michael Ross, "Made of the Write Stuff," *Sunday Times* (UK), March 11, 2007, Eire Culture, 4.

63 Steve Rogers to Jane S. Rogers, May 8, 1964.

64 Ibid.

65 Quoted in Don Shewey, "Rock-and-Roll Jesus with a Cowboy Mouth (Revisited)," *American Theatre* 21 (April 2004), 20–25, 82–84.

66 Joe Penhall, "The Outsider," *Guardian*, June 14, 2006.

67 Quoted in Don Shewey, "Rock-and-Roll Jesus with a Cowboy Mouth (Revisited)," *American Theatre* 21 (April 2004), 20–25, 82–84.

68 Sam Shepard, notebook, April to May 1981, HRC.

69 Quoted in Robert Goldberg, "Sam Shepard: Off-Broadway's Street Cowboy," *Rolling Stone College Papers*, Winter 1980, 44–45.

70 Quoted in Naseem Khan, "Free Form Playwright," *Time Out* (London), July 7–13, 1972, 30–31.

71 Quoted in Sylvie Drake, "Sam Shepard: A Play for Every Life Style," *Los Angeles Times*, October 21, 1979, Calendar, N1, 58, 62.

72 Quoted in Johnny Dark, "The 'True West' Interviews," *West Coast Plays* 9 (Summer 1981), 62.

73 Charles Mingus III, November 2, 2019.

74 Quoted in KC, 6.

75 Charles Mingus III, November 5, 2019; Charles Mingus III, November 2, 2019.

76 MC, 79; Quoted in PH, 92–93; MC, 79; Charles Mingus, November 2, 2019; MC, 80.

77 Biographical note for the "Playbill for the Premiere Production" of *Red Cross*, Judson Poets' Theatre, January 20, 1966, reprinted in *The New Underground Theatre*, ed. Robert J. Schroeder (New York: Bantam Books, 1968), 80; Quoted in JW, 80.

78 Ralph Cook, "Theatre Genesis," in *Eight Plays from Off-Off Broadway*, ed. Nick Orzel and Michael Smith, with an introduction by Michael Smith (New York: Bobbs-Merrill, 1966), 93, 94–95; Lee Kissman, July 25, 2024.

79 Quoted in "Sam Shepard: The Art of Theatre XII," interview by Mona Simpson, Jeanne McCullock, and Benjamin Howe, *Paris Review* (Spring 1997), reprinted in *The Paris Review: Playwrights at Work*, ed. George Plimpton, with an introduction by John Lahr (New York: Modern Library, 2000), 336.

80 Paul L. Montgomery, "'Study in Color,' a Trilogy, Opens," *New York Times*, August 1, 1964, 13; "St. Marks Welcomes the Unusual," *New York World-Telegram* and *The Sun*, October 10, 1964, 20; "*Cowboys* and *The Rock Garden*," program by Theater Genesis, St. Mark's Church in-the-Bowery, October 1964.

81 Sandy Rogers, July 28, 2023.

82 Quoted in TDS.

## CHAPTER 3 "JUNK MAGIC" AT THEATER GENESIS

1 Quoted in John Leland, "How Sam Shepard Hit Downtown New York and Reinvented Himself," *New York Times*, August 4, 2017, online.

2 Quoted in *California Typewriter*, directed by Doug Nichol (American Buffalo Pictures, 2017).

3 Lee Kissman, "The Playwrights Unit," unpublished manuscript, January 16, 2019; Charles Mingus III, January 9, 2025; Helen Rogers to Jane Rogers, May 4, 1965; Charles Mingus III, November 2, 2019.

4 Lee Kissman, November 24, 2024.

5 "Sam Shepard: The Art of Theatre XII," interview by Mona Simpson, Jeanne McCullock, and Benjamin Howe, *Paris Review* (Spring 1997), reprinted in *The Paris Review: Playwrights at Work*, ed. George Plimpton, with an introduction by John Lahr (New York: Modern Library, 2000), 336.

6 Along with Shepard's affiliation with Theatre 65, Theater Genesis's program for *Cowboys* and *The Rock Garden* lists the playwright as scheduled to produce a "new work produced at Café La MaMa Theatre." Shepard's next play with the Playwrights Unit would be *4-H Club*, based on his experience on Avenue C with Mingus and Richmond, which opened in workshop at the Village South Theatre on September 9, 1965, then moved to the Cherry Lane Theatre.

7 Steve Rogers to Jane S. Rogers, August 9, 1964.

8 Quoted in Bruce Weber, "Theater: Ralph Cook Is Dead at 85, Pioneer of Off-Off-Broadway," *New York Times*, October 21, 2013, D8.

9 Quoted in Sylvie Drake, "Sam Shepard: A Play for Every Life Style," *Los Angeles Times*, October 21, 1979, Calendar, 58.

10 *Cowboys* has been considered lost ever since, including by Shepard; but a couple of scripts did in fact exist. My deep gratitude to Lee Kissman for sharing with me, at his home in Glendale, California, his original performance copy of *Cowboys*, which now resides in the Lee Kissman Alternative Theater Collection at Washington University in St. Louis, Missouri.

11 Quoted in Samuel G. Freedman, "Theater Rebels of 60's Reminisce," *New York Times*, November 15, 1984, 24.

12 Quoted in Alexis Soloski, "True East," *Village Voice*, June 25–July 1, 2008, 28.

13 Douglas M. Davis, "The Expanding Arts: Success for Off-Off Broadway," *National Observer*, April 10, 1967, 20.

14 Georgia and Walter Hadler, October 19, 2019.

15 "Interview with Sam Shepard Conducted by Eric Marciano on the Subject of Ellen Stewart," October 6, 2011, Gershwin Hotel. Shepard was awarded the Ellen Stewart Award on October 17, 2011. My gratitude to Eric Marciano for sharing his unpublished interview with me.

16 This was La MaMa's second location, as the first, on the basement floor at 321 East Ninth Street, after multiple arrests and closings for alleged prostitution, was shut down for bogus fire-code violations.

17 Stephen J. Bottoms, *Playing Underground: A Critical History of the 1960s Off-Off-Broadway Movement* (Ann Arbor: University of Michigan Press, 2006), 194.

18 Quoted in Alexis Soloski, "True East," *Village Voice*, June 25–July 1, 2008, 28.

19 Stephen J. Bottoms, *Playing Underground: A Critical History of the 1960s Off-Off-Broadway Movement* (Ann Arbor: University of Michigan Press, 2006), 194.

20 There has been some question about whether Shepard's world premiere was held on October 10 or October 16. (See Lee Kissman, "50 Years On: Theater Genesis and

Sam Shepard," *Contemporary Theatre Review* 25, no. 4 [2015], 573–81, 580n, and JW, 73.) But the *New York World-Telegram* and *The Sun* reported on Saturday, October 10, that the play would "open tonight" (20), and Jerry Tallmer's *New York Post* review came out on Monday, October 12.

21 EO, 32.

22 EO, 32; quoted in Bruce Weber, "Theater: Ralph Cook Is Dead at 85, Pioneer of Off-Off-Broadway," *New York Times*, October 21, 2013, D8.

23 "St. Marks Welcomes the Unusual," *New York World-Telegram* and *The Sun*, October 10, 1964, 20; JA, 146.

24 Steve Rogers to Jane S. Rogers, August 9, 1964; Quoted in Carol Rosen, "'Silent Tongues': Sam Shepard's Explorations of Emotional Territory," *Village Voice*, August 4, 1992, 42.

25 FO, 134; Lee Kissman, January 8, 2019. In the published version of *The Rock Garden*, for which he dropped the article in the title, Shepard has a brief opening scene, with Man, Boy, and Girl (based on Sandy Rogers). For reasons that were unclear to Kissman, this scene was not performed at the premiere.

26 Ralph Cook, "Theatre Genesis," in *Eight Plays from Off-Off Broadway*, ed. Nick Orzel and Michael Smith, with an introduction by Michael Smith (New York: Bobbs-Merrill, 1966), 94. *The Rock Garden*'s final scene was revived in Kenneth Tynan's wildly popular sex revue *Oh, Calcutta!* in June 1969. After La MaMa put on a similar show, *The Dirtiest Show in Town*, Shepard wrote his own pornographic show, *Shaved Splits*, but with a revolutionary twist. *Shaved Splits* opened at La MaMa on July 27, 1970, with four back-to-back midnight performances. Lee Kissman starred with his girlfriend at the time, Madeleine le Roux; Bill Hart directed; Johnny Dodd designed the lighting; and the one-act play is notable for Shepard and Hart's innovative use of the PA system. Shepard also published it in *Screw: The Sex Review*, June 21, 1971.

27 Barbara Eda-Young, April 20, 2019.

28 Georgia Hadler, November 17, 2019.

29 Quoted in Kembrew McLeod, *The Downtown Pop Underground* (New York: Abrams, 2018), 135.

30 Quoted in Anne Waldman, "Sam Shepard 1943–1917: Sweet Vortex," *Poetry Project* 253 (December 2017/January 2018), 6.

31 Barbara Eda-Young, April 20, 2019; quoted in Oumano, 33; Lee Kissman, "50 Years On: Theater Genesis and Sam Shepard," *Contemporary Theatre Review* 25, no. 4 (2015), 580; EO, 33; Jerry Tallmer, "Across the Footlights: Tell Me About the Morons, George," *New York Post*, October 12, 1964, 17.

32 Michael Smith, April 9, 2022; JD.

33 Michael Smith, "Theatre: *Cowboys* and *The Rock Garden*," *Village Voice*, October 22, 1964, 13.

34 Ibid.; AD, 159.

35 Quoted in EO, 34; Lee Kissman, "50 Years On: Theater Genesis and Sam Shepard," *Contemporary Theatre Review*, 25, no. 4 (2015), 580.

36 JD; Murray Mednick, March 13, 2019.

37 Eleanor Lester, "The Pass-the-Hat Theater Circuit," *New York Times*, December 5, 1965, 100. It's unclear in context whether the scare quotes around "genius" are meant to be sarcastic or not; either way, Shepard wouldn't appear again in the "paper of record" for nearly five years.

38 EO, 34.

39 Lee Kissman, March 11, 2019.

40 Lee Kissman, "The Playwrights Unit," unpublished manuscript, January 16, 2019.

41 Quoted in Allan Wallach, "It's Act I for Early Stage Playwrights," *Newsday*, February 9, 1965, 3C; Joyce Aaron, August 2, 2022. Theatre 65 placed *Up to Thursday* on a triple bill with Paul Foster's *Balls* and Lanford Wilson's *Home Free!*.

42 Quoted in Allan Wallach, "It's Act I for Early Stage Playwrights," *Newsday*, February 9, 1965, 3C.

43 Quoted in Samuel G. Freedman, "Theater Rebels of 60's Reminisce," *New York Times*, November 15, 1984, 24; Joyce Aaron, August 2, 2022.

44 Deedee Moore, "Give Her Regards to Broadway," *Newsday*, August 5, 1967, 27W; Joyce Aaron, August 2, 2022; Terry Stoller, "Joyce Aaron: Actor, Director, Teacher," Westbeth Artists Residents Council, 2014, online.

45 Joseph Chaikin, "A Note on Sam Shepard," in CC, 81; Patti Hartigan, "Sam Shepard: The Legendary Playwright, Actor and Private Man of Action Sits Still for an Interview," *Boston Globe*, August 18, 1996, N5; Eileen Blumenthal, "Sam Shepard and Joseph Chaikin: Speaking in Tongues," in AD, 136.

46 Quoted in Eileen Blumenthal, *Joseph Chaikin: Exploring the Boundaries of Theater* (New York: Cambridge University Press, 1984), 171. Blumenthal provides a complete list of pieces Shepard wrote for the Open Theater.

47 Sam Shepard, interview by Steve Gomer, January 13, 1983, KS; quoted in Michael Smith, "The Good Scene: Off-Off-Broadway," *Tulane Drama Review* 1, no. 4 (Summer 1966), 167.

48 Sam Shepard to Joseph Chaikin, 1972, in JC, 7; quoted in TSD.

49 Quoted in Steve Gomer, "Interview with Sam Shepard," January 13, 1983, KS.

50 Sam Shepard to the Magic Theatre, April 29, 1998, WC.

51 Joyce Aaron, August 2, 2022.

52 Joyce Aaron, "Clues in Memory," AD, 173.

53 Leonard Harris, "Trio of 1-Acters at Cherry Lane," *New York World-Telegram* and *The Sun*, February 11, 1965, 22.

54 Richard J. Shepard, "Drama: 3 New Arrivals; Theater 1965 Offers Test for Writers," *New York Times*, February 11, 1965, 45.

55 Quoted in Michael Pye, "Dream Maverick," *Observer*, March 26, 1989, A5.

56 Joyce Aaron, August 2, 2022. These rehearsals for the draft board interview were integrated into an unproduced and unpublished play *Three and Melons*, which only garnered a staged reading in Boston the following fall at the new Theater Company

of Boston for production that spring. But after hearing the read-through, Shepard replaced it with a revival of *Icarus's Mother*. He didn't abandon *Three and Melons*, however, which is a strong play. The script is marked 1965, but it was copyrighted on June 9, 1966, and he returned to it in the 1970s for a production at the American Place Theatre. The New York Public Library, Billy Rose Theatre Division's script date is inaccurately recorded as 1974. *See also* DS: 44 and SB: 27.

57 Charles Mingus III, November 5, 2019.

58 Sam Shepard to Jane Rogers, January 26, 1968; JD; Charles Mingus III, December 8, 2024.

59 Charles Mingus III, November 19, 2019.

60 Charles Mingus III, November 2 and 19, 2019, and December 8, 2024.

61 Quoted in RG, 64; Joyce Aaron, August 2, 2022.

62 Quoted in KC, 6; quoted in EO, 40.

63 FOP, 156.

64 Ralph Cook, "Notes on *Chicago*," in Sam Shepard, *Five Plays* (Indianapolis: Bobbs-Merrill, 1967), 2.

65 Sam Shepard to Sam Rogers, May 26, 1965.

66 Biographical note for the "Playbill for the Premiere Production" of *Red Cross*, Judson Poets' Theatre, January 20, 1966, reprinted in *The New Underground Theatre*, ed. Robert J. Schroeder (New York: Bantam Books, 1968), 80.

67 Lee Kissman, November 24, 2024; Anne Waldman, "Sam Shepard 1943–1917: Sweet Vortex," *Poetry Project* 253 (December 2017/January 2018), 6; Lee Kissman, November 24, 2024.

68 Sam Shepard to Jane Rogers, May 3, 1965; Helen Rogers to Jane Rogers, May 4, 1965.

69 Helen Rogers to Jane Rogers, May 4, 1965.

70 Letter from Sam Shepard to Sam Rogers, May 26, 1965.

71 Ibid.; Sam Shepard to Sam Rogers, May 26, 1965.

72 Sam Shepard to Sam Rogers, May 26, 1965.

73 KC, 9.

74 Joyce Aaron, August 2, 2022. See also EO, 46–47; MC, 77.

75 Barbara L. Wilson, "Park Has Area Debut," *Philadelphia Inquirer*, June 13, 1965, sec. 5, 1.

76 Joyce Aaron, August 2, 2022; Lee Kissman, March 18, 2022; Joyce Aaron, August 2, 2022. *Red Cross* opened on January 20, 1966, starring Joyce Aaron as her own character and Lee Kissman as Shepard's, at Judson Poets' Theatre in the Judson Memorial Church, on Washington Square South, and was followed by Sophocles's *Antigone*.

77 Bill Morgan, *I Celebrate Myself: The Somewhat Private Life of Allen Ginsberg* (New York: Penguin Books, 2006), 300, 428; *Me and My Brother* premiered on September 1, 1968, at the Venice Film Festival.

78 George C. White, November 20, 2021; quoted in Robert Coe, "Saga of Sam Shepard," *New York Times Magazine*, November 23, 1980, 120; Murray Mednick, March 13, 2019.

## CHAPTER 4 LOS TURISTAS

1 JD; Joyce Aaron, August 2, 2022.
2 Quoted in Matthew Roudané, "Shepard on Shepard: An Interview," CC, 77.
3 Sylvie Drake, "Sam Shepard: A Play for Every Life Style," *Los Angeles Times*, October 21, 1979, Calendar, 58; Joyce Aaron, August 2, 2022.
4 JD; MC, 70; quoted in John O'Mahony, "The Write Stuff," *Guardian*, October 10, 2003, online.
5 MC, 70; "Papantla," in CP, 215.
6 Sylvie Drake, "Sam Shepard: A Play for Every Life Style," *Los Angeles Times*, October 21, 1979, Calendar, 58.
7 Sam Shepard, "Visualization, Language and the Inner Library," *Drama Review* 21, no. 4 (Playwrights and Playwriting issue, December 1977), 58.
8 EO, 45–46; Joyce Aaron, August 2, 2022.
9 Joyce Aaron, August 2, 2022.
10 Quoted in Naseem Khan, "Free Form Playwright," *Time Out* (London), July 7–13, 1972, 31.
11 Quoted in Samuel G. Freedman, "Theater Rebels of 60's Reminisce," *New York Times*, November 15, 1984, 24.
12 Douglas M. Davis, "The Expanding Arts: Success for Off-Off Broadway," *National Observer*, April 10, 1967, 20; Michael Smith, April 4, 2022.
13 Douglas M. Davis, "The Expanding Arts: Success for Off-Off Broadway," *National Observer*, April 10, 1967: 20; Michael Smith, April 4, 2022.
14 AD, 159; Eileen Blumenthal, *Joseph Chaikin: Exploring the Boundaries of Theater* (New York: Cambridge University Press, 1984), 173.
15 Michael Smith, "Theatre Journal," *Village Voice*, December 2, 1965, 24; AD, 161.
16 Edward Albee, "Theatre: Icarus' Mother," *Village Voice*, November 25, 1965, 19; Michael Smith, April 18, 2022; quoted in PH, 98.
17 Quoted in Samuel G. Freedman, "Theater Rebels of 60's Reminisce," *New York Times*, November 15, 1984, 24.
18 Shepard's one-act, *Fourteen Hundred Thousand*, along with van Itallie's *Pavane* and Paul Foster's *Recluse*, was filmed that summer by National Educational Television (NET) for their *NET Playhouse* series in an evening called "La MaMa Playwrights," which aired on January 20, 1967, with Joyce Aaron, Joe Chaikin, and Kevin O'Connor.
19 Bob Lundegaard, "They'll Let Works Talk for Them: Visiting Playwrights Duck Quiz," *Minneapolis Tribune*, March 6, 1966, 4E.
20 Ibid.; Walter Alford to Mrs. Carol Rogers of *Village Voice*, April 26, 1967, NYPL. Sam Shepard, untitled reminiscence, October 1978, WC; Joyce Aaron confirmed that they never secretly married. Joyce Aaron, May 2, 2023.
21 Bob Lundegaard, "They'll Let Work Talk for Them: Visiting Playwrights Duck Quiz," *Minneapolis Tribune*, March 6, 1966, 4E.

22 Quoted in Susan Spiegel, "Shephard [*sic*], van Itallie: Writers Knock Preconceptions," *Minnesota Daily*, March 10, 1966, 21.

23 KC, 9; see Stephen J. Bottoms, "The Garden in the Machine: Edward Albee, Sam Shepard, and the American Absurd," in *Rethinking the Theatre of the Absurd: Ecology, the Environment and the Greening of the Modern Stage*, ed. Carl Lavery and Clare Finburgh (London: Methuen Drama Engage, 2015), 77–104; playbill for *Fourteen Hundred Thousand* and *Where's de Queen?*, Firehouse Theater, Minneapolis, MN, March 11, 1966, UCD.

24 Lew Reeve, "Fourteen Hundred Thousand Times, No," *Minneapolis Star*, March 12, 1966, 5A.

25 Leo Lerman, "The Third Stream Off-Off-Broadway," *Mademoiselle*, March 1966, 146.

26 Quoted in Leo Lerman, "The Third Stream Off-Off-Broadway," *Mademoiselle*, March 1966, 146.

27 Quoted in Brian Case, "Slay 'Em Again, Sam," *Time Out* (London), no. 1350 (July 3–10, 1996), 26.

28 Quoted in *The New Underground Theatre*, ed. Robert J. Schroeder (New York: Bantam Books, 1968), x–xi; Sam Shepard, untitled typescript, one page, May 18, 1977, BU, box 3, folder 5.

29 PH, 95.

30 Quoted in *The New Underground Theatre*, ed. Robert J. Schroeder (New York: Bantam Books, 1968), 102; DS, 55; Sam Shepard, "Machismo Sagas," 1978, HRC.

31 Peter Stampfel, March 9, 2024; "Fear of the Fiddle," CP, 56; Peter Stampfel, "Tribute by Peter Stampfel, Part 1," *Perfect Sound Forever* (December 2017), online.

32 Peter Stampfel, March 9, 2024; "Fear of the Fiddle," CP, 56; Peter Stampfel, March 9, 2024; MG, 1969.

33 JD; Peter Stampfel, "Tribute by Peter Stampfel, Part 1," *Perfect Sound Forever* (December 2017), online; JD.

34 Quoted in Jeremy Gerard, *Wynn Place Show: A Biased History of the Rollicking Life & Extreme Times of Wynn Handman and the American Place Theatre* (Hanover, NH: Smith and Kraus, 2013), 63.

35 Quoted in Jeremy Gerard, "Wynn Handman, Unflappable Off-Broadway Champion," *American Theatre*, April 14, 2020, online; PH, 88; Robert Goldberg, "Sam Shepard: Off-Broadway's Street Cowboy," *Rolling Stone College Papers*, Winter 1980, 45.

36 Quoted in Jeremy Gerard, *Wynn Place Show: A Biased History of the Rollicking Life & Extreme Times of Wynn Handman and the American Place Theatre* (Hanover, NH: Smith and Kraus, 2013), 64.

37 Sam Shepard, *La Turista (a play in ~~three~~ two acts)*, actor's copy, NYPL. This copy is marked with Wynn Handman's note, "as performed the week of March 10th." Quoted in Jeremy Gerard, "Wynn Handman, Unflappable Off-Broadway Champion," *American Theatre*, April 14, 2020, online; SB, 52.

38 Quoted in Jeremy Gerard, *Wynn Place Show: A Biased History of the Rollicking Life & Extreme Times of Wynn Handman and the American Place Theatre* (Hanover, NH: Smith and Kraus, 2013), 65.

39 Sam Shepard, *La Turista (a play in ~~three~~ two acts)*, actor's copy, NYPL.

40 MG, 1969; SP, 298.

41 Jeremy Gerard, "Wynn Handman, Unflappable Off-Broadway Champion," *American Theatre*, April 14, 2020, online; Edward R. Bendet of Greenbaum, Wolff & Ernst to the American Place Theatre, January 31, 1967, NYPL.

42 Quoted in Jeremy Gerard, *Wynn Place Show: A Biased History of the Rollicking Life & Extreme Times of Wynn Handman and the American Place Theatre* (Hanover, NH: Smith and Kraus, 2013), 67.

43 Michael Smith, "Theatre Journal," *Village Voice*, March 9, 1967, 23.

44 Quoted in Lewis Funke, "Singing the Rialto Blues," *New York Times*, March 5, 1967, sec. 2, 5.

45 Jeremy Gerard, "Wynn Handman, Unflappable Off-Broadway Champion," *American Theatre*, April 14, 2020, online.

46 Jeremy Gerard, April 17, 2023; Elizabeth Hardwick, "Word of Mouth," *New York Review of Books*, April 6, 1967, online; Elizabeth Hardwick, introduction, in Sam Shepard, *La Turista* (New York: Bobbs-Merrill, 1968), x.

47 Quoted in Lewis Funke, "Singing the Rialto Blues," *New York Times*, March 5, 1967, sec. 2, 5; Elizabeth Hardwick, "Word of Mouth," *New York Review of Books*, April 6, 1967, online; Joyce Aaron, "Clues in Memory," AD, 174.

48 Quoted in Sylvia Drake, "Sam Shepard: A Play for Every Life Style," *Los Angeles Times*, October 21, 1979, Calendar, 58.

49 Sam Shepard to Sam Rogers, May 26, 1965.

50 In 1979, La MaMa director George Ferencz combined four of Shepard's "rock plays" into the first festival devoted to Shepard's "musicals." It was entitled *Shep in Rep (the Rock 'n Roll Plays)*, which included, along with *Melodrama Play*, his later plays *Cowboy Mouth*, *The Mad Dog Blues*, and *The Tooth of Crime*.

51 Quoted in Mel Gussow, "Off-Off Broadway: It's In," *Newsweek*, May 1, 1967, 90.

52 Joyce Aaron, May 2, 2023; Sam Shepard to Jane Rogers, January 26, 1968.

53 Joyce Aaron, August 2, 2022.

54 Quoted in Joe Penhall, "The Outsider," *Guardian* (UK), June 14, 2006, Culture, 19.

55 Roxanne Rogers, March 15, 2022; quoted in RG, 83.

## CHAPTER 5 THE ITALIAN JOB

1 Quoted in DS, 65; "Woodstock News: Major Offering Blues Program; Raga as Bonus," *Kingston Daily Freeman*, June 30, 1967, 5; Yvette Nachmias-Baeu, *Best Friends* (Morrisville, NC: Lulu Publishing, 2018), 137.

2 JD; Sam Shepard, "It Wasn't Proust," GDH, 79.

3 Yvette Nachmias-Baeu, *Best Friends* (Morrisville, NC: Lulu Publishing, 2018), 137.
4 Lee Kissman, November 24, 2024; Lee Kissman, February 3, 2019.
5 Tony Barsha, March 15, 2019; Lee Kissman, November 24, 2024; Murray Mednick, March 13, 2019.
6 Quoted in Mel Gussow, "Off-Off Broadway: It's In," *Newsweek*, May 1, 1967, 90.
7 Michael Smith, "Theatre Journal," *Village Voice*, January 11, 1968, 23; Lee Kissman, March 2, 2019; UH, 281.
8 Michael Smith, "Theatre Journal," *Village Voice*, January 11, 1968, 23. Smith shows that Shepard had first called the Oolan character O'Lan [*sic*], but changed it soon after. Murray Mednick, March 13, 2019.
9 *Operation Sidewinder* program, Lincoln Center for the Performing Arts, 1970, 15.
10 Johnny Dark, February 25, 2021.
11 Diane Haithman, "Inventing a World, One Note at a Time," *Los Angeles Times*, March 18, 2001, online.
12 Johnny Dark, July 19, 2020; SD.
13 Johnny Dark, July 22, 2020; SD.
14 Tony Barsha, March 15, 2019; Georgia and Walter Hadler, October 19, 2019.
15 SA, 28; quoted in Charles McNulty, "Sam Shepard, the Cowboy Playwright Who Rewrote the Rules of the American Stage," *Los Angeles Times*, July 31, 2017, online; Richard Gilman quoted in Jonathan Cott, "The Rolling Stone Interview: Sam Shepard," *Rolling Stone*, December 18, 1986–January 1, 1987, online.
16 Quoted in TW, 82.
17 Sam Shepard to Jane Rogers, January 26, 1968.
18 Ibid.
19 Anthony Foutz, February 2, 2023; Sam Shepard to Jane Rogers, January 26, 1968.
20 Quoted in MG, 1969.
21 Quoted in TW, 82–83.
22 Archivio Michelangelo Antonioni, Ferrara, Italy. There's also a fifteen-page MGM "Reader's Report" by Evelyn Scott at the Margaret Herrick Library (Academy Library) in Beverly Hills. My gratitude to Walter Romanus Donati for sending me copies of Shepard's scenes and a copy of the MGM report (Walter Romanus Donati, emails, January 28 and February 6, 2023).
23 *Newsweek*, August 3 and August 23, 1965; Wallace Turner, "Discontent and Hate Viewed as Factors in Coast Violence," *New York Times*, August 15, 1965, sec. IV, 1, 80. My thanks again to Walter Romanus Donati for sharing files that indicated the news sources at the Archivio Michelangelo Antonioni, Ferrara, Italy.
24 See Evelyn Scott, "Reader's Report: *Zabriskie Point* by Michelangelo Antonioni, Tonino Guerra, & Sam Shepard," April 23, 1968, the Margaret Herrick Library, 7–8.
25 *Zabriskie Point*, directed by Michelangelo Antonioni (MGM, 1970).
26 Evelyn Scott, "Reader's Report: *Zabriskie Point* by Michelangelo Antonioni, Tonino Guerra, & Sam Shepard," April 23, 1968, the Margaret Herrick Library.

27 Yvette Nachmias-Baeu, April 3, 2019.
28 Sam Shepard, interviewed by Jonathan Cott, "The Rolling Stone Interview: Sam Shepard," *Rolling Stone*, December 18, 1986–January 1, 1987, 166–72, 198, 200, HRC.
29 Quoted in TW, 83; Carey Gough, January 21, 2024.
30 Anthony Foutz, February 8, 2023; Sam Shepard and Anthony Foutz, "Maxagasm: A Distorted Western for Soul and Psyche," unpublished manuscript, 136 leaves, second draft (Los Angeles: Creative Management Associates, n.d.), University of California, Berkeley, Northern Regional Library Facility, Bancroft Library, iii.
31 Contract for *Maxagasm* written by Anthony Foutz and signed by Foutz and Shepard, May 31, 1968, UCD; Anthony Foutz, February 8, 2023.
32 Bill Wyman, *Stone Alone* (New York: Viking, 1990), 484; Anthony Foutz, February 2, 2023.
33 MC, 46; Anthony Foutz, February 2, 2023; SA, 28; Anthony Foutz, February 8, 2023.
34 Anthony Foust, February 2, 2023.
35 Phil Gerrow, July 31, 2019; SA, 28.
36 Sam Shepard and Anthony Foutz, "Maxagasm: A Distorted Western for Soul and Psyche," unpublished manuscript, 136 leaves, second draft (Los Angeles, CA: Creative Management Associates, n.d.), University of California, Berkeley, Northern Regional Library Facility, Bancroft Library, 125.
37 Anthony Foutz, February 2, 2023; Yvette Nachmias, personal calendar, 1968; Sam Shepard to Michelangelo Antonioni, February 16, 1968, Archivio Michelangelo Antonioni, Ferrara, Italy; *Queen Elizabeth II*, hospitality photograph of Sam Shepard and Nancy Mandel, March 12, 1968.
38 Quoted in Beverly Walker, "Michelangelo and the Leviathan: The Making of *Zabriskie Point*," *Film Comment* 28, no. 5 (September–October 1992), 37.
39 Quoted in Michael White, "Underground Landscapes," *Guardian*, February 20, 1972, 8; *Zabriskie Point*, directed by Michelangelo Antonioni (MGM, 1970); MG, 1969.
40 Peter Stampfel, March 9, 2024; advertisement, *San Francisco Chronicle*, August 2, 1968, 25.
41 Beverly Walker, January 29, 2023; Beverly Walker, "Michelangelo and the Leviathan: The Making of *Zabriskie Point*," *Film Comment* 28, no. 5 (September–October 1992), 44, 46.
42 Peter Stampfel, March 9, 2024; Anthony Foutz, February 8, 2023; SA, 6, 7, 28; Beverly Walker, January 23, 2023. The Hollywood house where Shepard wrote *Operation Sidewinder* is located at 2604 Glen Green Street.
43 SA, 6.
44 Phyllis Willner, March 10, 2025; Anthony Foutz, February 8, 2023; Beverly Walker, emails, January 30 and February 1, 2023; Peter Stampfel, "Tribute by Peter Stampfel, Part 1," *Perfect Sound Forever*, December 2017, online.
45 Quoted in SA, 6; Beverly Walker, January 29, 2023.
46 Beverly Walker, January 29, 2023; Beverly Walker, "Michelangelo and the Leviathan: The Making of *Zabriskie Point*," *Film Comment* 28, no. 5 (September–October 1992), 38, 44, 46.
47 Harrison Starr, August 19, 2019.

48 Quoted in "Shepard, Sam," *Current Biography Yearbook 1979*, ed. Charles Moritz, et al. (New York: H. W. Wilson, 1979), 35.

49 Quoted in SA, 6; Sam Shepard to Michelangelo Antonioni, January 8, 1972, Archives of Ferrara Museum, Ferrara, Italy; Beverly Walker, email, January 28, 2023.

50 Anthony Foutz, February 2, 2023.

51 Rudy Wurlitzer, February 14, 2020.

52 Sam Shepard to Lee Kissman, November 18, 1968; quoted in MG, 1969.

## CHAPTER 6 SAM AND O-LAN

1 Sam Shepard, "In Fondest Memory of Billy Hart," *Village Voice*, January 22, 2008.

2 Johnny Dark to Lee Kissman, February 6, 2017; MC, 75; Lee Kissman, April 21, 2023.

3 Quoted in Bruce Fretts, "A Man with the Right Stuff," *Closer Weekly*, August 21, 2017, 57.

4 Charles Mingus III, October 8, 2019.

5 Charles Mingus III, December 8, 2024, and October 8, 2019.

6 Lee Kissman, April 21, 2023.

7 D[avid]. B. [Tipmore], "Theatre: 3 at the Old Reliable," *Village Voice*, August 21, 1969, 24.

8 Cecil Smith, "'Muzeeka' Staged by Theatre Group," *Los Angeles Times*, October 11, 1967, online.

9 Tony Barsha, March 15, 2019.

10 O-Lan Jones, "Running Off with Sam," *American Theatre Magazine*, August 4, 2017, online.

11 Ibid.

12 Tony Barsha, March 15, 2019; "Tony Barsha," Doollee.com.

13 Tony Barsha, email, April 3, 2019.

14 Tony Barsha, email, April 8, 2019.

15 Lee Kissman, October 21, 2021; Lee Kissman to Johnny Dark, June 2012.

16 O-Lan Jones, "Running Off with Sam," *American Theatre Magazine*, August 4, 2017, online.

17 Ibid.; JD.

18 Lee Kissman, October 20, 2021; Tony Barsha, March 15, 2019.

19 Tony Barsha, March 15, 2019.

20 Sam Shepard, "Trips," HGC; MG, 1969; quoted in DS, 65; JD.

21 Albert Poland, October 8, 2023; Georgia and Walter Hadler, October 19, 2019; "Instant Animal," HM, 69.

22 Sam Shepard to Jane and Roxanne Rogers, November 9, 1969.

23 Albert Poland, October 8, 2023.

24 Georgia Hadler, January 10, 2019.

25 Mel Gussow, "Sam Shepard: Writer on the Way Up," *New York Times*, November 12, 1969, 42.

26 Quoted in EO, 78; Georgia and Walter Hadler, January 10, 2019.

27 Albert Poland, October 8, 2023; Georgia and Walter Hadler, January 10, 2019. Kathleen Cramer was O-Lan's maid of honor.

28 Sam Shepard to Jane and Roxanne Rogers, November 9, 1969.

29 Georgia and Walter Hadler, January 10, 2019; Sam Shepard to Jane and Roxanne Rogers, November 9, 1969.

## CHAPTER 7 STRANGERS VS. FRIENDS

1 MG, 1969.

2 "LA MaMa Troupe to Do Two at McCarter," *Central New Jersey Home News*, March 5, 1970, 44.

3 Sam Shepard, "Visualization, Language and the Inner Library," *Drama Review* 21, no. 4 (Playwrights and Playwriting issue, December 1977), 54.

4 Sam Rogers to Roxanne Rogers, March 8, 1974; Jane Rogers, "On Sam Rogers," n.d.

5 The name Moss, which he would also use as a replacement in *The Late Henry Moss* (2000), derived from a rodeo man, Shepard said, "who had a cattle dog named Moss. I guess I always loved that name." Quoted in Michael Phillips, "Sam Shepard's Family Values," *Los Angeles Times*, November 8, 2000, F1; UH, 323, 333.

6 Robert Rockwell, "Theatre Intime: 'The Curse of Apollo,'" *Daily Princetonian*, March 11, 1970, 2.

7 Quoted in Ruth Miller, "The Campus Scene: "New Troupe Plans Three Performances at College Little Theater Next Week," *Leader-Herald* (NY), March 13, 1970, 5.

8 MG, 1969.

9 *Operation Sidewinder* program, Lincoln Center for the Performing Arts, 1970, 4; Louis Mofsie, February 22, 2023.

10 Robert Brustein, *Making Scenes: A Personal History of the Turbulent Years at Yale, 1966–1979* (New York: Random House, 1981), 73; "The Editors Reply," *Yale Daily News*, April 1, 1969, 2.

11 Sam Shepard, "Operation Sidewinder," draft, 1969, Michael Douglas Papers, U.S. Mss 176AN, box 27, folder 24, Wisconsin Center for Film and Theater Research.

12 MG, 1969; Robert Brustein, *Making Scenes: A Personal History of the Turbulent Years at Yale, 1966–1979* (New York: Random House, 1981), 78; Sam Zolotow, "Black Students Block Yale Play: 'Operation Sidewinder' Off Drama School's Schedule," *New York Times*, December 27, 1968, 38.

13 KC, 8.

14 Barbara Eda-Young, April 20, 2019.

15 Mel Gussow, "Sam Shepard: Writer on the Way Up," *New York Times*, November 12, 1969, 42.

16 Barbara Eda-Young, March 4, 2019.

17 Quoted in Howard Taubman, "Lincoln Center Faces the Crucial 1970s," *New York Times*, March 20, 1970, 50.

18 Quoted in Mel Gussow, "Sam Shepard: Writer on the Way Up," *New York Times*, November 12, 1969, 42; Albert Poland, October 8, 2023.

19 Sam Shepard to Lee Kissman, November 18, 1968; Barbara Eda-Young, April 20, 2019; Sam Shepard to Tennessee Williams, August 26, 1971, HGC; Tennessee Williams to Sam Shepard, September 10, 1971, HGC.

20 Barbara Eda-Young, April 20, 2019; MG, 1969.

21 John Lahr, "Postscript: Sam Shepard, Who Brought Rage and Rebellion Onstage," *New Yorker*, July 31, 2017, online.

22 Ibid.

23 Jasper Rees, "When Sam Shepard Was a Londoner," theartsdesk.com, December 4, 2016; John Lahr, "Postscript: Sam Shepard, Who Brought Rage and Rebellion Onstage," *New Yorker*, July 31, 2017, online; Barbara Eda-Young, April 20, 2019.

24 John Lahr, "Postscript: Sam Shepard, Who Brought Rage and Rebellion Onstage," *New Yorker*, July 31, 2017, online.

25 Peter Stampfel, March 9, 2024; Barbara Eda-Young, April 20, 2019.

26 Barbara Eda-Young, Ibid.

27 Louis Mofsie, February 22, 2023.

28 John Lahr heard one of the dancers shouting, "I'm a real Indian—not one of those painted, wooden imitations. I'm real. I'm real!" This was Gregory Borst, Mofsie remembered, who blew up at the cast about one of the actor's improper behavior toward Muriel Miguel. If he'd threatened to walk out, as Lahr noted in his diary, it was only Borst, not the other dancers. (John Lahr, "Postscript: Sam Shepard, Who Brought Rage and Rebellion Onstage," *New Yorker*, July 31, 2017, online; Louis Mofsie, February 23, 2023.)

29 Louis Mofsie, February 23, 2023; Barbara Eda-Young, April 20, 2019.

30 Quoted in Jim Moore, "The Gospels According to Durang and Shepard," *Los Angeles Times*, April 10, 1977, 46.

31 JW, 130; Clive Barnes, "Theater: A Sam Shepard Double Bill: Dramatic Cartoons Are Displayed in the Village," *New York Times*, April 2, 1970, 43; George Oppenheimer, "Sensory Overkill," *Newsday*, March 13, 1970, 7A.

32 Quoted in Robert Goldberg, "Sam Shepard: American Original," *Playboy*, March 1984, 112.

33 Albert Poland, email, March 9, 2025; Clive Barnes, "Theater: A Sam Shepard Double Bill: Dramatic Cartoons Are Displayed in the Village," *New York Times*, April 2, 1970, 43.

34 Albert Poland, October 8, 2023.

35 Tony Barsha, March 15, 2019; Albert Poland, October 8, 2023.

36 Peter Stampfel, "Tribute by Peter Stampfel, Part 3," *Perfect Sound Forever*, October–December 2017, online; advertisement, *The Unseen Hand* and *Forensic and the Navigators*, April 1970; Elia Kazan to Albert Poland, telegram, n.d.

37 Clive Barnes, "Theater: A Sam Shepard Double Bill: Dramatic Cartoons Are Displayed in the Village," *New York Times*, April 2, 1970, 43.

38 Albert Poland, October 8, 2023; Tony Barsha, March 5, 2019; Tony Barsha and Sam Shepard, film treatment of *The Unseen Hand*, 1970, D-O55, box 8, folder 41, UCD.
39 Tony Barsha, March 5, 2019; Albert Poland, October 8, 2023.
40 Tony Barsha, March 16, 2022; Albert Poland, October 8, 2023.
41 Peter Stampfel, "Tribute by Peter Stampfel, Part 3," *Perfect Sound Forever*, October–December 2017, online.
42 Quoted in Michael Feeney Callan, *Robert Redford: The Biography* (New York: Random House, 2012), 185. *The Unseen Hand*'s screenplay, written in April 1970, is located at UCD, box 8, folder 40.
43 Sam Shepard to Jane and Roxanne Rogers, April 7, 1970.
44 Albert Poland, October 8, 2023.
45 Roxanne Rogers, July 22, 2020; JD and JW, 131.
46 John O'Mahony, "The Write Stuff," *Guardian*, October 10, 2003, 22; Sam Shepard to Jane and Roxanne Rogers, April 29, 1970; Barbara Eda-Young, April 20, 2019; PK.
47 Peter Stampfel, March 9, 2024; DS, 70.
48 Sam Shepard to Jane and Roxanne Rogers, April 29, 1970; Cumberland County Deeds, 268–463, June 29, 1970.
49 Rudy Wurlitzer, February 14, 2020.
50 Rudy Wurlitzer, February 19, 2020.
51 Sam Shepard to Jane and Roxanne Rogers, July 22, 1970.
52 Hill Top Farm is located at 3253 Highway 209; Rudy Wurlitzer, February 19, 2020.

## CHAPTER 8 THE GOTHIC CROW

1 Patti Smith, *Just Kids* (New York: Ecco, 2010), 171.
2 Quoted in Peter Stampfel, "Tribute by Peter Stampfel, Part 3," *Perfect Sound Forever*, October–December 2017, online.
3 Patti Smith, *Just Kids* (New York: Ecco, 2010), 171; Patti Smith, "Remembering Sam Shepard," St. Ann and the Holy Trinity Church, Brooklyn, NY, December 5, 2017; Patti Smith, interview by David Remnick, the New Yorker Festival, October 11, 2019.
4 Quoted in Michael Almereyda, "Sam Shepard," *Interview*, September 24, 2011, online.
5 PK.
6 Patti Smith, "My Albertine," in Albertine Sarrazzin, *Astragal*, 1965, trans. Patsy Southgate (New York: New Directions, 2013), xiii.
7 PK.
8 Ibid.
9 Quoted in Patricia Morrisroe, *Mapplethorpe: A Biography* (New York: Random House, 1995), 92.
10 PK.

11 *Please Kill Me: The Uncensored Oral History of Punk*, ed. Legs McNeil and Gillian McCain (New York: Grove Press, 1996), 105; Patti Smith, "Remembering Sam Shepard," St. Ann and the Holy Trinity Church, Brooklyn, NY, December 5, 2017.

12 Patti Smith, *Just Kids* (New York: Ecco, 2010), 171.

13 Quoted in ibid., 172–74.

14 Peter Stampfel, "Tribute by Peter Stampfel, Part 3," *Perfect Sound Forever*, October–December 2017, online.

15 Patti Smith, *Just Kids* (New York: Ecco, 2010), 172–74.

16 EO, 89.

17 Arthur Miller, *Timebends* (New York: Grove, 1987), 513.

18 Patricia Morrisroe, *Mapplethorpe: A Biography* (New York: Random House, 1995), 93. This poem would be expanded upon in her poem "Sam Shepard: 9 Random Years [7+2]," which was published in Shepard's *Angel City, Curse of the Starving Class & Other Plays* (1977).

19 Patti Smith, "Remembering Sam Shepard," St. Ann and the Holy Trinity Church, Brooklyn, NY, December 5, 2017.

20 Maureen Dowd, "Rock Star Patti Smith, Making Paris Swoon," *New York Times*, September 19, 2019, online.

21 My gratitude to Lucy Sante for providing me with the *New York Flyer* interview; I was first made aware of its existence while reading her article on Patti Smith, "The Mother Courage of Rock," *New York Review of Books*, February 9, 2012.

22 Quoted in "Patti Smith Susses Media," *New York Flyer* 81, April 29, 1971.

23 Ibid.

24 Quoted in Victor Bockris and Roberta Bayley, *Patti Smith: An Unauthorized Biography* (New York: Simon & Schuster, 1999), 69.

25 Patricia Morrisroe, *Mapplethorpe: A Biography* (New York: Random House, 1995), 92; "Monday's Muse: Vali Myers," anyonegirl.com, May 19, 2013; Sandy Daley and Josh Lawson (assistant), email, January 12, 2025. *Patti Having Her Knee Tattooed* premiered alongside *Robert Having His Nipple Pierced*, with Patti Smith as musical accompaniment, at the Museum of Modern Art's Cineprobe series in November 1971. Sandy Daley and Josh Lawson (assistant), email, March 10, 2025.

26 Patricia Morrisroe, *Mapplethorpe: A Biography* (New York: Random House, 1995), 92; Sandy Daley and Josh Lawson (assistant), emails, February 24 and 26, 2025.

27 JD.

28 Patti Smith, *Just Kids* (New York: Ecco, 2010), 184; Patti Smith, "Remembering Sam Shepard," St. Ann and the Holy Trinity Church, Brooklyn, NY, December 5, 2017.

29 Quoted in Patti Smith, *Just Kids* (New York: Ecco, 2010), 185.

30 Murray Mednick, March 13, 2019.

31 Quoted in Samantha Weinberg, "Pale Writer," *Harpers & Queen* (UK), December 1996, 153; Albert Poland, October 8, 2023.

32 Quoted in Allan Wallach, "Stage: Improvisational Frolic," *Newsday*, March 9, 1971, 60A; Bill Mohr, January 4, 2019; Albert Poland, October 8, 2023.

33 Tony Barsha, March 15, 2019.

34 Lee Kissman, March 4, 2023; Johnny Dark, July 22, 2020.

35 Andee Nathanson, February 21, 2023; quoted in Jeremy Gerard, *Wynn Place Show: A Biased History of the Rollicking Life & Extreme Times of Wynn Handman and the American Place Theatre* (Hanover, NH: Smith and Kraus, 2013), 64–65.

36 Roxanne Rogers, July 6, 2024.

37 Quoted in Maureen Dowd, "Rock Star Patti Smith, Making Paris Swoon," *New York Times*, September 19, 2019, online.

38 Quoted in Victor Bockris and Roberta Bayley, *Patti Smith: An Unauthorized Biography* (New York: Simon & Schuster, 1999), 71.

39 EO, 89; Georgia and Walter Hadler, October 19, 2019.

40 Peter Stampfel, "Tribute by Peter Stampfel, Part 3," *Perfect Sound Forever*, October–December 2017, online; Victor Bockris and Roberta Bayley, *Patti Smith: An Unauthorized Biography* (New York: Simon & Schuster, 1999), 75; BB, 91; Patti Smith, "My Buddy," *New Yorker*, August 1, 2017, online.

41 Patti Smith, *Just Kids* (New York: Ecco, 2010), 185.

42 Patti Smith, "Flash Flood. Water," PK.

43 Sam Shepard, "Long Night's Journey into Day," PK.

44 Robb Baker, "Off Off and Away: A Dead Crow on Her Belly," *After Dark* 7, no. 5 (September 1974), 77.

45 FFL, 145, 147; Pop Scene Service, "Fans Begin to See Her as a Girl: But Patti's Not the Usual Female Sex Symbol," *Columbia Record* (SC), July 31, 1971, 9B.

46 Quoted in Robert Goldberg, "Sam Shepard: Off-Broadway's Street Cowboy," *Rolling Stone College Papers*, Winter 1980, 44; Patti Smith, *Just Kids* (New York: Ecco, 2010), 185.

47 FFL, 157.

48 Quoted in Patti Smith, *Just Kids* (New York: Ecco, 2010), 185, 186.

49 Allen Wright, "Theatre," *Scotsman*, April 3, 1971; Cordelia Oliver, "Cowboy Mouth at the Traverse, Edinburgh," *Guardian*, April 3, 1971, 12; Michael Rudman to Toby Cole, June 2, 1971, National Library Scotland.

50 Quoted in EO, 90; Allen Wright, "Theatre," *Scotsman*, April 3, 1971; Cordelia Oliver, "*Cowboy Mouth* at the Traverse, Edinburgh," *Guardian*, April 3, 1971, 12; Michael Rudman to Toby Cole, June 2, 1971, National Library Scotland.

51 Program for *The Cowboy Mouth*, April 29, 1971; quoted in Leonard Lyons, "Lyons Den," *New York Post*, April 26, 1971; Sam Shepard, "Autobiography: Sam Shepard," *News of the American Place* III, no. 3 (April 1971), 1–2.

52 HM, 49–50.

53 The Holy Modal Rounders and the Velvet Underground played the weekend of January 9–11, 1969, at the Boston Tea Party in Boston, Massachusetts. For a description

of the show, see: Richie Unterberger, *White Light/White Heat: The Velvet Underground Day by Day* (London, UK: Jawbone Press, 2009): 223.

54 Tony Barsha, March 15, 2019. See Sam Shepard, *Back Bog Beast Bait* (University of Delaware, 1969).

55 Quoted in Bottoms, CC, 57; quoted in EO, 93.

56 Tony Barsha, March 15, 2019; Patti Smith, *Just Kids* (New York: Ecco, 2010), 186; EO, 91.

57 Michael Feingold, "The Punk Rock Cowboy," *Village Voice*, July 31, 2017; EO, 90.

58 Quoted in Deborah S. Greenhut, "Turn Up the Amp: Cowboy Mouth," *OOBR: The Off Off Broadway Review*, March 2004; quoted in RG, 136; EO, 89.

59 Georgia and Walter Hadler, January 10, 2019.

60 Tony Barsha, March 15, 2019; Peter Stampfel, March 9, 2024; Quoted in DS, 73.

61 Tony Barsha, March 15, 2019; TP, 63–64; Peter Stampfel, "Tribute by Peter Stampfel, Part 3," *Perfect Sound Forever*, October–December 2017, online.

62 HM, 54. Shepard published *Hawk Moon* from London in January 1973.

63 Quoted in Robb Baker, "Off Off and Away: A Dead Crow on Her Belly," *After Dark* 7, no. 5 (September 1974), 77; quoted in Victor Bockris and Roberta Bayley, *Patti Smith: An Unauthorized Biography* (New York: Simon & Schuster, 1999), 70; quoted in PH, 95.

## CHAPTER 9 THE LONDON FRINGE

1 Quoted in Brian Case, "Slay 'Em Again, Sam," *Time Out* (London), no. 1350 (July 3–10, 1996), 24.

2 Steven Putzel, "An American Cowboy on the English Fringe: Sam Shepard's London Audience," *Modern Drama* 36 (1993), 131; quoted in Brian Case, "Slay 'Em Again, Sam," *Time Out* (London), no. 1350 (July 3–10, 1996), 24.

3 Quoted in Jasper Rees, "American Playwright in London," *Independent* (London), June 26, 1996, 8; Michael White, "Underground Landscapes," *Guardian*, February 20, 1972, 8.

4 Nancy Meckler, May 10, 2023; quoted in Jasper Rees, "American Playwright in London," *Independent* (London), June 26, 1996, 8; Nancy Meckler, May 10, 2023; TP, 231.

5 Nancy Meckler, May 10, 2023.

6 Charles Marowitz, "America's Great Hopes, White or Black?," *New York Times*, April 13, 1969, D3; Sam Shepard to Jane and Roxanne Rogers, November 16, 1971.

7 Ibid.; Sam Shepard, "Song for Marlene." The song was recorded on Michael Moorcock and the Deep Fix's album *The New World's Fair* (1975); quoted in KC, 12.

8 RG, 104; Sam Shepard, "Preface to the Revised Edition," *Tooth of Crime (Second Dance)* (New York: Vintage, 2006), ix; Sam Shepard, "Tooth of Crime: Intro to New Re-write," 2005, HRC.

9 KC, 11.

10 Sam Shepard, "Preface to the Revised Edition," *The Tooth of Crime (Second Dance)* (New York: Vintage Books, 2006), x.

11 Charles Marowitz, "Sam Shepard: Sophisticate Abroad," *Village Voice*, September 7, 1972, 59; advertisement, *Los Angeles Times*, September 9, 1973, online; quoted in Stanley Eichelbaum, "The Dean of Counter Culture Theater," *San Francisco Chronicle*, April 23, 1975, 24.

12 TP, xi, 5; Lee Kissman, January 21, 2023; Lee Kissman, March 4, 2023; Sam Shepard to Roxanne Rogers, no day or month, 1972.

13 P. D. Ouspensky, *In Search of the Miraculous: Fragments of an Unknown Teaching* (New York: Harcourt, Brace & World, 1949), 219. Sam Shepard's copy.

14 Sam Shepard, notebook entitled "Fractured," Nova Scotia (Summer 1972): 17–19, box 27, folder 2, Sam Shepard Collection 1943–2017, HGC.

15 Roxanne Rogers, January 1, 2025; SP, 232.

16 Roxanne Rogers, email, February 3, 2020.

17 Nancy Meckler, May 10, 2023.

18 O-Lan Shepard to Roxanne Rogers, January 16, 1973.

19 Quoted in Naseem Khan, "The Other Theatre," *Evening Standard*, June 2, 1974, 13; Nancy Meckler, May 10, 2023.

20 Charles Marowitz, "Sam Shepard: Sophisticate Abroad," *Village Voice*, September 7, 1972, 59.

21 Ibid.; Sam Shepard, "Emotional Tyranny," in KC, 22.

22 Sam Shepard, Trans-American Journal, 1972, box 26, folder 1, Sam Shepard Collection 1943–2017, HGC.

23 TP, 223.

24 Roxanne Rogers, text message, December 19, 2024; Roxanne Rogers, July 9, 2024.

25 Sandy Rogers, July 28, 2023; "Woman Dies in Cajon Car Crash," *San Bernardino Sun*, November 15, 1971, 29. Sam Rogers and Ruth Maxwell were married in Los Angeles on September 30, 1969; Ruth remarried in 1972.

26 Robert Frost, 1905 or 1906, "The Death of the Hired Man."

27 Sam Shepard to Jane Elaine Rogers, October 9, 1972; Sam Shepard, Trans-American Journal, 1972, box 26, folder 1, Sam Shepard Collection 1943–2017, HGC.

28 Johnny Dark, July 22, 2020; JD; TP, 5.

29 P. D. Ouspensky, *The Psychology of Man's Possible Evolution* (New York: Vintage Books, 1974), 89.

30 Nancy Meckler, May 10, 2023; notebook entry, January 23, 2001, HRC; Jonathan Cott, Conversation with Sam Shepard, typescript of *Rolling Stone* article with revisions by Shepard and correspondence, March 1986, series IV, container 28.11, Sam Shepard Papers 1965–2009, HRC.

31 Murray Mednick, March 13, 2019. In London, Mednick introduced Shepard to William S. Burroughs, whom Mednick knew from the New York drug scene; the novelist got drunk and made passes at them, according to Mednick, so they fled.

32 Murray Mednick, March 13, 2019.

33 TP, 13.

34 Quoted in Brian Case, "Slay 'Em Again, Sam," *Time Out* (London), no. 1350 (July 3–10, 1996), 25.

35 Sam Shepard, "Less than Half a Minute," *Time Out* (London), July 12–18, 1974, 16–17. Patti Smith had covertly visited Shepard in London in November 1972.

36 FFL, 301.

37 FFL, 280.

38 FFL, 301; KC, 14; FFL, 282; "Theatre: Fringe," *Time Out* (London), March 1–7, 1974, 51.

39 JW, 82; Ralph Cook, "Notes on *Chicago*," in Sam Shepard, *Five Plays* (Indianapolis: Bobbs-Merrill, 1967), 2.

40 Quoted in Michael White, "Underground Landscapes," *Guardian*, February 20, 1972, 8; Sam Shepard, reminiscence of Stephen Rea, no title, March 2, 1984, HRC.

41 Quoted in Alexis Soloski, "True East," *Village Voice*, June 25–July 1, 2008, 30.

42 Ibid.; CS, 13; KC, 26.

43 Display ad, "Theatre: Fringe," *Time Out* (London), March 1–7, 1974, 51.

44 Shepard largely based the plot of *Geography of a Horse Dreamer* on the 1935 farce *Three Men on a Horse* by John Cecil Holm and George Abbott and D. H. Lawrence's short story "The Rocking-Horse Winner," later made into a short film by Michael Almereyda in 1997. See Joel Schechter, review of *Geography of a Horse Dreamer*, *Educational Theatre Journal* 26, no. 3 (October 1974), 401–3. *Geography of a Horse Dreamer* was filmed for TV with a different cast and aired on ITV on March 31, 1974.

45 KC, 24; Joel Schechter, review of *Geography of a Horse Dreamer*, *Educational Theatre Journal* 26, no. 3 (October 1974), 403.

46 Quoted in Jasper Rees, "Theatre: American Playwright in London," *Independent* (London), June 26, 1996, 8; O-Lan Jones, program note for *Action*, *Little Ocean*, and *The Unseen Hand*, Black Box Performing Arts Center, September 21–October 8, 2023.

47 Sam Shepard, *Little Ocean*, March 1974, Sam Shepard Collection 1943–2017, HGC, 8, 22.

48 Stephen Rea, "An Appreciation by the Actor Stephen Rea," *Guardian*, August 6, 2017, online.

49 Peter Ansorge, "*Cowboy Mouth/Little Ocean*," *Plays and Players* 21, no. 8 (May 1974), 45.

50 Roxanne Rogers, December 29, 2019.

51 Sam Shepard, "Visualization, Language and the Inner Library," *Drama Review* 21, no. 4 (Playwrights and Playwriting issue, December 1977), 57.

52 CS, 12; quoted in Gary Grant, "Writing as a Process of Performing the Self: Sam Shepard's Notebooks," *Modern Drama* 34, no. 4 (Winter 1991), 563.

53 FFL, 169; Jeanne Miller, "They Said His Novels Were Crazy . . . So He Writes Plays," *San Francisco Examiner*, March 7, 1975, 33.

54 Nancy Meckler, May 10, 2023.

55 TP, 15.

56 TP, 19.

## CHAPTER 10 CALIFORNIA DREAMING

1 TP, 228; MC, 121.

2 Philip Rhodes, email, Mill Valley Library, June 5, 2018; RT, 4; Scarlett Dark to Jane and Roxanne Rogers, January 11, 1975.

3 Bernard Weiner, "Playwright Sam Shepard Turns Director for His Plays," *San Francisco Examiner*, April 27, 1975, 13.

4 Sean Elder, "Sam Shepard at the Magic," *Backstage Bay Area, SF Gate*, May 12, 2014: Online.

5 Quoted in ibid.

6 *It Takes a Lunatic*, directed by Billy Lyons, Seth Isler, and Kim Ferraro (Exemplar Productions, 2019); Bernard Weiner, "Playwright Sam Shepard Turns Director for His Plays," *San Francisco Examiner*, April 27, 1975, 13.

7 Sam Shepard to the Magic Theatre, n.d., KS; Sam Shepard to Lee Kissman, May 24, 1975.

8 "Corte Maderan's Plays Win Fifth Theater Award," *Independent Journal* (Corte Madera, CA), May 23, 1975, 38; quoted in Jonathan Cott, typescript of *Rolling Stone* article with revisions by Shepard and correspondence, March 1986, series IV, container 28.11, Sam Shepard Papers 1965–2009, HRC.

9 Sam Shepard, "Fractured," unproduced screenplay, 1975, 27, 73. Courtesy of Michael Almereyda.

10 HM, 40.

11 Quoted in Sam Shepard interview on Criterion Collection DVD (2007) of *Days of Heaven*, directed by Terrence Malick, 1978.

12 Michael Pye, "Dream Maverick," *Observer*, March 26, 1989, A5; Patti Smith, "Sam Shepard: 9 Random Years [7+2]," in AC, 242; quoted in Patti Hartigan, "Sam Shepard: The Legendary Playwright, Actor and Private Man of Action Sits Still for an Interview," *Boston Globe*, August 18, 1996, N5; Sam Shepard, "Fractured," unproduced screenplay, 1975, 22, 27. Courtesy of Michael Almereyda.

13 Johnny Dark, July 19, 2020.

14 Quoted in Kristopher Tapley, "Christian Bale and Sam Rockwell on Early Acting Days and Reuniting for 'Vice,'" *Variety*, December 13, 2018, online; Sandy Rogers, July 28, 2023.

15 Quoted in Sam Shepard and John Lion, transcript of interview with *Newsweek*, July 26, 1976, carton 4, folder 4.54 (BANC MSS 81/184), Magic Theatre records, Bancroft Library, University of California, Berkeley.

16 Sam Shepard, "Man Fly," unpublished play, 1975, American Place Theatre Company records 1953–2010, NYPL. The result of this period was Shepard's two-act remake of Marlowe's *Doctor Faustus* called *Man Fly (A Play, with Music, in Two Acts)*, which the American Place Theatre rejected and was never produced or published.

17 RT, 4; undated note from O-Lan, Howard Gotlieb Center. On page 4 of the *Rolling Thunder Logbook*, Shepard rewrites the note: "Dylan called—will call back later."

18 RT, 5.

19 RT, 6.

20 Julien Levy, "My Father Was Left Out of Martin Scorsese's Bob Dylan Movie," *Vice*, September 18, 2019, online; interview with Sam Shepard, *Rolling Thunder Revue: A Bob Dylan Story*, directed by Martin Scorsese (Grey Water Park Productions, 2019); Robert Goldberg, "Sam Shepard: Off-Broadway's Street Cowboy," *Rolling Stone College Papers*, Winter 1980, 44; Sam Shepard, "Rolling Thunder" notebook, 1975, box 4, folder E, HGC.

21 List of tour personnel, Rolling Thunder Revue, 1975, container 24.8, HRC; quoted in Chris O'Dell, with Katherine Ketcham, *Miss O'Dell: My Hard Days and Long Nights with the Beatles, the Stones, Bob Dylan, Eric Clapton, and the Women Who Loved Them* (New York: Simon & Schuster, 2009), 320, 321.

22 Quoted in Chris O'Dell, with Katherine Ketcham, *Miss O'Dell: My Hard Days and Long Nights with the Beatles, the Stones, Bob Dylan, Eric Clapton, and the Women Who Loved Them* (New York: Simon & Schuster, 2009), 321; interview with Bob Dylan, *Rolling Thunder Revue: A Bob Dylan Story*, directed by Martin Scorsese (Grey Water Park Productions, 2019).

23 David Remnick, "Let's Celebrate the Bob Dylan Nobel Win," *New Yorker*, October 13, 2016, online.

24 Interview with Sam Shepard for *Rolling Thunder Revue: A Bob Dylan Story* by Martin Scorsese, 2019.

25 *Renaldo and Clara*, directed by Bob Dylan (Circuit Films, 1978).

26 RT, 17, 76.

27 David Sterritt, "Two Sam Shepard Plays Inventively Done at La MaMa," *Christian Science Monitor*, October 19, 1983, online; RT, 76.

28 Sam Shepard, *The Sad Lament of Pecos Bill on the Eve of Killing His Wife* (stage play), July 1976, series I, container 12, Sam Shepard Papers 1965–2011, HRC. *The Sad Lament* premiered at the inaugural Bay Area Playwrights Festival in San Francisco in October 1976, directed by Robert Woodruff.

29 Quoted in Chris O'Dell, with Katherine Ketcham, *Miss O'Dell: My Hard Days and Long Nights with the Beatles, the Stones, Bob Dylan, Eric Clapton, and the Women Who Loved Them* (New York: Simon & Schuster, 2009), 326.

30 RT, 132.

31 Ben Brantley, "Sam Shepard, Whose Plays Forged a New Frontier, Dies at 73," *New York Times*, August 1, 2017, A20; Sam Shepard, "Rolling Thunder" notebook, 1975, box 4, folder E, HGC; quoted in Chris O'Dell, with Katherine Ketcham, *Miss O'Dell: My Hard Days and Long Nights with the Beatles, the Stones, Bob Dylan, Eric Clapton, and the Women Who Loved Them* (New York: Simon & Schuster, 2009), 327.

32 Quoted in ibid., 327–28.

33 Quoted in ibid., 329–30.

34 Quoted in David Yaffe, *Reckless Daughter: A Portrait of Joni Mitchell* (New York: Sarah Crichton Books, 2017), 204, 206–7.

35 RT, 174; quoted in Ruthie Fierberg, "Actor Ethan Hawke Makes the Case for Sam Shepard's Genius," *Playbill*, January 19, 2019, online.

36 Quoted in Johnny Dark, "Sam Shepard on Myths and Heroes," *San Francisco*, September 1983, 70; Sam Shepard, "Rolling Thunder" notebook, 1975, box 4, folder E, HGC. "Everything counts" was one of Johnny Dark's favorite sayings. See SD.

37 RT: 176, 177.

38 RT, 176, 177.

39 TSD; RT, 98.

40 RT, 4.

41 Michael Meyer, Scott Goldberg, and Karen Johnson, "The Flying Y Ranch," Diaries and Ranches folder, Mill Valley Library History Room.

42 Heidi Benson, "Sam Shepard's Kid in Writing Game," *San Francisco Chronicle*, February 2, 2003, online.

43 Mike Davis, *Ecology of Fear: Los Angeles and the Imagination of Disaster*, 1988 (Vintage Books, 1999).

44 Davis, *Ecology of Fear*; quoted in Sam Shepard and John Lion, transcript of interview with *Newsweek*, July 26, 1976, carton 4, folder 4.54 (BANC MSS 81/184), Magic Theatre records, Bancroft Library, University of California, Berkeley; Jim Moore, "The Gospels According to Durang and Shepard," *Los Angeles Times*, April 10, 1977, 46.

45 Shepard wrote another Hollywood play in the fall of 1976, which was not as successful, titled *Seduced*, about the aeronautical tycoon Howard Hughes, who fell into madness. *Seduced* premiered at Trinity Repertory Company's Lederer Theater in Providence, Rhode Island, on April 21, 1978. It opened in New York on January 29, 1979, directed by Jack Gelber at the American Place Theatre, with Rip Torn as Henry Hackamore.

46 Quoted in Sam Shepard and John Lion, transcript of interview with *Newsweek*, July 26, 1976, carton 4, folder 4.54 (BANC MSS 81/184), Magic Theatre records, Bancroft Library, University of California, Berkeley; Sam Shepard, "Angel City (A Moving Picture Show) in Two Acts," undated typescript, from the library of the dramaturge Norman Frisch, online.

47 FFL, 68–69.

48 Quoted in Naseem Khan, "Free Form Playwright," *Time Out* (London), July 13–17, 1972, 31.

49 Quoted in Bruce Weber, "Spring Theater/Visions of America; An Unusual Case of Role Reversal," *New York Times*, February 27, 2000, sec. 2, 10; quoted in Bernard Weiner, "Shepard Takes On Hollywood," *San Francisco Chronicle*, July 2, 1976, 41.

50 Quoted in Alan Licht, "An Interview with Rudy Wurlitzer," *Believer* 98 (May 1, 2013), online; TP, 227.

51 Ibid.

52 Sam Shepard, "Sweet Bed-Ridden," September 1976, series II, box 4, folder C, Sam Shepard Collection 1943–2017, HGC; quoted in Michael Almereyda, "After the Rehearsal: Flirting with *Disaster*: Discussing *Days of Heaven* and Dylan Classics with Sam Shepard," *Village Voice*, April 20, 2004, online.

53 DS, 159; quoted in Michael Almereyda, "After the Rehearsal: Flirting with *Disaster*: Discussing *Days of Heaven* and Dylan Classics with Sam Shepard," *Village Voice*, April 20, 2004, online.

54 TP, 29; quoted in JW, 198.

55 TP, 30; quoted in Jordan Raup, "Brooke Adams on the Enduring Beauty of *Days of Heaven* and Terrence Malick's Method," *Film Stage*, December 7, 2023, online; DS, 159.

56 Quoted in Jordan Raup, "Brooke Adams on the Enduring Beauty of *Days of Heaven* and Terrence Malick's Method," *Film Stage*, December 7, 2023, online.

57 Gene Seymour, "Sam Shepard Could Do Everything," CNN.com, August 1, 2017.

58 Lee Kissman, November 24, 2024. Shepard joined the faculty of the Padua Writers Workshop (later the Padua Hills Playwrights' Festival) in the first week of July 1978 in Claremont, California. It was a three-week program led by Murray Mednick, who'd received a teaching job at nearby La Verne University. Other attendees from OOB included Lee Kissman, Barbara Eda-Young, Walter Hadler, Bob Glaudini, Michael Smith, María Irene Fornés, John Steppling, and John O'Hara. At Padua, Shepard wrote *Red Woman*, which was performed by Bob Glaudini, a comical monologue named for the red stone statue of a genuflecting Mexican woman on the campus. The future Pulitzer Prize– and Tony Award–winning playwright David Henry Hwang was a student there, and he performed jazz violin to accompany *Red Woman*. "I learned to be a playwright at Padua," Hwang told me. David Henry Hwang, July 16, 2023.

## CHAPTER 11 **BLOOD LINES**

1 Jack Suderman, May 23, 2018; Johnny Dark to Lee Kissman, March 29, 2013; "Sam Shepard, Actor and Playwright, Dies at 73," *Independent Journal* (Corte Madera, CA), August 1, 2017, online; Don Shirley, "Searching for Sam Shepard," *Washington Post*, January 14, 1979, online.

2 Quoted in Michael VerMeulen, "Sam Shepard: Yes, Yes, Yes," *Esquire*, February 1980, 86; quoted in Jennifer Dunning, "A Nagrin Dance to a Shepard Libretto," *New York Times*, May 31, 1979, C13. *Jacaranda* opened at St. Clement's Church in New York on June 7, 1979.

3 Quoted in SB; Johnny Dark, July 22, 2020. After *Koko*, Shepard wrote *Inacoma*, a three-hour jazz opera, with sixteen actors accompanied by eight members of the San Francisco Jazz Ensemble, inspired by the Karen Ann Quinlan euthanasia controversy in 1975. *Inacoma*, which never had a formal script, opened at the Magic Theatre under Shepard's direction on March 18, 1977, and was largely well received.

4 Johnny Dark, July 19, 2020.

5 CS, 39; Jack Suderman, May 23, 2018; Johnny Dark to Lee Kissman, February 6, 2017; Sam Shepard to Johnny Dark, August 29, 2005, WC; Johnny Dark, July 19, 2020; TP, 60.

6 Johnny Dark, *People I May Know: The Uncollected Essays, Photographs, Letters, Notebooks, Commentaries and Tales of Johnny Dark* (New York: Little Bear Press, 2006), n.p.

7 Johnny Dark to Lee Kissman, June 12, 2013; O-Lan Shepard to Sam Shepard, March 22, 1977, HGC.

8 Johnny Dark, July 19, 2020.

9 Sam Shepard, "Fractured," unproduced screenplay, 84.

10 Sam Shepard to Roxanne Rogers, December 8, 1979.

11 TP, 321.

12 CS, 40.

13 Quoted in Roger Downey, "Inside the Words," *Time Out* (London), April 22–28, 1977, 11.

14 Sam Rogers to Sam Shepard, January 4, 1976, and February 24, 1976, HGC.

15 Quoted in JA, 148.

16 Sam Shepard et al., "American Experimental Theatre: Then and Now," *Performing Arts Journal* 2, no. 2 (Autumn 1977), 14. Robert Brustein commissioned *Suicide in* $B^{\flat}$ for Yale Rep, where it opened on October 15, 1976.

17 Sam Shepard to Brandeis University, 1976, online; Sam Shepard et al., "American Experimental Theatre: Then and Now," *Performing Arts Journal* 2, no. 2 (Autumn 1977), 14. Shepard would be honored with a second Brandeis Creative Arts Award in April 1984.

18 Quoted in JA, 148.

19 Sam Shepard and John Lion, transcript of interview with *Newsweek*, July 26, 1976, carton 4, folder 4.54 (BANC MSS 81/184), Magic Theatre records, Bancroft Library, University of California, Berkeley; quoted in Roger Downey, "Inside the Words," *Time Out* (London), April 22–28, 1977, 11; Dan Sullivan, "Shepard's 'Starving Class' in London," *Los Angeles Times*, May 27, 1977, View, 1.

20 SP, 163.

21 Michiko Kakutani, "Myths, Dreams, Realities: Sam Shepard's America," *New York Times*, January 29, 1984, B26.

22 Sam Shepard and John Lion, transcript of interview with *Newsweek*, July 26, 1976, carton 4, folder 4.54 (BANC MSS 81/184), Magic Theatre records, Bancroft Library, University of California, Berkeley.

23 SP, 155, 167, 173, 174.

24 Quoted in Mel Gussow, "Papp Halves New Season at Beaumont," *New York Times*, August 24, 1976, 20; quoted in Roger Downey, "Inside the Words," *Time Out* (London), April 22–28, 1977, 11; Nancy Meckler, email, May 29, 2023.

25 Nancy Meckler, email, May 29, 2023; Victoria Radin, "Small Rooms—Open Spaces," *Observer*, April 24, 1977, 26; Michael Billington, "Curse of the Starving Class," *Guardian*, April 22, 1977, 10.

26 Douglas Watt, "In the End, Emptiness," *Daily News*, March 3, 1978, 55.

27 Sam Shepard, "Long Gone," May 11, 1971, PK.

28 Sandy Rogers, July 28, 2023.

29 Roxanne Rogers, email, February 3, 2020; JW, 170; Roxanne Rogers, email, January 31, 2020.

30 TP, 223; SP, 117.

31 Sandy Rogers, July 28, 2023.

32 Walter V. Addiego, "A Hilarious One-Act by Shepard," *San Francisco Examiner*, October 26, 1976, 27; quoted in Sara Holdren, "Director Robert Woodruff Remembers Sam Shepard," *Vulture*, August 1, 2017, online.

33 Alexis Soloski, "Sam Shepard Takes Stock of *Buried Child* and the Writer's Life," *New York Times*, January 31, 2016, Late edition (East Coast), AR5.

34 Al, 45; SP, 89; AL, 6, 44.

35 Chris Jones, May 24, 2021.

36 Alexis Soloski, "An Urban Cowboy Returns to Broadway," *New York Times*, January 31, 2016, AR5; quoted in Carol Rosen, *Sam Shepard: A "Poetic Rodeo"* (New York: Palgrave Macmillan, 2004), 230–31.

37 Thomas P. Adler, "Repetition and Regression in *Curse of the Starving Class* and *Buried Child*," in CC, 121; SP, 122, 124.

38 Alexis Soloski, "An Urban Cowboy Returns to Broadway," *New York Times*, January 31, 2016, AR5; Peter Marks, "Sam Shepard Is Happy to Be on Broadway but It's Just a Visit," *New York Times*, May 28, 1996, C11; Irene Oppenheim, "Sam Shepard and Bob Dylan," *Threepenny Review* 1 (Winter–Spring 1980), 20.

39 Quoted in Sylvie Drake, "Sam Shepard: A Play for Every Life Style," *Los Angeles Times*, October 21, 1979, Calendar, N1.

40 BB, 25.

41 SB; Jeff Gordinier, "Q&A with Sam Shepard," *Details,* July 2008, online; Gwynne Watkins, "Sam Shepard Gives a Rare Interview, Thinks Safe House Could've Been Better," *GQ*, June 11, 2012, online.

42 David Ansen, "The Reluctant Saint," *Newsweek*, November 17, 1980, 117.

43 Quoted in JW, 220.

44 Johnny Dark to Sam Shepard, February 16, 1979, HGC.

45 O-Lan Shepard to Sam Shepard, February 6, 1979, HGC.

46 Sam Shepard, "4/79—Santa Fe, N.M.," WC; quoted in SB; Roxanne Rogers, email, December 29, 2019.

47 Jane Rogers, "On Sam Rogers," n.d.; quoted in Robert Coe, "Saga of Sam Shepard," *New York Times Magazine*, November 23, 1980, 123; TP, 48.

## CHAPTER 12 THE WOLF AND THE SHEEP

1 Eileen Blumenthal, *Joseph Chaikin: Exploring the Boundaries of Theater* (New York: Cambridge University Press, 1984), 171, 172.

2 CS, 43; Sam Shepard, "Snake Eyes," 1974, box 22, folder 4, Sam Shepard Collection 1943–2017, HGC.

3 Stanley Eichelbaum, "The Avant-Garde Speaks in 'Tongues,'" *San Francisco Examiner*, June 9, 1978, 25; Mel Gussow, "A Shepard Joint Effort," *New York Times*, November 16, 1979, C6; Mel Gussow, "Intimate Monologues That Speak to the Mind and Heart," *New York Times*, December 9, 1979, D3.

4 *Tongues* opened at the Magic Theatre, performed by Chaikin with music and dialogue by Shepard, on June 7, 1978.

5 Sam Shepard to Roxanne Rogers, December 8, 1979.

6 MC, 127–28.

7 MC, 129, 133.

8 MC, 140.

9 Johnny Dark, July 19, 2020.

10 MC, 140–41; see MC, 76–77.

11 Sam Shepard to Roxanne Rogers, December 8, 1979; MC, 142.

12 SD; Sam Shepard, "Knowledge of the Seven Steps (Synthetic Tears)," stage play handwritten draft, November 1979, series I, container 8.1, Sam Shepard Papers 1965–2011, HRC.

13 Quoted in Ann McFerran, "Poet of Post-War Americana," *Time Out*, December 4-10, 1981, 24-25: 25; Quoted in Johnny Dark, "The 'True West' Interviews," *West Coast Plays* 9 (Summer 1981), 59.

14 SP, 9.

15 SP, 3.

16 SP, 49, 57.

17 *California Typewriter*, directed by Doug Nichol (American Buffalo Pictures, 2017).

18 Michiko Kakutani, "Myths, Dreams, Realities: Sam Shepard's America," *New York Times*, January 29, 1984, B1; quoted in Don Shewey, "The True Story of 'True West,'" *Village Voice*, November 30, 1982, 115; Bruce Weber, "Spring Theater/Visions of America; An Unusual Case of Role Reversal," *New York Times*, February 27, 2000, online.

19 John McDaniel, August 1, 2019; Johnny Dark, July 19, 2020.

20 Graeme Wood, "Sam Shepard Saw It All Coming," *Atlantic*, August 2019, online; MG, 2002.

21 Quoted in Stephen Applebaum, "Poet of the Badlands," *Independent* (UK), April 28, 2006, Film, 9.

22 "True West (Symbiosis)," August 1979, WC; Michael Pye, "Dream Maverick," *Observer*, March 26, 1989, A6. Shepard is referring to a Gurdjieff line in *Meetings with Remarkable Men*; see also TP, 62.

23 Ethan Hawke, December 28, 2021; SP, 59.

24 Quoted in Michael VerMeulen, "Sam Shepard: Yes, Yes, Yes," *Esquire*, February 1980, 80.

25 Ibid., 79; quoted in Sean Elder, "Sam Shepard at the Magic," *CT Insider*, May 7, 2014, online.

26 JD; quoted in Johnny Dark, "The 'True West' Interviews," *West Coast Plays* 9 (Summer 1981), 58.

27 Quoted in Johnny Dark, "The 'True West' Interviews," *West Coast Plays* 9 (Summer 1981), 58; quoted in Berna Rauch, "A Non-Symbolic Sam Shepard," *Berkeley Barb* (CA), May 9–15, 1975, 16; quoted in Carol Rosen, "'Silent Tongues': Sam Shepard's Explorations of Emotional Territory," *Village Voice*, August 4, 1992, 40.

28 Quoted in SM.

29 Steve Winn, "The Magic Theater Is Exploring New Turf," *San Francisco Sunday Examiner and Chronicle*, September 21, 1980, 24.

30 Quoted in Don Shewey, "The True Story of 'True West,'" *Village Voice*, November 30, 1982, 115; Robert Coe, "Saga of Sam Shepard," *New York Times Magazine*, November 23, 1980, 58; quoted in John Lion, "Rock n' Roll Jesus with a Cowboy Mouth: Sam Shepard Is the Inkblot of the '80s," *American Theatre*, April 1984, 8.

31 Mel Gussow, "Stage: Shepard's 'True West' Revived and Restored," *New York Times*, October 18, 1982, C18; KT, 501.

32 Quoted in Johnny Dark, "The 'True West' Interviews," *West Coast Plays* 9 (Summer 1981), 55.

33 Quoted in KT, 501.

34 Barbara Bright, June 16, 2018; quoted in KT, 498, 500, 501.

35 Quoted in Michael Feingold, "Papp's 'True West' False, Says Shepard," *Village Voice*, December 10–16, 1980, 112; quoted in Fred Ferretti, "Joseph Papp: A 'Divisive Force' or a 'Healing' One?: Producer's Eye . . . ," *New York Times*, December 20, 1980, 16; quoted in KT, 495.

36 Ben Brantley, "Sam Shepard, Storyteller," *New York Times*, November 13, 1994, Arts and Leisure, 26.

37 Quoted in Michael Feingold, "Papp's 'True West' False, Says Shepard," *Village Voice*, December 10–16, 1980, 112; Frank Rich, "Shepard's 'True West': Myths vs. Reality," *New York Times*, December 24, 1980, C9; Donal Henahan, "Woodruff Disclaims Public's 'True West,'" *New York Times*, December 13, 1980, 18; quoted in KT, 497.

38 Richard Christiansen, "Steppenwolf's 'True West' a Rompin,' Stompin' Success," *Chicago Tribune*, June 28, 1982, sec. 2, 6.

39 Richard Christiansen, "'True West' Is a True Hit," *Chicago Tribune*, June 28, 1982, sec. 2, 7.

40 Ibid.; Chris Jones, May 24, 2021.

41 Ibid.; Chris Jones, email, November 1, 2022; see also Chris Jones, "It Feels like End of 'In-Yer-Face' Era in Chicago Theater," *Chicago Tribune*, August 3, 2017, online; Ethan Hawke, December 28, 2021; Chris Jones, May 24, 2021.

42 Dominic Cavendish, "'He Was a True One-Off': John Malkovich on the Genius of Sam Shepard," *Telegraph* (UK), November 4, 2018, online; Richard Christiansen, "'True West' Conquers East," *Chicago Tribune*, November 4, 1982, sec. 2, 4.

43 Richard Christiansen, Ibid., 1; Mel Gussow, "Stage: Shepard's 'True West' Revived and Restored," *New York Times*, October 18, 1982, C18.

## CHAPTER 13 THE AVIATOR

1 Quoted in Ruthe Stein, "A Marriage of Luck and Chemistry," *San Francisco Chronicle*, July 20, 1981, 15.

2 Matt Zoller Seitz, "Made for Jessica Lange," *Vulture*, February 28, 2024, online; Johnny Dark, July 22, 2020.

3 Quoted in Harry Haun, "The Last American Hero," *Daily News*, October 16, 1983, 7.

4 Quoted in RG, 250. Dale Pollock, "Screen Biography of Actress Frances Farmer Scheduled," *Los Angeles Times*, April 21, 1981, Part IV: 1.

5 Quoted in Anthony Uzarowski, *Jessica Lange: An Adventurer's Heart* (Lexington: University Press of Kentucky, 2023), 77.

6 Quoted in NC, 186; JD.

7 Anthony Uzarowski, *Jessica Lange: An Adventurer's Heart* (Lexington: University Press of Kentucky, 2023), 76; quoted in Roderick Mann, "The Postman Always Rings Twice for Jessica," *Los Angeles Times*, January 16, 1983, Calendar, 19.

8 Quoted in Anthony Uzarowski, *Jessica Lange: An Adventurer's Heart* (Lexington: University Press of Kentucky, 2023), 76–77.

9 Quoted in JD.

10 Quoted in NC, 234.

11 Quoted in NC, 186.

12 Quoted in Roderick Mann, "The Postman Always Rings Twice for Jessica," *Los Angeles Times*, January 16, 1983, Calendar, 19.

13 Matt Zoller Seitz, "In Conversation: Made for Jessica," *Vulture*, 28 February 2024; MC, 121.

14 O-Lan founded, with the director Julie Hébert, the Marin-based Overtone Theatre in late 1980. O-Lan and Hébert developed an impressionistic musical theater piece called *Superstitions* with material from *Motel Chronicles*. On July 3, 1981, *Superstitions* opened at San Francisco's Intersection for the Arts Theater. The Overtones coproduced *Superstitions* with New Writers at the Westside, and it would be produced on a double bill with *Sad Lament of Pecos Bill*, with O-Lan as Sluefoot Sue and Mark Petrakis as Bill, at La MaMa in September 1983; it also aired on KQED TV (San Francisco's PBS channel) on December 18, 1984.

15 Blanche McCrary Boyd, "The Natural," *American Film: Magazine of the Film and Television Arts*, October 1984, 22–26, 91–92: 91.

16 Wim Wenders, Sam Shepard, and L. M. Kit Carson, "Interview with Wim Wenders, Director," April 1984, in *Paris, Texas* (New York: Ecco, 1984), 117.

17 Quoted in BB, 91; quoted in Wim Wenders, Sam Shepard, and L. M. Kit Carson, "Interview with Wim Wenders, Director," April 1984, in *Paris, Texas* (New York: Ecco, 1984), 117.

18 MC, 104.

19 Quoted in Wim Wenders, Sam Shepard, and L. M. Kit Carson, "Interview with Wim Wenders, Director," April 1984, in *Paris, Texas* (New York: Ecco, 1984), 127–28; MC , 127.

20 Quoted in John O'Mahony, "The Write Stuff," *Guardian*, October 10, 2003.

21 The reading took place on February 19, 1980. "Readings by Bly, Shepard," *San Francisco Chronicle*, February 7, 1980, 33.

22 Philip Kaufman, "Sam Shepard Remembered by 'The Right Stuff' Director Philip Kaufman: Half Jackrabbit, Best Chili Maker," *Variety*, August 1, 2017, online; quoted in Philip Kaufman, as told by Gregg Kilday, "'The Right Stuff' Filmmaker Remembers Sam Shepard: He Was 'Born with the Gift of a Golden Ear,'" *Hollywood Reporter*, August 1, 2017, online; Jack Kroll, with Constance Guthrie in New York and Janet Huck in Los Angeles, "Who's That Tall, Dark Stranger?," *Newsweek*, November 11, 1985, 72.

23 Johnny Dark, "Sam Shepard on Myths and Heroes: The Right Stuff Is Best Defined by What It Isn't," ed. and with an introduction by Hal Gelb, *San Francisco*, September 1983, 70; quoted in Robert Goldberg, "Sam Shepard: American Original," *Playboy*, March 1984, 193.

24 Quotations from this and the previous paragraph: BB, 25; quoted in "Sam Shepard," interview by Terry Gross, *Fresh Air*, March 31, 1998; quoted in Alex and Howie Kahn French, "Punch a Hole in the Sky: An Oral History of *The Right Stuff*," *Wired*, November 18, 2014, online; quoted in James Brady, "In Step with Sam Shepard," *San Francisco Chronicle*, January 10, 1999, 23.

25 Philip Kaufman, "Sam Shepard Remembered by 'The Right Stuff' Director Philip Kaufman: Half Jackrabbit, Best Chili Maker," *Variety*, August 1, 2017, online.

26 Jack Kroll, with Constance Guthrie in New York and Janet Huck in Los Angeles, "Who's That Tall, Dark Stranger?," *Newsweek*, November 11, 1985, 72.

27 Quoted in Robert Goldberg, "Sam Shepard: American Original," *Playboy*, March 1984, 193; Bernard Weiner, "Shepard: Waiting for a Western," *San Francisco Chronicle*, February 9, 1983, 55.

28 Ross Wetzsteon, "'Unknown Territory,'" *Village Voice*, December 10, 1985, 55.

29 Sandy Rogers, July 28, 2023.

30 Matthew Roudané, "Shepard on Shepard: An Interview," in CC, 73.

31 FFL, 24; Sandy Rogers, July 28, 2023; quoted in Ruthe Stein, "Sibling Revelry," *San Francisco Chronicle*, January 6, 1986, 17. In *Synthetic Tears*, Shepard's character is Eddie, and Sandy's is May. Eddie was named after a three-foot-tall childhood doll of Sandy's.

32 TP, 45.

33 Nancy Scott, "A Winning 'Fool,'" *San Francisco Examiner*, February 11, 1983, E13.

34 Harry Haun, "The Image Maker," *Playbill*, November 1985, 81; Edith Oliver, "Off Broadway," *New Yorker*, June 6, 1983, 110; quoted in Lawrence DeVine, "Maverick Playwright in New York Canyons," *Detroit Free Press*, August 31, 1983, 6B. Ed Harris was replaced by Will Patton, then Bruce Willis, then Aidan Quinn. "If you don't like this play": Clive Barnes, "Theater: A Sam Shepard Double Bill: Dramatic Cartoons Are Displayed in the Village," *New York Times*, April 2, 1970, 43.

35 Johnny Dark, July 19, 2020; SOC, 172–73.

36 Quoted in JW, 257; SOC, 182; Johnny Dark, July 19, 2020.

37 TP, 65; Johnny Dark, July 19, 2020; Sandy Rogers, July 28, 2023.

38 TP, 69–70.

39 Quoted in David Rosenthal, "Jessica Lange's Latest Life," *Rolling Stone*, March 17, 1983, 12.

40 "New Duluthian: Actress Jessica Lange," *Duluth Reader*, March 29, 2012, online; TP, 67. The location of Jessica Lange's cabin has been incorrectly identified in previous studies of Shepard's life, but I refrain from including the address here out of respect for the family's privacy, as they still occupy the property.

41 TP, 69, 80.

42 Johnny Dark, July 19, 2020; Johnny Dark to Lee Kissman, March 25, 2017.

43 Sam Shepard to Jane Rogers, April 29, 1983.

44 TP, 71; recording of Johnny Dark interviewing Sam Shepard in Iowa while Shepard was shooting *Country*, 1983, WC/SD. The house in Santa Fe that Shepard and Jessica first occupied was located at 923 1/2 Acequia Madre.

45 SOC, 34.

46 SOC, 34, 36.

47 "Jessica, Shepard Selling Home," *Santa Fe New Mexican*, April 11, 1986, C1; Office of the Santa Fe County Assessor; TP, 76. Their house in Santa Fe during this period was located at 14 Brass Horse Road.

48 JD; BB, 26; Kevin Sessums, "Digitized Dialogues: Sam Shepard," 1988, online.

## CHAPTER 14 "JUST SAM"

1 Quoted in Matt Zoller Seitz, "Made for Jessica Lange," *Vulture*, February 28, 2024, online.

2 TP, 70.

3 Quoted in PRLA, 22; TP, 88; PRLA; quoted in JW, 275.

4 CS, 155. Their rental was located at 270 Sheridan Road in Waterloo.

5 Quoted in PRLA, 22; quoted in PRLA, 19; Julia Cameron, "Jessica Lange," *American Film*, January–February 1983, 33.

6 Michael Pye, "Dream Maverick," *Observer*, March 26, 1989, A5; PRLA, 18.

7 Sam Shepard, notebook, 1988–1989, January 2, 1989, box 15, folder 2, HRC; recording of Johnny Dark and Sam Shepard in Iowa while Shepard was shooting *Country*, 1983, WC/SD.

8 BB, 25–26; Kevin Sessums, "Digitized Dialogues: Sam Shepard," 1988, online.

9 TP, 99; quoted in AP; "Lange Decries the Advent of the 'Disposable' Family," *Newsday*, September 28, 1988, 11.

10 Quoted in Michael Ross, "Made of the Write Stuff," *Sunday Times* (UK), March 11, 2007, Eire Culture, 4; JD.

11 Mark Matousek, "Harry Dean Stanton on *Paris, Texas*: For the First Time, I Got the Girl," *Interview*, May 5, 2018, online; quoted in Wim Wenders, Sam Shepard, and L. M. Kit Carson, "Interview with Wim Wenders, Director," April 1984, in *Paris, Texas* (New York: Ecco, 1984), 117; quoted in David Gordon, "Harry Dean Stanton, the Man We Couldn't Stop Watching," *GQ*, November 8, 2010, online.

12 Quoted in Claire Dwyer-Hogg, "Sam Shepard: 'The Good Guy and Bad Guy Stuff Just Doesn't Interest Me,'" *Guardian* (UK), December 1, 2013, online.

13 Quoted in *Harry Dean Stanton: Partly Fiction*, directed by Sophie Huber (New York, 2013).

14 Quoted in Wim Wenders, Sam Shepard, and L. M. Kit Carson, "Interview with Wim Wenders, Director," April 1984, in *Paris, Texas* (New York: Ecco, 1984), 117.

15 Quoted in JW, 264.

16 Chris Peachment, "American Hero," *Time Out*, August 23–29, 1984, 17.

17 Quoted in Gregorio Belinchón, "Forty Years On from 'Paris, Texas': Wim Wenders Tells the Story of the Making of His Masterpiece About the West and Sadness," *El País*, May 13, 2023, online.

18 Quoted in Wim Wenders, Sam Shepard, and L. M. Kit Carson, "Interview with Wim Wenders, Director," April 1984, in *Paris, Texas* (New York: Ecco, 1984), 129.

19 Michael Agresta, "Texas' Strange Brand of Cool: Revisiting *Paris, Texas*, the Film That Made Nowhere Hip," *Texas Observer*, April 4, 1916, online.

20 Ben Brantley, "Sam Shepard, Storyteller," *New York Times*, November 13, 1994, Arts and Leisure, 26.

21 Mark Muro, "Sam About Town: Bostonians Pine for a Glimpse of the Mythical Shepard," *Boston Globe*, February 7, 1984, 11; JA, 143.

22 Quoted in Lianne Stevens, "Joseph Chaikin: Triumph over Irony," *Los Angeles Times*, December 21, 1985, Part V, 5.

23 Sam Shepard, July 2008, notebook, April 2008–February 2009, box 17, folder 1, HRC.

24 Sandy Rogers, July 28, 2023; Roxanne Rogers, 18 March 2025.

25 Sam Rogers to Roxanne Rogers, October 15, 1974; Sam Shepard, "Synthetic Tears," *Motel Chronicles* notebook, April–June 1981, HRC; CP, 145; Sam Shepard, "Sangre de Cristo" (unfinished), spiral notebook, August 25, 1989, WC. Shepard makes clear in the documentary *This So-Called Disaster* that this last visit to his father was "about three weeks" before he died.

26 Sam Shepard, "Synthetic Tears," *Motel Chronicles* notebook, April–June 1981, HRC; TSD. Shepard's Sonoma County ranch was located on a parcel that combined what is now 4442 and 4452 Arlington Avenue in Santa Rosa, California.
27 MG, 2002.
28 Quoted in SGF, 20.
29 Ibid.
30 TSD.
31 "Steve Sandoval," *New Mexican* (Santa Fe), May 28, 1989, B2; Sam Shepard, "Between 2 Deaths," notebook, April 10, 1984, HRC. Shepard refers to Sandoval by his full name in *Motel Chronicles* and as Esteban in his short story "See You in My Dreams," "Sangre de Cristo," and *The Late Henry Moss.*
32 Sam Shepard, "Sangre de Cristo" (unfinished), spiral notebook, August 25, 1989, WC; CP, 143, 144, italics mine.
33 CP, 141.
34 CP, 142. Shepard discusses this person in Sam Sr.'s life in *Cruising Paradise*, *The Late Henry Moss*, and "Sangre de Cristo," respectively.
35 SOC, 45. Several of the stories in SOC were revised and published in CP.
36 "Bernalillo," DD, 245.
37 SOC, 46; University of New Mexico Office of the Medical Investigator, Report of Findings on Sam Rogers, March 25, 1984. Shepard believed it was higher, .337 (Sam Shepard, "Between 2 Deaths," notebook, April 10, 1984, HRC).
38 Alejandro Aragonez (New Mexico Office of the Medical Investigator), email, August 6, 2024; University of New Mexico Office of the Medical Investigator, Report of Findings on Sam Rogers, March 25, 1984.
39 Sam Shepard, "Between 2 Deaths," notebook, April 10, 1984, HRC.
40 FO, 24; CP, 146; CP, 149.
41 Shepard also wrote a screenplay about the funeral in the spring of 1984 called "Denial," which includes O-Lan's character, Cassie, arriving at the funeral proceedings with a gun, hell-bent on killing her ex-husband, Jake (Shepard), HRC.
42 SOC, 50, 51.
43 TSD; quoted in SGF, 20.
44 SOC, 53.
45 Quoted in Michael Ross, "Made of the Write Stuff," *Sunday Times* (UK), March 11, 2007, Eire Culture, 4.

## CHAPTER 15 LEGENDS OF LOVE

1 Quoted in PRLA, 22.
2 Quoted in "Shepard Doesn't Want His Plays in NM," *Santa Fe New Mexican*, October 7, 1984, 3.

3 Albert Poland, *Stages: A Theater Memoir*, with a foreword by Michael Reidel (Self-published, 2019), 229.

4 Quoted in PH, 78, 102.

5 Quoted in NC, 234.

6 Nick Roddick, "On the Road with Robert Altman," *Cinema Papers* (Melbourne, Australia), September 1986, 24–27.

7 Ruthe Stein, "Sibling Revelry," *San Francisco Chronicle*, January 6, 1986, 16; Sandy Rogers, July 28, 2023.

8 Quoted in SGF, 20.

9 Quoted in Vincent Canby, "Shepard's 'Fool for Love,'" *New York Times*, December 6, 1985, C2; Jack Kroll, "Who's That Tall, Dark Stranger?," *Newsweek*, November 11, 1985, 72.

10 Quotations from this and the previous paragraph quoted in JW, 284.

11 TP, 105.

12 Quoted in PR, 345.

13 Sam Shepard, *Fool for Love* (San Francisco: City Lights Books, 1983) (also contains the libretto and music for *The Sad Lament of Pecos Bill on the Eve of Killing His Wife*), 85, 86; FFL, 45.

14 CS, 114, 115.

15 Ibid.

16 LM, 14–15.

17 CC, 230; LM, 58. Shepard wrote a script titled "Denial," which he wrote over the spring of 1984, then rewrote it the following fall as *A Lie of the Mind.* Much of "Denial" takes place in a cabin in the "Great North Woods," i.e., Minnesota, before he changed it to Montana. Sam Shepard, "Brown notebook," includes material for 'Denial,' 'The War in Heaven,' January–April 1984, series I, container 14.13, Sam Shepard Papers 1965–2011, HRC.

18 LM, 77–78.

19 LM, 95.

20 Roxanne Rogers, January 21, 2021; Michael Kuchwara (AP), "Country Boys Answer Call to the Stage," *The Day* [New London, CT], March 23, 1986, B3–B4: B3; "Music Notes," in LM, 7; Stephen Fay, "Renaissance Man Rides Out of the West," *Sunday Times Magazine*, August 26, 1984, 19; Ross Wetzsteon, "'Unknown Territory,'" *Village Voice*, December 10, 1985, 56.

21 Frank Rich, "'A Lie of the Mind,' by Sam Shepard," *New York Times*, December 6, 1985, C3.

22 Albert Poland, *Stages: A Theater Memoir*, with a foreword by Michael Reidel (Self-published, 2019), 231.

23 JD; Albert Poland, *Stages: A Theater Memoir*, with a foreword by Michael Reidel (Self-published, 2019), 232.

24 Tony Richardson, *The Long-Distance Runner* (New York: William Morrow, 1993), 289; quoted in Carol Rosen, "'Silent Tongues': Sam Shepard's Explorations of Emotional Territory," *Village Voice*, August 4, 1992, 35.

25 Quoted in Carole Cadwalladr, "Sam Shepard Opens Up," *Guardian*, March 20, 2010, 11.

26 Associated Press, "Hollywood Pair Joining Virginia's Landed Gentry," *Roanoke Times & World News*, April 23, 1986, B1. The house was called "the Helm," located at 325 Caswell Beach Road, Oak Island, North Carolina.

27 David Richards, "SSsshhhh! It's Sam Shepard; Secretive and Publicity-Shy, with No Regrets About His 'Far North,'" *Washington Post*, December 12, 1988, C1. Totier Creek Farm is located at 7548 Totier Creek Farm Road in Scottsville, Virginia.

28 Heidi Benson, "Sam Shepard's Kid in Writing Game," *San Francisco Chronicle*, February 2, 2003, online; Johnny Dark, July 22, 2020. Jesse Shepard was a wrangler and stuntman on *Silent Tongue* and, later, on movies his father acted in, *Good Old Boys*, *Streets of Laredo*, and *Don't Come Knocking*, where he doubled for Shepard on horseback in the first scene.

29 Sam Shepard, in an interview with Lenny Shulman, in Lenny Shulman, *Head to Head: Conversations with a Generation of Horse Racing Legends* (Lexington: University Press of Kentucky, 2021), 96; "Grade II Winner Two Trail Sioux Retired," *Blood-Horse Daily*, February 13, 2006, online; "Sam Shepard Dead at 73," *Thoroughbred Daily News*, July 31, 2017, online.

30 Bob Dylan, interviewed by Sam Shepard, recordings, June 5, 1986, WC. The date is not specified but is based on the fact that Shepard mentioned that it was a Thursday and that Hannah, born in January, was six months old; it's also the only date Dylan would have had free time during his True Confessions tour with Tom Petty.

31 Roxanne Rogers, December 29, 2020.

32 Quoted in Jonathan Cott, conversation with Sam Shepard, typescript of *Rolling Stone* article with revisions by Shepard and correspondence, March 1986, series IV, container 28.11, Sam Shepard Papers 1965–2009, HRC. John McEnroe and his family, not Bob Dylan, appeared on the *Esquire* cover.

33 Shepard later published *True Dylan* as *Short Life of Trouble* in 2012. FO, 57–78.

34 John Lahr, "The Imperfectionist," *New Yorker*, December 1, 1996, online; Woody Allen to Sam Shepard, May 6, 1987, HRC; quoted in JA, 148.

35 TP, 111; Jonathan Cott, "Strong Words: An Interview with Sam Shepard by Jonathan Cott," *Vogue*, September 1988, 681.

36 TP, 112.

37 Quoted in JA, 144.

38 Kevin Sessums, "Digitized Dialogues: Sam Shepard," 1988, online.

39 Quoted in Jonathan Cott, "Strong Words: An Interview with Sam Shepard by Jonathan Cott," *Vogue*, September 1988, 681, 756.

40 Quoted in ibid., 756.

41 TP, 113; Jerry Roberts, "Actors Get a Good Ride in 'Far North,'" *News-Pilot*, November 9, 1988, C16; Sheila Benson, "'Far North' Gets Lost in Every Direction," *Los Angeles*

*Times,* November 9, 1988, Part IV, 2; Janet Maslin, "'Far North': Sam Shepard Ventures into Directing," *New York Times*, November 9, 1988, C18

42 TP, 113–14.

43 TP, 114.

## CHAPTER 16 "HORRORS OF THE ROAD"

1 Sam Shepard, "Such a Man," February 1989, HRC.

2 Quoted in NC, 236.

3 Vincent Canby, "A Variation on the Oedipus Theme," *New York Times*, January 31, 1992, C6; Julie Delpy, September 22, 2023.

4 SOC; Julie Delpy, interviewed by Marc Maron, *WTF with Marc Maron* (podcast), October 24, 2021; Ethan Hawke, December 28, 2021; Julie Delpy, September 22, 2023.

5 SOC, 135; HRC.

6 Claudia Steinberg, "Volker Schlöndorff," *BOMB* 32 (Summer 1990), online; Julie Delpy, September 22, 2023.

7 TP, 123.

8 Quoted in CR, 39.

9 Quoted in MG, 1969; Sam Shepard, "Fractured," typescript, n.d., circa 1972, box 23, folder 4, HGC.

10 SFS, 39.

11 Fintan O'Toole, "A Nod from One Sam to Another," *Irish Times*, February 24, 2007, Arts, 1.

12 SFS, 5; quoted in CR, 39; SFS, 29, 31.

13 Anne Militello, email, August 7, 2023.

14 Quoted in CR, 42; quoted in Dominic Cavendish, "'He Was a True One-Off': John Malkovich on the Genius of Sam Shepard," *Telegraph* (UK), November 4, 2018, online.

15 See Mimi Kramer, "Toxic Shock," *New Yorker*, June 3, 1991, 78; Richard Hornby, "Broadway Economics," *Hudson Review* 44, no. 3 (Autumn 1991), 459; Ben Brantley, "Sam Shepard, Storyteller," *New York Times*, November 13, 1994, Arts and Leisure, 26.

16 Newsweek Staff, "Sam Shepard Tosses a Grenade," *Newsweek*, May 26, 1991, online.

17 Sam Shepard, "The Devouring Lion," November 6, 1992, WC; Sam Shepard, "Separation (Horrors of the Road)," September 1, 1992, WC.

18 Sam Shepard, "One Last Favor," September 3, 1992, WC; TP, 135, 136.

19 Quoted in CR, 39.

20 Quoted in Wolf Schneider, "Back Home . . . on the Range," *Los Angeles Times*, July 16, 1992, Calendar, F8.

21 See *Reel Injun*, directed by Neil Diamond (Rezolution Pictures, 2010); Brian Young, "Why I Won't Wear War Paint and Feathers in a Movie Again," *Zócalo Public Square*, June 11, 2015, online.

22 Quoted in Russell Smith, "Sam Shepard—A Star Who Prefers to Shine Quietly," *Monitor* (McAllen, TX), February 28, 1993, 4F.

23 Elgy Gillespie, "True Sam: True West," *San Francisco Review of Books*, Fall 1992, 13.

24 Peter Travers, "Silent Tongue," *Rolling Stone*, February 1, 1994, online; Sam Shepard, "One Last Favor," September 3, 1992, WC.

25 Jane Galbraith, "'Silent Tongue' to Speak for River Phoenix," *Los Angeles Times*, November 14, 1993, Calendar, 7.

26 Caryn James, "Sam Shepard's Spiritual, Imagistic Vision of the Old West," *New York Times*, February 25, 1994, C3.

27 MG, 1993.

28 Aaron Ryder, July 11, 2023; quoted in Graham Fuller, "Broadway Babies," *Interview*, June 1996, 76.

29 MG, 1993.

30 Ibid.

31 "Jessica Lange Wins Best Actress: 1995," Oscars, YouTube. https://www.youtube.com/watch?v=RZDbJHC1uxs&t=1s.

32 Caryn James, "Strong, Vulnerable; Vulnerable, Strong," *New York Times*, May 21, 1989, H28.

33 Gigi Hanna, "Pasadena Schoolteacher Gave a Lot of Love to her Students," *Pasadena Star-News*, March 17, 1994, A6.

34 Roxanne Rogers, November 17, 2022; quoted in TW, 31.

35 MG, 1993.

36 Ibid.

37 Laurie Winer, "It's a Public with a Punch," *Los Angeles Times*, November 27, 1994, Calendar, 46.

38 The story in the first act is based on a short piece about himself and "J.D." (Johnny Dark), which he later published in *Cruising Paradise* under the title "Thin Skin."

39 Sam Shepard, *Simpatico* (New York: Vintage, 1996), 53, 54, 57, 109.

40 Jack Kroll, "Shepard the Thoroughbred," *Newsweek*, November 27, 1994, 68.

41 Sam Shepard, "Peter Handke's Inner Self," *Vanity Fair*, September 1984, 106; quoted in TW, 143, 144.

42 Sam Shepard to Johnny Dark, November 28, 1995, and March 10, 1995, WC.

43 Sam Shepard, "Separation (Horrors of the Road)," September 1, 1992, WC.

44 Charles and Mary Jane Nuckols, August 2, 2019; Sam Shepard to Johnny Dark, November 28, 1995; Stephen Schiff, "Showcase: Shepard on Broadway," *New Yorker*, April 22, 1996, 84–86. The Stillwater house was located at 903 Fourth Street North. Jessica purchased a farm in Wisconsin with money from *King Kong* years before, and the Kinnickinnic ranch may be the same property.

45 MG, 2002; "Sam Shepard," 1997, *The Paris Review: Playwrights at Work*, ed. George Plimpton, with an introduction by John Lahr (New York: Modern Library, 2000), 333.

46 TP, 140.

## CHAPTER 17 THOSE SO-CALLED DISASTERS

1 TP, 219.

2 TP, 143, 219; Phil Gerrow, July 31, 2019. Gerrow told me that Shepard and Jessica Lange later sold the property because the Biosphere was owned by the Mexican government, and the zoning restrictions became too burdensome.

3 Hedy Weiss, "Sam Shepard's Tales Cover a Lot of Ground," *Chicago Sun-Times*, May 8, 1996.

4 Quoted in MG, 2002.

5 Stephen Schiff, "Showcase: Shepard on Broadway," *New Yorker*, April 22, 1996, 85; Peter Marks, "On Stage, and Off: Sam Shepard Blitz," *New York Times*, March 29, 1996, C2.

6 Quoted in Peter Marks, "Sam Shepard Is Happy to Be on Broadway but It's Just a Visit," *New York Times*, May 28, 1996, C15.

7 Nick Offerman, *Where the Deer and the Antelope Play: The Pastoral Observations of One Ignorant American Who Loves to Walk Outside* (New York: Dutton, 2021), xiv, xv; quoted in Jeff Ruby, "The Delicious Life of Nick Offerman," *Chicago*, September 25, 2013, online.

8 Ethan Hawke, December 28, 2021.

9 Ibid.

10 Quoted in Peter Marks, "Sam Shepard Is Happy to Be on Broadway but It's Just a Visit," *New York Times*, May 28, 1996, C15; quoted in Neal Justin, "Playwright Sam Shepard Speaks His Mind; 'U' Students Soak It Up," *Star-Tribune* (Minneapolis), May 24, 1996, B5.

11 Quoted in Kathy Henderson, "Shepherding Sam: Terry Kinney Directs the World Premiere of Sam Shepard's *Eyes for Consuela* at the Manhattan Theatre Club," *In Theater*, February 1998, 24.

12 Patti Hartigan, "Sam Shepard: The Legendary Playwright, Actor and Private Man of Action Sits Still for an Interview," *Boston Globe*, August 18, 1996, N5.

13 Dan Hulbert, "World Awaits 'Green': Shepard-Chaikin Team Has the Right Stuff for High Drama," *Atlanta Journal-Constitution*, July 19, 1996, 45.

14 Ben Brantley, "Sam Shepard, Storyteller," *New York Times*, November 13, 1994, Arts and Leisure, online.

15 LHM, 195, 201, 219.

16 Quoted in Patti Hartigan, "Sam Shepard: The Legendary Playwright, Actor and Private Man of Action Sits Still for an Interview," *Boston Globe*, August 18, 1996, N5.

17 Quoted in Dan Hulbert, "World Awaits 'Green': Shepard-Chaikin Team Has the Right Stuff for High Drama," *Atlanta Journal-Constitution*, July 19, 1996, 45.

18 Patti Hartigan, "Arts Give Games Their Soul," *Boston Globe*, August 2, 1996, E1; LHM, 190. *When the World Was Green (A Chef's Fable)* was commissioned by 7 Stages, where Chaikin was then artist-in-residence, and it was performed at the 14th Street Playhouse Mainstage in Atlanta.

19 Patti Hartigan, "Arts Give Games Their Soul," *Boston Globe*, August 2, 1996, E9.

20 Quoted in Don Shewey, "Patriot Acts," *Village Voice*, November 17–23, 2004, online.

21 Quoted in Dave Hoekstra, "Burnett's Identity Found in the Woods," *Chicago Sun-Times*, May 21, 2006, D7.

22 Boaty Boatwright, May 10, 2023.

23 Jasper Rees, "When Shepard Was a Londoner," theartsdesk.com, December 4, 2016, online; PR, 333. For the timing of his extended break from alcohol, see TP, 185, 233–35.

24 PR, 333; TP, 156, 215, 217; quoted in George Rush and Joanna Molloy, "Despite Reviews, It's Still a 'Cape' of Good Hopes," *Daily News*, February 1, 1998, 14.

25 TP, 154; Roxanne Rogers, January 1, 2025; JD; TP, 154.

26 TP, 156.

27 Fintan O'Toole, "New Shepard Play 'Eyes' Is a Must-See," *Daily News*, February 11, 1988, 42; LHM, 145.

28 LHM, 140, 148–49, 161.

29 Johnny Dark, July 19, 2020.

30 Sandy Rogers, July 28, 2023.

31 Fintan O'Toole, "New Shepard Play 'Eyes' Is a Must-See," *Daily News*, February 11, 1988, 42; Vincent Canby, "A 'Three Sisters' with a Poignant Russian Forecast," *New York Times*, February 15, 1998, AR26.

32 Ben Brantley, "When Love Is Blinding as Well as Blind," *New York Times*, February 11, 1998, E1.

33 Quoted in Kathy Henderson, "Shepherding Sam: Terry Kinney Directs the World Premiere of Sam Shepard's *Eyes for Consuela* at the Manhattan Theatre Club," *In Theater*, February 1998, 24; "Sam Shepard," interview by Terry Gross, *Fresh Air*, March 31, 1998.

34 Michael Almereyda, preface to *William Shakespeare's Hamlet*, with an introduction by Ethan Hawke (London: Faber and Faber, 2000), vii-xii: xi.

35 Quoted in Eric Grode, "Stage to Screen: Documenting a Shepard Play and 'The Producers,'" *Playbill*, March 28, 2004, online.

36 Michael Almereyda, "Sam Shepard: The All-American Cultural Icon at 50," *Arena*, May/June 1994, 66–69; Michael Almereyda, preface to *William Shakespeare's Hamlet*, with an introduction by Ethan Hawke (London: Faber and Faber, 2000), xi, xii.

37 Ethan Hawke, "Ethan Hawke on a New Biography of the Elusive Sam Shepard," *Washington Post*, April 11, 2023, online.

38 Ethan Hawke, December 28, 2021.

39 Michael Almereyda, preface to *William Shakespeare's Hamlet*, with an introduction by Ethan Hawke (London: Faber and Faber, 2000), xi–xii.

40 Sam Shepard to Michael Almereyda, March 13, 2000. Courtesy of Michael Almereyda.

41 Chris Hewitt, "Play It Again, Sam," *Saint Paul Pioneer Press*, May 17, 2000, Express, 2E.

42 See JW, 324–25, 333; Michael Phillips, "Sam Shepard's Family Values," *Los Angeles Times*, November 8, 2000, F1.

43 After completing *The Late Henry Moss*, he also wrote an adaptation of *King Lear* set in Texas. (See James Brady, "In Step with Sam Shepard," *San Francisco Chronicle*, January 10, 1999, 23.)

44 TP, 188; Brian Bartels, "Sam Shepard's Master Class in Playwriting," *Missouri Review*, Spring 2007, 78; MG, 2002; TP, 220. The legendary production was directed by Matthew Warchus, who directed the film *Simpatico.*

45 TP, 188; Sam Shepard, "News Blues," *Time Out* (London), no. 222 (May 31–June 6, 1974), 17; See Sam Shepard, "News Blues," *Time Out* [London] 222, May 31–June 6, 1974, 17. quoted in Matthew Roudané, "Shepard on Shepard: An Interview," CC, 69.

46 TP, 149, 151; Frank O'Connor, "The Late Henry Conran," 1931, *Guests of the Nation* (Dublin: Poolbeg Press, 1979), 175, 177.

47 TSD.

48 Quoted in Matthew Roudané, "Shepard on Shepard: An Interview," CC, 67.

49 Edward Guthmann, "Sam Shepard Talks a Bit About His Latest," *San Francisco Chronicle*, November 5, 2000, Datebook, 43; quoted in Kevin Berger, "Being Sam Shepard," *San Francisco*, November 2000, 86.

50 Quoted in Paul Iorio, "Cheech Marin Tries Something Different," *San Francisco Chronicle*, November 5, 2000, Datebook, 42.

51 Quoted in Kevin Berger, "Being Sam Shepard," *San Francisco*, November 2000, 91.

52 Quoted in Hillary Weston, "The Music of Memory: A Conversation with Michael Almereyda," *Current*, August 2, 2017, online; Will Blythe, "The Side of Denis Johnson You Never Knew," *Playbill*, December 20, 2022, online.

53 Michael Almereyda, n.d., "Notes on the Making of *This So-Called Disaster*," HRC; quoted in Eric Grode, "Stage to Screen: Documenting a Shepard Play and 'The Producers,'" *Esquire*, March 28, 2004, online.

54 Quoted in Kevin Berger, "Being Sam Shepard," *San Francisco*, November 2000, 89; Matthew Roudané, "Sam Shepard's *The Late Henry Moss*," in CC, 280.

55 MG, 2002.

56 Robert Hurwitt, "Stars on Stage," *San Francisco Examiner*, November 15, 2000, B4.

57 Eugene O'Neill, *Long Day's Journey into Night*, ed. Travis Bogard, 1941, Vol. 3. *O'Neill: Complete Plays, 1932–1943* (New York: Library of America, 1988), 714.

58 Hal Gelb, "Long Playwright's Journey," *Nation*, December 25, 2000, 37.

## CHAPTER 18 TRIGGER WORDS

1 Sam Shepard, "At Home," December 26, 2000, HRC; TP, 233.

2 TP, 234, 235.

3 Quoted in David Fear, "The Last Word: Jessica Lange on Buddhism, Photography and 'American Horror Story,'" *Rolling Stone*, March 2019, online.

4 Sam Shepard, "At Home," December 26, 2000, HRC.

5 Quoted in "Black Hawk Down: Production Notes," n.d., Cinema.com.

6 Clark Middleton, December 31, 2018; Sam Shepard to Johnny Dark, September 10–12, 2010, WC.

7 Sam Shepard to Johnny Dark, September 10–12, 2010, WC.

8 Ethan Hawke, December 28, 2021.

9 Ibid.

10 Donald Lyons, "Sibling Story Misses with Lack of Detail," *New York Post*, September 25, 2001, online; Charles Isherwood, "The Late Henry Moss," *Variety*, September 24, 2001, online; John Simon, "Don't Play It Again," *New York*, October 8, 2001, online; David Dominguez, "'Moss' a Shepard Re-Peat," *Daily News*, September 25, 2001, 55; Ben Brantley, "No-Good Dad Whose Tale Is Told Repeatedly," *New York Times*, September 25, 2001, E1; Jacques Le Sourd, "A Moss-Gatherer from Shepard," *Journal News* (White Plains, NY), September 25, 2001, 1E, 2E.

11 Ethan Hawke, December 28, 2021.

12 Roxanne Rogers, July 6, 2024.

13 Johnny Dark, July 22, 2020; MG, 2002.

14 TP, 227.

15 Sam Shepard, "Berlin Wall Piece," GDH, 20.

16 MG, 2002; quoted in TW, 108–9.

17 Jeff Strickler, "'Don't Come Knocking' Was Hammered Out in Twin Cities," *Star Tribune* (Minneapolis), April 7, 2006, 1F; Chris Kaltenbach, "Wim Wenders Takes On American West Again," *Baltimore Sun*, May 21, 2006, 3E.

18 Jeff Strickler, "'Don't Come Knocking' Was Hammered Out in Twin Cities," *Star Tribune* (Minneapolis), April 7, 2006, 1F.

19 Quoted in Euan Kerr, "Creating Howard Spence," Minnesota Public Radio News, April 7, 2006, online; Sam Shepard, "'Don't Come Knocking'—Intro," n.d., HRC; quoted in Stephen Farber, "East Meets West, Take 2," *New York Times*, March 12, 2006, online.

20 Ethan Hawke, December 28, 2021.

21 Sam Shepard to Clark Middleton, September 21, 2003.

22 Quoted in Dominick Cavendish, "Sam Plays It Again," *Telegraph* (UK), September 25, 2004, online; Sam Shepard to Johnny Dark, January 23, 2004, WC.

23 Sam Shepard to Johnny Dark, February 2 and 4, 2004, WC; Don Ricker, "Sam Shepard Takes Lead in Two New Films," *Hartford Courant*, July 31, 2005, G7.

24 Sam Shepard to Johnny Dark, February 4, 2004, WC.

25 Michael O'Sullivan, "Wim Wenders: How the West Won Him Over," *Washington Post*, April 14, 2006, 29; Sam Shepard, "'Don't Come Knocking'—Intro," n.d., HRC.

26 Quoted in Euan Kerr, "Creating Howard Spence," Minnesota Public Radio News, April 7, 2006, online.

27 Quoted in "Don't Come Knocking," HanWay Films press kit, 2005.

28 Wim Wenders to Sam Shepard, August 28, 2004, HRC.

29 Quoted in Don Ricker, "Sam Shepard Takes Lead in Two New Films," *Hartford Courant*, July 31, 2005, G7; quoted in Christina M. Hinke, "Don't Come Knocking Says Jessica Lange," *New York Cool*, April 2006, online.

30 TP, 265; quoted in Don Ricker, "Sam Shepard Takes Lead in Two New Films," *Hartford Courant*, July 31, 2005, G7; TP, 265.

31 Quoted in "Don't Come Knocking," HanWay Films press kit, 2005.

32 Stephen Holden, "Another True West Tale of Phantom Family Ties," *New York Times*, March 17, 2006, E1; quoted in Kevin Sessums, "Lange on Life," *Vanity Fair*, March 1995, 151; quoted in Jasper Rees, "Acting Has to Be an Emotional Experience," *Daily Telegraph* (UK), February 5, 2007, 29.

33 Jesse McKinley, "Pointed New Shepard Play to Arrive Just Before Election," *New York Times*, October 4, 2004, E1.

34 TP, 259; Don Shewey, "Patriot Acts," *Village Voice*, November 17–23, 2004, online.

35 Quoted in Jesse McKinley, "Pointed New Shepard Play to Arrive Just Before Election," *New York Times*, October 4, 2004, E1.

36 Ibid.; quoted in Mel Gussow, "From Plays to Fiction: Thanks, Dad; Sam Shepard's Rascals Are Inspired by Memories of a Mysterious Father," *New York Times*, October 15, 2002, E1.

37 Quoted in Don Shewey, "Patriot Acts," *Village Voice*, November 17–23, 2004, online.

38 Quoted in Boris Kachka, "How the West Was Lost: Sam Shepard Takes On Cowboy Poseurs—and His Own Iconhood," *New York*, June 22, 2008, online.

39 Patrick Pacheco, "Truth, Justice vs. America's Way," *Los Angeles Times*, June 25, 2006, E38.

40 Quoted in Don Shewey, "Patriot Acts," *Village Voice*, November 17–23, 2004, online.

41 Ibid.; Sam Shepard, *The God of Hell* (New York: Vintage, 2005), 10.

42 Sam Shepard, *The God of Hell* (New York: Vintage, 2005): 92.

43 Quoted in Patrick Pacheco, "Truth, Justice vs. America's Way," *Los Angeles Times*, June 25, 2006, E38; quoted in Jesse McKinley, "Pointed New Shepard Play to Arrive Just Before Election," *New York Times*, October 4, 2004, E1.

44 Linda Winer, "Irresistible Satire by the Grace of 'God,'" *Newsday*, November 17, 2004, B5; Terry Teachout, "Parochial School Duel; 'Moonstruck' Author Pens Powerful Play on Abuse; Woody Allen's Kitchen Sink," *Wall Street Journal*, November 26, 2004, W1; Ben Brantley, "That's No Girl Scout Selling Those Cookies," *New York Times*, November 17, 2004, E1.

45 Quoted in David Kilpatrick, "Same Difference: On Caryl Churchill's *A Number*," *Brooklyn Rail*, November 2004, online; quoted in Don Shewey, "Rock-and-Roll Jesus with a Cowboy Mouth (Revisited)," *American Theatre* 21 (April 2004), online.

46 Quoted in Don Shewey, "Patriot Acts," *Village Voice*, November 2004, 17–23, online; quoted in Ted Sod, "A Conversation with Director James Macdonald," Roundabout Theatre Company, January 19, 2019, online; quoted in Allie Shah, "Lange's Stillwater

House Has Sold for $1.825 million," *Star Tribune* (Minneapolis), September 26, 2008, online; Howard Kissel, "Acting Expands Slim 'Number,'" *Daily News*, December 8, 2004, 50; Ben Brantley, "My 3 Sons: Cloning's Unexpected Results," *New York Times*, December 8, 2004, E1, E7.

47 Quoted in Allie Shah, "Lange's Stillwater House Has Sold for $1.825 Million," *Star Tribune* (Minneapolis), September 26, 2008, online. They first rented a brownstone at 119 Waverly Place; then, in early April 2005, they bought a ninth-floor apartment a block away at One Fifth Avenue, Apt. 9GF. (Morgan Halberg, "Jessica Lange Made a Feud-Free Purchase on Fifth Avenue," *Observer*, June 5, 2018, online).

48 Roxanne Rogers, July 6, 2024; Jeff Gordinier, "Q+A with Sam Shepard," *Details*, July 2008, online.

49 Sam Shepard, "Green spiral notebook, includes material for cabin play, Dead Horse, fishing play, Sway, 2005," series I, container 16.1, Sam Shepard Papers 1965–2011, HRC.

50 Ibid.

51 Sam Shepard, *Sway*, corrected script, January 2006, box 12, folder 14, HRC; quoted in Patrick Healy, "Getting Faster with Age: Sam Shepard's New Velocity," *New York Times*, February 12, 2010, C1; Ethan Hawke, December 28, 2021.

52 TP, 341; Richard H. Schein, July 30, 2019.

53 Richard H. Schein, July 30, 2019; Phil Gerrow, July 31, 2019; Sam Shepard, July 2008, notebook, April 2008–February 2009, box 17, folder 1, HRC; "Sam Shepard," interviewed by Lenny Shulman, *Head to Head: Conversations with a Generation of Horse Racing Legends* (Lexington: University Press of Kentucky, 2021), 97. The property is in Scott County at 800 Fishers Mill Road, just across the South Elkhorn Creek from Midway. For the location of the house as that of Jesse James's mother Zerelda Cole's family, see J. Dooley Rodgers, "James Boys Not Natives of Woodford," *Lexington Herald-Leader*, June 30, 1938, 9.

54 Charles and Mary Jane Nuckols, August 2, 2019; Henry Wombles, August 1, 2019; Laura Wolfrom, August 18, 2019. The property price included another parcel of fifty-five acres a few miles away at 5380 Bethel Road.

55 Herman Daniel Farrell III, August 3, 2019; Richard H. Schein, July 30, 2019; TP, 274.

56 Sam Shepard to Johnny Dark, May 8, 2006, WC/SD.

57 John McDaniel, "Sam Shepard in Midway," *Midway Messenger*, August 2, 2017, online.

58 John McDaniel, August 1, 2019; Midway shop owner, July 31, 2019; Phil Gerrow, July 31, 2019.

59 Phil Gerrow, July 31, 2019; Sam Shepard, "Promising Two-Year-Old," DD, 190.

## CHAPTER 19 AT HOME AT THE ABBEY

1 Roxanne Rogers, January 1, 2025; Fiach Mac Conghail, December 29, 2023.

2 Fiach Mac Conghail, December 29, 2023.

3 Ibid. The retrospective never happened, Mac Conghail told me, because the Abbey ran out of time and money. Shepard would later be involved in the Abbey's New Playwrights Programme and perform at a fundraiser for them with Patti Smith in April 2012.

4 Fiach Mac Conghail, December 29, 2023.

5 Kevin Cullen, "Staging a Turnaround in Dublin," *Boston Globe*, April 15, 2007, N2, N3; Fiach Mac Conghail, December 29, 2023; quoted in Donald Clark, "Sam Shepard, RIP: Was This a Man? You're Damn Right It Was," *Irish Times*, July 31, 2017, online.

6 Stephen Rea, foreword, in Sam Shepard, *Kicking a Dead Horse* (New York: Vintage Books, 2008), ix, x; Stephen Rea, "Sam Shepard 1943–2017," *Guardian*, August 6, 2017, online.

7 Fiach Mac Conghail, December 29, 2023; Sam Shepard, "Dead Horse," October 7, 2005, HRC.

8 Sam Shepard, *Kicking a Dead Horse* (New York: Vintage, 2008), 12. Shepard specifies in the play (page 41) that Hobart is stuck "right nearby" where Crazy Horse was killed—Fort Robinson, Nebraska.

9 Quoted in Alexis Soloski, "True East," *Village Voice*, June 25–July 1, 2008, 30.

10 Quoted in Colin Murphy, "To the Abbey and Beyond," *Village*, April 4, 2007, online.

11 Fiach Mac Conghail, December 29, 2023.

12 Fintan O'Toole, "A Nod from One Sam to Another," *Irish Times*, February 24, 2007, online.

13 Michael Ross, "Made of the Write Stuff," *Sunday Times* (UK), March 11, 2007, Eire Culture, 4; Alexis Soloski, "True East," *Village Voice*, June 25–July 1, 2008, 30; Fintan O'Toole, "A Nod from One Sam to Another," *Irish Times*, February 24, 2007, online.

14 Quoted in Celia McGee, "A Lone King Lear on the Lone Prairie," *New York Times*, June 22, 2008, Arts and Entertainment, 8; Sam Shepard, *Kicking a Dead Horse* (New York: Vintage, 2008), 9.

15 Celia McGee, "A Lone King Lear on the Lone Prairie," *New York Times*, June 22, 2008, Arts and Entertainment, 8; quoted in Morgan Falconer, "Straight from the Horse's Mouth," *Times* (UK), August 30, 2008, Stage, 14.

16 Sam Shepard, *Kicking a Dead Horse* (New York: Vintage, 2008), 24, 42.

17 Shepard, *Kicking a Dead Horse*, 8.

18 Fiach Mac Conghail, December 29, 2023; Catherine Foley, "Kicking Up a Storm Onstage," *Irish Times*, March 17, 2007.

19 Richard Ford, emails, April 4, 2020, and September 10, 2023.

20 Hilton Als, "Fantasy Suite," *New Yorker*, July 28, 2008, online.

21 Karen Fricker, "Kicking a Dead Horse," *Variety*, March 16, 2007, online; Joe Penhall, "The Outsider," *Guardian* (UK), June 14, 2006, Culture, 21.

22 TP, 295.

23 FO, 6.

24 FO, 15, 24, 25.

25 TP, 296.

26 TP, 284.

27 TP, 289; Sam Shepard to Johnny Dark, February 24, 2006, WC.

28 Bill Flick, "Welcome to B-N's Unofficial Tour of Famed Sites," *Pantagraph* (Bloomington-Normal, IL), March 6, 2009, D1; TP, 317; Edith Brady-Lunny, "Shepard Apologizes for Driving Drunk," *Pantagraph* (Bloomington-Normal, IL), February 12, 2009, A3.

29 TP, 316; Sam Shepard, "Normal (Highway 39 South)," DD, 210–11.

30 LuAnn Walther to Sam Shepard, January 16, 2009, HRC; LuAnn Walther to Jennings Law Firm, January 16, 2009, HRC.

31 Staterecords.org. He was pulled over for reckless driving on November 14, 2008; quoted in Carole Cadwalladr, "Sam Shepard Opens Up," *Guardian*, March 20, 2010, online.

32 TP, 309.

33 TP, 317, 316.

34 Edith Brady-Lunny, "Shepard Apologizes for Driving Drunk," *Pantagraph* (Bloomington-Normal, IL), February 12, 2009, A3; Edith Brady-Lunny, "Actor Sam Shepard Completes Service Requirements for Local DUI," *Pantagraph* (Bloomington-Normal, IL), February 25, 2010, A3; TP, 342–43.

35 TP, 318.

36 Sam Shepard to Johnny Dark, December 14, 2009, WC.

37 TP, 310.

38 Allison Bray, "Stars Flock to See Shepard's Play in Abbey Premiere," *Irish Independent*, March 3, 2009, online. Roddy Doyle published a short story of Shepard's, "After the Gunfight," in his 2012 collection *Fighting Words*.

39 Stephen Rea, "Waiting for the New Beckett Is Over," *Irish Times*, February 28, 2009, online.

40 "Land of the Living" was first published in the September 21, 2009, issue of the *New Yorker*.

41 TP, 336.

42 TP, 307.

43 Patrick Healy, "Getting Faster with Age: Sam Shepard's New Velocity," *New York Times*, February 12, 2010, C1.

44 Ethan Hawke, December 28, 2021.

45 Ibid.

46 Sam Shepard, notebook, December 22, 2009, HRC.

47 TP, 365; Sam Shepard to Johnny Dark, July 12, 2011, WC/JD; quoted in Carole Cadwalladr, "Sam Shepard Opens Up," *Guardian*, March 20, 2010, online.

48 Staff, PageSix.com, "That's a Porch?," *New York Post*, October 3, 2011, online.

49 Sam Shepard to Johnny Dark, August 9, 2010, WC/JD.

50 FO, 50.

51 Sam Shepard, *Heartless* (New York: Vintage, 2013), 75.

52 FO, 56.

53 Sam Shepard to Johnny Dark, July 12, 2011, WC/JD; Johnny Dark, March 3, 2021; Sam Shepard to Johnny Dark, November 3, 2011, WC.

54 Quoted in JW, 222.

55 "Treva Wurmfeld," interviewed by Scott Macaulay, *Filmmaker*, Fall 2022, online. When I wrote to Treva Wurmfeld, she suggested I read her book *Tangents* in lieu of an interview (Treva Wurmfeld, email, December 2, 2022).

56 Johnny Dark, January 13, 2022; they sold the collection to the archive for around a quarter million dollars each, and Dark used it to buy annuities for retirement. SD.

57 Johnny Dark, January 13, 2022; TW, 37; Johnny Dark, February 27, 2021.

58 Johnny Dark, July 22, 2020.

59 Quoted in Christie Evangelisto, "In Between Sam Shepard Worlds," *Signature Stories* 3, Summer 2012, 9.

60 Quoted in David Krakauer, "Tribute to Sam Shepard," Santa Fe Institute, August 1, 2017, online.

61 Jamie Brisick, "Day of Days: Sam Shepard's Long Ride," *Wrestling Elephants*, December 11, 2013, online.

62 Quoted in Eric Killelea, "Sam in Santa Fe: From the Mailbox of a Great American Playwright," August 30, 2017, online.

63 Sam Shepard to Johnny Dark, July 20, 2010, WC/JD.

64 JD; TW, 105.

65 Johnny Dark, untitled memoir (Texas State University, 2011).

66 Johnny Dark to Lee Kissman, March 28, 2013 (courtesy of Lee Kissman); TP, 369; JD; SD.

67 "A Tangent: Director Treva Wurmfeld Talks with Sam Shepard," *Filmmaker*, Fall 2022, online.

68 Scott Macaulay, "Treva Wurmfeld," *Filmmaker*, Fall 2022, online.

69 Jamie Brisick, "Day of Days: Sam Shepard's Long Ride," *Wrestling Elephants*, December 11, 2013, online.

70 Johnny Dark, March 3, 2021; Michael Almereyda, June 22, 2024.

71 Quoted in Christie Evangelisto, "In Between Sam Shepard Worlds," *Signature Stories* 3, Summer 2002, 10–11.

72 TW, 155.

73 Sam Shepard to Johnny Dark, October 14, 2011, WC/JD; Johnny Dark, October 16, 2020, and March 3, 2021; JD.

74 Sam Shepard, *Heartless* (New York: Vintage, 2013), 61; Roxanne Rogers, July 6, 2024.

75 Notebook entry, n.d. [summer 2011], uncatalogued box, HRC; Sam Shepard, *Heartless* (New York: Vintage, 2013), 44, 51.

76 Notebook entry, n.d. [summer 2011], uncatalogued box, HRC; OI, 102.

77 Ibid.; quoted in Jamie Brisick, "Day of Days: Sam Shepard's Long Ride," *Wrestling Elephants*, December 11, 2013, online.

78 Sam Shepard, *Heartless* (New York: Vintage, 2013), 107.

79 Betty Gilpin, interviewed by Marc Maron, *WTF with Marc Maron* (podcast), August 26, 2019; quoted in Jamie Brisick, "Day of Days: Sam Shepard's Long Ride," *Wrestling Elephants*, December 11, 2013, online.

80 Sam Shepard, notebook entry, June 27, 2011, uncataloged box, HRC.

81 Sam Shepard to Johnny Dark, March 7, 2012, WC/JD. Shepard's house in Santa Fe while he was at SFI was located at 38 Sudeste Place.

82 Sophocles, *The Oedipus Cycle*, ed. and trans., Dudley Fitts and Robert Fitzgerald (New York: Harcourt Brace, 2002), 16.

83 Sam Shepard, "Tragedy," November 20, 2013, Field Day program for *A Particle of Dread.*

84 TP, 80; Sam Shepard, "Things You Learn from Others," DD, 250.

85 Notebook entry, n.d. [summer 2011], uncataloged box, HRC; Jonathan Cott, "The Rolling Stone Interview: Sam Shepard," *Rolling Stone*, December 18, 1986–January 1987, online; quoted in TW, 92.

86 Sam Shepard, "Guilt," n.d., circa 1972, HGC.

87 Quoted in TW, 92.

88 Ibid.; Sam Shepard to Johnny Dark, July 2, 2010, WC/JD.

89 Quoted in "Like Father," *Time Out* (Chicago), November 11, 2010, online; Patti Smith, "My Buddy," *New Yorker*, August 1, 2017, online.

90 "Actor and Playwright Sam Shepard Reads at Trinity College Dublin," Trinity College, December 11, 2012, online.

91 Quoted in Emma Creedon, *Sam Shepard and the Aesthetics of Performance* (New York: Palgrave Macmillan, 2015), 166; Nicola Anderson, "Playwright Shepard Honoured by TCD," *Irish Independent*, December 8, 2012, online; quoted in Michael Coveney, "Sam Shepard: The Playwright Remembered," WhatsOnStage.com, November 15, 2018.

92 Quoted in Beth Whitaker, "Sam Shepard: A Fascination with Fate," *Signature Stories* 10 (Autumn 2014), 16.

93 Quoted in Sara Rose Leonard, "Variations on a Theme: Director Nancy Meckler on *A Particle of Dread*," *Signature Stories* 10 (Autumn 2014), 18, 19.

94 Nancy Meckler, May 10, 2023; see "Things You Learn from Others," DD, 250.

95 JD; Peter Crawley, "*A Particle of Dread (Oedipus Variations)*," *Irish Times*, December 2, 2023, online.

96 Nancy Meckler, May 10, 2023; Matthew Murphy, "'A Particle of Dread (Oedipus Variations),'" *Hollywood Reporter*, November 23, 2014, online.

97 Ben Brantley, "Call Out the Patricide Squad," *New York Times*, November 23, 2014, online.

98 Quoted in Alexis Soloski, "An Urban Cowboy Returns to Broadway," *New York Times*, January 31, 2016, AR5.

## CHAPTER 20 "COYOTE FADES"

1 OI, 119; Roxanne Rogers, July 22, 2020.

2 Carey Gough, January 21, 2024; Sam Shepard to Johnny Dark, August 1, 2012, WC/JD.

3 Carey Gough, January 21, 2024; JD.

4 Sam Shepard, notes on *The One Inside*, JD; quoted in Laura Barton, "Sam Shepard: 'America Is on Its Way Out as a Culture,'" *Guardian* (UK), September 7, 2014, online.

5 Sam Shepard, "Notebook Entitled Fractured," Nova Scotia (Summer 1972): 17–19, box 27, folder 2, HGC.

6 Quoted in Laura Barton, "Sam Shepard: 'America Is on Its Way Out as a Culture,'" *Guardian* (UK), September 7, 2014, online.

7 In March 2015, Shepard also performed a small part in James Franco's *In Dubious Battle*, a film adaptation of John Steinbeck's 1936 novel about exploited California apple pickers. Though *In Dubious Battle* appeared before *Never Here* (his last film appearance), this was the last time Shepard performed in front of a movie camera.

8 Patti Smith, *Year of the Monkey* (New York: Alfred A. Knopf, 2019), 89; Bruno Schulz, "Dodo," *Sanatorium Under the Sign of the Hourglass*, 1937, trans. Celina Wieniewska (New York: Walker and Company, 1978), 142, 148. Patti Smith most likely encouraged the title change from "Stacked" to "The One Inside" (Carey Gough, January 21, 2024).

9 OI, 3.

10 OI, 3, 41.

11 OI, 155.

12 TW, 92.

13 OI, 25, 96, 115. The character Lucy in *Heartless*, Sally's sister whom Roscoe eventually leaves with, is based on another girlfriend, a thirty-five-year-old waitress from Santa Fe's Coyote Cafe who stole his heart in July 2011. He referred to her as "little Luci," and characterized her as an opium smoker with a strong air of the Indigenous shaman about her (Sam Shepard to Johnny Dark, July 9, 2010, WC/JD).

14 Sam Shepard to Johnny Dark, July 15, 2015, WC/JD; OI, 129, 130.

15 Sam Shepard to Johnny Dark, September 23 and 30, 2012, WC/JD.

16 Roxanne Rogers, July 6, 2024; Carey Gough, January 21, 2024.

17 JD.

18 JD; Sam Shepard, notes on *The One Inside*, JD.

19 JD; Carey Gough, January 21, 2024; Roxanne Rogers, January 24, 2023.

20 JD; Sam Shepard, notebook, February 10, 2015, WC; Roxanne Rogers, January 24, 2023; Sam Shepard, notebook, March 17, 2015, CW.

21 JD; Carey Gough, January 21, 2024.

22 Carey Gough, January 21, 2024; Johnny Dark, November 21, 2020.

23 Sam Shepard to Johnny Dark, August 1, 2012, CW/JD.
24 JD.
25 Michael Almereyda, *Tesla: All My Dreams Are True* (New York: OR Books, 2022), 48. *Tesla* was released in 2020. Almereyda removed Mark Twain from the script. "The idea of building a Twain subplot collapsed," he wrote. "I didn't care to think of anyone filling Sam's shoes" (*Tesla*, 52).
26 Sam Shepard to Johnny Dark, July 15, 2015; Carey Gough, January 21, 2024.
27 Carey Gough, January 21, 2024; Reuters, "U.S. Playwright, Actor Sam Shepard Arrested on Drunken Driving Charge," May 26, 2015, online; Shelby Perea, "Dash-cam Video Captures Sam Shepard's Arrest," KRQE (Santa Fe, NM), May 27, 2015, online; JD.
28 JD.
29 JD; Carey Gough, January 21, 2024.
30 Carey Gough, January 21, 2024; JD; Johnny Dark, July 19, 2020.
31 Patti Smith returned several more times to help finalize the manuscript for *The One Inside*, including on Thanksgiving, for the Kentucky Derby in May, in August, and the following winter in California.
32 Carey Gough, January 21, 2024; quoted in Sandy Rogers, July 28, 2023.
33 Patti Smith, interviewed by David Remnick, New Yorker Festival, October 11, 2019; Patti Smith, *Year of the Monkey* (New York: Alfred A. Knopf, 2019), 118, 119; Carey Gough, January 21, 2024.
34 Carey Gough, January 21, 2024; quoted in Chris Wiegand, "'It Was Like Meeting a Cowboy': Ed Harris, Kathy Burke and Others Remember Sam Shepard," *Guardian*, August 2, 2017, online; JD.
35 Molly Haskell, "Masculinity and Its Perils," *New York Times*, February 26, 2017, Sunday Book Review, 9.
36 Sam Shepard, *Spy of the First Person*, draft, June 2, 2016, HRC; Patti Smith, foreword, OI, xi.
37 Carey Gough, January 21, 2024.
38 Sam Shepard, *Spy of the First Person*, draft, June 2, 2016, HRC.
39 "A Celebration of Sam Shepard: Curse of the Starving Class," New Group, 92nd Street Y, January 16, 2025.
40 Michael Almereyda, email, September 2, 2024.
41 Roxanne Rogers, December 29, 2020, and July 6, 2024; Michael Almereyda, email, September 3, 2024.
42 Michael Almereyda, emails, September 2, 2024.
43 Quoted in "Remembering Lou Reed: Tributes from Fans and Followers," *Rolling Stone*, November 7, 2013, 48.
44 David Foster Wallace, *Brief Interviews with Hideous Men*, 1999 (New York: Back Bay Books/Little, Brown, 2007), 256.
45 Sam Shepard, "Signature," February 26, 2016. Courtesy of Michael Almereyda.

46 Sam Shepard, "Signature," translation unknown, February 26, 2016. Courtesy of Michael Almereyda.

47 TOI, 67.

48 Carey Gough, January 21, 2024.

49 Quoted in Alexandra Alter, "A Final Work by Sam Shepard Reveals His Struggle with Lou Gehrig's Disease," *New York Times*, December 4, 2017, online; Sam Shepard, *Spy of the First Person*, draft, June 2, 2016, HRC.

50 Roxanne Rogers, July 6, 2024.

51 Roxanne Rogers, December 29, 2020.

52 Quoted in Caryn James, "How a Dying Sam Shepard Wrote 'Spy of the First Person,'" *Wall Street Journal*, December 4, 2017, online; Alexandra Alter, "A Final Work by Sam Shepard Reveals His Struggle with Lou Gehrig's Disease," *New York Times*, December 4, 2017, online.

53 Quoted in Alexandra Alter, "A Final Work by Sam Shepard Reveals His Struggle with Lou Gehrig's Disease," *New York Times*, December 4, 2017, online; quoted in Caryn James, "How a Dying Sam Shepard Wrote 'Spy of the First Person,'" *Wall Street Journal*, December 4, 2017, online.

54 CS, 40; Ernie Earnshaw, "Sam Shepard: A Memorial Performance," video, Bootleg Theater, Los Angeles, October 2, 2017 (courtesy of Guy Zimmerman); Sam Shepard, *Spy of the First Person* (New York: Alfred A. Knopf, 2017), 12.

55 Ibid., 56; Quoted in Caryn James, "How a Dying Sam Shepard Wrote 'Spy of the First Person,'" *Wall Street Journal*, December 4, 2017, online.

56 Sam Shepard, *Spy of the First Person* (New York: Alfred A. Knopf, 2017), 80, italics mine; quoted in JW, 345. See also Juan Rulfo epigraph of CP.

57 Alexandra Alter, "Sam Shepard Novel Set for December Release," *New York Times*, October 19, 2017, C3; quoted in Alexandra Alter, "A Final Work by Sam Shepard Reveals His Struggle with Lou Gehrig's Disease," *New York Times*, December 4, 2017, online.

58 Roxanne Rogers, December 29, 2020, and July 6 and 9, 2024; Carey Gough, January 21, 2024.

59 JD; Carey Gough, January 21, 2024; quoted in TP, 359; Sandy Rogers, July 28, 2023; Roxanne Rogers, January 1, 2025.

60 Quoted in Patti Smith, *Year of the Monkey* (New York: Alfred A. Knopf, 2019), 88.

## EPILOGUE **A PULSE IN THE DARK**

1 Matthew Paul Olmos, "Backpages 27.4," *Contemporary Theatre Review* 27 (4), 2017, 536–46: 545; David Henry Hwang, email, July 16, 2023.

2 Charles McNulty, "Sam Shepard, the Cowboy Playwright Who Rewrote the Rules of the American Stage," *Los Angeles Times*, July 31, 2017, online; Nancy Melich, "Sundance Playwrights Lab Applies Scalpel to the Mindless Mediocrity of Broadway," *Salt Lake Tribune*, July 3, 1994, Arts, E2.

3 Quoted in Chris Wiegand, "'It Was Like Meeting a Cowboy': Ed Harris, Kathy Burke and Others Remember Sam Shepard," *Guardian*, August 2, 2017, online.

4 Quoted in "Authors, Directors, Projects at Sundance Playwrights Lab," *Salt Lake Tribune*, July 3, 1994, E2; Carson Kreitzer, "Backpages 27.4," *Contemporary Theatre Review*, 2017, 536–46: 542, 543.

5 Quoted in Hedy Weiss, "Actor, Pulitzer-Winning Playwright Sam Shepard Dies at 73," *Chicago Sun-Times*, July 31, 2017, online; Philip Kaufman, "Sam Shepard Remembered by 'The Right Stuff' Director Philip Kaufman: Half Jackrabbit, Best Chili Maker," *Variety*, August 1, 2017, online; Michael Feingold, "The Punk Rock Cowboy," *Village Voice*, July 31, 2017, online; quoted in Michael Coveney, "Sam Shepard: the Playwright Remembered," WhatsOnStage.com, November 15, 2018.

6 Richard Ridge, "Inside Opening Night of *True West*," Broadway World, January 24, 2019, YouTube.

7 Geri Thoma, email, October 21, 2017; Roxanne Rogers, December 29, 2020; Patti Smith, "My Buddy," *New Yorker*, August 1, 2017, online.

8 Quoted in Anthony Uzarowski, *Jessica Lange: An Adventurer's Heart* (Lexington: University Press of Kentucky, 2023), 191.

9 Joyce Aaron, August 2, 2022; "Sam Shepard: A Great Recognition," invitation by the Shepard family. Courtesy of Joyce Aaron; JD.

10 Johnny Dark, February 25, 2021; JD.

11 Phil Gerrow, July 31, 2019.

12 Ibid.; Carey Gough, January 21, 2024; Sam Shepard, "Repeat," CP, 111.

13 Roxanne Rogers, January 1, 2025; Carey Gough, January 21, 2024; MG, 2002.

14 Roxanne Rogers, July 6, 2024; Carey Gough, January 21, 2024.

15 Quoted in Chris Wiegand, "'It Was Like Meeting a Cowboy': Ed Harris, Kathy Burke and Others Remember Sam Shepard," *Guardian*, August 2, 2017, online.

16 Roxanne Rogers, January 1, 2025; Carey Gough, January 21, 2024; Richard H. Schein, July 30, 2019.

17 Sandy Rogers, "Sam Shepard: A Memorial Performance," video, Bootleg Theater, Los Angeles, October 2, 2017. Courtesy of Guy Zimmerman.

18 Quoted in BB, 92; quoted in Jeff Gordinier, "Wiseguy: The Iconic Playwright-Actor Discusses the Effect He Has on Women, His Oscarphobia, and Why He's an Agent's Nightmare," *Details*, September 2008, 252.

# INDEX

NOTE: Page references starting with *P* refer to photo insert. For example, *P1* refers to first page of insert.

# IMAGE CREDITS

Page 1, top: Courtesy of Roxanne Rogers
Page 1, bottom: Sam Rogers
Page 2, top: Courtesy of Roxanne Rogers
Page 2, middle: Sam Rogers
Page 2, bottom: Grace Upton
Page 3, top: Grace Upton
Page 3, bottom: Roxanne Rogers
Page 4, top left: *Halconado* '62, Duarte High School, Duarte, California
Page 4, top right: Roxanne Rogers
Page 4, middle: Bob Greene
Page 4, bottom: Duane Michals / La MaMa Archives
Page 5, top: Chuck Gould
Page 5, bottom: Bruce Davidson / Archivio Michelangelo Antonioni
Page 6, top: Michael Evans / *The New York Times*
Page 6, bottom: Martha Swope / © Billy Rose Theatre Division, The New York Public Library for the Performing Arts
Page 7, top: Sandy Daley
Page 7, bottom: Gerard Malanga
Page 8, top left: Alpaslan Ataman
Page 8, top right: Johnny Dark / Sam Shepard & Johnny Dark Collections, The Wittliff Collections, Texas State University
Page 8, bottom: Sam Shepard & Johnny Dark Collections, The Wittliff Collections, Texas State University
Page 9, top: Ken Regan / Camera 5 via Contour by Getty Images
Page 9, bottom: Theodore Shank
Page 10, top: Johnny Dark / Sam Shepard & Johnny Dark Collections, The Wittliff Collections, Texas State University

Page 10, middle: Johnny Dark / Sam Shepard & Johnny Dark Collections, The Wittliff Collections, Texas State University

Page 10, bottom: Martha Swope / © Billy Rose Theatre Division, The New York Public Library for the Performing Arts

Page 11, top: Warner Bros / Everett Collection

Page 11, bottom: Studiocanal Films / Alamy Stock Photo

Page 12, top: Johnny Dark

Page 12, bottom: AJ Pics / Alamy Stock Photo

Page 13, top: Nick Ut / AP

Page 13, bottom: Douglas Kent Hall / Princeton University Library Special Collections

Page 14, top: Lynn Davis

Page 14, middle: Michael Almereyda

Page 14, bottom: Michael Almereyda

Page 15, top: © Donata Wenders

Page 15, middle: Jamie McCarthy / Everett Collection via Getty Images

Page 15, bottom: Ros Kavanagh

Page 16: Saeed Ayani / Netflix

# ABOUT THE AUTHOR

**Robert M. Dowling** is professor of English at Central Connecticut State University. He is the author of *Slumming in New York: From the Waterfront to Mythic Harlem* and the biography *Eugene O'Neill: A Life in Four Acts*, which was a Los Angeles Times Book Prize finalist for biography in 2015. He has also coedited the 2021 compendium of interviews *Conversations with Sam Shepard*. As an authority on American drama, he has been featured in *The New York Times*, *The Wall Street Journal*, and *The Boston Globe*, among other publications.